"Look for Me
All Around You"

AFRICAN AMERICAN LIFE SERIES

*A complete listing of the books in this series
can be found online at http://wsupress.wayne.edu*

Series Editors

MELBA JOYCE BOYD
Department of Africana Studies
Wayne State University

RONALD BROWN
Department of Political Science
Wayne State University

"Look for Me
All Around You"

Anglophone Caribbean Immigrants in the Harlem Renaissance

Edited by
LOUIS J. PARASCANDOLA

WAYNE STATE UNIVERSITY PRESS   DETROIT

09 08 07 06   5 4 3 2

Library of Congress Cataloging-in-Publication Data

"Look for me all around you" : anglophone Caribbean immigrants in the Harlem
Renaissance / edited by Louis J. Parascandola.
p. cm.—(African American life series)
Includes bibliographical references and index.
ISBN 0-8143-2987-X (pbk. : alk. paper)
1. American literature—Caribbean American authors.   2. Caribbean Area—Emigration
and immigration—Literary collections.   3. West Indies—Emigration and immigration—
Literary collections.   4. West Indian Americans—Literary collections.   5. Caribbean
Americans—Literary collections.   6. American literature—20th century.   7. Harlem
Renaissance.   I. Parascandola, Louis J., 1952–   II. Series.
PS508.C27L66 2005

2004021791

Acknowledgments are indicated following each piece.
Any errors or omissions are unintentional. The publisher, if notified,
will be pleased to make any corrections at the earliest opportunity.

My parents, Louis and Ann Parascandola, both children of immigrants, did not finish the journey with me physically yet were with me every step of the way. This book is dedicated to them.

I cannot praise, for you have passed from praise,
    I have no tinted thoughts to paint you true;
But I can feel and I can write the word;
    The best of me is but the least of you.

    Claude McKay, "Heritage"

CONTENTS

PART 2. SOCIALISTS

PART 3. COMMUNISTS

PART 4. LITERARY FIGURES

PART 5. HISTORIANS

ACKNOWLEDGMENTS

This project had its genesis some seven years ago when I was completing a manuscript on Eric Walrond. In doing research on Walrond, I realized how much influence the Caribbean community wielded in New York City during the Harlem Renaissance and how much, despite a spate of fine work on this burgeoning group (notably by Irma Watkins-Owens and Winston James), was still left unexplored. My journey, like that of these immigrants, was often a longer (I started out with ten authors) and bumpier trip than expected. I would like to thank the following, who were with me for some or all of this sojourn, now finally complete. You eased my arrival at this destination considerably. Walk good.

The many institutions that made material available, including Diana Lachantere and the staff at the Schomburg Center for Research in Black Culture; the staff at the James Weldon Johnson Collection at ˜Yale University; Thomas C. Battle and the staff at the Moorland-Spingarn Research Center at Howard University; Karen Jefferson and the staff at the Robert W. Woodruff Library at Atlanta University Center; the staff at the copyright office at the Library of Congress; Robert Bone, Carl Wade, Mark Solomon, Robert A. Hill, Jeffrey B. Perry, Amritjit Singh, Winston James, Joyce Moore Turner, George Hutchinson, and Tony Martin, who offered advice, encouragement, inspiration, and/or permission to reprint works; the several anonymous reviewers of this manuscript, who urged some ultimately necessary emendations to the introduction and inclusions to the contents; the West Indian man who accidentally picked up part of the manuscript at the photocopy store and, after keeping it several days without telling me so that he could read it, offered four pages of handwritten comments; my friends at Mid-Manhattan Library, including Deborah Hirsch and Richard Reyes-Gavilan, particularly those in Literature and Language; my colleagues at Long Island University, including those in the Honors Program, the Latin American and Caribbean

Program, and the English Department, particularly my chair, Leah Dilworth; my students at Long Island University, especially those in three different classes on West Indians in the Harlem Renaissance; Dean David Cohen and Provost Gale Stevens-Haynes for fostering an environment that allows creative work to go on; the staff at Wayne State University Press, including Brandon Kelley for publicity, Series Editor Melba Joyce Boyd, and my ever faithful and patient editors Kristin Harpster Lawrence and (again) Kathy Wildfong; copyeditor Sandra Judd for picking so many nits; Jacqueline Brown for proofreading; Bonny McLaughlin for indexing; Susan Rothschild, Joan Goldsmith, and Harold Goebel; Denise Foulkes, for her friendship and the cover; Canje, my study buddy; my sisters, Maryann and Judy, and my brother, John, for their unending advice and support; my extended Caribbean family, the Neros; and my wife, Shondel Nero, who spent inordinate (and at times heroic) amounts of time and love addressing the needs both of this manuscript and its author.

EDITOR'S NOTE

Since anglophone Caribbean immigrants played a prominent role in both the literary and the political activities of the Harlem Renaissance, this collection brings together a representative selection of their literary and nonliterary works: fiction, poetry, drama, and essays. Both the literary and the political works show the spirit of the New Negro, one emphasizing racial pride, self-definition, and aesthetic consciousness. This anthology presents both commentary on and a selection of original pieces for those interested in the Harlem Renaissance and the larger Black or Caribbean contribution to cultural and political thinking. It is the first to integrate political and literary writings, facilitating a fuller understanding of the period. As Barbara Foley posits in *Spectres of 1919*, attempts to see the Harlem Renaissance as "a cultural phenomenon, only peripherally influenced by leftist [and Black nationalist for that matter] politics" have always been problematic (Urbana: U of Illinois P, 2003, 3); the cultural and political aspects must be examined hand in hand.

In choosing the material, I selected pieces on a wide range of subjects relevant to both the authors' times and our own. Out of a desire to respect the integrity of the pieces, excerpts have been avoided as much as possible and, when given, are intended only to provide the "taste" of a long, essential text (e.g., *Home to Harlem* and *From Superman to Man*) or, in a few cases, to delete what to modern readers would be extraneous material from a work. Some of the topics covered include immigration and assimilation, Garveyism, racial prejudice, socialism and communism, Black pride, the role of women in cultural and political arenas, the New Negro movement, and Caribbean immigrants' relationships with American Blacks. The fifteen writers chosen address these topics from a diversity of literary, political, and social perspectives. They also hail from a variety of geographic regions: Jamaica, Barbados, the Virgin Islands, British Guiana, Nevis, Puerto Rico, Dutch Guiana, and Trinidad.

The categorization of the authors (Garveyites, Socialists, Communists, Literary Figures, Historians) is, by necessity, somewhat permeable, as these are complex figures with often overlapping affiliations. Virtually all of those included were at one time or another connected with Garvey, principally through an involvement with his periodical the *Negro World*, even if they were not members of his organization, the Universal Negro Improvement Association. Similarly, almost all of the communists were at an earlier time socialists. Furthermore, the literary figures and historians, of course, also had their political allegiances. Claude McKay, for example, published with the *Negro World* but was also connected, in various incarnations, with socialism and communism. Thus, the authors have been arranged under the headings with which it was felt they are best represented.

The texts contained here are from numerous publications, each with its own editorial policies. While a few obvious errors have been corrected, sometimes indicated by brackets or in a note, I have not attempted to regularize spelling, italics, or capitalization. My general goal has been to adhere to the texts as they were originally published. Several small omissions have been made in the nonfiction, indicated in the text by three asterisks, when it was felt that material would be irrelevant or confusing to readers. I have selectively provided annotations, marked by a single asterisk.

Introduction

Marcus Garvey, on the verge of being imprisoned in Atlanta in 1925, told his followers to "[l]ook for me in the whirlwind or the storm, look for me all around you." Garvey's words, urging his followers not to despair during his absence, are reflective not only of his condition but also of the situation of anglophone Caribbean people in Harlem in the early part of the twentieth century.[1] During the 1920s, the height of what was dubbed the era of the New Negro movement, historically associated with African Americans, one in four Harlemites was foreign-born, mostly from the anglophone Caribbean (Osofsky 131). Despite their ubiquity, as these immigrants have gradually died, moved away, or assimilated into New York's African American community, their achievements have been rendered virtually invisible. In fact, aside from Marcus Garvey and Claude McKay, the names of most of the Caribbean pioneers have held, until recently, scant significance for most people, including many scholars of the period. This anthology allows us to redress this significant lacuna in literary, political, and cultural history by collecting the writings of a variety of Caribbean authors in one place and in some cases reprinting their works for the first time since their original publication.

In the words of critic Roy Simon Bryce-Laporte, Anglophone Caribbean immigrants have suffered a "double invisibility . . . as *blacks* and as *black foreigners*" (31). Even major figures such as Garvey and McKay have not been generally thought of in relation to the large Caribbean community of which they were a part. Notwithstanding differences in their backgrounds and philosophies, these writers were linked by a common heritage and bound together in a new city, a new land, at a critical juncture. It was the age of the Harlem Renaissance, when the New Negro began to assert the necessity for political and economic equality for Blacks and to resist accommodation.[2] It was a period that produced an artistic movement unlike any Black America had previously known. Above all, it was a time that emphasized newness and "signified a manifestation that blurred the boundaries

1

between aesthetics, politics, and life style" (Watson 8). Caribbean immigrants were key contributors to the burgeoning developments of this seminal era, cogently adding their unique voice to a variety of issues, including race and image building, the development of a Black aesthetic, progressive politics, and the struggle to define the status of Blacks in America.

Anglophone Caribbean Immigrants during the Harlem Renaissance: An Overview

In order to better understand the contributions of these early figures, we must realize the status of Caribbean immigrants in New York City: why they came, who they were, what their concerns were. Migration has long been a way of life in the Caribbean; indeed, the area's history has been "a succession of waves of migration" (D. Marshall 15). The region's origin itself was one of uprootedness, born out of slavery and indentured labor. Emancipation throughout the British Empire in 1834 only increased migration, as it was one of the limited options by which West Indians could display their newly won liberation. They had been migrating within the region throughout the nineteenth and early twentieth centuries, to work on the sugar estates in Trinidad, Cuba, and British Guiana; on banana plantations and the rail system in Costa Rica; and on the building of the Panama Canal (Chaney 7). Some twenty thousand had even come to the United States by 1900, particularly after the United Fruit Company began importing bananas in the 1880s, paving the way for fairly inexpensive travel (and increased tourism) between the Caribbean and the United States. By 1860, 20 percent of Black Bostonians had been born in the Caribbean (James, "Explaining Afro-Caribbean" 219). The number of immigrants to reach the shores of the United States increased rapidly between 1900 and 1930. Several factors were responsible for this increase, but the chief reasons, as always, were economic and political. Many of the islands were chronically overcrowded, with high unemployment rates and little land available (particularly for Blacks) for agriculture. The plantocratic system established by the colonial powers had helped create a system with pervasive class discrimination, allowing few opportunities for advancement. Natural disasters, including earthquakes, hurricanes, and droughts, made conditions even worse. The completion in 1914 of the Panama Canal, built primarily by Caribbean laborers in a highly segregated society, largely ended migration to that part of the region. For all these reasons immigrants now turned to America (Holder 7–12; Palmer 1–8; James, *Holding Aloft* 9–49).

Caribbean immigrants viewed the United States as a land of opportunity and their favorite destination was New York City. The foreign-born Black population in the city increased steadily, from 3,552 in 1900 to almost 60,000 in 1930 (Holder 9).[3] Anglophone Caribbean immigrants began moving to New York about the same time that Black Americans began migrating from the South in large numbers. Hundreds of thousands of southern Blacks migrated to the North and West from 1916 to 1918 (Marks). The Caribbean immigrants and Black southern migrants joined with an already existent African American population to form the Black capital of America.

Harlem was occupied almost exclusively by Whites until the early twentieth century; however, several events in the first decade of the new century radically transformed this demographic picture. Race riots in 1900 and 1905 made many Blacks, a number of whom lived in midtown Manhattan in the Tenderloin and San Juan Hill sections, fear for their safety. At about this same time many Blacks were being forced out of their homes by new construction projects such as the Pennsylvania Station. These people needed to find a place quickly to live, one close to where they worked and expansive enough to accommodate their rapidly increasing numbers. Harlem seemed the perfect fit. First, the opening of the IRT subway line in 1904 made the area accessible to a large number of people. In addition, the economic downturn of 1903–04 enabled African American real estate brokers such as Philip A. Payton to buy large amounts of property in Harlem (J. W. Johnson 145–59). Following a frequent though unfortunate pattern in American urban development, as Blacks began moving into the area, Whites living there rapidly sold their property. As a result, by 1930 the area from 128th to 145th streets bounded by Fifth and Seventh avenues was almost exclusively inhabited by Blacks (Watkins-Owens, *Blood Relations* 39–53; De Jongh 5–14).

Race, Identity, and "Otherness"

The foreign-born Blacks moving into Harlem had all the problems of other immigrants adjusting to a different way of life; however, in addition to these obstacles, Black immigrants were forced to negotiate a racial "otherness" most had never before encountered. This intersection of ethnicity and race was (and still is) at the nexus of the Black immigrant experience in the United States. Compounding this "otherness" was the hybridity of the anglophone Caribbean immigrant. While W. E. B. Du Bois, in *The Souls of Black Folk* (1903), spoke of the "double consciousness" of African Americans, the Caribbean immigrant took this one step further, loosely combining features of European, African, and American cultures into what critic Paul Gilroy has termed "the black Atlantic." These immigrants had "a desire to escape the restrictive bonds of ethnicity, national identification, and sometimes even 'race' itself" (19). They exhibited a fluidity of identity, describing themselves as Black, as West Indian or Caribbean, as British, as Jamaican (or whatever their homeland was), and, when it suited their purpose, American, and feeling no need to choose between these multiple identities. This, however, often left them feeling not as if they belonged to all of these worlds but rather that they did not quite fit in any of them. Upon coming to the United States, many Caribbean immigrants felt a displacement, "a transformation," as Heather Hathaway suggests, "that can leave one forever distanced and different from the land and people of one's origin, if also from the land of one's adoption" (2).

Once in the United States, these immigrants were often misunderstood by other Americans. West Indians were thought of as a monolithic group despite the significant historical and cultural differences between those from different homelands. To think of the many lands in the Caribbean as a uniform whole is a vast oversimplification. Despite a number of commonalities among the peoples of these lands, there are cultural and linguistic differences between them (attributable in part to the various colonial powers in the region) too subtle for most Americans to detect but readily apparent to anyone from the Caribbean. Often separated by different classes at home, even those from the same land did not fit well when thrust together in America. As Jervis Anderson observes, Caribbean immigrants "clung to the regional and insular attitudes of their particular backgrounds, and there were almost as many rivalries among them as there were between them and the majority of black Americans in Harlem—who viewed the West Indians with a mixture of reserve and resentment" (299).

As if the tensions among these immigrants were not enough, anglophone Caribbean immigrants also had to confront the often-contradictory stereotypes that were held by Americans. Caribbean immigrants were considered to be crafty, intelligent, sensitive, hot tempered, proud, aggressive, ambitious, clannish, and frugal, stereotypes that continue today (Reid 107–08). These perceptions, of course, frequently depended upon the viewer and the particular situation. In some cases West Indians were looked upon more favorably by White Americans than were American-born Blacks. Author Claude McKay, for example, recounts an incident when, while relaxing in a cafe in Pittsburgh largely frequented by African Americans, he was rounded up in a police dragnet intended to catch "draft dodgers and vagrants." After the judge had given out numerous sentences to the American-born Blacks, McKay's turn came. He gave a short defense, after which the judge inquired whether he had been born in Jamaica. When McKay answered affirmatively, the judge replied, "Nice place. I was there a couple of seasons ago," and dismissed the case. Thereafter, McKay decided "to cultivate more my native accent" (7–9).

The experiences of Caribbean immigrants in America, however, were often not so benign as McKay's. Many anglophone Caribbean immigrants had their first encounters with racial prejudice in the United States. In their homelands, even if they had not been in a position of power, they had been part of the majority. At home, although class and skin color (a lighter pigmentation defined social status in many Caribbean islands, particularly Jamaica) might have determined the level of advancement they could attain, their lives had not been circumscribed solely by race. In fact, the bipolar distinction of Black and White was alien to many Caribbean immigrants who had been brought up with many gradations between groups based upon racial complexion and class (Waters 29–31; N. Foner 12–13). They had been taught that advancement would come through hard work and merit and to deemphasize race as a means to social advancement. These immigrants soon realized, however, that in the United States upward mobility did not necessarily shield them from racism (Vickerman 5–6, 112–13). McKay succinctly explains this realization of the intractability of racism: "the first time I had ever come face to face with such manifest, implacable hate of my race . . . my feelings were indescribable" (286, this volume).

The prejudice against Caribbean immigrants as both foreigners and Blacks caused them to resist assimilation assiduously. They held tenaciously to their dress, culture, and religion (most American Blacks were Baptists or Methodists, while anglophone Caribbeans tended to be Episcopalian or Roman Catholic). They also retained their ties to Great Britain, with more than five thousand of them attending a celebration for King George VI's coronation in 1937 (Reid 126–28). Confused and angered by American racism, West Indians often cried out in despair (generally in vain) to the British consulate. Many longed to return to their homelands, and, in fact, a great many did. They often thought of their stay in the United States, even if protracted, as merely "a visit," desperately holding on to the belief that they would someday be able to return to their land of birth (Reid 179). Tellingly, West Indians had the lowest rate of naturalization of any immigrant group. According to the 1930 census, 25.6 percent of foreign-born Blacks twenty-one years of age and older had become citizens, compared to 60.4 percent of foreign-born Whites (Walter, "Caribbean Immigrant" 539). Much of the resistance to assimilation among Caribbeans, no doubt, was due to the vicious racial prejudice they suffered as Blacks in America. Mary Waters, in speaking of contemporary anglophone Caribbean immigrants, makes a telling remark about the effects of racism that is equally applicable to their early-twentieth-century predecessors: "For these immigrants becoming American also entails becoming American black, which they perceive as lower social status than staying a West Indian" (93).

Anglophone Caribbean immigrants faced bias not only from White Americans. The juncture of West Indians and Black Americans from the South in northern urban areas was not always a harmonious one. The immigrants sometimes boasted about the progress they had made in their new land. Some also felt that African Americans were poorly educated and lacking in ambition, not fully understanding the difficulties they experienced every day in dealing with American racism, which often denied them proper education, housing, and career opportunities (Hathaway 21–22). Many American-born Blacks, on the other hand, maintained that anglophone Caribbean immigrants thought of themselves as superior. Their emphasis on schooling and on owning property, and their pride in their British training and in speaking "proper" English, made some American Blacks think they were arrogant. The main source of conflict between the groups was a perceived "competition for jobs, control of black businesses, political influence, and status in general" (Hellwig 185). The result was a frequent antagonism between anglophone Caribbean immigrants and American Blacks. Caribbeans were referred to as "monkey-chasers."

The lyrics to "The West Indies Blues," a popular song of the era, included lines such as "I'll make my livin' sure's you born, / A-divin' after qua'ters" and reflected these negative feelings (qtd. in Reid 114).

While ethnic differences between American Blacks and foreign-born Blacks caused friction between the groups, it would be misleading to suggest that there was constant conflict between them. Some Black Americans were even enthralled by what the immigrants brought to America. Langston Hughes, for instance, praised what he witnessed in anglophone Caribbean Harlem, calling it "warm, rambunctious, sassy . . . little pockets of tropical dreams in alien tongues" (qtd. in Anderson 300). Carter Woodson hailed the spirit of cooperation that often unified those within the Caribbean community (9). Moreover, social conditions frequently forced the two groups into what Jamaican W. A. Domingo described as "reconciling contacts." These conditions brought West Indians into common, albeit tenuous, political and social alliances with Black Americans. As a result of these conflicting impulses, a complex dynamic arose between African Americans and West Indians, whereby the immigrants attempted to distance themselves from Black Americans because of perceived differences over cultural values while simultaneously bonding with them on issues of race (Vickerman 137–60). As Philip Kasinitz observes, "Caribbean New Yorkers of the 1920s and 1930s might have been immigrants in a city of immigrants, but it was race that structured their life chances. Being black determined where they lived and could not live, where they could and could not go to school, what type of job they could get and the way they were treated by Americans of all colors" (8).[4]

Success and the Myth of the Model Minority

Despite the obstacles they encountered, many immigrants flourished. Their success was often facilitated by their background and abetted by the strong bonds of community that prevailed. Caribbean immigrants, perhaps because of their familiarity with migration, often developed remarkably flexible survival skills in their new environment (Henke 38–42). The success of these immigrants is easily documented. For example, in *Who's Who in Colored America* (1930), 6 percent of those listed were foreign-born Blacks, although they made up less than 1 percent of the Black population nationally (Walter and Ansheles 51–52). Black periodicals were peppered with stories of their various achievements. They particularly excelled in business, from the wealthy funeral director Howard A. Howell to the prosperous numbers banker Casper Holstein.[5] Indeed, there was a common expression in Harlem that "[w]hen a West Indian got 'ten cents above a beggar' . . . he opened a business" (qtd. in Osofsky 133). Many did struggle to open businesses, sometimes foraying into areas once off-limits for Blacks, yet their achievements were often tempered by the stranglehold of Whites in business.

This relative success does not mean, however, that Caribbean immigrants, as conservative African American critic Thomas Sowell has contended, were a "model minority," one whose members through hard work and grit alone could (unlike their American Black brethren) succeed despite their skin color. This image of success was one that developed, in part, due to a careful cultivation by West Indians themselves (see, for example, W. A. Domingo's "Gift of the Black Tropics" and Hubert H. Harrison's "Prejudice Growing Less and Cooperation More, Says Student of Question" in this volume).

It is important to consider some of the differences between these immigrants and most members of the African American community. In business, for example, Caribbean immigrants did not face in their home countries the harsh racism that many African Americans endured; therefore, when they came to the United States, "[s]tarting a business could be a realistic goal for those who had capital and experience" (Watkins-Owens, *Blood Relations* 127). In addition, many Caribbean immigrants were far better off than their countrymen and women at home. The cost of transportation alone excluded the poorest members of Caribbean society from the ranks of immigrants to the United States.

While most Caribbean immigrants were far from wealthy, and they were often forced to take domestic positions, their immigration was, on the whole, from a higher social strata of educated and skilled individuals. This was especially true after the Literacy Act of 1917 was passed. Between 1918 and 1932, only about a third of anglophone Caribbean immigrants could be classed as unskilled (Holder 7–12). Between 1924 and 1932, more than 98 percent of Caribbeans immigrating to the United States were literate, a percentage far exceeding that of the general population in their homelands as well as that of the native-born American population, both Black and White (Walter, "Caribbean Immigrant" 524–28).

Winston James reminds us, "[w]hatever the virtues of a sound English common school education, not everyone in the British

Caribbean received one" ("Explaining Afro-Caribbean" 238). The typical Caribbean immigrant to the United States in the early part of the twentieth century, however, was from the segment of the population that did receive a quality education. In fact, it was the disparity in the Caribbean between the more prosperous, better-educated population and those less well off that prompted many to leave their homeland. Thus, it is not surprising that these early Caribbean immigrants often thrived in business and demonstrated upward social mobility.[6]

Gender Issues

Between 1900 and 1930, 48,135 foreign-born Negro women arrived in America, compared to 57,887 men (Reid 236). There are a number of reasons why fewer women than men joined the ranks of the immigrants in this period, unlike today, when women make up the majority of New York's Caribbean population (Scott A1). Some families were reluctant to allow single women to migrate, and the U.S. government, fearing that such women might turn to prostitution, was reluctant to grant them visas. Though their numbers were smaller, Caribbean women who emigrated often tended to stay in the country more permanently than did men, in part because they were more likely to enter the country legally (Watkins-Owens, "Early-Twentieth-Century" 29).

Caribbean women made substantial contributions to the social network of the immigrant community, though the subject has received little critical attention to date. In some cases, they were the first members of their families to arrive in America, helping to pave the way for others. Hubert Harrison, Cyril Briggs, W. A. Domingo, and Richard B. Moore, for example, all joined female family members upon first arrival in the United States.

While gender restrictions often had curtailed their educational opportunities in their home countries, most of the female immigrants from the Caribbean had received a primary school education or had some training in a skilled trade. In America, these women typically worked as domestics or laundry workers or in the higher-paying jobs in the garment industry (as finishers, dressmakers, and needlepointers). The more entrepreneurial women sought employment in hairdressing, real estate, nursing, or even the illegal numbers games. Like most Black workers, however, their earnings were limited despite their job skills. Whatever their earnings, women worked to help provide "the down payment on a brownstone house, a college education for their children, and the much coveted middle-class status these achievements represented" (P. Marshall 83). In addition, women, particularly mothers, were expected to provide remittances, an essential resource for those back home.

Women also were often central figures in the numerous benevolent and rotation credit associations (a means of building capital by pooling resources) that helped foster growth in the local community and provided support for those in their native lands. Furthermore, as will be explored in more detail later in my introduction, they also were frequent contributors to the political and literary arenas (Watkins-Owens, "Early-Twentieth-Century").

The Decline and Revival of the Caribbean Community

Although West Indian immigrants achieved great success in the first three decades of the twentieth century, hostility toward immigrants, and particularly toward people of color, increased markedly during and after World War I, as is evidenced by the anti-immigrant Alien Act of 1918. The effects of this hostility are also reflected in the Immigration Act of 1924, which greatly reduced immigration quotas for all but Northern Europeans. As a result of the Immigration Act, foreign-born Black immigration to the United States fell from 12,243 in 1924 to 791 in 1925 (Walter, "The Caribbean Immigrant" 542). Despite the obvious racism in the legislation, however, there was little American-born Black opposition. Fred R. Moore, for example, in an editorial in the conservative African American newspaper the *New York Age*, denounced newer West Indians for "flaunt[ing] their British allegiance" and for making "disloyal utterances." W. E. B. Du Bois, who had earlier written that he was "proud" of his own Caribbean heritage, essentially washed his hands of the whole matter: "The Nordic champions undoubtedly put one over on us in the recent immigration bill. If our West Indian friends had watched more carefully and warned us, we might have been able to take some effective step" (qtd. in Watkins-Owens, *Blood Relations* 28).[7]

The 1924 act signaled the end of the first great wave of anglophone Caribbean immigration to the United States. The decline was hastened considerably by the onset of the Great Depression and the subsequent shortage of jobs. By 1933, as was the case with many immigrant groups at the time, more West Indians were leaving the

United States than were entering The number of Caribbean immigrants remained fairly small until the passage in 1965 of the Hart-Cellar Immigration and Nationality Act. This act and the subsequent amendments to it made it much easier for the next generation of anglophone Caribbean immigrants to come to America. Indeed, they continue to come, in remarkable numbers, often to New York City, just as their predecessors did. Jamaica and Guyana, for example, despite having relatively small populations, remain among the top five countries sending immigrants to New York (Dugger A1).

The continuing surge of immigration has caused many "to rethink, if not reconceive, the notion of *diasporic citizenship* so as to take stock of the newer facets of the globalization process" (Laguerre 5). As Holger Henke has stated, "While the rest of the world is only beginning to experience globalization, Caribbean people have been located at the center of this maelstrom for several hundred years" (153). The Caribbean person is almost from birth taught to look outward, because of overcrowding, political and environmental events, or limited educational and economic opportunities at home. Migration is thus a natural part of the Caribbean psyche.

The seeds of transnationalism were already present, then, in the early Caribbean immigrants. Their correspondence, remittances, rotating credit systems, and participation in nationalistic organizations (ranging from small groups such as the Montserrat Progressive Society to the broader Universal Negro Improvement Association) helped them maintain ties with their countries (or region) of origin at the same time that they were establishing themselves in their new lands. The close proximity of their native lands and the constant influx of new immigrants abetted this process, and this has increased exponentially over the past thirty-five years (Sutton 15–29; N. Foner 7–10; Thomas 45–58; Basch, Schiller, and Blanc). In these times of ever increasing global movement, as Michelle Stephens notes, historicizing the Caribbean experience can "teach us something new about the very construction and use of hegemonic categories of race, nation and ethnicity throughout the [twenty-first] century" (594).

Political and Social Aspects: The "Making" of a Radical

The America that the anglophone Caribbean immigrant entered at the turn of the twentieth century was one filled with racial tension. Jim

Crow laws were pervasive and Blacks had little political clout. Booker T. Washington, founder of the Tuskegee Institute in Alabama, remained a powerful presence. Washington, an often maligned but complex figure, advocated racial accommodation, believing that conditions for American Blacks could best be advanced by industrial and agricultural expertise rather than agitation toward civil rights. Despite the opposition of other Black leaders, including W. E. B. Du Bois and Ida B. Wells Barnett, Washington's position, which had its base in the rural South, held sway in the late nineteenth century and the early years of the twentieth century.[8]

This period was among the most blatantly racist in America's history. Legal decisions such as *Plessy v. Ferguson* (1896) legitimized Jim Crow. Popular author Thomas Dixon celebrated the Ku Klux Klan in his novel *The Clansman* (1905), which was the basis for D. W. Griffith's classic film, *The Birth of a Nation* (1915). In fact, the Klan reorganized itself in 1915, emerging more virulent than ever in both the North and the South. Workplace discrimination was rampant, and lynching continued unabated. As the United States entered World War I, deep racial unrest divided the nation, culminating in a race riot in East St. Louis on July 2, 1917.

Black leaders were divided over whether Blacks should serve in World War I, but many, such as Du Bois, ultimately urged them to "close ranks" with White America and to participate in the struggle (the *Crisis*, July 1918). The hopes of many Black leaders were raised by President Woodrow Wilson's famous Fourteen Points speech on January 8, 1918, with its proposal for self-determination of subject peoples. Their aspirations, however, were quickly dashed when Wilson turned out to be unsympathetic to demands for equality at home.

Though close to 400,000 Blacks fought in the War, after its finish in 1918 many saw that their sacrifices had largely been in vain. This was particularly difficult to accept for those who had served in France, with its somewhat more egalitarian views on race. The North, too, was a source of disillusionment for the New Negro. Many Blacks, seeing the increased demand for labor during the war years and seeking escape from poverty, lynching, and Jim Crow, sought refuge in the North only to encounter de facto segregation there. Harlem was rife with social ills of its own, including overcrowding, job discrimination, a scarcity of Black-owned businesses, crime, and high tuberculosis and infant mortality rates (Wintz 24–29).

Thoroughly disillusioned, many Blacks began to fight back, particularly during the so-called Red Summer of 1919, when there were bloody uprisings in a number of cities, including Chicago and Washington (Lewis, *When Harlem* 3–24). The government waged an intensive war against those groups it considered radical—in the case of Blacks, essentially anyone advocating "racial change of which they [Whites] disapproved" (Kornweibel, *No Crystal Stair* 69). During the "Red Scare" of 1919–20, Attorney General A. Mitchell Palmer ordered a series of raids in which over ten thousand people were arrested and some three hundred deported. Many people were under surveillance, radical organizations were routinely infiltrated with government informers, and publications were examined and in some cases detained by the mail service. Black publications such as the *Messenger,* the *Negro World,* the *Crusader,* and even the more moderate organ of the National Association for the Advancement of Colored People (NAACP), the *Crisis,* were deemed seditious. In November 1919, Palmer submitted a report on Black periodicals to the Justice Department that was a scathing indictment of the revolutionary tendencies of these publications. In that same year, New York State Senator Clayton R. Lusk headed a committee to trace the impact of "Bolshevism" in New York and the dangers it posed. Lusk conducted his research by making illegal raids on the socialist Rand School, seizing material, and reporting on the committee's research in 1920 (P. Foner, *American Socialism* 292–315; Kornweibel, *No Crystal Stair* 66–104).[9] In such a climate, when any Black who dared aspire to full equality with Whites was branded a radical, only the boldest (or most disaffected) would choose to belong to subversive groups.

Many of those who did so were Caribbean immigrants; in fact, Kelly Miller, conservative dean of Howard University, said that by definition, a Negro radical is "an *over*-educated West Indian without a job" (James, *Holding Aloft* 2). The large-scale involvement of Caribbean immigrants in radical American political movements is remarkable, especially when one considers that since many were not citizens, they could not vote, hold office, or even register in a political party. This radicalism chiefly manifested itself through a somewhat permeable involvement in militant trade unions, Black nationalist, or socialist or communist organizations (Walter, "Black Immigrants" 131).[10]

There has been much discussion of the reasons for anglophone Caribbean radicalism. Kelly Miller, for example, believed that

Caribbeans were conservative while in their home countries but became "radical abroad" (qtd. in Henry 29). Ira Reid, Harold Cruse, Dennis Forsythe, and Keith Henry all, to varying degrees, advance a similar theory of political transformation on the part of Caribbean migrants. There are several flaws, however, in such reasoning. First, it is inaccurate to assume the submissiveness of Caribbean people at home. Caribbean rebelliousness has a long history, dating back to the Maroons, runaway slaves who established their own communities. Many Caribbean immigrants, such as Marcus Garvey and W. A. Domingo, had already exhibited radical tendencies in the West Indies, having been part of trade unions or nationalist organizations. The seeds for their behavior were planted in their homelands, only to reach fruition under differing conditions in their new land.

Upon arriving in the United States, anglophone Caribbean people, like many immigrants, felt a loss of status and prestige from what they had known in their homelands. Black immigrants, having been among the elite in the Caribbean, had generally received a solid primary and secondary school education and job training, giving them the skills that would allow them to expect good positions; therefore, many were genuinely shocked when they faced discrimination in America that they had not endured at home. They had been unaccustomed in their homelands to Jim Crow laws, let alone more heinous crimes such as lynching.

In addition, because they often had been forced to move abroad due to limited higher educational and employment opportunities, Caribbean immigrants, like other immigrants who tended to be at the fore of radical politics, generally had a more international viewpoint than many native-born Americans. The experience of seeing life in other countries and interacting with other Blacks helped lead Caribbean immigrants to a more Pan-African perspective. Furthermore, the immigrants, unlike most Black Americans, who were linked to the Republican party, felt no special allegiance to any one political party and had few qualms about aligning themselves with other parties (James, *Holding Aloft* 50–91; Walter, "Caribbean Immigrant" 532–35).

Garveyism

Marcus Mosiah Garvey was a major figure in the Caribbean community during the Harlem Renaissance. This is not meant to suggest that all his supporters were Caribbean; more than half in the United States were, in fact, African Americans (James, *Holding Aloft* 134–35). It is no coincidence that Garvey's message found resonance when it did, during a time when many Blacks felt betrayed and prone to militancy. This atmosphere of discontent provided fertile soil for Garvey's philosophy, which combined Booker T. Washington's belief in Black economic self-empowerment with a growing sense of Black nationalism. It was an amalgam that synergized Black America in the 1920s.

Garvey's appeal was not to Du Bois, who felt that the best way to uplift the masses was through an educated elite—the "Talented Tenth." Instead, Garvey courted the common person directly. He published his weekly newspaper, the *Negro World*, at a price working people could afford, and sections of it were published in Spanish and French in order to appeal to a wider audience. He established the Negro Factories Corporation, which managed many Black businesses, including restaurants, laundries, a hotel, a printing press, and a doll factory. He held huge annual conventions. He sold shares (only to Blacks) in his Black Star Steamship Line, a Black-run business that transported Blacks throughout the world. He encouraged the establishment of branches of the organization he helped found, the Universal Negro Improvement and Conservation Association and African Communities (Imperial) League (UNIA), internationally. As a result, he succeeded in galvanizing the largest mass movement in Black history.

Garvey's message, reiterated over and over, is readily apparent in some of the most famous catch-phrases of his movement, including "Race First," "Africa for the Africans," "Up, You Mighty Race!" and "One Aim! One God! One Destiny!" Garvey steadfastly believed that Blacks had been responsible for many of the greatest accomplishments in world history, and he constantly appealed to the racial pride of his audience.

Like Du Bois and other Black leaders, Garvey embraced the concept of Pan-Africanism, an attempt to unify Blacks throughout the diaspora, but Garvey, unlike most of these other leaders, did not advocate assimilation into American culture. Instead, he proposed a separate Black state to be established in Africa. Garvey's separatist beliefs were a direct challenge to those like Du Bois who espoused integration within the larger community. Although Garvey was not the first to launch a "Back to Africa" movement (those preceding him included Martin Delany and Alexander Crummell), he was the first to gain such an international response. This does not mean that Garvey believed all Blacks should be living in Africa—he himself had never visited the continent—or that his followers all desired to return to the Motherland (most did not). Garvey's movement stressed "African redemption," the liberation of Africa from foreign powers, maintaining that it was essential for the benefit of Blacks worldwide to have a powerful, independent Black state in Africa.

At first, Garvey's movement met with incredible success. The conferences he held were enormous and his meeting place, Liberty Hall, was regularly packed for his speeches. Soon, however, cracks began to appear. Many of his early supporters questioned his strong-arm tactics and his financial abilities as well as his perceived resistance to the widening Marxist movements of the 1920s. Others, like Du Bois, felt he was crude and did not understand the complicated situation of Blacks in America. White Americans saw him as dangerous, stirring up the Black masses. He had, in fact, been under investigation by the government since 1919 (Kornweibel, "Seeing Red" 100–31). In the face of such overwhelming opposition, it was inevitable that Garvey's empire would soon crumble. The end came with the federal investigation of his activities, culminating in his indictment in 1922 on charges of mail fraud involving the sale of Black Star Line stock, his imprisonment in 1925, and his eventual deportation in 1927.

Evaluating what happened to cause Garvey's downfall and assessing his achievements is difficult. Garvey was neither a flawless saint nor, to use Du Bois's phrase, a "lunatic or a traitor" (the *Crisis*, May 1924). Certainly many of his strategies backfired. He ran his organization with an iron fist, which turned away some supporters. He did not fully comprehend the history of the Negro in America. The military uniforms he and his followers wore and the ceremonial titles he bestowed (Garvey gave himself the title of "Provisional President of Africa") were meant to instill pride, an essential component of his program, but were seen as pompous and ridiculous by his opponents. His skills as a fiscal manager were questionable, as was readily apparent in his purchase of decaying vessels for the Black Star Line, depleting the UNIA of funds; however, in Garvey's defense, his hands were tied, since virtually no one would agree to sell him any ships. His greatest miscalculation was in meeting with the Ku Klux Klan in 1922 to discuss attitudes toward race. Garvey felt that "potentially, every whiteman is a Klansman," so he maintained that the "honesty" of the

Klan made them "better friends of the race" than the integrationists were (67, this volume). Although the Klan was as fervent as Garvey was in expediting the departure of Blacks from America, the vast majority of Black Americans did not wish any "assistance" from the Grand Wizardry. No matter what one's views on this controversial figure, however, few Black leaders in history have had the large-scale impact of Garvey, one that influenced the Black Nationalist movement of the 1960s, the Rastafarians, and the Nation of Islam.

Women in the Garveyite Movement

Garvey, of course, did not run the organization alone. He was ably assisted by numerous loyal supporters, including his two wives, Amy Ashwood and Amy Jacques. Women, in fact, played a significant part in the UNIA. In the words of novelist Paule Marshall, not only did the women regularly contribute money to the UNIA, "but they attended meetings, marched in parades, and served as members of the nurses' brigade" (84). Still, the UNIA essentially saw "the woman not as worker or professional but as helpmate and partner to the man, a moral influence, a charitable volunteer, and an educator of children" (Bair 159). However, the ideal UNIA Race Mother was expected to assume responsibilities extending beyond the domestic sphere. As Beryl Satter observes, "Garveyite women who tried to follow the New Negro Woman model of both creating a perfect home life and actively serving the UNIA inevitably found themselves exhausted by the multiple demands on their lives" (50–51).

In the highly segregated UNIA world, women had clearly defined roles. Most chapters had separate meetings for women and men. The women would elect a "lady president" for their chapter, who would then report to the male president, who in turn reported to Garvey. While they desired to be supportive of Black men in advancing the nationalist cause and believed that their role in rearing the children helped uplift the community, women often resisted the secondary status they were assigned.

Despite the Garveyite movement's sexist trappings, the UNIA appealed to many women. Their participation allowed some, for the first time, "to engage in public sphere leadership outside their immediate community" (Watkins-Owens, "Early-Twentieth-Century" 46). There were significant all-female divisions, including the Black Cross

Nurses and the Universal African Motor Corps. In addition, several women rose to key positions, including Audley Moore, Maymie Turpeau de Mena, and Henrietta Vinton Davis.[11]

Most prominent among these women were Garvey's two wives. Though there is little published material by Amy Ashwood Garvey, she played a role in establishing the UNIA, including the formation of a ladies' division. Her unpublished biography of her husband, a portion of which is included in this anthology, vividly describes her views on the founding of the movement. The indomitable Amy Jacques Garvey published her thoughts regularly in her *Negro World* column "Our Women and What They Think" from 1924 to 1927, where she tackled a host of issues ranging from motherhood to Black nationalism. She also spread the Garveyite message by editing *The Philosophy and Opinions of Marcus Garvey*.

Black and Red

While Garvey's separatist Black nationalism might seem antithetical to Black involvement in Marxism, with its general emphasis (in theory if not always in practice) on integration between workers regardless of race, the two were actually different strands of Black radicalism stemming from a similar source: widespread disaffection caused by the position of Blacks in America. While Black Marxists may have disagreed with Garvey's racial exclusiveness, his support of capitalism, and his quasi-imperialist views on Africa, they lauded his appeal to Black pride and marveled at his success in appealing to the masses. It should, therefore, come as no surprise that many Black Marxists initially were Garvey supporters. Garvey had "leaped into the ocean of black unhappiness at a most timely moment for a savior" (Ottley 69). Socialist and communist supporters hoped to tap into this same feeling of Black discontent in recruiting new adherents. As noted by William J. Maxwell, "Migratory black intellectuals clashed over much but jointly regarded the oppression of blacks as a transnational ill requiring transnational remedies" (21).

The possible "remedies" were readily evidenced in the "stepladder" or "soapbox" tradition. Venturing along Lenox Avenue in Harlem most evenings between 1910 and 1930, one was likely to encounter any number of speakers engaged in fiery political rhetoric. Many of the speakers, including Hubert H. Harrison, Richard B. Moore, Frank

R. Crosswaith, George Padmore, Elizabeth Hendrickson, Helena Benta, and Bonita Williams, were Caribbean immigrants.[12] These radicals, coming from a culture which had long valued skills in elocution, spoke out on a variety of issues, including women's suffrage, birth control, workers' rights, and Black rights.

Socialism

One way in which Caribbean radicalism took shape was within the socialist movement. Socialism in America has a long, complex history with various strands dating back to antebellum days. While it is reductive to consider it as a monolithic whole, generally socialism stresses that workers' conditions are determined by economics, not race, and that when the conditions for exploited workers of all races improve, racial problems will be eliminated. Such a view emphasizes class rather than race. Although the national Socialist Party expressed scant desire to recruit Blacks, by the beginning of World War I in Europe in 1914, the Socialist Party chapter in New York, with its anti-war beliefs, its emphasis on trade unionism, and its support for the working class, garnered growing support among Blacks. As a result, the Socialist Party candidate for mayor in 1917, Morris Hillquit, gained 25 percent of the votes in Harlem (P. Foner, *American Socialism* 1–93, 279).

An important early Black radical was Hubert H. Harrison, from the Virgin Islands, whose philosophy blended socialism and Black nationalism. Although he eventually broke with the Socialist Party because of its White chauvinism, Harrison influenced a number of Blacks toward socialism through his articles and speeches, including southerners A. Philip Randolph and Chandler Owen, who would form the *Messenger* magazine in 1917.

The *Messenger* group—opposed to American involvement in World War I, strong advocates of Black membership in trade unions, and supportive of socialism—would include a number of prominent Blacks, including Caribbeans Frank R. Crosswaith and W. A. Domingo. Crosswaith was instrumental in working with A. Philip Randolph to organize the Brotherhood of Sleeping Car Porters and Maids (BSCP).[13] Called the "Negro Eugene Debs," Crosswaith devoted his life to incorporating Blacks into the labor movement. Domingo, a loyal socialist, was one of the editors of the *Messenger* and worked with the periodical for several years until breaking with it over its representation of Caribbeans in 1923. Of all the *Messenger* group, Domingo "continually linked the antiracist class struggle in the United States with movements against colonialism around the globe" (Foley, *Spectres* 51). Domingo also was assisted by Randolph and Owen in establishing his own short-lived socialist, anti-Garveyite publication, the *Emancipator* (1920).

Despite the forceful presence of such Black leaders as Harrison, Crosswaith, and Domingo, the Socialist Party was generally not able to shed its paternalistic views of Blacks. Even Socialist Party leader Eugene Debs, who later condemned his party's lack of support for Black concerns, had said as early as 1903, "We have nothing special to offer the Negro, and we cannot make separate appeals to all the races" (qtd. in Draper 316). The party's philosophy was best summed up by James Oneal's pamphlet *The Next Emancipation* (1922), the only socialist publication between 1919 and 1935 dealing exclusively with the Black condition. Oneal opposed any "social equality" between the races, fearing a southern backlash, and essentially maintained "that there was no special Negro problem" (P. Foner, *American Socialism* 321). Many Blacks, while agreeing with socialists that racial prejudice was largely based on economics, felt that special attention must be given to the condition of racial minorities. Du Bois stated that the "The Negro Problem . . . is the great test of the American Socialist" ("Socialism" 140). If that is the case, then the socialists generally did not score high grades in the early decades of the twentieth century.

Communism

The Russian Revolution of 1917 would lead to a split within the Socialist Party between those who felt such a rebellion would be possible in the United States and those who did not foresee such an event in the immediate future. The former, more radical group became communists who took hope in the Soviet Union's anti-imperialist, anti-colonial stance and in actions taken to stop pogroms against Jews in Russia. These early communists included Caribbean immigrants Claude McKay, Otto Huiswoud, George Padmore, Richard B. Moore, and Cyril Briggs. Huiswoud and McKay even traveled to Russia and spoke at the Fourth Congress of the comintern in Moscow in 1922, where they received a warm welcome. As McKay's biographer, Wayne Cooper, points out, "The official stance of the

Comintern [Communist International] regarding blacks in 1922 was influenced by West Indians, who were simultaneously much more nationalistic, class conscious, and international-minded than were American-born blacks" (180–81).

Blacks were not always as openly embraced, however, in the Communist Party in the United States. When the Communist Party of America was formed in 1919, the party's views on the "Negro problem" were similar to those of the socialists, placing little emphasis on race and maintaining that racial prejudice stemmed from capitalism and would be eradicated when the system was overthrown by workers of all races.[14] However, fearing that Blacks would become strike breakers, the large unions began to make efforts to unionize Black labor. As a result, the American Federation of Labor (AFL) Convention in 1919 had the largest delegation of Blacks (twenty-three) in its history. Seeing these gains by labor and prodded by the Soviets in Russia and by Blacks within the party, by the early 1920s the Communist Party in America slowly sought to gain Black recruits.

Some of the leading members of the communist group were Cyril Briggs, Richard B. Moore, and Otto Huiswoud. Briggs, a native of Nevis (now St. Kitts and Nevis), penned a series of fiery editorials in the *Amsterdam News*. An advocate of Black nationalism, Briggs initially was drawn to Garvey, but the two disagreed about communism. Barbadian Richard B. Moore, an eloquent speaker, was deeply concerned with the rights of workers and tenants. Later he would take up the cause of the Scottsboro Boys, arguing for the release of a group of Black youths unfairly accused of raping two white women in Alabama in 1931. Otto Huiswoud, from Dutch Guiana (now Suriname), was one of the earliest Black communists and wrote for such radical periodicals as the *Communist*.

Briggs, Moore, and Huiswoud were among the driving forces behind the African Blood Brotherhood for African Liberation and Redemption (ABB), first announced in the October 1919 issue of Briggs's radical periodical the *Crusader*. No agenda was set forth, no phone number even provided, just a call for those who were "willing to go the limit" (James, *Holding Aloft* 168–69). The response to this brief notice was immediate, with enthusiastic letters coming from around the globe. Just as the initial call provides scant information on the group, however, so does much about the ABB remain wrapped in secrecy, this despite the increasing attention that has been paid to this pivotal organization. The ABB was a paramilitary organization founded in response to the race riots during the Red Summer of 1919 and drew its name from the symbolic blood-sharing ceremony performed by some African tribes. The ABB credo, largely drawn from articles within the *Crusader*, merged Black nationalism with Marxism, espousing workers' rights, Black liberation, and anti-imperialism. Perhaps its most distinctive characteristic was its support for armed Black self-defense.

Because of its secretive nature, it is hard to know exactly how many adherents the ABB had. Most likely, however, there were never more than three thousand, with a significantly smaller core group. The leaders were almost exclusively Caribbean; indeed, without its Caribbean members, the ABB would scarcely have existed. In addition to Briggs, who was the executive head, Moore, and Huiswoud, its members included Domingo, McKay, and Grace Campbell.[15] There remains considerable debate as to whether the organization was founded by the communists, but regardless, it soon became affiliated with the party.

Although it attempted to win over members from the UNIA, attending the organization's conference in 1920, the ABB could never attain this goal. The ABB's lack of a charismatic presence such as Garvey, its extreme views, its lack of funding, and its secretive nature militated against its gaining widespread popularity. With little to sustain it, the ABB's membership gradually dissipated, until it was dissolved in 1925 into the Workers' Party, a group to which most of the ABB members had already belonged. Soon it would be replaced by the Communist Party with the American Negro Labor Congress (ANLC). Despite its brief existence and small membership, the ABB was an important force in the history of communism in America, as its cadre of loyal followers would be instrumental in recruiting new members to the party during its heyday in the late 1930s.

The ANLC was envisioned as "a centralized movement of black protest led by labor" (Solomon 52). Formed in 1925 from what was left of the ABB, it included many of the same members, such as Huiswoud, Briggs, Moore, and Campbell. However, the ANLC was doomed to failure almost from the start, for several reasons. First, the average Black worker remained skeptical of it, perceiving it as a repository for disgruntled Black communists being manipulated by Whites. This perception was reinforced by the very visible presence of Whites in the organization. Second, the American Federation of Labor looked askance at a large radical organization trying to unify Black workers. Third, the government was cracking down hard on the labor movement, particularly groups that smacked of Bolshevik influence. As a result, the ANLC soon was reduced to a small hard-core group of radical labor unionists and was disbanded by the party in 1929.

Despite its relatively early demise, the impact of the ANLC should not be discounted. The ANLC took up many causes, from the local Harlem Tenants League, spearheaded by Moore, which effectively confronted landlords and their political backers over issues such as high rents and substandard living conditions, to the Caribbean Jamaican Trades and Labor Union, co-founded by Huiswoud. Furthermore, although the ANLC was not able to get many new recruits, those they were able to attract included African American James W. Ford (later a key party member) and Trinidadian George Padmore, who would go on to work for the International Trade Union Committee of Negro Workers and to edit the organization's journal, the *Negro Worker*. He would also be the author of the important anti-imperialist tract *The Life and Struggles of Negro Toilers*. As Mark Solomon observes, "The ANLC's fundamental belief in the importance of black workers to the cause of unionism and social progress reemerged in the left-wing National Negro Labor Council under Coleman Young in the 1950s, in [A. Philip] Randolph's black labor coalition in the 1960s, and in the present-day Coalition of Black Trade Unionists" (67).

Seeing that their strategies were not attracting many Blacks, the communists took more drastic measures. The Soviet Communist Party, noting the lure of Black nationalism as represented by the UNIA, wished to tap into this appeal now that Garvey's movement was in disarray. At the Sixth World Congress of the Comintern, the Soviets, with some key Black supporters such as African American Harry Haywood, proposed a resolution, passed October 26, 1928, that American Blacks were an oppressed nation and, in the counties of the Black Belt South from Virginia to Texas where they were a majority, deserved the right of self-determination. The resolution drew resistance from White chauvinists and divided the ranks of Black members of the party. Many, like Huiswoud, opposed it, feeling that though Blacks were oppressed, they were not a subject nation. Others, however, such as Briggs and Moore, embraced it, though it left many specifics unclear (e.g., whether the founding of this Black nation would be through violence, who would lead the struggle to create it, and whether it would become a sovereign nation or a self-governing region within the United States). Some, though skeptical of the resolution, felt that a clear mandate had been given by Moscow to involve Blacks more directly in party activity and to banish White chauvinism. The resolution, though it had little effect on Blacks' right to self-determination, did spotlight race and increasingly emboldened Blacks to demand their own unions and organizations (Draper 342–53; Haywood 332–38; Solomon 68–91; E. Hutchinson 43–58; Record 54–119).

The party's gradual development of a Negro program began to show gains in the 1930s. No doubt Black support of the party was abetted to some extent by the downturn of the economy during the Depression, which was particularly harsh on Blacks (Naison 5–31). By 1932, one of every two Blacks in New York was unemployed (E. Hutchinson 59). Communist sympathy for the Scottsboro Boys also gained support for the party within the Black community.[16] Despite these gains, however, many White members of the party remained adamant about not allowing Blacks real autonomy. The party established the League of Struggle for Negro Rights in 1930 and made Briggs editor of its newspaper, the *Liberator*, but its insistence that the organization appeal only to Negro issues undoubtedly contributed to its demise by 1934 (Kelley 110–11).

Assessing the Marxist-Black Connection

Despite the efforts of Marxist groups, the number of Blacks attracted to socialism and particularly communism were fairly small in the 1920s and early 1930s. Most Americans remained wary of Marxism, seeing it as a means for foreigners to take over the government. Some Blacks rejected Marxism because they believed it remained possible for them through capitalism to achieve part of the American dream. For others, this rejection was a matter of survival; they simply felt it was too dangerous to be both Black and "red."

Evaluations of the relationship between Blacks and the Communist Party have not been completely fair. Critics such as Harold Cruse and Wilson Record saw the Communist (Workers') Party as being dominated by the Soviet Union. Cruse, in particular, made a harsh indictment of the role of Caribbean intellectuals within radical American politics (see James, *Holding Aloft* 262–91 for a reasoned rebuke of Cruse). Record and Cruse, and to a lesser extent Theodore Draper, maintained that the socialist and communist organizations were dominated by Whites and addressed Black issues only when it was convenient for their own purposes. Any changes that took place, these critics felt, were only at the prodding of the Soviet Union.

While these accusations are not completely baseless, recent critics such as William Maxwell, Winston James, Barbara Foley, and Mark Solomon provide a more balanced viewpoint, arguing that the communists did not just follow in lockstep with Soviet Russia, nor were Blacks mere pawns of the party. Leading Black spokespersons such as Briggs, Moore, and Huiswoud were often unafraid to voice their opposition. At times, this led to their censure or even dismissal from the party. In general, though, Black Marxist leaders believed that the best way to advance Black concerns was through solidarity with the larger White proletariat. By eliminating the capitalist system, they felt they could lessen some of the economic disparities that suppressed Blacks and encouraged the growth of imperialism.

Black immigrants played an important role in shaping the radical movement in American politics. The Communist Party in particular "probed neglected areas of African American history, especially militant and nationalist currents, the sordid legacy of white racism, and connections between black Americans and blacks around the world" (Solomon 87). The discussion of "the Negro Question" by the Comintern in 1928 stirred many Black radicals and progressive Whites, no matter what their position on the proposal. Despite these gains, Black communists were often stymied by the pervasive "white chauvinism" within the Communist Party in America, a bias that helped to deter Blacks from joining the party. Nevertheless, as Philip S. Foner and James S. Allen observe, "throughout the 1920s the Communists did make significant advances beyond the old Socialist stand, developing on their own the elements of a program that would eventually recognize the national quality of the 'Negro question'" (xi). Whatever progress was made was in large part due to this small group of pioneering radicals. In fact, the face of Marxist politics in post–World War One America in general would have been vastly different without the presence of people like Harrison, Domingo, Moore, Huiswoud, and Briggs, who helped to lay the groundwork for the cross-racial, cross-cultural coalitions at the base of many of today's trade unions and radical political movements. Their involvement helped lead to a surge of interest in Marxism that would reach its apex in the late 1930s, when as many as ten thousand Blacks would belong to the Communist Party (Vincent, *Voices* 169).

Literature and Culture

Anglophone Caribbean immigrants, coming from a tradition that put great stock in literacy, emphasized the importance of reading as part of the racial struggle.[17] Hubert H. Harrison, Richard B. Moore, J. A. Rogers, and Arthur Schomburg were some of the great collectors of Black books. As Schomburg's biographer, Elinor Des Verney Sinnette, points out, such bibliophiles "viewed their collecting as another facet of the continuing struggle against social, economic, and cultural prejudice" (76). They and others such as Marcus Garvey, Amy Jacques Garvey, and Cyril Briggs espoused the necessity of reading in order to advance the race (James, *Holding Aloft* 78–80). Perhaps this goal is stated best by Harrison in *When Africa Awakes*.

> It is not with our teeth that we will tear the white man out of our ancestral land. It isn't with our jaws that we can ring from his hard hands consideration and respect. It must be done by the upper and not by the lower parts of our heads. Therefore, I have insisted ever since my entry into the arena of racial discussion that we Negroes must take to reading. (123)

Periodicals

Periodicals were the literary and political material most widely read by Blacks during the Harlem Renaissance. While magazines such as the *New Republic, American Mercury,* and the *Nation* published some Black writers, it was the Black journals—including the *Crisis* (1910–), the *Messenger* (1917–28), *Opportunity* (1923–49), and the *Negro World* (1918–33), all of which were ostensibly political in scope—that largely nurtured the Harlem Renaissance. Any grasp of the movement necessitates an understanding of these periodicals; indeed, it could not have risen to the level that it did without them.

It should come as no surprise that politics and culture were so closely intertwined in the period. In speaking of the African Blood

Brotherhood, Ted Vincent points out the links between the two: "The brotherhood represented those who felt revolution had to encompass not just new economic relationships, but new relationships in all fields of life—cultural, artistic, musical and philosophical. The logic of the dialectical outlook led Briggs and his cohorts to be cultural as well as economic and political radicals" (*Keep Cool* 146).

All of the leading figures of the Harlem Renaissance—including Du Bois, Charles S. Johnson, James Weldon Johnson, Walter White, Jessie Fauset, Alain Locke, Randolph, Garvey, and Briggs—to varying degrees and looking through different lenses, saw the potency of culture in advancing political ends. No matter their particular agenda, because of the overlap between politics and aesthetics, all the leading journals, in addition to social and political writings, included reviews of books and theater as well as original poetry, plays, fiction, and literary criticism. Most also sponsored literary contests and gave away books.

The NAACP's organ the *Crisis* was under the firm hand of Du Bois from 1910–34 with the assistance of the astute Jessie Fauset as literary editor from 1919–26. The journal, and Du Bois's own literary output, reflected his dictum that "all Art is propaganda" ("Criteria" 103), essentially expressing the belief that art was a race-building tool, one that should express a political content. The *Crisis* was the most influential Black magazine of the period, with a peak circulation of 100,000 copies. Virtually all of the major names of the period were published there, including Countee Cullen, Langston Hughes, and Zora Neale Hurston. A number of Claude McKay's works were also included, until a harsh review of *Home to Harlem* (1928) in which Du Bois expressed the need to bathe after reading the novel. Such a view is reflective of Du Bois's increasingly strong belief "that Afro-American literature could shape public opinion in a constructive way only if it dealt primarily with the black middle class" (Johnson and Johnson 64). It was a view that alienated him from many of the younger, more radical, New Negro writers, who did not see their artistic productions linked entirely to civil rights.[18]

Although it never exceeded a circulation of eleven thousand, *Opportunity*, the house publication of the National Urban League, was likely the journal that best fostered the younger writers. Charles S. Johnson, the editor from the magazine's inception until September 1928, encouraged interracial cooperation and maintained that it was through the power of art and literature that the intellectual and social parity of the race could be established. Johnson, trained as a sociologist, believed "that art and life are inseparable, that art serves the enrichment of everyday experience of the common world, and thus ultimately the improvement of that world for enhanced living—art is, in the widest possible sense, 'use-full'" (G. Hutchinson 177). Johnson's philosophy, which stressed "freedom and self-expression for the creative writer" (Johnson and Johnson 51), was favored by many of the younger, radical writers of the period, including Eric Walrond (who served as business manager from August 1925 to February 1927). Walrond lobbied to include these writers, and he himself published several stories and reviews in *Opportunity*, including "The Stone Rebounds," the first piece of fiction to be published in the journal. While serving as business manager, he helped to broaden the international scope of the journal, particularly in a special November 1926 issue focusing on the Caribbean. Walrond also facilitated financial assistance from Caribbean businessman Casper Holstein, described by Hubert Harrison as New York's sole Black patron of the arts, who for a time funded the influential Opportunity Awards.

Johnson arranged the famous Civic Club dinner of March 21, 1924, presided over by Howard University professor Alain Locke and attended by over a hundred influential Black and White authors and publishers. The dinner helped lead to a special issue of the journal *Survey Graphic* (March 1925), which was expanded into the groundbreaking anthology *The New Negro* (1925) edited by Locke.

Described by Claude McKay as a "remarkable chocolate soufflé of art and politics," *The New Negro* is filled with optimism, largely based on Locke's hope of growing racial cooperation between "the enlightened minorities of both race groups" fostered through the "artistic endowments and cultural contributions, past and prospective" of Blacks. Because of its emphasis on racial integration, Black nationalism and Marxist politics are largely neglected. However, the anthology, with its inclusion of five Caribbean authors—Domingo, McKay, Walrond, Schomburg, and Rogers—does reveal "a Harlem multiculturalism" (Charras 271). In fact, Locke's linkage between Harlem and Dublin as cultural centers even presents an international perspective (Singh and Schmidt 21). Domingo's "Gift of the Black Tropics" praises (perhaps overmuch) the Caribbean presence in America, particularly "the insistent assertion of their manhood in an environment that demands too much servility and unprotesting acquiescence from men of African blood." McKay's poems "Baptism" and "The Tropics in New York" deal with the complex process of acclimating to a new environment. His poem "The White House" may be the angriest piece in the anthology despite Locke's attempt to mute its force by changing the title to "White Houses," much to McKay's consternation. Rogers's "Jazz at Home" maintains that despite "its present vices and vulgarizations," jazz, a quintessential American art form, "with more wholesome growth in the future . . . may . . . truly democratize" by breaking down racial boundaries. Walrond's "The Palm Porch" provides an early, impressionistic draft of one of the stories that would be included in his collection *Tropic Death*. Schomburg's "The Negro Digs Up His Past" explains the need for the American Black to "remake his past in order to make his future."[19]

The voices of labor unionism and socialism may have been omitted from *The New Negro*, but they were at the fore of the *Messenger*, founded by A. Philip Randolph and Chandler Owen. Although long overshadowed by its rivals the *Crisis* and *Opportunity*, the *Messenger* published most of the leading literary figures of the Harlem Renaissance, including many who were just starting to establish literary reputations. Its editorial staff included Domingo, who was initially involved in the paper's "Garvey Must Go" campaign until he felt the paper took on an anti-Caribbean tone. Historian J. A. Rogers regularly contributed biographical sketches of great figures in Black history. Radical in nature, the magazine regularly roused the ire of government agents. Attorney General A. Mitchell Palmer, for example, labeled one issue containing McKay's poem "If We Must Die" and an inflammatory essay by Domingo as being "insolently offensive" (qtd. in Daniel 243). Although its emphasis, particularly in its early years, was clearly on "socioeconomic issues," the magazine was an advocate of the arts, especially between 1925–28, when novelist and essayist George Schuyler, drama editor Theophilus Lewis, and, briefly, novelist Wallace Thurman dominated its editorial policies (Ikonné 106).

Unlike the *Crisis*, *Opportunity*, and the *Messenger*, all monthly magazines, the UNIA's the *Negro World*, which at its apex had a circulation approaching 200,000, was a weekly newspaper. The *Negro World* had an able editorial staff that in addition to Garvey included at one time or another Domingo, Walrond, Harrison, Amy Jacques Garvey, and veteran African American journalists John Edward Bruce, T. Thomas Fortune, and William Ferris. Domingo and particularly Harrison helped to shape the early editorial policies and format of the paper, and, as Cary D. Wintz points out, "The years of Walrond's involvement with the paper corresponded with the peak of Garvey's literary activity, some of which anticipated the developments several years later that launched the Harlem Renaissance" (148).

Though Garvey shared Du Bois's belief that literature had a propagandistic value, the *Negro World* reflected Garvey's philosophy of appealing to a wider audience than just the educated elite. Garvey believed, "We must encourage our own black authors who have character, who are loyal to their race, who feel proud to be black, and in every way let them feel that we appreciate their efforts to advance our race through healthy and decent literature." In the words of Garvey biographer Tony Martin, "The *Negro World* did not only bring literature and art to the masses; it gave the masses a chance to express themselves artistically" (xvi). Thus, the paper published pieces by well-known figures as well as rank-and-file Garveyites in such regular sections as the "Poetry for the People" column. Garvey himself dabbled in poetry and included some in the *Negro World*.[20]

While some critics have felt that communism has had a "stultifying" effect on Black writers because of the emphasis on using proletarian realism to advance party dogma (Young passim), communist magazines, including Briggs's the *Crusader* and *Liberator*, attempted to advance Black culture through their publication of regular theater reviews, poetry, and drama, and their emphasis on music, especially jazz, a popular art form generally denigrated by the Black press. Although it goes beyond the scope of this book to discuss the effects of communism on Black writers, one must acknowledge that both well-known and obscure Black authors regularly published in communist periodicals. These journals together served as a wellspring for "a renascent black nationalist literary movement" whose concerns "combined class consciousness, prevailing Pan-African ideas, and an emphasis on struggle as a form of masculine redemption," issues that resonated in the Caribbean as well as African American community (Kelley 111). As William Maxwell has noted, "It is no accident that the headiest days of U.S. anticapitalism were those of its tightest rapport with black art" (12).[21]

Caribbean Writers

Claude McKay once wryly commented that his critics found his poetry "too daring" and his prose "too dirty." These assessments were typified in reactions to what are probably his two most famous works, the fiercely militant poem "If We Must Die" and the bestselling novel *Home to Harlem*, an exploration of the lives of working-class urban Blacks. Yet these two often seemingly disparate sides of McKay, joined by his overarching emphasis on racial consciousness, are what characterize his writings.

McKay, a seminal figure of the Harlem Renaissance as a poet, as an essayist, and as a fiction writer, was a man of many contradictory impulses. He could be warm, making friends easily, yet he was often abrasive and alienated many people. He was generous but constantly in need of money himself. He felt a need to belong to organizations but would not be confined by their beliefs. He consistently praised the ways of rural Black folks although generally living in urban environments surrounded by White radical thinkers. He wished to be thought of as an artist, not a political spokesman, but he was closely aligned with radical political movements. Because of these conflicting tendencies, McKay has often been misread. He was a complex figure who was more than the sum of all his sometimes warring parts. What was consistent about him, however, was his belief in the strength and vitality of common Black people.

Eric Walrond's career paralleled that of McKay in many ways. Both lived migratory lives and drifted in and out of several literary and cultural movements, never really finding a home in any of them. Born in British Guiana (now Guyana), Walrond migrated to Barbados when he was eight and to Panama when he was ten. His experiences in all three locations kindled his literary imagination. Walrond became one of the leading lights of the Harlem Renaissance, serving as an influential editor for some time at both Garvey's *Negro World* and the Urban League's *Opportunity*. Walrond's chief literary achievement, however, was *Tropic Death* (1926), which holds a unique place in Black literature. In it Walrond wrote of the migratory nature of many Caribbean people, the oppressive colonial system that had been established in the area, the colorism that White racism had facilitated, the changes wrought by industrialization, the beauty and harshness of the land, and the maintenance of traditional culture such as folklore, songs, and obeah (a folk belief in magic). He was particularly concerned with the language of the people, and he took great pains to recreate the many dialects of the anglophone Caribbean, as well as the francophone islands and Spanish-speaking Panama, often succeeding with remarkable dexterity.

Like Walrond and McKay, Eulalie Spence was interested in Black pride. Spence, from Nevis, stood apart in several ways from the other Black female playwrights of the Harlem Renaissance. Alone among them, Spence set most of her plays in Harlem and wrote in the Harlem vernacular, realistically portraying the speech of her characters. She took great care to dramatize "tenderly the day-to-day lives of these Harlemites of the twenties" (Brown-Guillory 16). Despite their flaws, Spence's characters were always treated with dignity and sympathy.

While the work of Spence, Walrond, and McKay often helped to dispel Black stereotypes, no one worked harder toward this end than Jamaican J. A. Rogers. His fictionalized account of the conversation between an educated Black porter and a racist U.S. passenger in *From Superman to Man* (1917) was a vehicle for Rogers to debunk a number of stereotypes. In some sixteen books and pamphlets and hundreds of articles written over fifty years, Rogers recorded the accomplishments of people of African descent, often left out of standard histories.

Rogers's friend Arturo (Arthur) Schomburg also championed the cause of Black culture in a global frame. Schomburg, a native of Puerto Rico, deeply absorbed the culture of his mother, a native of the Virgin Islands. Best known for his work as a bibliophile, Schomburg also authored a number of articles that celebrate the importance of Black history, most notably "The Negro Digs Up His Past."

Common Issues

Assessing the literary and cultural contributions of these Caribbean authors is a complex task, particularly because of the range of nationalities and personalities presented as well as the various forums in which the works were displayed. There is, of course, no single distinguishing characteristic that marks one as a "Caribbean" writer. Nevertheless, one may suggest some common issues shared by such authors as McKay, Walrond, Spence, Rogers, and Schomburg, including (im)migration, race, and language. Interest in these areas, to be sure, was not limited to anglophone Caribbeans. The subjects mentioned were of prime concern to African Americans as well, including Du Bois and Locke, but Caribbean immigrants' focus on such issues helped to broaden the discussion (Pedersen 265).

Because of the nature of slavery and its enduring legacy, African Americans have had a history of migration, often involuntary. The desire to escape lynching and Jim Crow laws and the hope of better employment opportunities drove Blacks to the North, a frequent subject in the literature and music of Black peoples. Thus, during the years of the Great Migration from the South and thereafter the theme of transplantation is frequent in African American fiction, perhaps the finest examples from the Harlem Renaissance being Jean Toomer's *Cane* (1923), Nella Larsen's *Quicksand* (1928), and the short stories of Rudolph Fisher.[22]

The theme of migration is also dominant in the writings of McKay and a number of other Caribbean literary vagabonds. As Robert Bone states in speaking of Walrond, "Human transplantation is [his] essential theme" (177). The writings of Caribbean authors reflect the lives of many in the region who have become permanent migrants, "always having a sense of home while simultaneously feeling the loss of it" (Parascandola 36). This seeming contradiction is often what adds power and poignancy to their work, a dilemma demonstrated, for example, in McKay's "The Tropics in New York," where the narrator recalls wistfully the lost days of home, and Walrond's "City Love," where the protagonist tries clumsily to understand the rules in his new land.

Whereas African Americans were moving within the borders of their own country, West Indians were, because of the relatively small size of and limited opportunities within their homelands, forced to look beyond their islands. Authors such as Walrond, McKay, and Rogers, because of their upbringing, could feel quite at home writing about people of their own and different ethnicities in the United States, the Caribbean, Latin America, and Europe. Walrond, for example, would, besides writing about the Caribbean and England, encourage inclusion of writers from diverse regions when editing *Opportunity*. McKay would write of the Soviet Union, Jamaica, France, and Northern Africa. Ray, a character in *Home to Harlem* and *Banjo*, provides "a diasporic interpretation of black world history" (Pedersen 262). Rogers would discuss Blacks' achievements globally and have a regular column, "Paris Pepperpot," in the *Pittsburgh Courier.* Schomburg, too, was interested in Blacks worldwide. This international perspective is one of the Caribbean immigrants' major contributions to the Harlem Renaissance (Rahming 68–69).

The perception of race and the search for self-identity is another area of mutual concern to West Indians and African Americans. Caribbean immigrants were shocked by the housing and employment discrimination they saw in the Jim Crow system established in the United States, something they had never before encountered. Many immigrants had been brought up to work as civil servants, being taught to disdain manual labor. Upon their arrival in America, West Indians were appalled at the positions they were often forced to take as porters or elevator operators and strove to improve their conditions. These frustrations are palpably manifested in Walrond's essay "The Black City," in which the false promise of America for Blacks is fully revealed, and in his sketch "On Being Black," where the narrator, a skilled newspaperman, is unable to get a job because of discrimination. Both McKay, in *Home to Harlem*, and Rogers, in *From Superman to Man*, depict the frustrations of highly educated men forced to take jobs as railroad porters, jobs the authors themselves had at one time taken out of necessity.

McKay writes of being stunned by the type of mindless prejudice, "the most primitive animal hatred," he encountered in America. He responded with defiant messages such as "If We Must Die," "The White House," and "America," in which the author utilized the traditional sonnet form to undermine the societal status quo. This same racism came as a shock to the other writers surveyed here as well, and they attempted to combat it in different ways, as in Eulalie Spence's "Her," where the vengeful ghost of an immigrant woman wreaks revenge upon her abusive, greedy American husband. The forceful messages of these Caribbean immigrants, so unprepared for what they found in America, helped to raise a powerful voice of protest.

The authors also emphasized racial pride, a key component of the New Negro Movement. The essays and research of Rogers and Schomburg (as well as others such as Marcus and Amy Jacques Garvey) constantly reaffirm the proud history and achievements of the race. The assertion of a positive self-image for Blacks helped to negate the distortions of Blacks and their omission by Whites from American history and culture. This emphasis on racial pride would help create the Negritude movement in the 1930s, also led by Blacks (in this case largely from the francophone Caribbean and Africa) who had been alienated by the colonial regime.

Although interested in affirming Black pride, many of the writers, like such African American authors as Bruce Nugent, Zora Neale Hurston, Langston Hughes, and Wallace Thurman, resisted writing propaganda literature. The portrayals of colorism, sexism, prostitution, gambling, drug running, and violence in the works of McKay, Spence, and Walrond often made the Talented Tenth cringe. Indeed, as Chidi Ikonné notes, "Most of the subjects treated by Walrond are matters which a large part of the black literati of the West Indies and the United States would have liked to leave unrevealed" (179). The people these authors tended to write about were ordinary Black folk, both urban and rural, not the "dicty," snobbish, upper class, yet the characters, no matter how reprehensible some of their actions, are treated sympathetically. They are merely trying to survive in an often hostile environment, something, no doubt, that is reflective of the authors' own experiences and observations.

One way in which Caribbean writers helped to depict Black folk realistically was through their use of the vernacular in their works. Caribbean authors, like such African American authors as Zora Neale Hurston and Langston Hughes, used the vernacular for several purposes, including verisimilitude, humor, and to pay respect to and help preserve their heritage. Their works reflect an effort by Blacks to define their own reality rather than have others do it for them. Spence, McKay, and Walrond, whether employing the African American English of their new home or their native Caribbean English, all authentically evoke the voice of the people they are writing about, providing them the respect that they were not often accorded by White writers, who did not understand the nuances of the vernacular. The anglophone Caribbean authors' use of language faithfully renders the various sociolinguistic factors, including class, ethnicity, education, and rural/urban provenance of their speakers. The result is not always easily comprehensible for outside readers, but it is one with ample rewards, expanding the use of English in our literature and language. Walrond and McKay (in his Jamaican poems) were among the pioneers in using Caribbean English, helping to lead the way for other writers such as Louise Bennett and Edward Kamau Brathwaite in using what Brathwaite called Nation Language. This "fattening" of

English, to use contemporary Trinidadian author Kelvin Christopher James's term, is one of the major contributions of the Caribbean authors.[23]

Concluding Remarks

Trinidad-born aviator Hubert Julian, known as "The Black Eagle," was one of the most famous Harlemites of the 1920s. A UNIA officer, he made several spectacular, if not always successful, parachute jumps into Harlem. Perhaps his most notorious incident occurred on July 4, 1924, when he attempted a flight from New York to Africa. He made it only as far as Queens, crashing into Flushing Bay, where he ended up with a broken leg. He is remembered today only by an aging handful of Harlemites (Lewis, *When Harlem* 111–12).[24]

Julian's flight, in some ways, mirrors the fate of many of those early anglophone Caribbean immigrants who enjoyed a fleeting moment of fame before receding from public memory until their deeds were virtually forgotten. This is particularly unfortunate because, more so than Julian's, their achievements were truly soaring, helping to spur the cultural advances of the Harlem Renaissance and changing forever the nature of Black politics in America. Only in the past decade or so have scholars begun to recognize their unacknowledged debt to the first large wave of Caribbean immigrants to America. It is hoped that this recent research and the future work built on it will secure these immigrants the rightful place in history they deserve.

NOTES

1. I have used the term "anglophone Caribbean" to describe people from the predominantly English-speaking Caribbean, including the mainland nations of Guyana and Belize and the English-speaking Black diasporic communities of officially Spanish- and Dutch-speaking countries. I have often simply reduced this to "Caribbean." The term "West Indian" was (and still is) also often used to define people from this region. Immigrants of Indic descent are not included here since their presence in New York, though substantial today, was fairly negligible during the period covered in this anthology. Race and ethnicity, of course, are problematic concepts. For some interesting distinctions, see Kasinitz 3–6. See also Michael Omi and Howard Winart, *Racial*

Formation in the United States: From the 1960s to the 1990s, 2d ed. (New York: Routledge, 1994). It should also be noted that in the 1920s people of African descent were generally called Negro (or negro), Aframerican, Colored, or Afro-American. I have generally preferred to use the terms "Black" or "African American."

2. The term "Harlem Renaissance" has been given varying parameters by historians. I have used David Levering Lewis's defining dates 1917 to 1935 (*Portable* xiii–xv). The year 1917 marks several significant events: (1) the beginning of U.S. involvement in World War I; (2) the silent protest parade on July 28, when more than ten thousand Blacks marched down New York's Fifth Avenue in silent protest over lynchings and a devastating riot in East St. Louis; (3) the April 5 premiere in the Provincetown Playhouse in New York City of White playwright Ridgely Torrence's *Three Plays for a Negro Theater*, one of the earliest serious dramatic renderings of Black life, and produced with all-Black casts; and (4) the publication of J. A. Rogers's *From Superman to Man*, Hubert Harrison's *The Negro and the Nation*, and Claude McKay's poems in the *Seven Arts*, possibly the initial work by a Black author in a White publication in the twentieth century. The year 1935 marked the March 19 Harlem riot, which was triggered by the deepening frustration of Harlemites over their conditions; McKay wrote of the incident in "Harlem Runs Wild" (*Nation* April 3, 1935).

The "Renaissance," of course, was not only a Harlem phenomenon but also included other locations, such as Philadelphia, Washington, Boston, and Chicago. The writers included in this anthology, however, were all centered in New York City for at least several years during the period treated. I do not mean to suggest that the Caribbean population in New York was restricted to Harlem. There were pockets of Caribbean people throughout the city, particularly in Brooklyn.

3. Statistics on foreign Black immigrants are difficult to gauge since they were not generally broken down by specific region.

4. For more on Caribbean and American Black relations, see Hellwig 179–209; Reid 107–24; Ottley 45–46; Osofsky 131–35; James, *Holding Aloft* 1–5; Kornweibel, *No Crystal Stair* 132–75; and Vickerman passim.

5. For more on anglophone Caribbean immigrants in business, see Watkins-Owens, *Blood Relations* 126–48. For more on Holstein, a native of the Virgin Islands, see Lewis (*When Harlem*), who includes him as one of the notables fostering the Harlem Renaissance. See also Geraldo Guirty's *Harlem's Danish-American West Indians, 1899–1964* (New York: Vantage, 1989) 36–49, and Rufus Chatzberg's *Black Organized Crime in Harlem, 1920–1930* (New York: Garland, 1993) 103–05. Holstein, an early Universal Negro Improvement Association (UNIA) supporter, also wrote several articles on

the condition of Virgin Islanders, including one highly critical of the United States' management of the islands, "The Virgin Islands" *Opportunity* 3 (October 1925): 304–06.

6. The myth of the model Caribbean immigrant is actively debated today by such critics as Suzanne Model in "Caribbean Immigrants: A Black Success Story?" *International Migration Review* 25 (1991): 248–76 and "West Indian Prosperity: Fact or Fiction?" *Social Problems* 42 (1995): 535–53.

7. Du Bois had written to Domingo on January 18, 1923, that "I, myself am of West Indian descent and am proud of the fact" (*The Correspondence of W. E. B. Du Bois: Volume I Selections, 1877–1934,* ed. Herbert Aptheker [U of Massachusetts P, 1973] 263). Other prominent Harlem Renaissance figures with Caribbean ancestry include James Weldon Johnson, Nella Larsen, and William Stanley Braithwaite.

8. For more on Washington, see Louis R. Harlan's *Booker T. Washington: The Wizard of Tuskegee 1901–1915* (New York: Oxford UP, 1982) and Houston A. Baker Jr.'s *Turning South Again: Re-reading Booker T* (Durham, NC: Duke UP, 2001) and *Modernism and the Harlem Renaissance* (Chicago: U of Chicago P, 1987). Harlan also edited *The Booker T. Washington Papers* (Urbana: U of Illinois P, 1972–89).

9. For more on the government's infiltration of Black radical groups, see Kornweibel's *"Seeing Red"* and the monumental twenty-five-microfilm-reel work Kornweibel edited, *Federal Surveillance of Afro-Americans (1917–1925): The First World War, the Red Scare, and the Garvey Movement* (Frederick, MD: University Publications of America, 1986). Ironically, the only remaining copies of some of this radical material are contained as evidence in the government's own cases.

10. By radical, I use Winston James's definition: "avowed anti-capitalists . . . as well as adherents of varieties of Black Nationalism" (*Holding Aloft* 292). This does not mean, however, that Caribbean immigrants were innately militant. As Cary Wintz says about the New Negro, "their values and objectives were basically middle class; all they demanded was an end to American racial prejudice and the institution of equal opportunity and social justice. However, they often assumed a posture of militancy when they voiced these demands" (30). Many West Indians were actually involved in mainstream politics, including Republicans William Derrick, John W. A. Shaw, and H. Adolph Howell and Democrat W. T. R. Richardson. See Calvin B. Holder, "The Rise of the West Indian Politician in New York City, 1900–1952," *Afro-Americans in New York Life and History* 4 (January 1980): 45–59, and Watkins-Owens, *Blood Relations* 75–91. A significant number of others refrained from any active participation in politics at all in their new land. For more on the Red Summer, see William M. Tuttle Jr. *Race Riot: Chicago in the Red Summer of 1919* (New York: Atheneum, 1970) and Barbara

Foley, *Spectres of 1919: Class and Nation in the Making of the New Negro* (Urbana: U of Illinois Press, 2003).

11. Moore, often called Queen Mother, was born in Louisiana and was a noted stepladder speaker who in later years shifted from Garveyism to communism. De Mena, born in Nicaragua, was Garvey's lieutenant while he was imprisoned. Davis, a native of Maryland, was a prominent speaker who regularly presided over "monster rallies" at Madison Square Garden and Carnegie Hall. Women writers and artists were also encouraged to participate at the UNIA conventions. The most prolific of the Garveyite poets was Ethel Trew Dunlap, an African American. Several of her poems are included in Tony Martin's *African Fundamentalism.* For more on the subject, see Martin, "Women in the Garveyite Movement," *Garvey: His Work and Impact,* ed. Rupert Lewis and Patrick Bryan (Trenton, NJ: Africa World P, 1991) 67–72; Honor Ford-Smith, "Women and the Garvey Movement in Jamaica," *Garvey: His Work and Impact,* ed. Rupert Lewis and Patrick Bryan (Trenton, NJ: Africa World P, 1991) 73–83; and William Seraile, "Henrietta Vinton Davis and the Garvey Movement," *Afro-Americans in New York Life and History* 7 (July 1983): 7–24.

12. Elizabeth Hendrickson was president of the American West Indian Ladies Aid Society and a spokesperson for the Harlem Tenants League. Helena Benta was secretary of the Montserrat Progressive Society. Bonita Williams, leader of the Communist Workers' Alliance, led protests against high prices in Harlem markets during the Depression. As Watkins-Owens observes, "Women were often the liaisons between leftist organizations, speakers, and bedrock community institutions. They were also financial backers of important social movements growing out of the street corner tradition" (*Blood Relations* 93). Yet few of their speeches or writings have been preserved and little information remains on them. For an exception see Helena Benta's "Address to a Group of Benevolent Associations" in Myrtle Evangeline Pollard's "Harlem As Is," master's thesis, City College of New York, 1937. Trinidadian Claudia Jones, an important member of the Communist Party, postdates the boundaries of this anthology. Born in 1915, Jones wrote most of her essays in the 1940s and 1950s. See Buzz Johnson's *"I Think of My Mother": Notes on the Life and Times of Claudia Jones* (London: Karia P, 1985) for more on her.

13. For more on Randolph and the BSCP, see Paula F. Pfeffer's *A. Philip Randolph: Pioneer of the Civil Rights Movement* (Baton Rouge: Louisiana State UP, 1990) and Jervis Anderson's *A. Philip Randolph: A Biographical Portrait* (New York: Harcourt, Brace, Jovanovich, 1973).

14. The history of the communists in America is a somewhat tangled one, with several branches, both open and underground. These include the Communist Workers' (Communist) Party and the Communist Party of

America. When I use the term "communist" I am referring to any of these groups unless specified differently in my text. For more see Draper, *American Communism and Soviet Russia.*

15. Campbell, often thought to have been Jamaican, was born in Georgia and had a Jamaican father. Though she was a master organizer, we have little written work by or about her. She was a founding member of the African Blood Brotherhood in addition to establishing the Friendly Shelter for unwed mothers. For more on her, see James, *Holding Aloft* 173–77. For more on the ABB, see Kornweibel, *"Seeing Red"* 140–48; Theman Thomas, "Cyril Briggs and the African Blood Brotherhood: Another Radical View of Race and Class During the 1920s," Ph.D. dissertation, University of California, Santa Barbara, 1981, 99–112; James, *Holding Aloft* 155–84; Theodore G. Vincent, *Black Power and the Garvey Movement* (San Francisco: Ramparts P, 1972) 74–85; Solomon 9–31; Haywood 122–31; and Robert A. Hill, introduction, *The Crusader,* vol. 1 (New York: Kraus, 1987).

16. For more on the Scottsboro Boys see Naison 57–94; Haywood Patterson and Earl Conrad, *Scottsboro Boy* (Garden City, NY: Doubleday, 1950); Dan T. Carter, *Scottsboro: A Tragedy of the American South*, rev. ed. (Baton Rouge: Louisiana State UP, 1979); and James Haskins, *The Scottsboro Boys* (New York: Henry Holt, 1994).

17. Although this anthology is limited to written works, Caribbean immigrants contributed to American culture in numerous ways. One would be remiss not to mention the many Calypsonians (most were Trinidadian) such as Sam Manning who recorded extensively in New York City in the 1920s and had a large base of support there. Caribbeans were also influential in film and theater. Most famous of these performers was Bahamian Bert Williams (c. 1874–1922), who teamed with African American George Walker. Williams, who often performed in blackface, starred in such shows as *In Dahomey* (1903). After Walker's death in 1909, Williams performed in the Ziegfeld Follies between 1909 and 1919. Although Williams was seen by some as perpetuating negative stereotypes of Blacks, his performances were presented with great compassion. For more on Williams, see Ann Charters's *Nobody: The Story of Bert Williams* (New York: Macmillan, 1970) and Eric Ledell Smith's *Bert Williams: A Biography of the Pioneer Black Comedian* (Jefferson, NC: McFarland, 1992). Two Caribbean writers of note not included in this anthology are George R. Margetson, from St. Kitts, and Walter Adolphe Roberts, from Jamaica. Margetson authored several volumes of poetry between 1906 and 1916. He came to the United States in 1897 and lived most of his life in Boston. He falls outside the geographic and chronological scope of this anthology. W. Adolphe Roberts was a journalist who wrote two volumes of raceless verse, but he is best known for his nov-

els, including *The Haunting Hand* (1926), one of the earliest mystery novels by a Black author. Although he lived in New York, because of the absence of Black characters or racial themes in his work, Roberts is not generally identified with the Harlem Renaissance (Kellner 305).

18. For a good sampling of the writing in the *Crisis, Opportunity,* and the *Messenger,* see the following three anthologies edited by Sondra Kathryn Wilson: *The Crisis Reader: Stories, Poetry, and Essays from the NAACP's Crisis Magazine* (New York: Modern Library, 1999); *The Opportunity Reader: Stories, Poetry, and Essays from the Urban League's Opportunity Magazine* (New York: Modern Library, 1999); and *The Messenger Reader: Stories, Poetry, and Essays from the Messenger Magazine* (New York: Modern Library, 2000). Histories of the journals are included in Abby Arthur Johnson and Ronald Maberry Johnson, *Propaganda and Aesthetics: The Literary Politics of Afro-American Magazines;* Chidi Ikonné, *From Du Bois to Van Vechten: The Early New Negro Literature, 1903–1926;* and Walter C. Daniel, *Black Journals of the United States.*

19. A recent reprint of *The New Negro* is Alain Locke, ed., *The New Negro* (1925; New York: Atheneum 1992), with an introduction by Arnold Rampersad. For more on Locke see Jeffrey Stewart, ed., *The Critical Temper of Alain Locke: A Selection of His Essays on Art and Culture* (New York: Garland, 1983); Russell Linnemann, ed., *Alain Locke: Reflections on a Modern Renaissance Man* (Baton Rouge: Louisiana State UP, 1982); and Talmadge C. Guy, "Adult Education and Propaganda: Alain Locke's Views on Culture, Propaganda, and Race Progress," *Langston Hughes Review* 13.2 (1995): 68–76. For more on Johnson see George Hutchinson, *The Harlem Renaissance in Black and* White; David Levering Lewis, *When Harlem Was in* Vogue; and Patrick J. Gilpin, "Charles S. Johnson: Entrepreneur of the Harlem Renaissance," *The Harlem Renaissance Remembered,* ed. Arna Bontemps (New York: Dodd, Mead, 1972) 215–46.

20. See Martin's *African Fundamentalism* for selections from *Negro World* literature and Martin's *Literary Garveyism: Garvey, Black Arts and the Harlem Renaissance* (Dover, MA: Majority P, 1983) for a discussion of the Garveyite contribution to literature. Garvey himself composed two volumes of poetry, *The Tragedy of White Injustice* (1927) and *Selections from the Poetic Meditations of Marcus Garvey* (1927). Martin also edited *The Poetical Works of Marcus Garvey* (Dover, MA: Majority P, 1983). For an assessment of Garvey's poetry, see Martin, *Literary Garveyism* 139–55 and Carolyn Cooper, "Unorthodox Prose: The Poetical Works of Marcus Garvey," *Garvey: His Work and Impact,* ed. Rupert Lewis and Patrick Bryan (Trenton, NJ: Africa World P, 1991) 113–21.

21. For more on the communist impact on Black literature see Naison 203–13; Maxwell 13–124; Ted Vincent, *Keep Cool* 106–72; and Foley, *Radical*

Representations 170–212. Also see Bill V. Mullen and James Smethurst, eds., *Left of the Color Line: Race, Radicalism, and Twentieth Century Literature of the United States* (Chapel Hill: U of North Carolina P, 2003).

22. For more on the African American migration novel see Farrah Jasmine Griffin, *Who Set You Flowin'?: The African American Migration Novel* (New York: Oxford UP, 1995), and Lawrence R. Rodgers *Canaan Bound: The African-American Great Migration Novel* (Urbana: U of Illinois P, 1997).

23. Debates about the portrayal of folk and the use of vernacular have raged since the time of Paul Laurence Dunbar. For some discussion, see Henry Louis Gates Jr., *The Signifying Monkey: A Theory of African-American Literary Criticism* (New York: Oxford UP, 1988) and J. Martin Favor, *Authentic Blackness: The Folk in the New Negro Renaissance* (Durham, NC: Duke UP, 1999). For more on the impact of Caribbean English on literature, see J. Edward Chamberlain, *Come Back to Me My Language: Poetry and the West Indies* (Urbana: U of Illinois P, 1993); Kenneth R. Ramchand, *The West Indian Novel and Its Background*, 2nd ed. (London: Heinemann, 1983); and Edward Kamau Brathwaite, *History of the Voice: The Development of Nation Language in Anglophone Caribbean Poetry* (London: New Beacon, 1984).

24. On a less soaring note, Julian sold alcohol during Prohibition and later became an arms dealer. For more on him, see John Peer Nugent, *The Black Eagle* (New York: Stein and Day, 1971) and Hubert F. Julian, *Black Eagle: Colonel Hubert Julian*, as told to John Bullock (London: Jarrolds, 1964).

BIBLIOGRAPHY

Anderson, Jervis. *This Was Harlem: A Cultural Portrait, 1900–1950.* New York: Farrar, Straus, Giroux, 1982.

Bair, Barbara. "True Women, Real Men: Gender, Ideology, and Social Roles in the Garvey Movement." *Gendered Domains: Rethinking Public and Private in Women's History.* Ed. Dorothy O. Helly and Susan M. Reverby. Ithaca, NY: Cornell UP, 1992. 154–66.

Basch, Linda, Nina Glick Schiller, and Cristina Szanton Blanc. *Nations Unbound: Transnational Projects and the Deterritorialized Nation-State.* Langhorne, PA: Gordon and Breach, 1994.

Bone, Robert. *Down Home: Origins of the Afro-American Short Story.* 1975. New York: Columbia UP, 1988.

Brown-Guillory, Elizabeth. *Their Place on the Stage: Black Women Playwrights in America.* New York: Praeger, 1990.

Bryce-Laporte, Roy Simon. "Black Immigrants: The Experience of Invisibility and Inequality." *Journal of Black Studies* 3 (1972): 29–56.

Chaney, Elsa M. "The Context of Caribbean Migration." *Caribbean Life in New York City: Sociocultural Dimensions.* Ed. Constance R. Sutton and Elsa M. Chaney. New York: Center for Migration Studies of New York, 1994. 3–14.

Charras, Françoise. "The West Indian Presence in Alain Locke's *The New Negro* (1925)." *Temples for Tomorrow: Looking Back at the Harlem Renaissance.* Ed. Geneviève Fabre and Michael Feith. Bloomington: Indiana UP, 2001. 270–87.

Cooper, Wayne F. *Claude McKay: Rebel Sojourner in the Harlem Renaissance, A Biography.* Baton Rouge: Louisiana State UP, 1987.

Cruse, Harold. *The Crisis of the Negro Intellectual.* 1967. New York: Quill, 1984.

Daniel, Walter C. *Black Journals of the United States.* Westport, CT: Greenwood P, 1982.

De Jongh, James. *Vicious Modernism: Black Harlem and the Literary Imagination.* New York: Cambridge UP, 1990.

Draper, Theodore. *American Communism and Soviet Russia: The Formative Period.* 1960. New York: Vintage, 1986.

Du Bois, W. E. B. "Criteria of Negro Art." *The Portable Harlem Renaissance Reader.* Ed. David Levering Lewis. New York: Penguin, 1994. 100–05.

———. "Socialism and the Negro Problem." *New Review* Feb. 1, 1913: 138–41.

———. *The Souls of Black Folk: Essays and Sketches.* Chicago: McClurg, 1903.

Dugger, Celia W. "City of Immigrants Becoming More So in 90s." *New York Times* Jan. 9, 1997: A1+.

Foley, Barbara. *Radical Representations: Politics and Form in U.S. Proletarian Fiction, 1929–1941.* Durham, NC: Duke UP, 1993.

———. *Spectres of 1919: Class and Nation in the Making of the New Negro.* Urbana: U of Illinois P, 2003.

Foner, Nancy. "West Indian Migration to New York: An Overview." *Islands in the City: West Indian Migration to New York.* Ed. Nancy Foner. Berkeley: U of California P, 2001. 1–22.

Foner, Philip S. *American Socialism and Black Americans: From the Age of Jackson to World War II.* Westport, CT: Greenwood P, 1977.

Foner, Philip S., and James S. Allen, eds. *American Communism and Black Americans: A Documentary History, 1919–1929.* Philadelphia: Temple UP, 1987.

Forsythe, Dennis. "West Indian Radicalism in America: An Assessment of Ideologies." *Ethnicity in the Americas.* Ed. Frances Henry. The Hague: Mouton, 1976. 301–32.

Gilroy, Paul. *The Black Atlantic: Modernity and Double Consciousness.* Cambridge: Harvard UP, 1993.

Harrison, Hubert H. *When Africa Awakes*. New York: Porro P, 1920.

Hathaway, Heather. *Caribbean Waves: Relocating Claude McKay and Paule Marshall*. Bloomington: Indiana UP, 1999.

Haywood, Harry. *Black Bolshevik: Autobiography of an Afro-American Communist*. Chicago: Liberator P, 1978.

Hellwig, David J. "The Afro-American and the Immigrant, 1880–1930: A Study of Black Social Thought." Diss. Syracuse U, 1973.

Henke, Holger. *The West Indian Americans*. Westport, CT: Greenwood P, 2001.

Henry, Keith S. "Caribbean Migrants in New York: The Passage from Political Quiescence to Radicalism." *Afro-Americans in New York Life and History* 2 (July 1978): 29–44.

Holder, Calvin B. "The Causes and Composition of West Indian Immigration to New York City, 1900–1952." *Afro-Americans in New York Life and History* 11 (Jan. 1987): 7–26.

Huggins, Nathan. *Harlem Renaissance*. New York: Oxford UP, 1971.

Hutchinson, Earl Ofari. *Blacks and Reds: Race and Class in Conflict 1919–1990*. East Lansing: Michigan State UP, 1995.

Hutchinson, George. *The Harlem Renaissance in Black and White*. Cambridge: Belknap Press of Harvard UP, 1995.

Ikonné, Chidi. *From Du Bois to Van Vechten: The Early New Negro Literature, 1903–1926*. Westport, CT: Greenwood P, 1981.

James, Winston. "Explaining Afro-Caribbean Social Mobility in the United States: Beyond the Sowell Thesis." *Comparative Studies in Society and History* 44 (April 2002): 218–62.

———. *Holding Aloft the Banner of Ethiopia: Caribbean Radicalism in Early-Twentieth-Century America*. New York: Verso, 1998.

Johnson, Abby Arthur, and Ronald Maberry Johnson. *Propaganda and Aesthetics: The Literary Politics of Afro-American Magazines in the Twentieth Century*. Amherst: U of Massachusetts P, 1979.

Johnson, James Weldon. *Black Manhattan*. 1930. New York: Da Capo, 1991.

Kasinitz, Philip. *Caribbean New York: Black Immigrants and the Politics of Race*. Ithaca, NY: Cornell UP, 1992.

Kelley, Robin D. G. *Race Rebels: Culture, Politics, and the Black Working Class*. New York: Free Press, 1994.

Kellner, Bruce, ed. *The Harlem Renaissance: A Historical Dictionary for the Era*. Westport, CT: Greenwood P, 1984.

Kornweibel, Theodore, Jr. *No Crystal Stair: Black Life and the "Messenger," 1917–1928*. Westport, CT: Greenwood P, 1975.

———. *"Seeing Red": Federal Campaigns against Black Militancy, 1919–1925*. Bloomington: Indiana UP, 1998.

Laguerre, Michel S. *Diasporic Citizenship: Haitian Americans in Transnational America*. New York: St. Martin's P, 1998.

Lewis, David Levering, ed. and intro. *The Portable Harlem Renaissance Reader.* New York: Penguin, 1994.

———. *When Harlem Was in Vogue.* 1979. New York: Oxford UP, 1981.

Marks, Carole. *Farewell—We're Good and Gone: The Great Black Migration.* Bloomington: Indiana UP, 1989.

Marshall, Dawn. "A History of West Indian Migrations: Overseas Opportunities and 'Safety-Valve' Policies." *The Caribbean Exodus.* Ed. Barry B. Levine. New York: Praeger, 1987. 15–31.

Marshall, Paule. "Black Immigrant Women in *Brown Girl, Brownstones.*" *Caribbean Life in New York City: Sociocultural Dimensions.* Ed. Constance R. Sutton and Elsa M. Chaney. New York: Center for Migration Studies of New York, 1994. 81–85.

Martin, Tony, ed. *African Fundamentalism: A Literary and Cultural Anthology of Garvey's Harlem Renaissance.* Dover, MA: Majority P, 1991.

Maxwell, William J. *New Negro, Old Left: African-American Writing and Communism between the Wars.* New York: Columbia UP, 1999.

McKay, Claude. *A Long Way from Home.* 1937. New York: Harcourt Brace, 1970.

Naison, Mark. *Communists in Harlem during the Depression.* Urbana: U of Illinois P, 1983.

Osofsky, Gilbert. *Harlem: The Making of a Ghetto, Negro New York, 1890–1930.* New York: Harper, 1966.

Ottley, Roi. *"New World A-Coming."* 1943. New York: Arno P, 1968.

Palmer, Ransford W. *Pilgrims from the Sun: West Indian Migration to America.* New York: Twayne, 1995.

Parascandola, Louis J., intro. and ed. *"Winds Can Wake Up the Dead": An Eric Walrond Reader.* Detroit: Wayne State UP, 1998.

Pedersen, Carl. "The Tropics in New York: Claude McKay and the New Negro Movement." *Temples for Tomorrow: Looking Back at the Harlem Renaissance.* Ed. Geneviève Fabre and Michael Feith. Bloomington: Indiana UP, 2001. 259–69.

Rahming, Melvin B. *The Evolution of the West Indian's Image in the Afro-American Novel.* Millwood, NY: Associated Faculty P, 1986.

Record, Wilson. *The Negro and the Communist Party.* Chapel Hill: U of North Carolina P, 1951.

Reid, Ira De A. *The Negro Immigrant: His Background, Characteristics and Social Adjustment, 1899–1937.* 1939. New York: AMS P, 1970.

Satter, Beryl. "Marcus Garvey, Father Divine and the Gender Politics of Race Difference and Race Neutrality." *American Quarterly* 48 (March 1996): 43–76.

Scott, Janny. "In Brooklyn Woman's Path, A Story of Caribbean Striving." *New York Times* June 26, 2003: A1+.

Singh, Amritjit, and Peter Schmidt. "On the Borders between U.S. Studies and Postcolonial Theory." *Postcolonial Theory and the United States: Race, Ethnicity, and Literature.* Ed. and intro. Amritjit Singh and Peter Schmidt. Jackson: UP of Mississippi, 2000. 3–69.

Singh, Amritjit, William S. Shiver, and Stanley Brodwin, eds. *The Harlem Renaissance: Revaluations.* New York: Garland P, 1989.

Sinnette, Elinor Des Verney. *Arthur Alfonso Schomburg: Black Bibliophile and Collector.* New York: New York Public Library; Detroit: Wayne State UP, 1989.

Solomon, Mark. *The Cry Was Unity: Communists and African Americans, 1917–36.* Jackson: UP of Mississippi, 1998.

Sowell, Thomas, ed., with the assistance of Lynn D. Collins. *Essays and Data on American Ethnic Groups.* Washington, DC: Urban Institute, 1978.

Stephens, Michelle A. "Black Transnationalism and the Politics of National Identity: West Indian Intellectuals in Harlem in the Age of War and Revolution." *American Quarterly* 50.3 (1998): 592–608.

Sutton, Constance R. "The Caribbeanization of New York City and the Emergence of a Transnational Sociocultural System." *Caribbean Life in New York City: Sociocultural Dimensions.* Ed. Constance R. Sutton and Elsa M. Chaney. New York: Center for Migration Studies of New York, 1994. 15–29.

Thomas, Bert J. "Historical Functions of Caribbean-American Benevolent/ Progressive Associations." *Afro-Americans in New York Life and History* 12 (July 1988): 45–58.

Vickerman, Milton. *Crosscurrents: West Indian Immigrants and Race.* New York: Oxford UP, 1999.

Vincent, Ted. *Keep Cool: The Black Activists Who Built the Jazz Age.* London: Pluto P, 1995.

Vincent, Theodore G., ed. *Voices of a Black Nation: Political Journalism in the Harlem Renaissance.* 1973. Trenton, NJ: Africa World P, 1990.

Walter, John C. "Black Immigrants and Political Radicalism in the Harlem Renaissance." *Western Journal of Black Studies* (June 1977): 131–41.

———. "The Caribbean Immigrant Impulse in American Life: 1900–1930." *Revista/Review Interamericana* (1981): 522–44.

Walter, John C., and Jill Louise Ansheles. "The Role of the Caribbean Immigrant in the Harlem Renaissance." *Afro-Americans in New York Life and History* 1 (Jan. 1977): 49–64.

Waters, Mary C. *Black Identities: West Indian Immigrant Dreams and American Realities.* New York: Russell Sage Foundation, 1999.

Watkins-Owens, Irma. *Blood Relations: Caribbean Immigrants and the Harlem Community, 1900–1930.* Bloomington: Indiana UP, 1996.

————. "Early-Twentieth-Century Caribbean Women: Migration and Social Networks in New York City." *Islands in the City: West Indian Migration to New York.* Ed. Nancy Foner. Berkeley: U of California P, 2001. 25–51.

Watson, Steven. *The Harlem Renaissance: Hub of African-American Culture, 1920–1930.* New York: Pantheon, 1995.

Wintz, Cary D. *Black Culture and the Harlem Renaissance.* Houston: Rice UP, 1988.

Woodson, Carter G. "The Contribution of the West Indian to America; A Topic of the Historical Meeting in New York City." *New York Age* Oct. 31, 1931: 9.

Young, James O. *Black Writers of the Thirties.* Baton Rouge: Louisiana State UP, 1973.

1
GARVEYITES

Marcus Garvey

Marcus Mosiah Garvey, often described as the Black Moses, was born of working-class parents in St. Ann's Bay, Jamaica, on August 17, 1887. His upbringing in this humble environment—the pride in his race instilled in him by his parents and his belief in the worth of the common folk—would provide the foundation for his establishment of the Universal Negro Improvement and African Communities (Imperial) League (UNIA), the largest Black mass movement in America to that time, having at its peak several million followers.[1]

When he was fourteen, after having received an elementary school education supplemented by private tutoring, Garvey became apprenticed to a printer. He moved to Kingston two years later and found employment as a printer, but he lost his position after siding with the laborers in a strike. Blacklisted from his profession, Garvey sailed to Costa Rica in 1910, working for the United Fruit Company and establishing a newspaper, *La Nación*. His editorials urging better working conditions for laborers angered the authorities and he was forced to leave the country. He traveled throughout Latin America working for laborers wherever he went.

In 1912, Garvey moved to England, working for Duse Mohamed Ali's *Africa Times and Orient Review*, a leading Pan-African journal. Garvey's stay in England was an enlightening one, allowing him to experience the disparities between life in England and that in its colonies. Upon his return to Jamaica two years later, he launched the UNIA. Initially the organization garnered little support, meeting stiff resistance from many middle-class Jamaicans. As a result, after receiving a promise of support from Booker T. Washington (who would die before Garvey's arrival), Garvey moved on to the United States, arriving on March 23, 1916.

Soon after his arrival in New York, Garvey began to deliver his electrifying speeches and to establish the UNIA in his new land. Since his accomplishments and failings and the opposition to his organization have already been taken up at some length in my introduction (see pages 14–17), only brief mention will be made of them here. Garvey seldom wrote about himself, but perhaps his most significant self-assessment is contained in "The Negro's Greatest Enemy." Here Garvey describes his upbringing and the development of and opposition to the UNIA.

Garvey's far-ranging program included establishing the newspaper the *Negro World*, managing businesses through the Negro Factories Corporation, and starting up the Black Star Shipping Line. The Black Star Line ultimately became Garvey's opponents' vehicle for ridding themselves of him. He was accused, without much solid evidence, of using the mail to defraud contributors to the shipping line. Acting as his own attorney, Garvey lost his case and was ordered in 1925 to serve a five-year prison term. Following appeals made on his behalf, the sentence was shortened, but he was deported in 1927.

After his deportation, Garvey returned to Jamaica. He continued his work, establishing two newspapers, the *Black Man* and the *New Jamaican*. When he ran for Legislative Council in 1930, he was jailed. In this inhospitable climate, Garvey migrated to England in 1934, where he continued to publish the *Black Man*. He also traveled throughout Canada and the Caribbean. After suffering a series of strokes, he died in London on June 10, 1940.

Garvey's message carried on long after his death. It emphasized several key tenets: race first, Black self-reliance, and Black nationalism. These ideas are encapsulated in the fifty-four planks of the "Declaration of Rights of the Negro Peoples of the World" drafted and adapted at the UNIA Convention in 1920. This defiant statement clearly spelled out the offenses committed against Blacks worldwide and the steps necessary to remedy them. These remedies included equal treatment under the law, the right of Blacks to use any means necessary to protect themselves, free speech, and self-determination. This document also declared "the colors Red, Black, and Green to be the colors of the Negro race."

Garvey was able to garner popular support not only through his message, with its enormous appeal to the masses, but also through the delivery of that message. The greatest means for Garvey to express his vision was through his weekly column on the front page of the *Negro World*. Many of these columns were reprinted in the two-volume *Philosophy and Opinions of Marcus Garvey* (1923, 1925), edited by Amy Jacques Garvey. In his best works he is effectively able to convey his considerable oratorical skills onto the printed page. An examination of two of Garvey's seminal essays will serve as an introduction not only to his ideas but also to his use of rhetorical strategies, something almost totally ignored by his biographers and critics.[2]

"The Future as I See It" reiterates a number of common Garveyite themes: the need for African redemption, and the necessity to liberate Blacks from economic bondage, avoid false leaders, and revel in Black pride. The cadences of the essay masterfully rise to a crescendo in the final section, "An Inspiring Vision":

> I have a vision of the future, and I see before me a picture of a redeemed Africa, with her dotted cities, with her beautiful civilization, with her millions of happy children, going to and fro. Why should I lose hope, why should I give up and take a back place in this age of progress? Remember that you are men, that God created you Lords of this creation. Lift up yourselves, men, take yourselves out of this mire and hitch your hopes to the stars; yes, rise as high as the very stars themselves. Let no man destroy your ambition, because man is but your companion, your equal; man is your brother; he is not your lord; he is not your sovereign master.

The passage employs many of the devices notable in Black preaching both in the Caribbean and in America. The "vision," in fact, both harkens back to the Bible and anticipates the famous "I Have a Dream" speech of Martin Luther King. There are also echoes of American transcendentalist Ralph Waldo Emerson in the phrase "hitch your hopes [wagon] to the stars." The passage is a virtual exhortation, hypnotic in its rhythm, replete with rhetorical questions, repetition, and parallel structures, all devices typically employed by Black preachers and frequently evident in Garvey's writing and speeches. It is a stirring, uplifting pronouncement. The effect on the reader or the listener is powerful to this day.

We get another instance of Garvey's bold oratory in the energizing "First Message to the Negroes of the World from Atlanta Prison." This upbeat message, delivered February 10, 1925, near the time of Garvey's incarceration, was intended to advise Garvey's followers to avoid his enemies, particularly Du Bois, and to urge them to support Amy Jacques Garvey in his absence. Most important, it is meant to reassure them that no matter what he will always remain with them, even in death:

> If I die in Atlanta my work shall then only begin, but I shall live, in the physical or spiritual to see the day of Africa's glory. When I am dead wrap the mantle of the Red, Black and Green around me, for in the new life I shall rise with God's grace and blessing to lead the millions up the heights of triumph with the colors that you well know. Look for me in the whirlwind or the storm, look for me all around you, for, with God's grace, I shall come and bring with me countless millions of black slaves who have died in America and the West Indies and the millions in Africa to aid you in the fight for Liberty, Freedom and Life.

Again, Garvey uses such devices as repetition, inversion, and the parallelism of the final sentence. At the moment of greatest despair for the man, and by extension the movement, Garvey boldly asserts that, like Moses, he will lead his people to the promised land even if he is unable physically to pass over with them. Thus, he and they will ultimately triumph. There is, in fact, a messianic quality to the piece, with the apotheosis of Garvey, rising to lead a ghostly army of enslaved Blacks to assist their oppressed descendants in the fight for freedom.

Garvey's oratory in the passages cited here, with its inflated language and style, has the ring of heroic poetry, and it is epic poetry to which it is most suited. It is also fitting that a frequent concern of the epic is the birth of a race or nation and the struggles involved, for Garvey had no greater concern than Black nation building.

NOTES

The largest collections of Garvey papers are in the National Library of Jamaica, the Schomburg Center in New York, and Fisk University in Nashville, Tennessee.

1. Exact figures are impossible to come by. Estimates vary from several thousand to over ten million.

2. For an exception, see Robert Hill and Barbara Bair's introduction to *Marcus Garvey: Life and Lessons.*

BIBLIOGRAPHY

Clarke, John Henrik, ed., with the assistance of Amy Jacques Garvey. *Marcus Garvey and the Vision of Africa.* New York: Vintage, 1974.

Cronon, E. David. *Black Moses: The Story of Marcus Garvey and the Universal Negro Improvement Association.* Madison: U of Wisconsin P, 1955.

Hill, Robert A., ed. *The Marcus Garvey and Universal Negro Improvement Association Papers.* 9 vols. Berkeley: U of California P, 1983–.

Hill, Robert, and Barbara Bair, eds. *Marcus Garvey: Life and Lessons.* Berkeley: U of California P, 1987.

Jacques Garvey, Amy. *Garvey and Garveyism.* 1963. London: Collier Books, 1970.

Lewis, Rupert. *Marcus Garvey: Anti-Colonial Champion.* Trenton, NJ: Africa World P, 1988.

Martin, Tony. *Race First: The Ideological and Organizational Struggles of Marcus Garvey and the Universal Negro Improvement Association.* Dover, MA: Majority P, 1976.

Rogers, J. A. "Marcus Garvey: 'Provisional President of Africa' and Messiah." *World's Great Men of Color.* Vol. 2. 1947. New York: Simon & Schuster, 1996. 415–31. 2 vols.

Stein, Judith. *The World of Marcus Garvey: Race and Class in Modern Society.* Baton Rouge: Louisiana State UP, 1986.

Vincent, Theodore G. *Black Power and the Garvey Movement.* Rev. ed. San Francisco: Ramparts P, 1972.

Africa for the Africans

For five years the Universal Negro Improvement Association has been advocating the cause of Africa for the Africans—that is, that the Negro peoples of the world should concentrate upon the object of building up for themselves a great nation in Africa.

When we started our propaganda toward this end several of the so-called intellectual Negroes who have been bamboozling the race for over half a century said that we were crazy, that the Negro peoples of the western world were not interested in Africa and could not live in Africa. One editor and leader went so far as to say at his so-called Pan-African Congress* that American Negroes could not live in Africa, because the climate was too hot. All kinds of arguments have been adduced by these Negro intellectuals against the colonization of Africa by the black race. Some said that the black man would ultimately work out his existence alongside of the white man in countries founded and established by the latter. Therefore, it was not necessary for Negroes to seek an independent nationality of their own. The old time stories of "African fever," "African bad climate," "African mosquitos," "African savages," have been repeated by these "brainless intellectuals" of ours as a scare against our people in America and the West Indies taking a kindly interest in the new program of building a racial empire of our own in our Motherland. Now that years have rolled by and the Universal Negro Improvement Association has made the circuit of the world with its propaganda, we find eminent statesmen and leaders of the white race coming out boldly advocating the cause of colonizing Africa with the Negroes of the western world. A year ago Senator MacCullum* of the Mississippi Legislature introduced a resolution in the House for the purpose of petitioning the Congress of the United States of America and the President to use their good influence in securing from the Allies sufficient territory in Africa in liquidation of the war debt, which territory should be used for the establishing of an independent nation for American Negroes. About the same time Senator France of Maryland* gave expression to a similar desire in the Senate of the United States. During a speech on the "Soldiers' Bonus[,]" [h]e said: "We owe a big debt to Africa and one which we have too long ignored. I need not enlarge upon our peculiar interest in the obligation to the people of Africa. Thousands of Americans have for years been contributing to the missionary work which has been carried out by the noble men and women who have been sent out in that field by the churches of America."

Germany to the Front

This reveals a real change on the part of prominent statesmen in their attitude on the African question. Then comes another suggestion from Germany, for which Dr. Heinrich Schnee, a former Governor of German East Africa,* is author. This German statesman suggests in an interview given out in Berlin, and published in New York, that

America takes over the mandatories of Great Britain and France in Africa for the colonization of American Negroes. Speaking on the matter, he says[,] "As regards the attempt to colonize Africa with the surplus American colored population, this would in a long way settle the vexed problem, and under the plan such as Senator France has outlined, might enable France and Great Britain to discharge their duties to the United States, and simultaneously ease the burden of German reparations which is paralyzing economic life."

With expressions as above quoted from prominent world statesmen, and from the demands made by such men as Senators France and McCullum [sic], it is clear that the question of African nationality is not a far-fetched one, but is as reasonable and feasible as was the idea of an American nationality.

A "Program" at Last

I trust that the Negro peoples of the world are now convinced that the work of the Universal Negro Improvement Association is not a visionary one, but very practical, and that it is not so far fetched, but can be realized in a short while if the entire race will only co-operate and work toward the desired end. Now that the work of our organization has started to bear fruit we find that some of these "doubting Thomases" of three and four years ago are endeavoring to mix themselves up with the popular idea of rehabilitating Africa in the interest of the Negro. They are now advancing spurious "programs" and in a short while will endeavor to force themselves upon the public as advocates and leaders of the African idea.

It is felt that those who have followed the career of the Universal Negro Improvement Association will not allow themselves to be deceived by these Negro opportunists who have always sought to live off the ideas of other people.

The Dream of a Negro Empire

It is only a question of a few more years when Africa will be completely colonized by Negroes, as Europe is by the white race. What we want is an independent African nationality, and if America is to help the Negro peoples of the world establish such a nationality, then we welcome the assistance.

It is hoped that when the time comes for American and West Indian Negroes to settle in Africa, they will realize their responsibility and their duty. It will not be to go to Africa for the purpose of exercising an over-lordship over the natives, but it shall be the purpose of the Universal Negro Improvement Association to have established in Africa that brotherly co-operation which will make the interests of the African native and the American and West Indian Negro one and the same, that is to say, we shall enter into a common partnership to build up Africa in the interests of our race.

Oneness of Interests

Everybody knows that there is absolutely no difference between the native African and the American and West Indian Negroes, in that we are descendants from one common family stock. It is only a matter of accident that we have been divided and kept apart for over three hundred years, but it is felt that when the time has come for us to get back together, we shall do so in the spirit of brotherly love, and any Negro who expects that he will be assisted here, there or anywhere by the Universal Negro Improvement Association to exercise a haughty superiority over the fellows of his own race, makes a tremendous mistake. Such men had better remain where they are and not attempt to become in any way interested in the higher development of Africa.

The Negro has had enough of the vaunted practice of race superiority as inflicted upon him by others, therefore he is not prepared to tolerate a similar assumption on the part of his own people. In America and the West Indies, we have Negroes who believe themselves so much above their fellows as to cause them to think that any readjustment in the affairs of the race should be placed in their hands for them to exercise a kind of an autocratic and despotic control as others have done to us for centuries. Again I say, it would be advisable for such Negroes to take their hands and minds off the now popular idea of colonizing Africa in the interest of the Negro race, because their being identified with this new program will not in any way help us because of the existing feeling among Negroes everywhere not to tolerate the infliction of race or class superiority upon them, as is the desire of the self-appointed and self-created race leadership that we have been having for the last fifty years.

The Basis of an African Aristocracy

The masses of Negroes in America, the West Indies, South and Central America are in sympathetic accord with the aspirations of the native Africans. We desire to help them build up Africa as a Negro Empire, where every black man, whether he was born in Africa or in the Western world, will have the opportunity to develop on his own lines under the protection of the most favorable democratic institutions.

It will be useless, as before stated, for bombastic Negroes to leave America and the West Indies to go to Africa, thinking that they will have privileged positions to inflict upon the race that bastard aristocracy that they have tried to maintain in this Western world at the expense of the masses. Africa shall develop an aristocracy of its own, but it shall be based upon service and loyalty to race. Let all Negroes work toward that end. I feel that it is only a question of a few more years before our program will be accepted not only by the few statesmen of America who are now interested in it, but by the strong statesmen of the world, as the only solution to the great race problem. There is no other way to avoid the threatening war of the races that is bound to engulf all mankind, which has been prophesied by the world's greatest thinkers; there is no better method than by apportioning every race to its own habitat.

The time has really come for the Asiatics to govern themselves in Asia, as the Europeans are in Europe and the Western world, so also is it wise for the Africans to govern themselves at home, and thereby bring peace and satisfaction to the entire human family.

From *The Philosophy and Opinions of Marcus Garvey* (1923)

The Future as I See It

It comes to the individual, the race, the nation, once in a life time to decide upon the course to be pursued as a career. The hour has now struck for the individual Negro as well as the entire race to decide the course that will be pursued in the interest of our own liberty.

We who make up the Universal Negro Improvement Association have decided that we shall go forward, upward and onward toward the great goal of human liberty. We have determined among ourselves that all barriers placed in the way of our progress must be removed, must be cleared away for we desire to see the light of a brighter day.

The Negro Is Ready

The Universal Negro Improvement Association for five years has been proclaiming to the world the readiness of the Negro to carve out a pathway for himself in the course of life. Men of other races and nations have become alarmed at this attitude of the Negro in his desire to do things for himself and by himself. This alarm has become so universal that organizations have been brought into being here, there and everywhere for the purpose of deterring and obstructing this forward move of our race. Propaganda has been waged here, there and everywhere for the purpose of misinterpreting the intention of this organization; some have said that this organization seeks to create discord and discontent among the races; some say we are organized for the purpose of hating other people. Every sensible, sane and honest-minded person knows that the Universal Negro Improvement Association has no such intention. We are organized for the absolute purpose of bettering our condition, industrially, commercially, socially, religiously and politically. We are organized not to hate other men, but to lift ourselves, and to demand respect of all humanity. We have a program that we believe to be righteous; we believe it to be just, and we have made up our minds to lay down ourselves on the altar of sacrifice for the realization of this great hope of ours, based upon the foundation of righteousness. We declare to the world that Africa must be free, that the entire Negro race must be emancipated from industrial bondage, peonage and serfdom; we make no compromise, we make no apology in this our declaration. We do not desire to create offense on the part of other races, but we are determined that we shall be heard, that we shall be given the rights to which we are entitled.

The Propaganda of Our Enemies

For the purpose of creating doubts about the work of the Universal Negro Improvement Association, many attempts have been made to cast shadow and gloom over our work. They have even written the most uncharitable things about our organization; they have spoken so unkindly of our effort, but what do we care? They spoke unkindly and uncharitably about all the reform movements that have helped in the betterment of humanity. They maligned the great movement of the Christian religion; they maligned the great liberation movements of America, of France, of England, of Russia; can we expect, then, to escape being maligned in this, our desire for the liberation of Africa and the freedom of four hundred million Negroes of the world?

We have unscrupulous men and organizations working in opposition to us. Some trying to capitalize the new spirit that has come to the Negro to make profit out of it to their own selfish benefit; some are trying to set back the Negro from seeing the hope of his own liberty, and thereby poisoning our people's mind against the motives of our organization; but every sensible far-seeing Negro in this enlightened age knows what propaganda means. It is the medium of discrediting that which you are opposed to, so that the propaganda of our enemies will be of little avail as soon as we are rendered able to carry to our peoples scattered throughout the world the true message of our great organization.

"Crocodiles" as Friends

Men of the Negro race, let me say to you that a greater future is in store for us; we have no cause to lose hope, to become faint-hearted. We must realize that upon ourselves depend our destiny, our future; we must carve out that future, that destiny, and we who make up the Universal Negro Improvement Association have pledged ourselves that nothing in the world shall stand in our way, nothing in the world shall discourage us, but opposition shall make us work harder, shall bring us closer together so that as one man the millions of us will march on toward that goal that we have set for ourselves. The new Negro shall not be deceived. The new Negro refuses to take advice from anyone who has not felt with him, and suffered with him. We have suffered for three hundred years, therefore we feel that the time has come when only those who have suffered with us can interpret our feelings and our spirit. It takes the slave to interpret the feelings of the slave; it takes the unfortunate man to interpret the spirit of his unfortunate brother; and so it takes the suffering Negro to interpret the spirit of his comrade. It is strange that so many people are interested in the Negro now, willing to advise him how to act, and what organizations he should join, yet nobody was interested in the Negro to the extent of not making him a slave for two hundred and fifty years, reducing him to industrial peonage and serfdom after he was freed; it is strange that the same people can be so interested in the Negro now, as to tell him what organization he should follow and what leader he should support.

Whilst we are bordering on a future of brighter things, we are also at our danger period, when we must either accept the right philosophy, or go down by following deceptive propaganda which has hemmed us in for many centuries.

Deceiving the People

There is many a leader of our race who tells us that everything is well, and that all things will work out themselves and that a better day is coming. Yes, all of us know that a better day is coming; we all know that one day we will go home to Paradise, but whilst we are hoping by our Christian virtues to have an entry into Paradise we also realize that we are living on earth, and that the things that are practiced in Paradise are not practiced here. You have to treat this world as the world treats you; we are living in a temporal, material age, an age of activity, an age of racial, national selfishness. What else can you expect but to give back to the world what the world gives to you, and we are calling upon the four hundred million Negroes of the world to take a decided stand, a determined stand, that we shall occupy a firm position; that position shall be an emancipated race and a free nation of our own. We are determined that we shall have a free country; we are determined that we shall have a flag; we are determined that we shall have a government second to none in the world.

An Eye for an Eye

Men may spurn the idea, they may scoff at it; the metropolitan press of this country may deride us; yes, white men may laugh at the idea of Negroes talking about government; but let me tell you there is going to be a government, and let me say to you also that whatsoever you give, in like measure it shall be returned to you.* The world is sinful, and therefore man believes in the doctrine of an eye for an eye, a tooth for a tooth.* Everybody believes that revenge is God's, but at the same time we are men, and revenge sometimes springs up, even in the most Christian heart.

Why should man write down a history that will react against him? Why should man perpetrate deeds of wickedness upon his brother which will return to him in like measure? Yes, the Germans maltreated the French in the Franco-Prussian war of 1870, but the French got even with the Germans in 1918. It is history, and history will repeat itself. Beat the Negro, brutalize the Negro, kill the Negro, burn the Negro, imprison the Negro, scoff at the Negro, deride the Negro, it may come back to you one of these fine days, because the supreme destiny of man is in the hands of God. God is no respecter of persons, whether that person be white, yellow or black. Today the one race is up, tomorrow it has fallen; today the Negro seems to be the footstool of the other races and nations of the world; tomorrow the Negro may occupy the highest rung of the great human ladder.

But, when we come to consider the history of man, was not the Negro a power, was he not great once? Yes, honest students of history can recall the day when Egypt, Ethiopia and Timbuctoo towered in their civilizations, towered above Europe, towered above Asia. When Europe was inhabited by a race of cannibals, a race of savages, naked men, heathens and pagans, Africa was peopled with a race of cultured black men, who were masters in art, science and literature; men who were cultured and refined; men who, it was said, were like the gods. Even the great poets of old sang in beautiful sonnets of the delight it afforded the gods to be in companionship with the Ethiopians. Why, then, should we lose hope? Black men, you were once great; you shall be great again. Lose not courage, lose not faith, go forward. The thing to do is to get organized; keep separated and you will be exploited, you will be robbed, you will be killed. Get organized, and you will compel the world to respect you. If the world fails to give you consideration, because you are black men, because you are Negroes, four hundred millions of you shall, through organization, shake the pillars of the universe and bring down creation, even as Samson brought down the temple upon his head and upon the heads of the Philistines.*

An Inspiring Vision

So Negroes, I say, through the Universal Negro Improvement Association, that there is much to live for. I have a vision of the future, and

I see before me a picture of a redeemed Africa, with her dotted cities, with her beautiful civilization, with her millions of happy children, going to and fro. Why should I lose hope, why should I give up and take a back place in this age of progress? Remember that you are men, that God created you Lords of this creation. Lift up yourselves, men, take yourselves out of this mire and hitch your hopes to the stars;* yes, rise as high as the very stars themselves. Let no man pull you down, let no man destroy your ambition, because man is but your companion, your equal; man is your brother; he is not your lord; he is not your sovereign master.

We of the Universal Negro Improvement Association feel happy; we are cheerful. Let them connive to destroy us; let them organize to destroy us; we shall fight the more. Ask me personally the cause of my success, and I say opposition; oppose me, and I fight the more, and if you want to find out the sterling worth of the Negro, oppose him, and under the leadership of the Universal Negro Improvement Association he shall fight his way to victory, and in the days to come, and I believe not far distant, Africa shall reflect a splendid demonstration of the worth of the Negro, of the determination of the Negro, to set himself free and to establish a government of his own.

From *The Philosophy and Opinions of Marcus Garvey* (1923)

The Negro, Communism, Trade Unionism and His (?) Friend*

"Beware of Greeks Bearing Gifts"

If I must advise the Negro workingman and laborer, I should warn him against the present brand of Communism or Workers' Partizanship as taught in America, and to be careful of the traps and pitfalls of white trade unionism, in affiliation with the American Federation of white workers or laborers.

It seems strange and a paradox, but the only convenient friend the Negro worker or laborer has, in America, at the present time, is the white capitalist. The capitalist—being selfish—seeking only the largest profit out of labor—is willing and glad to use Negro labor wherever possible on a scale "reasonably" below the standard white union wage. He will tolerate the Negro in any industry (except those that are necessarily guarded for the protection of the whiteman's material, racial and assumed cultural dominance) if he accepts a lower standard of wage than the white union man; but, if the Negro union-izes himself to the level of the white worker, and, in affiliation with him, the choice and preference of employment is given to the white worker, without any regard or consideration for the Negro.

White Unionism is now trying to rope in the Negro and make him a standard wage worker, then, when it becomes generally known that he demands the same wage as the white worker, an appeal or approach will be made to the white capitalist or employer, to alienate his sympathy or consideration for the Negro, causing him, in the face of all things being equal, to discriminate in favor of the white worker as a race duty and obligation. In this respect the Negro if not careful to play his game well, which must be done through and by his leaders, is between "hell and the powder house."

The danger of Communism to the Negro, in countries where he forms the minority of the population, is seen in the selfish and vicious attempts of that party or group to use the Negro's vote and physical numbers in helping to smash and over-throw, by revolution, a system that is injurious to them as the white under dogs, the success of which would put their majority group or race still in power, not only as com-munists but as whitemen. To me there is no difference between two roses looking alike, and smelling alike, even if some one calls them by different names. Fundamentally what racial difference is there between a white Communist, Republican or Democrat? On the appeal of race interest the Communist is as ready as either to show his racial ascendancy or superiority over the Negro. He will be as quick and eager as any to show the Negro that he is white, and by Divine right of assumption has certain duties to perform to the rest of us mortals, and to defend and protect certain racial ideals against the barbarian hordes that threaten white supremacy.

I am of the opinion that the group of whites from whom Com-munists are made, in America, as well as trade unionists and members of the Worker's party, is more dangerous to the Negro's welfare than any other group at present. Lynching mobs and wild time parties are generally made up of 99 1/2 per cent. of such white people. The Negro should keep shy of Communism or the Worker's party in America. Since they are so benevolent let them bring about their own reforms and show us how different they are to others. We have been bitten too many times by all the other parties,—"Once bitten, twice shy"—Negroes have no right with white people's fights or quarrels, except, like the humble, hungry, meagre dog, to run off with the bone when both contestants drop it, being sure to separate himself from the big, well fed dogs, by a good distance, otherwise to be overtaken, and then completely outdone.

If the Negro takes my advice he will organize by himself and always keep his scale of wage a little lower than the whites until he is able to become, through proper leadership, his own employer; by so doing he will keep the good will of the white employer and live a little longer under the present scheme of things. If not, between Communism, white trade unionism and worker's parties he is doomed in the next 25, 50 or 100 years to complete economic and general extermination.

The Negro needs to be saved from his (?) "Friends," and beware of "Greeks bearing gifts." The greatest enemies of the Negro are among those who hypocritically profess love and fellowship for him, when, in truth, and deep down in their hearts, they despise and hate him. Pseudo-philanthropists and their organizations are killing the Negro. White men and women of the Morefield Storey, Joel Spingarn, Julius Rosenwald, Oswald Garrison Villard, Congressman Dyer and Mary White Ovington* type, in conjunction with the above mentioned agencies, are disarming, dis-visioning, dis-ambitioning and fooling the Negro to death. They teach the Negro to look to the whites in a false direction. They, by their practices are endeavoring to hold the Negroes in check, as a possible dangerous minority group, and yet point them to the impossible dream of equality that shall never materialize, as they well know, and never intended; at the same time distracting the Negro from the real solution and objective of securing nationalism. By thus decoying and deceiving the Negro and side-tracking his real objective, they hope to gain time against him in allowing others of their race to perfect the plan by which the blacks are to be completely destroyed as a competitive permanent part of white majority civilization and culture. They have succeeded in enslaving the ignorance of a small group of so-called "Negro intellectuals" whom they use as agents to rope in the unsuspicious colored or Negro people. They have become resentful and bitter toward the Ku Klux Klan, and use the influence of their controlled newspapers (white and colored) to fight them, not because they so much hate the Klan, where the Negro is concerned, but because the Klan, through an honest expression of the whiteman's attitude toward the Negro, prepares him to help himself.

This hypocritical group of whites, like Spingarn and Storey, have succeeded an earlier group that fooled the Negro during the days of Reconstruction. Instead of pointing the Negro to Africa, as Jefferson and Lincoln did, they sought to revenge him, for the new liberty given him, by imprisoning him in the whiteman's civilization; to further rob his labor, and exploit his ignorance, until he is subsequently ground to death by a newly developed superior white civilization. The plot of these Negro baiters is wretched to contemplate, hence their hatred of me and their influence to crush me in my attempt to save the black race.

Between the Ku Klux Klan and the Morefield Storey National Association for the Advancement of "Colored" People group, give me the Klan for their honesty of purpose towards the Negro. They are better friends to my race, for telling us what they are, and what they mean, thereby giving us a chance to stir for ourselves, than all the hypocrites put together with their false gods and religions, notwithstanding. Religions that they preach and will not practise; a God they talk about, whom they abuse every day—away with the farce, hypocrisy and lie. It smells, it stinks to high heaven. I regard the Klan, the Anglo-Saxon Clubs and White American Societies, as far as the Negro is concerned, as better friends of the race than all other groups of hypocritical whites put together. I like honesty and fair play. You may call me a Klansman if you will, but, potentially, every whiteman is a Klansman, as far as the Negro in competition with whites socially, economically and politically is concerned, and there is no use lying about it.

From *The Philosophy and Opinions of Marcus Garvey* (1925)

The Negro's Greatest Enemy

This Article, Which Is Largely a Chapter of Autobiography, Appeared in Current History Magazine, *September, 1923*

I was born in the Island of Jamaica, British West Indies, on August 17, 1887. My parents were black Negroes. My father was a man of brilliant intellect and dashing courage. He was unafraid of consequences. He took human chances in the course of life, as most bold men do, and he failed at the close of his career. He once had a fortune; he died poor. My mother was a sober and conscientious Christian, too soft and good for the time in which she lived. She was the direct opposite of my father. He was severe, firm, determined, bold and strong, refusing to yield even to superior forces if he believed he was right. My mother, on the other hand, was always willing to return a smile for a blow, and ever ready to bestow charity upon her enemy. Of this strange combination I was born thirty-six years ago, and ushered into a world of sin, the flesh and the devil.

I grew up with other black and white boys. I was never whipped by any, but made them all respect the strength of my arms. I got my education from many sources—through private tutors, two public schools, two grammar or high schools and two colleges. My teachers were men and women of varied experiences and abilities; four of them were eminent preachers. They studied me and I studied them. With some I became friendly in after years; others and I drifted apart, because as a boy they wanted to whip me, and I simply refused to be whipped. I was not made to be whipped. It annoys me to be defeated; hence to me, to be once defeated is to find cause for an everlasting struggle to reach the top.

I became a printer's apprentice at an early age, while still attending school. My apprentice master was a highly educated and alert man. In the affairs of business and the world he had no peer. He taught me many things before I reached twelve, and at fourteen I had enough intelligence and experience to manage men. I was strong and manly, and I made them respect me. I developed a strong and forceful character, and have maintained it still.

To me, at home in my early days, there was no difference between white and black. One of my father's properties, the place where I lived most of the time, was adjoining that of a white man. He had three girls and two boys; the Wesleyan minister, another white man, whose church my parents attended, also had property adjoining ours. He had three girls and one boy. All of us were playmates. We romped and were happy children, playmates together. The little white girl whom I liked most knew no better than I did myself. We were two innocent fools who never dreamed of a race feeling and problem. As a child, I went to school with white boys and girls, like all other

Negroes. We were not called Negroes then. I never heard the term Negro used once until I was about fourteen.

At fourteen my little white playmate and I parted. Her parents thought the time had come to separate us and draw the color line. They sent her and another sister to Edinburgh, Scotland, and told her that she was never to write or try to get in touch with me, for I was a "nigger." It was then that I found for the first time that there was some difference in humanity, and that there were different races, each having its own separate and distinct social life. I did not care about the separation after I was told about it, because I never thought all during our childhood association that the girl and the rest of the children of her race were better than I was; in fact, they used to look up to me. So I simply had no regrets.

After my first lesson in race distinction, I never thought of playing with white girls any more, even if they might be next-door neighbors. At home my sisters' company was good enough for me, and at school I made friends with the colored girls next to me. White boys and I used to frolic together. We played cricket and baseball, ran races and rode bicycles together, took each other to the river and to the sea beach to learn to swim, and made boyish efforts while out in deep water to drown each other, making a sprint for shore crying out "Shark, shark, shark!" In all our experiences, however, only one black boy was drowned. He went under on a Friday afternoon after school hours, and his parents found him afloat, half eaten by sharks, on the following Sunday afternoon. Since then we boys never went sea bathing.

"You Are Black"

At maturity the black and white boys separated, and took different courses in life. I grew then to see the difference between the races more and more. My schoolmates as young men did not know or remember me any more. Then I realized that I had to make a fight for a place in the world, that it was not so easy to pass on to office and position. Personally, however, I had not much difficulty in finding and holding a place for myself, for I was aggressive. At eighteen I had an excellent position as manager of a large printing establishment, having under my control several men old enough to be my grandfathers. But I got mixed up with public life. I started to take an interest in the politics of my country, and then I saw the injustice done to my race because it was black, and I became dissatisfied on that account. I went traveling to South and Central America and parts of the West Indies to find out if it was so elsewhere, and I found the same situation. I set sail for Europe to find out if it was different there, and again I found the stumbling block—"You are black." I read of the conditions in America. I read "Up from Slavery," by Booker T. Washington,* and then my doom—if I may so call it—of being a race leader dawned upon me in London after I traveled through almost half of Europe.

I asked: "Where is the black man's Government?" "Where is his King and his kingdom?" "Where is his President, his country, and his ambassador, his army, his navy, his men of big affairs?" I could not find them, and then I declared, "I will help to make them."

Becoming naturally restless for the opportunity of doing something for the advancement of my race, I was determined that the black man would not continue to be kicked about by all the other races and nations of the world, as I saw it in the West Indies, South and Central America and Europe, and as I read of it in America. My young and ambitious mind led me into flights of great imagination. I saw before me then, even as I do now, a new world of black men, not peons, serfs, dogs and slaves, but a nation of sturdy men making their impress upon civilization and causing a new light to dawn upon the human race. I could not remain in London any more. My brain was afire. There was a world of thought to conquer. I had to start ere it became too late and the work be not done. Immediately I boarded on a ship at Southampton for Jamaica, where I arrived on July 15, 1914. The Universal Negro Improvement Association and African Communities (Imperial) League was founded and organized five days after my arrival, with the program of uniting all the Negro peoples of the world into one great body to establish a country and Government absolutely their own.

Where did the name of the organization come from? It was while speaking to a West Indian Negro who was returning home to the West Indies from Basutoland* with his Basuto wife, that I further learned of the horrors of native life in Africa. He related to me such horrible and pitiable tales that my heart bled within me. Retiring to my cabin, all day and the following night I pondered over the subject matter of that conversation, and at midnight, lying flat on my back, the vision and thought came to me that I should name the organization the Universal Negro Improvement Association and African Communities (Imperial) League. Such a name I thought would embrace the purpose of all black humanity. Thus to the world a name was born, a movement created, and a man became known.

I really never knew there was so much color prejudice in Jamaica, my own native home, until I started the work of the Universal Negro Improvement Association. We started immediately before the war. I had just returned from a successful trip to Europe, which was an exceptional achievement for a black man. The daily papers wrote me up with big headlines and told of my movement. But nobody wanted to be a Negro. "Garvey is crazy; he has lost his head." "Is that the use he is going to make of his experience and intelligence?"—such were the criticisms passed upon me. Men and women as black as I, and even more so, had believed themselves white under the West Indian order of society. I was simply an impossible man to use openly the tern "Negro"; yet every one beneath his breath was calling the black man a nigger.

I had to decide whether to please my friends and be one of the "black-whites" of Jamaica, and be reasonably prosperous, or come out openly, and defend and help improve and protect the integrity of the black millions, and suffer. I decided to do the latter, hence my offense against "colored-black-white" society in the colonies and America. I was openly hated and persecuted by some of these colored men of the island who did not want to be classified as Negroes, but as white. They hated me worse than poison. They opposed me at every step, but I had a large number of white friends, who encouraged and helped me. Notable among them were the then Governor of the Colony, the Colonial Secretary and several other prominent men. But they were afraid of offending the "colored gentry" that passed for white. Hence my fight had to be made alone. I spent hundreds of pounds (sterling) helping the organization to gain a footing. I also gave up all my time to the promulgation of its ideals. I became a marked man, but I was determined that the work should be done.

The war helped a great deal in arousing the consciousness of the colored people to the reasonableness of our program, especially after the British at home had rejected a large number of West Indian colored men who wanted to be officers in the British army. When they were told that Negroes could not be officers in the British army they started their own propaganda, which supplemented the program of the Universal Negro Improvement Association. With this and other contributing agencies a few of the stiff-necked colored people began to see the reasonableness of my program, but they were firm in refusing to be known as Negroes. Furthermore, I was a black man and therefore had absolutely no right to lead; in the opinion of the "colored" element, leadership should have been in the hands of a yellow or a very light man. On such flimsy prejudices our race has been retarded. There is more bitterness among us Negroes because of the caste of color than there is between any other peoples, not excluding the people of India.

I succeeded to a great extent in establishing the Association in Jamaica with the assistance of a Catholic Bishop, the Governor, Sir John Pringle, the Rev. William Graham, a Scottish clergyman, and several other white friends. I got in touch with Booker Washington and told him what I wanted to do. He invited me to America and promised to speak with me in the Southern and other States to help my work. Although he died in the Fall of 1915, I made my arrangements and arrived in the United States on March 23, 1916.

Here I found a new and different problem. I immediately visited some of the then so-called Negro leaders, only to discover, after a close study of them, that they had no program but were mere opportunists who were living off their so-called leadership while the poor people were groping in the dark. I traveled through thirty-eight States and everywhere found the same condition. I visited Tuskegee and paid my respects to the dead hero, Booker Washington, and then returned to New York, where I organized the New York division of the Universal Negro Improvement Association. After instructing the people in the aims and objects of the Association, I intended returning to Jamaica to perfect the Jamaica organization, but when we had enrolled about 800 or 1,000 members in the Harlem district and had elected the officers, a few Negro politicians tried to turn the movement into a political club.

Political Faction Fight

Seeing that these politicians were about to destroy my ideals, I had to fight to get them out of the organization. Then it was that I made my first political enemies in Harlem. They fought me until they smashed the first organization and reduced its membership to about fifty. I started again, and in two months built up a new organization of about 1,500 members. Again the politicians came and divided us into two factions. They took away all the books of the organization, its treasury and all its belongings. At that time I was only an organizer, for it was not then my intention to remain in America, but to return to Jamaica. The organization had its proper officers elected, and I was not an officer of the New York division, but President of the Jamaica branch.

On the second split in Harlem thirteen of the members conferred with me and requested me to become President for a time of the New York organization so as to save them from the politicians. I consented and was elected President. There then sprang up two factions, one led by the politicians with the books and the money, and the other led by me. My faction had no money. I placed at their disposal what money I had, opened an office for them, rented a meeting place, employed two women secretaries, went on the street[s] of Harlem at night to speak for the movement. In three weeks more than 2,000 new members joined. By this time I had the Association incorporated so as to prevent the other faction using the name, but in two weeks the politicians had stolen all the people's money and had smashed up their faction.

The organization under my Presidency grew by leaps and bounds. I started The Negro World. Being a journalist, I edited this paper free of cost for the Association, and worked for them without pay until November, 1920. I traveled all over the country for the Association at my own expense and established branches until in 1919 we had about thirty branches in different cities. By my writings and speeches we were able to build up a large organization of over 2,000,000 by June, 1919, at which time we launched the program of the Black Star Line.

To have built up a new organization, which was not purely political, among Negroes in America was a wonderful feat, for the Negro politician does not allow any other kind of organization within his race to thrive. We succeeded, however, in making the Universal Negro Improvement Association so formidable in 1919 that we encountered more trouble from our political brethren. They sought the influence of the District Attorney's office of the County of New York to put us out of business. Edwin P. Kilroe,* at that time an Assistant District Attorney, on the complaint of the Negro politicians, started to investigate us and the association. Mr. Kilroe would constantly and continuously call me to his office for investigation on extraneous matters without coming to the point. The result was that after the eighth or ninth time I wrote an article in our newspaper, The Negro World, against him. This was interpreted as a criminal libel for which I was indicted and arrested, but subsequently dismissed on retracting what I had written.

During my many tilts with Mr. Kilroe, the question of the Black Star Line was discussed. He did not want us to have a line of ships. I told him that even as there was a White Star Line, we would have, irrespective of his wishes, a Black Star Line. On June 27, 1919, we incorporated the Black Star Line of Delaware, and in September we obtained a ship.

The following month (October) a man by the name of Tyler came to my office at 56 West 135th Street, New York City, and told me that Mr. Kilroe had sent him to "get me," and at once fired four shots at me from a .38-calibre revolver. He wounded me in the right leg and the right side of my scalp. I was taken to the Harlem Hospital, and he was arrested. The next day it was reported that he committed suicide in jail just before he was to be taken before a City Magistrate.

Record-Breaking Convention

The first year of our activities for the Black Star Line added prestige to the Universal Negro Improvement Association. Several hundred thousand dollars worth of shares were sold. Our first ship, the steamship Yarmouth, had made three voyages to the West Indies and Central America. The white press had flashed the news all over the world. I, a young Negro, as President of the corporation, had become famous. My name was discussed on five continents. The Universal Negro Improvement Association gained millions of followers all over the world. By August, 1920, over 4,000,000 persons had joined the movement. A convention of all the Negro peoples of the world was called to meet in New York that month. Delegates came from all parts of the known world. Over 25,000 persons packed the Madison Square Garden on August 1 to hear me speak to the first International Convention of Negroes. It was a record-breaking meeting, the first and the biggest of its kind. The name of Garvey had become known as a leader of his race.

Such fame among Negroes was too much for other race leaders and politicians to tolerate. My downfall was planned by my enemies. They laid all kinds of traps for me. They scattered their spies among the employes of the Black Star Line and the Universal Negro Improvement Association. Our office records were stolen. Employes started to be openly dishonest; we could get no convictions against them; even if on complaint they were held by a Magistrate, they were dismissed by the Grand Jury. The ships' officers started to pile up thousands of dollars of debts against the company without the knowledge of the officers of the corporation. Our ships were damaged at sea, and there was a general riot of wreck and ruin. Officers of the Universal Negro Improvement Association also began to steal and be openly dishonest. I had to dismiss them. They joined my enemies, and thus I had an endless fight on my hands to save the ideals of the Association and carry out our program for the race. My Negro enemies, finding that they alone could not destroy me, resorted to misrepresenting me to the leaders of the white race, several of whom, without proper investigation, also opposed me.

With robberies from within and from without, the Black Star Line was forced to suspend active business in December, 1921. While I was on a business trip to the West Indies in the Spring of 1921, the Black Star Line received the blow from which it was unable to recover. A sum of $25,000 was paid by one of the officers of the corporation to a man to purchase a ship, but the ship was never obtained and the money was never returned. The company was defrauded of a further sum of $11,000. Through such actions on the part of dishonest men in the shipping business, the Black Star Line received its first setback. This resulted in my being indicted for using the United States mails to defraud investors in the company. I was subsequently convicted and sentenced to five years in a Federal penitentiary. My trial is a matter of history. I know I was not given a square deal, because my indictment was the result of a "frame-up" among my political and business enemies. I had to conduct my own case in court because of the peculiar position in which I found myself. I had millions of friends and a large number of enemies. I wanted a colored attorney to handle my case, but there was none I could trust. I feel that I have been denied justice because of prejudice. Yet I have an abundance of faith in the courts of America, and I hope yet to obtain justice on my appeal.

Association's 6,000,000 Membership

The temporary ruin of the Black Star Line has in no way affected the larger work of the Universal Negro Improvement Association, which now has 900 branches with an approximate membership of 6,000,000. This organization has succeeded in organizing the Negroes all over the world, and we now look forward to a renaissance that will create a new people and bring about the restoration of Ethiopia's ancient glory.

Being black, I have committed an unpardonable offense against the very light-colored Negroes in America and the West Indies by making myself famous as a Negro leader of millions. In their view, no black man must rise above them, but I still forge ahead determined to give to the world the truth about the new Negro who is determined to make and hold for himself a place in the affairs of men. The Universal Negro Improvement Association has been misrepresented by my enemies. They have tried to make it appear that we are hostile to other races. This is absolutely false. We love all humanity. We are working for the peace of the world, which we believe can only come about when all races are given their due.

We feel that there is absolutely no reason why there should be any differences between the black and white races, if each stop to adjust and steady itself. We believe in the purity of both races. We do not believe the black man should be encouraged in the idea that his highest purpose in life is to marry a white woman, and we do believe that the white man should be taught to respect the black woman in the same way as he wants the black man to respect the white woman. It is a vicious and dangerous doctrine of social equality to urge, as certain colored leaders do, that black and white should get together, for that would destroy the racial purity of both.

We believe that the black people should have a country of their own, where they should be given the fullest opportunity to develop politically, socially and industrially. The black people should not be encouraged to remain in white people's countries and expect to be Presidents, Governors, Mayors, Senators, Congressmen, Judges and social and industrial leaders. We believe that with the rising ambition of the Negro, if a country is not provided for him in another 50 or 100 years, there will be a terrible clash that will end disastrously to him and disgrace our civilization. We desire to prevent such a clash by pointing the Negro to a home of his own. We feel that all well-disposed and broad-minded white men will aid in this direction. It is because of this belief no doubt that my Negro enemies, so as to prejudice me further in the opinion of the public, wickedly state that I am a member of the Ku Klux Klan, even though I am a black man.

I have been deprived of the opportunity of properly explaining my work to the white people of America, through the prejudice worked up against me by jealous and wicked members of my own race. My success as an organizer was much more than rival Negro leaders could tolerate. They, regardless of consequences, either to me or to the race, had to destroy me by fair means or foul. The thousands of anonymous and other hostile letters written to the editors and publishers of the white press by Negro rivals to prejudice me in the eyes of public opinion are sufficient evidence of the wicked and vicious opposition I have had to meet from among my own people, especially among the very light colored. But they went further than the press in their attempts to discredit me. They organized clubs all over the United States and the West Indies, and wrote both open and anonymous letters to city, State and Federal officials of this and other Governments to induce them to use their influence to hamper and destroy me. No wonder, therefore, that several Judges, District Attorneys and other high officials have been opposing me without knowing me. No wonder, therefore, that the great white population of this country and of the world has a wrong impression of the aims and objects of the Universal Negro Improvement Association and of the work of Marcus Garvey.

The Struggle of the Future

Having had the wrong education as a start in his racial career, the Negro has become his greatest enemy. Most of the trouble I have had in advancing the cause of the race has come from Negroes. Booker Washington aptly described the race in one of his lectures by stating that we were like crabs in a barrel that none would allow the other to climb over, but on any such attempt all would combine to pull back into the barrel the one crab that would make the effort to climb out. Yet, those of us with vision cannot desert the race, leaving it to suffer and die.

Looking forward a century or two, we can see an economic and political death struggle for the survival of the different race groups. Many of our present-day national centres will have become overcrowded with vast surplus populations. The fight for bread and position will be keen and severe. The weaker and unprepared group is bound to go under. That is why, visionaries as we are in the Universal Negro Improvement Association, we are fighting for the founding of a Negro nation in Africa, so that there will be no clash between black and white and that each race will have a separate existence and civilization all its own without courting suspicion and hatred or eyeing each other with jealousy and rivalry within the borders of the same country.

White men who have struggled for and built up their countries and their own civilizations are not disposed to hand them over to the Negro, or any other race, without let or hindrance. It would be unreasonable to expect this. Hence any vain assumption on the part of the Negro to imagine that he will one day become President of the Nation, Governor of the State, or Mayor of the City in the countries of white men, is like waiting on the devil and his angels to take up their residence in the Realm on high and direct there the affairs of Paradise.

From *The Philosophy and Opinions of Marcus Garvey* (1925)

Declaration of Rights of the Negro Peoples of the World

Drafted and adopted at Convention held in New York, 1920, over which Marcus Garvey presided as Chairman, and at which he was elected Provisional President of Africa.

(Preamble)

"Be it Resolved, That the Negro people of the world, through their chosen representatives in convention assembled in Liberty Hall, in the City of New York and United States of America, from August 1 to August 31, in the year of our Lord, one thousand nine hundred and twenty, protest against the wrongs and injustices they are suffering at the hands of their white brethren, and state what they deem their fair and just rights, as well as the treatment they propose to demand of all men in the future."

We complain:

I. "That nowhere in the world, with few exceptions, are black men accorded equal treatment with white men, although in the same situation and circumstances, but, on the contrary, are discriminated against and denied the common rights due to human beings for no other reason than their race and color."

"We are not willingly accepted as guests in the public hotels and inns of the world for no other reason than our race and color."

II. "In certain parts of the United States of America our race is denied the right of public trial accorded to other races when accused of crime, but are lynched and burned by mobs, and such brutal and inhuman treatment is even practised upon our women."

III. "That European nations have parcelled out among themselves and taken possession of nearly all of the continent of Africa, and the natives are compelled to surrender their lands to aliens and are treated in most instances like slaves."

IV. "In the southern portion of the United States of America, although citizens under the Federal Constitution, and in some states almost equal to the whites in population and are qualified land owners and taxpayers, we are, nevertheless, denied all voice in the making and administration of the laws and are taxed without representation by the state governments, and at the same time compelled to do military service in defense of the country."

V. "On the public conveyances and common carriers in the Southern portion of the United States we are jim-crowed and compelled to accept separate and inferior accommodations and made to pay the same fare charged for first-class accommodations, and our families are often humiliated and insulted by drunken white men who habitually pass through the jim-crow cars going to the smoking car."

VI. "The physicians of our race are denied the right to attend their patients while in the public hospitals of the cities and states where they reside in certain parts of the United States."

"Our children are forced to attend inferior separate schools for shorter terms than white children, and the public school funds are unequally divided between the white and colored schools."

VII. "We are discriminated against and denied an equal chance to earn wages for the support of our families, and in many instances are refused admission into labor unions, and nearly everywhere are paid smaller wages than white men."

VIII. "In Civil Service and departmental offices we are everywhere discriminated against and made to feel that to be a black man in Europe, America and the West Indies is equivalent to being an outcast and a leper among the races of men, no matter what the character and attainments of the black man may be."

IX. "In the British and other West Indian Islands and colonies, Negroes are secretly and cunningly discriminated against, and denied those fuller rights in government to which white citizens are appointed, nominated and elected."

X. "That our people in those parts are forced to work for lower wages than the average standard of white men and are kept in conditions repugnant to good civilized tastes and customs."

XI. "That the many acts of injustices against members of our race before the courts of law in the respective islands and colonies are of such nature as to create disgust and disrespect for the white man's sense of justice."

XII. "Against all such inhuman, unchristian and uncivilized treatment we here and now emphatically protest, and invoke the condemnation of all mankind."

"In order to encourage our race all over the world and to stimulate it to a higher and grander destiny, we demand and insist on the following Declaration of Rights:

1. "Be it known to all men that whereas, all men are created equal and entitled to the rights of life, liberty and the pursuit of happiness, and because of this we, the duly elected representatives of the Negro peoples of the world, invoking the aid of the just and Almighty God do declare all men[,] women and children of our blood throughout the world free citizens, and do claim them as free citizens of Africa, the Motherland of all Negroes."

2. "That we believe in the supreme authority of our race in all things racial; that all things are created and given to man as a common possession; that there should be an equitable distribution and apportionment of all such things, and in consideration of the fact that as a race we are now deprived of those things that are morally and legally ours, we believe it right that all such things should be acquired and held by whatsoever means possible.["]

3. "That we believe the Negro, like any other race, should be governed by the ethics of civilization, and, therefore, should not be deprived of any of those rights or privileges common to other human beings."

4. "We declare that Negroes, wheresoever they form a community among themselves, should be given the right to elect their own representatives to represent them in legislatures, courts of law, or such institutions as may exercise control over that peculiar community."

5. "We assert that the Negro is entitled to even-handed justice before all courts of law and equity in whatever country he may be found, and when this is denied him on account of his race or color such denial is an insult to the race as a whole and should be resented by the entire body of Negroes."

6. "We declare it unfair and prejudicial to the rights of Negroes in communities where they exist in considerable numbers to be tried by a judge and jury composed entirely of an alien race, but in all such cases members of our race are entitled to representation on the jury."

7. "We believe that any law or practice that tends to deprive any African of his land or the privileges of free citizenship within his country is unjust and immoral, and no native should respect any such law or practice."

8. "We declare taxation without representation unjust and tyrannous, and there should be no obligation on the part of the Negro to obey the levy of a tax by any law-making body from which he is excluded and denied representation on account of his race and color."

9. "We believe that any law especially directed against the Negro to his detriment and singling him out because of his race or color is unfair and immoral, and should not be respected."

10. "We believe all men entitled to common human respect, and that our race should in no way tolerate any insults that may be interpreted to mean disrespect to our color."

11. "We deprecate the use of the term 'nigger' as applied to Negroes, and we demand that the word 'Negro' be written with a capital 'N.'"

12. "We believe that the Negro should adopt every means to protect himself against barbarous practices inflicted upon him because of color."

13. "We believe in the freedom of Africa for the Negro people of the world, and by the principle of Europe for the Europeans and Asia for the Asiatics; we also demand Africa for the Africans at home and abroad."

14. "We believe in the inherent right of the Negro to possess himself of Africa, and that his possession of same shall not be regarded as an infringement on any claim or purchase made by any race or nation."

15. "We strongly condemn the cupidity of those nations of the world who, by open aggression or secret schemes, have seized the territories and inexhaustible natural wealth of Africa, and we place on record our most solemn determination to reclaim the treasures and possession of the vast continent of our forefathers."

16. "We believe all men should live in peace one with the other, but when races and nations provoke the ire of other races and nations by attempting to infringe upon their rights, war becomes inevitable, and the attempt in any way to free one's self or protect one's rights or heritage becomes justifiable.["]

17. "Whereas, the lynching, by burning, hanging or any other means, of human beings is a barbarous practice, and a shame and disgrace to civilization, we therefore declare any country guilty of such atrocities outside the pale of civilization."

18. "We protest against the atrocious crime of whipping, flogging and overworking of the native tribes of Africa and Negroes everywhere. These are methods that should be abolished, and all means should be taken to prevent a continuance of such brutal practices."

19. "We protest against the atrocious practice of shaving the heads of Africans, especially of African women or individuals of Negro blood, when placed in prison as a punishment for crime by an alien race."

20. "We protest against segregated districts, separate public conveyances, industrial discrimination, lynchings and limitations of political privileges of any Negro citizen in any part of the world on account of race, color or creed, and will exert our full influence and power against all such."

21. "We protest against any punishment inflicted upon a Negro with severity, as against lighter punishment inflicted upon another of an alien race for like offense, as an act of prejudice and injustice, and should be resented by the entire race."

22. "We protest against the system of education in any country where Negroes are denied the same privileges and advantages as other races."

23. "We declare it inhuman and unfair to boycott Negroes from industries and labor in any part of the world."

24. "We believe in the doctrine of the freedom of the press, and we therefore emphatically protest against the suppression of Negro newspapers and periodicals in various parts of the world, and call upon Negroes everywhere to employ all available means to prevent such suppression."

25. "We further demand free speech universally for all men."

26. "We hereby protest against the publication of scandalous and inflammatory articles by an alien press tending to create racial strife and the exhibition of picture films showing the Negro as a cannibal."

27. "We believe in the self-determination of all peoples."

28. "We declare for the freedom of religious worship."

29. "With the help of Almighty God, we declare ourselves the sworn protectors of the honor and virtue of our women and children, and pledge our lives for their protection and defense everywhere, and under all circumstances from wrongs and outrages."

30. "We demand the right of unlimited and unprejudiced education for ourselves and our posterity forever."

31. "We declare that the teaching in any school by alien teachers to our boys and girls, that the alien race is superior to the Negro race, is an insult to the Negro people of the world."

32. "Where Negroes form a part of the citizenry of any country, and pass the civil service examination of such country, we declare them entitled to the same consideration as other citizens as to appointments in such civil service."

33. "We vigorously protest against the increasingly unfair and unjust treatment accorded Negro travelers on land and sea by the agents and employees of railroad and steamship companies and

insist that for equal fare we receive equal privileges with travelers of other races."

34. "We declare it unjust for any country, State or nation to enact laws tending to hinder and obstruct the free immigration of Negroes on account of their race and color."

35. "That the right of the Negro to travel unmolested throughout the world be not abridged by any person or persons, and all Negroes are called upon to give aid to a fellow Negro when thus molested."

36. "We declare that all Negroes are entitled to the same right to travel over the world as other men."

37. "We hereby demand that the governments of the world recognize our leader and his representatives chosen by the race to look after the welfare of our people under such governments."

38. "We demand complete control of our social institutions without interference by any alien race or races."

39. "That the colors, Red, Black and Green, be the colors of the Negro race."

40. "Resolved, That the anthem 'Ethiopia, Thou Land of Our Fathers,' etc., shall be the anthem of the Negro race."

The Universal Ethiopian Anthem

*(Poem by Burrell and Ford)**

I

Ethiopia, thou land of our fathers,
Thou land where the gods loved to be,
As storm cloud at night suddenly gathers
Our armies come rushing to thee.
We must in the fight be victorious
When swords are thrust outward to gleam;
For us will the vict'ry be glorious
When led by the red, black and green.

Chorus
Advance, advance to victory,
Let Africa be free;
Advance to meet the foe

With the might
Of the red, the black and the green.

II
Ethiopia, the tyrant's falling,
Who smote thee upon thy knees,
And thy children are lustily calling
From over the distant seas.
Jehovah, the Great One has heard us,
Has noted our sighs and our tears,
With His spirit of Love he has stirred us
To be One through the coming years.
Chorus—Advance, advance, etc.

III
O Jehovah, thou God of the ages
Grant unto our sons that lead
The wisdom Thou gave to Thy sages
When Israel was sore in need.
Thy voice thro' the dim past has spoken,
Ethiopia shall stretch forth her hand,
By Thee shall all fetters be broken,
And Heav'n bless our dear fatherland.
Chorus—Advance, advance, etc.

41. "We believe that any limited liberty which deprives one of the complete rights and prerogatives of full citizenship is but a modified form of slavery."

42. "We declare it an injustice to our people and a serious impediment to the health of the race to deny to competent licensed Negro physicians the right to practise in the public hospitals of the communities in which they reside, for no other reason than their race and color."

43. "We call upon the various governments of the world to accept and acknowledge Negro representatives who shall be sent to the said governments to represent the general welfare of the Negro peoples of the world."

44. "We deplore and protest against the practice of confining juvenile prisoners in prisons with adults, and we recommend that

such youthful prisoners be taught gainful trades under humane supervision."

45. "Be it further resolved, that we as a race of people declare the League of Nations null and void as far as the Negro is concerned, in that it seeks to deprive Negroes of their liberty."

46. "We demand of all men to do unto us as we would do unto them, in the name of justice; and we cheerfully accord to all men all the rights we claim herein for ourselves."

47. "We declare that no Negro shall engage himself in battle for an alien race without first obtaining the consent of the leader of the Negro people of the world, except in a matter of national self-defense."

48. "We protest against the practice of drafting Negroes and sending them to war with alien forces without proper training, and demand in all cases that Negro soldiers be given the same training as the aliens."

49. "We demand that instructions given Negro children in school include the subject of 'Negro History,' to their benefit."

50. "We demand a free and unfettered commercial intercourse with all the Negro people of the world."

51. "We declare for the absolute freedom of the seas for all peoples."

52. "We demand that our duly accredited representatives be given proper recognition in all leagues, conferences, conventions or courts of international arbitration wherever human rights are discussed."

53. "We proclaim the 31st day of August of each year to be an international holiday to be observed by all Negroes."

54. "We want all men to know we shall maintain and contend for the freedom and equality of every man, woman and child of our race, with our lives, our fortunes and our sacred honor."

These rights we believe to be justly ours and proper for the protection of the Negro race at large, and because of this belief, we, on behalf of the four hundred million Negroes of the world, do pledge herein the sacred blood of the race in defense, and we hereby subscribe our names as a guarantee of the truthfulness and faithfulness hereof in the presence of Almighty God, on the 13th day of August, in the year of our Lord one thousand nine hundred and twenty.

The document was signed by 122 delegates from the convention, including Garvey himself and many important members of the movement, such as Henrietta Vinton Davis, Arnold Josiah Ford, and Garvey's secretaries, Janie Jenkins and Mary E. Johnson.

From *The Philosophy and Opinions of Marcus Garvey* (1925)

First Message to the Negroes of the World from Atlanta Prison

February 10, 1925

Fellow Men of the Negro Race, Greetings:

I am delighted to inform you, that your humble servant is as happy in suffering for you and our cause as is possible under the circumstances of being viciously outraged by a group of plotters who have connived to do their worst to humiliate you through me, in the fight for real emancipation and African Redemption.

I do trust that you have given no credence to the vicious lies of white and enemy newspapers and those who have spoken in reference to my surrender. The liars plotted in every way to make it appear that I was not willing to surrender to the court. My attorney advised me that no mandate would have been handed down for ten or fourteen days, as is the custom of the courts, and that would have given me time to keep speaking engagements I had in Detroit, Cincinnati and Cleveland. I hadn't left the city for ten hours when the liars flashed the news that I was a fugitive. That was good news to circulate all over the world to demoralize the millions of Negroes in America, Africa, Asia, the West Indies and Central America, but the idiots ought to know by now that they can't fool all the Negroes at the same time.

I do not want at this time to write anything that would make it difficult for you to meet the opposition of the enemy without my assistance. Suffice it to say that the history of the outrage shall form a splendid chapter in the history of Africa redeemed, when black men will no longer be under the heels of others, but have a civilization and country of their own.

The whole affair is a disgrace, and the whole black world knows it. We shall not forget. Our day may be fifty, a hundred or two hundred years ahead, but let us watch, work and pray, for the civilization of injustice is bound to crumble and bring destruction down upon the heads of the unjust.

The idiots thought that they could humble me personally, but in that they are mistaken. The minutes of suffering are counted, and when God and Africa come back and measure out retribution these minutes may multiply by thousands for the sinners. Our Arab and Riffian* friends will be ever vigilant, as the rest of Africa and ourselves shall be. Be assured that I planted well the seed of Negro or black nationalism which cannot be destroyed even by the foul play that has been meted out to me.

Continue to pray for me and I shall ever be true to my trust. I want you, the black peoples of the world, to know that W. E. B. Du Bois and that vicious Negro-hating organization known as the Association for the Advancement of "Colored" People are the greatest enemies the black people have in the world. I have so much to do in the next few minutes at my disposal that I cannot write exhaustively on this or any other matter, but be warned against these two enemies. Don't allow them to fool you with fine sounding press releases, speeches and books; they are the vipers who have planned with others the extinction of the "black" race.

My work is just begun, and when the history of my suffering is complete, then future generations of Negroes will have in their hands the guide by which they shall know the "sins" of the twentieth century. I, and I know you, too, believe in time, and we shall wait patiently for two hundred years, if need be, to face our enemies through our posterity.

You will cheer me much if you will now do even more for the organization than when I was among you. Hold up the hands of those who are carrying on. Help them to make good, so that the work may continue to spread from pole to pole.

I am also making a last minute appeal for support to the Black Cross Navigation and Trading Company. Please send in and make your loans so as to enable the directors to successfully carry on the work.

All I have I have given to you. I have sacrificed my home and my loving wife for you. I entrust her to your charge, to protect and defend her in my absence. She is the bravest little woman I know. She has suffered and sacrificed with me for you; therefore, please do not desert her at this dismal hour, when she stands alone. I have left her penniless and helpless to face the world, because I gave you all, but her courage is great, and I know she will hold up for you and me.

After my enemies are satisfied, in life or death I shall come back to you to serve even as I have served before. In life I shall be the same; in death I shall be a terror to the foes of Negro liberty. If death has power, then count on me in death to be the real Marcus Garvey I would like to be. If I may come in an earthquake, or a cyclone, or plague, or pestilence, or as God would have me, then be assured that I shall never desert you and make your enemies triumph over you. Would I not go to hell a million times for you? Would I not like Macbeth's ghost walk the earth forever for you? Would I not lose the whole world and eternity for you? Would I not cry forever before the footstool of the Lord Omnipotent for you? Would I not die a million deaths for you? Then, why be sad? Cheer up, and be assured that if it takes a million years the sins of our enemies shall visit the millionth generation of those that hinder and oppress us.

Remember that I have sworn by you and my God to serve to the end of all time, the wreck of matter and the crash of worlds. The enemies think that I am defeated. Did the Germans defeat the French in 1870? Did Napoleon really conquer Europe? If so, then I am defeated, but I tell you the world shall hear from my principles even two thousand years hence. I am willing to wait on time for my satisfaction and the retribution of my enemies. Observe my enemies and their children and posterity, and one day you shall see retribution settling around them.

If I die in Atlanta my work shall then only begin, but I shall live, in the physical or spiritual to see the day of Africa's glory. When I am dead wrap the mantle of the Red, Black and Green around me, for in the new life I shall rise with God's grace and blessing to lead the millions up the heights of triumph with the colors that you well know. Look for me in the whirlwind or the storm, look for me all around you, for, with God's grace, I shall come and bring with me countless millions of black slaves who have died in America and the West Indies and the millions in Africa to aid you in the fight for Liberty, Freedom and Life.

The civilization of today is gone drunk and crazy with its power and by such it seeks through injustice, fraud and lies to crush the unfortunate. But if I am apparently crushed by the system of influence and misdirected power, my cause shall rise again to plague the conscience of the corrupt. For this I am satisfied, and for you, I repeat, I am glad to suffer and even die. Again, I say, cheer up, for better days are ahead. I shall write the history that will inspire the millions that are coming and leave the posterity of our enemies to reckon with the hosts for the deeds of their fathers.

With God's dearest blessings, I leave you for awhile.

From *The Philosophy and Opinions of Marcus Garvey* (1925)

African Fundamentalism*

Fellow Men of the Negro Race, Greeting:

The time has come for the Negro to forget and cast behind him his hero worship and adoration of other races, and to start out immediately to create and emulate heroes of his own.

We must canonize our own saints, create our own martyrs, and elevate to positions of fame and honor black men and women who have made their distinct contributions to our racial history. Sojourner Truth is worthy of the place of sainthood alongside of Joan of Arc; Crispus Attucks and George William Gordon* are entitled to the halo of martyrdom with no less glory than that of the martyrs of any other race. Toussaint L'Ouverture's brilliancy as a soldier and statesman outshone that of a Cromwell, Napoleon and Washington; hence, he is entitled to the highest place as a hero among men. Africa has produced countless numbers of men and women, in war and in peace, whose lustre and bravery outshine that of any other people. Then why not see good and perfection in ourselves?

Ours the Right to Our Doctrine

We must inspire a literature and promulgate a doctrine of our own without any apologies to the powers that be. The right is ours and God's. Let contrary sentiment and cross opinions go to the winds. Opposition to race independence is the weapon of the enemy to defeat the hopes of an unfortunate people. We are entitled to our own opinions and not obligated to or bound by the opinions of others.

A Peep at the Past

If others laugh at you, return the laughter to them; if they mimic you, return the compliment with equal force. They have no more right to dishonor, disrespect and disregard your feeling and manhood than you have in dealing with them. Honor them when they honor you; disrespect and disregard them when they vilely treat you. Their arrogance is but skin deep and an assumption that has no foundation in morals or in law. They have sprung from the same family tree of obscurity as we have; their history is as rude in its primitiveness as ours; their ancestors ran wild and naked, lived in caves and in branches of trees, like monkeys, as ours; they made human sacrifices, ate the flesh of their own dead and the raw meat of the wild beast for centuries even as they accuse us of doing; their cannibalism was more prolonged than ours; when we were embracing the arts and sciences on the banks of the Nile their ancestors were still drinking human blood and eating out of the skulls of their conquered dead; when our civilization had reached the noon-day of progress they were still running naked and sleeping in holes and caves with rats, bats and other insects and animals. After we had already unfathomed the mysteries of the stars and reduced the heavenly constellations to minute and regular calculus they were still backwoodsmen, living in ignorance and blatant darkness.

Why Be Discouraged?

The world today is indebted to us for the benefits of civilization. They stole our arts and sciences from Africa. Then why should we be ashamed of ourselves? Their *modern improvements* are but *duplicates* of a grander civilization that we reflected thousands of years ago, without the advantage of what is buried and still hidden, to be resurrected and reintroduced by the intelligence of our generation and our posterity. Why should we be discouraged because somebody laughs at us today? Who [can] tell what tomorrow will bring forth? Did they not laugh at Moses, Christ and Mohammed? Was there not a Carthage, Greece and Rome? We see and have changes every day, so pray, work, be steadfast and be not dismayed.

Nothing Must Kill the Empire Urge

As the Jew is held together by his *religion*, the white races by the assumption and the unwritten law of *superiority*, and the Mongolian by the precious tie of *blood*, so likewise the Negro must be united in one *grand racial hierarchy*. Our *union must know no clime, boundary, or nationality*. Like the great Church of Rome, Negroes the world over *must practice one faith*, that of Confidence in themselves, with One God! One Aim! One Destiny! Let no religious scruples, no political machinations divide us, but let us hold together under all climes and in every country, making among ourselves a Racial Empire upon which "the sun shall never set."

Allegiance to Self First

Let no voice but your own speak to you from the depths. Let no influence but your own raise you in time of peace and time of war. Hear all, but attend only that which concerns you.

Your first allegiance shall be to your God, then to your family, race and country. Remember always that the Jew in his political and economic urge is always first a Jew; the white man is first a white man under all circumstances, and you can do no less than being first and always a Negro, and then all else will take care of itself. Let no one inoculate you with evil doctrines to suit their own conveniences. There is no humanity before that which starts with yourself. "Charity begins at home." First, to thyself be true, and "thou canst not then be false to any man."*

We Are Arbiters of Our Own Destiny

God and Nature first made us what we are, and then out of our own creative genius we make ourselves what we want to be. Follow always that great law.

Let the sky and God be our limit, and Eternity our measurement. There is no height to which we cannot climb by using the active intelligence of our own minds. Mind creates, and as much as we desire in Nature we can have through the creation of our own minds. Being at present the scientifically weaker race, you shall treat others only as they treat you; but in your homes and everywhere possible you must teach the higher development of science to your children; and be sure to develop a race of scientists par excellence, for in science and religion lies our only hope to withstand the evil designs of modern materialism. Never forget your God.

Remember, we live, work and pray for the establishing of a great and binding *racial hierarchy*, the founding of a *racial empire* whose only natural, spiritual and political limits shall be God and "Africa, at home and abroad."

From the *Negro World* June 6, 1925

The Black Woman

Black queen of beauty, thou hast given color to the world!
Among other women thou art royal and the fairest!
Like the brightest of jewels in the regal diadem,
Shin'st thou, Goddess of Africa, Nature's purest emblem!

Black men worship at thy virginal shrine of truest love,
Because in thine eyes are virtue's steady and holy mark,
As we see in no other, clothed in silk or fine linen,
From ancient Venus, the Goddess, to mythical Helen.

When Africa stood at the head of the elder nations,
The Gods used to travel from foreign lands to look at
     thee:
On couch of costly Eastern materials, all perfumed,
Reclined thee, as in thy path flow'rs were strewn—
     sweetest that bloomed.
Thy transcendent marvelous beauty made the whole
     world mad,
Bringing Solomon to tears as he viewed thy comeliness;
Anthony and the elder Caesars wept at thy royal feet,
Preferring death than to leave thy presence, their foes to
     meet.

You, in all ages, have attracted the adoring world,
And caused many a bloody banner to be unfurled:
You have sat upon exalted and lofty eminence,
To see a world fight in your ancient African defence.

Today you have been dethroned, through the weakness of
     your men,
While, in frenzy, those who of yore craved your smiles
     and your hand—
Those who were all monsters and could not with love
     approach you—
Have insulted your pride and now attack your good
     virtue.

Because of disunion you became mother of the world,
Giving tinge of robust color to five continents,
Making a greater world of millions of colored races,
Whose claim to beauty is reflected through our black
     faces.

From the handsome Indian to the European brunette,
There is a claim for that credit of their sunny beauty
That no one can e'er take from thee, O Queen of all
    women
Who have borne trials and troubles and racial burden.

Once more we shall, in Africa, fight and conquer for you,
Restoring the pearly crown that proud Queen Sheba did
    wear:
Yes, it may mean blood, it may mean death; but still we
    shall fight,
Bearing our banners to Vict'ry, men of Afric's might.

Superior Angels look like you in Heaven above,
For thou art fairest, queen of the seasons, queen of our
    love:
No condition shall make us ever in life desert thee,
Sweet Goddess of the ever green land and placid blue
    sea.

From *Selections from the Poetic Meditations of Marcus Garvey* (New York: A. J. Garvey, 1927)

"Home to Harlem," Claude McKay's Damaging Book, Should Earn Wholesale Condemnation of Negroes

Fellowmen of the Negro Race, Greeting:

It is my duty to bring to your attention this week a grave evil that afflicts us as a people at this time. Our race, within recent years, has developed a new group of writers who have been prostituting their intelligence, under the direction of the white man, to bring out and show up the worst traits of our people. Several of these writers are American and West Indian Negroes. They have been writing books, novels, and poems, under the advice of white publishers, to portray to the world the looseness, laxity and immorality that are peculiar to our group, for the purpose of these publishers circulating the libel against us among the white people of the world, to further hold us up to ridicule and contempt and universal prejudice.

McKay's "Home to Harlem"

Several of these books have been published in America recently, the last of which is Claude McKay's "Home to Harlem," published by Harper Bros. of New York. This book of Claude McKay's is a damnable libel against the Negro. It is doing a great deal of harm in further creating prejudice among the white people against the Negro.*** Claude McKay, the Jamaican Negro, is not singular in the authorship of such books. W. E. B. Du Bois, of America; Walter White, [James] Weldon Johnson, Eric Waldron [*sic*], of British Guiana, and others, have written similar books, while we have had recently a large number of sappy poems from the rising poets.

White Publishers Use Negroes

The white people have these Negroes to write the kind of stuff that they desire to feed their public with so that the Negro can still be regarded as a monkey or some imbecilic creature. Whenever authors of the Negro race write good literature for publication the white publishers refuse to publish it, but wherever the Negro is sufficiently known to attract attention he is advised to write in the way that the white man wants. That is just what has happened to Claude McKay. The time has come for us to boycott such Negro authors whom we may fairly designate as "literary prostitutes." We must make them understand that we are not going to stand for their insults indulged in to suit prejudiced white people who desire to hold the Negro up to contempt and ridicule. We must encourage our own black authors who have character, who are loyal to their race, who feel proud to be black, and in every way let them feel that we appreciate their efforts to advance our race through healthy and decent literature.

Writers to Fight Negro Cause

We want writers who will fight the Negro's cause, as H. G. Wells of the white race fights for the cause of the Anglo-Saxon group. Let us imagine Wells prostituting his intelligence and ability as an author to suit Negro publishers, as against the morals or interest of the Anglo-Saxon race. It is impossible. Yet there are many Negro writers who have prostituted their intelligence to do the most damaging harm to the morals and reputations of the Black race.*

Proud Blood of the Negro

In the autobiography Claude McKay tries to make out that his parents were from Madagascar, and that they were so proud as to have gone on a death strike against being enslaved. I do not believe this. I don't believe McKay can trace his ancestry back to Madagascar. It is most likely that he came from the Congo. Negroes who are descendants from proud ancestors generally retain some of their proud blood. No proud man of any race ever debases his race. It is always those of low ancestry who are always willing to play the monkey for the satisfaction of others. But it is a trait of those libellers against the black race to always suggest when they come in contact with white people that they represent the best blood of the Negro.

Du Bois' Royal House

If I am not mistaken, a friend told me that Du Bois stated and suggested that he has claim to the ancestry of a Royal House in East Africa. It is rather amusing to hear these libellers of the race talking about their royal ancestry when they represent the lowest type of ancestry. Negroes of royal ancestry always want to be proud of their race; they do not think any race better than their own. Yet Du Bois called a black man an ugly man simply because he was black. Those of you who remember his article in the "Century Magazine" in 1920* will remember that he positively stated that to be black was to be ugly. The black royal blood of East Africa believes in the honor and integrity of the black race. Du Bois to the contrary believes that the standard of beauty is to be found in the white man.

Something Funny

It is funny that these writers are always suggesting that they are from royal black blood and yet they are prostituting their intelligence and ability as authors and writers against their race for the satisfaction of white people.

We are calling a halt on these libelous writers so that we may develop authors and poets worthy of our race and who will fight for the cause of the race.

From the *Negro World* September 29, 1928

Amy Ashwood Garvey

Amy Ashwood Garvey, the first wife of Marcus Garvey, has often been credited as being the co-founder of the Universal Negro Improvement Association (UNIA). She writes poignantly in her fragmented, unpublished biography of Garvey about conceiving the organization with him, culminating in their mutual pledge to support one another: "Marcus Garvey stood before me and said in a very earnest voice, 'Amy Ashwood, I appoint you secretary of the Universal Negro Improvement Association.' I replied with an equal earnestness, 'And Marcus Garvey, I appoint you president.'" Though it is difficult to verify her claims of co-founding the UNIA, she was at the very least a seminal figure in developing the organization and helping to nourish it in its early years.[1]

Ashwood was born in Port Antonio, Jamaica, on January 18, 1897. In her youth, she lived in Panama and Jamaica. Ashwood met Marcus Garvey in 1914 and the UNIA was formed shortly thereafter. As Garvey was building the fledgling movement, Ashwood accompanied him on trips throughout Jamaica and was involved in establishing a ladies' division. Ashwood's parents, who did not approve of her relationship with Garvey, a dreamer from a lower class, arranged for her to travel to Panama in 1916. She did not encounter him again until 1918, when she arrived in New York. At this point she thrust herself into work on the UNIA, giving speeches, recruiting, helping with the management of the *Negro World* and the Black Star Line. According to an agent of the Bureau of Investigation (who had been investigating the couple), she was Garvey's "chief assistant, a kind of managing boss" (Hill 2: 15). She is also alleged to have saved Garvey's life by thwarting a would-be assassin in 1919.

Ashwood and Garvey were married in an elaborate ceremony on December 25, 1919. In her biography of Garvey, Ashwood records their courtship, he being the Napoleon to her Josephine, in storybook language. Yet the tale did not have a happy ending. Two such strong-willed people inevitably clashed. Within months the marriage was riven by rancorous accusations on both sides. She was said to be an alcoholic, an adulterer, and an embezzler. He was charged with infidelity and being domineering. After bitter court proceedings, the marriage ended in divorce in 1922, whereupon Garvey quickly married Ashwood's childhood friend and her chief bridesmaid, Amy Jacques. Ashwood never accepted the divorce and accused Garvey of bigamy.

After leaving the UNIA, she collaborated with Trinidadian Calypsonian Sam Manning on the musicals *Brown Sugar*, *Hey! Hey!*, and *Black Magic*, which all had short runs at the Lafayette Theatre in New York and other venues. The plays, with story lines intended to foster better relationships between West Indians and African Americans, featured top performers, including Fats Waller as the bandleader in *Brown Sugar*.[2]

Ashwood journeyed to London in 1929 and, with Manning, opened the Florence Mills Nightclub, which became the center of the Pan-African movement in England, with such illustrious patrons as C. L. R. James, George Padmore, Kwame Nkrumah, and Jomo Kenyatta. In 1945 she co-chaired, with W. E. B. Du Bois, the Fifth Pan-African Congress, in Manchester, organized by Padmore and Nkrumah. At the congress, Ashwood voiced her feminist concerns, calling for a greater attention to the needs of Black women, including the need for increased wages.

Returning to New York in 1944, she campaigned on behalf of Adam Clayton Powell Jr. and met with prominent Black communists such as Paul Robeson. Such activity again brought her to the attention of the Federal Bureau of Investigation.

Ashwood, like Garvey an ardent Pan-African, eventually traveled to the Motherland, unlike her ex-husband. In the late 1940s she journeyed throughout West Africa, with stops in Liberia, Sierra Leone, Senegal, Nigeria, and the Cameroons. In the Gold Coast (present-day Ghana), she traced her ancestry back to Ashanti.

The remainder of her life was spent in constant travel through-out the United States, England, the Caribbean, and West Africa, advocating on behalf of various causes. She founded the Association for the English Advancement of Coloured People in London in 1958 in response to the Notting Hill riots. She was involved in the ceremony that brought Garvey's remains to Jamaica from England in 1964. She spoke on behalf of Liberia and established a close relationship with William Tubman, president of that country. One thing she was unable to do, however, was to publish her biography of Garvey. This is unfortunate, as the brief portions that are available provide insight into the origins of the UNIA. Ashwood died in poverty in Jamaica on May 3, 1969, fighting to the end on behalf of her people.

NOTES

Ashwood's papers are largely in the National Library of Jamaica and in private collections.

1. Lionel Yard's biography remains the best source of information on Ashwood, but it borders at times on hagiography.

2. Manuscripts of the musicals do not seem to have survived. For a brief review of *Hey! Hey!* see the *Amsterdam News* November 10, 1926.

BIBLIOGRAPHY

Ashwood Garvey, Amy. *"Up You Mighty Race": Recollections of Marcus Garvey.* Songs by Thelma Massy and Lord Obstinate. LP. Garvey Records, [1968].

Bennett, Lerone Jr. "The Ghost of Marcus Garvey: Interviews with Crusader's Two Wives." *Ebony* 15 (March 1960): 53–61.

Hill, Robert, ed. *The Marcus Garvey and Universal Negro Improvement Association Papers.* 9 vols. Berkeley: U of California P, 1983–.

Martin, Tony. "Amy Ashwood Garvey: Wife No. 1." *Jamaica Journal* 20 (Aug.–Oct. 1987): 32–36.

———. "Discovering African Roots: Amy Ashwood Garvey's Pan-Africanist Journey." *Comparative Studies of South Asia, Africa, and the Middle East* 17 (1997): 118–26.

Parker, Kevin. "Amy Ashwood Garvey." *Encyclopedia of African American Culture and History.* Ed. Jack Salzman, David Lionel Smith, and Cornel West. New York: Macmillan, 1996. 1089–90.

Yard, Lionel M. *Biography of Amy Ashwood Garvey, 1897–1969, Co-Founder of the Universal Negro Improvement Association.* [Washington, DC]: Associated P, [198?].

The Birth of the Universal Negro Improvement Association

A few months after his arrival from Britain it seemed to Garvey that for a time he might be chasing a will o' the wisp. Dreaming of greatness in itself alone failed to satisfy Garvey for long. His ardent spirit and passionate devotion to an ideal clamored for action. He wanted to see his race marching triumphantly in the human conclave ever onwards; he wanted officers and co-workers around him who had caught his spirit and would thus prove loyal bodyguards. Grandiose schemes would avail naught unless they could be translated into reality. If as he considered, he was a Napoleon, he would need a Josephine. He had reached that moment in the life of all great men when the testing period between ideas and their execution became more challenging and acute. This is the period of well-nigh frustration through which all leaders must pass—the potter's fire of the refining gold and the elimination of the dross therefrom. It was a phase that was causing him to champ at the stirrup.

It was just at this period that our paths met. Marcus Garvey and I met for the first time as if by some design of fate and conspiracy of destiny. It was no casual meeting, for its timing was significant for both of us. It changed much in the life of each of us.

The occasion was a simple one. It was my custom at that time to attend the weekly literary debate at the Baptist Church Hall in Kingston, Jamaica. On that particular Tuesday evening in the late July of 1914, I had proposed the motion that "Morality does not increase with civilization." I had argued my case as strongly as I could, and then sat down to hear what my opponents had to say. As the debate progressed I had become so absorbed in the literary thrusts and parries that I paid little if any attention to the individual speakers themselves, not even among my own supporters, one of whom had been a pronouncedly outspoken young man.

When the meeting had dispersed, I went off to catch the usual train home. But waiting at the stop was a stocky figure with slightly drooping shoulders. He seemed vaguely familiar, and then I realised that he was the gentleman who had argued so forcibly for my point of view. At closer quarters the stranger arrested my attention. Excitement over the debate had vanished, and I saw clearly that an intense light shone from the eyes of my unknown supporter. In that evening light they were such black twinkling eyes. A world shone from them.

Then followed the greatest surprise of my life. The bold stranger came forward impulsively, and without any invitation addressed me in the most amazing fashion.

"At last," he said in his rich deep voice, "I have found my star of destiny! I have found [my] Josephine!"

Not even the romantic spell of the Caribbean night could banish or conceal my astonishment on hearing so startling a declaration. Who was this strange Romeo who had appeared as if by magic out of the night? Yet I must admit that I was inwardly thrilled by such an amorous outburst of gallantry. Other admirers had paid me compliments, but none of them had equalled him in his sheer audacity, dash, and flattery of approach.

I was seventeen years old upon the occasion of this unusual tribute of affection, an age when I could have easily been swept off my feet. Yet somehow I managed to keep my balance and, I remember courteously declining his offer that evening to see me home. Such was my meeting with the imperious, young and daring Marcus Garvey in the springtime of our youth. True to his nature Marcus swept on regardlessly. Here was no timid suitor. The very next day, at eight in the morning to be precise, he was knocking at the door of my home. On that morning, I too felt a strange unaccountable sense of elation. It was a happy sunny morning. The birds were mingling merrily with the flowers and all nature seemed friendly; for me, there was an atmosphere of great expectations about the day.

Marcus spent no time talking of trivialities. Almost at once he plunged into relating his life to me, seemingly pressed by a sense of urgency. His manner of speaking fascinated me. Throughout the whole flow of his story there was never any suggestion nor visible consciousness that he was addressing one whom he had hardly known. He might have known me for years. The complete story of his heart, an outpouring of his most intimate self [sic].* At times he would stumble for the most fitting or appropriate words, but, nothing was hid and he was obviously sincere. How vividly he recalled the scenes of his unruly boyhood days, the nature and disposition of his parents, his father's prophecy, his first struggles to gain a livelihood, and how his heart went out to the Colored masses so oppressed by poverty and ignorance—his yearnings, hopes and aspirations for their betterment.

Continuing his story, Marcus went on to relate how he came to admire men who had fought their way to the top. Toussaint L'Ouverture, Napoleon, Antonio Maceo,* Booker T. Washington—all serving their race in their own way and according to their own lights in the circumstances of their particular times. He glowed with pride when he spoke of the Jamaican Maroons and the many slaves who had fought all their years to keep alive the spirit of freedom and resistance to the shackles amongst their people. Listening to all this I instinctively felt that love for the African race was a powerful influence on his life.

The narration poured forth like some turbulent stream, gaining in power and depth and warmth of intensity as it flowed. The hiddenmost recesses of his heart were revealed to me. Marcus spoke of the inner-compelling force driving him to the devotion of his mortal life to the awakening of his race and people. He earnestly desired to see them all obtain a higher social, political, cultural, and economic standard of living. One could sense his deep sorrow for the sad condition of so many West Indians; and what angered him to the core was the fact that they accepted their lot in life so fatalistically. Why did not a mighty roar of protest arise from their midst? Had Toussaint, the Maroons and other Afro-American leaders fought their battles for freedom merely that the descendants of the slaves might decay in frustration and apathy?

The "Napoleon" was now boiling over with indignation. He maintained forcibly that although the Afro-American people were legally "free" as a people, something of the slave mentality was still characteristic of them. Mentally they were still in chains on account of the crippling effect of an inferiority complex. Somehow the sunlight must be allowed to flood in the dark confines of their minds, so that they could be truly free and truly men, confident of holding their own with men of other races. The logic and simplicity of his contention needed no illumination.

It was obvious that Marcus had penetrated to the very core of the afflictions of the man of African origin. He divined accurately and precisely the cause and effect of the spirit of his people being broken and distraught, and he was intent on finding an elixir—a drastic remedy to heal the festered and chronic wound. He denounced all those who had placed obstacles in their path. By what sanction, human or divine, he asked, were his people prevented from taking their rightful place in the onward march of mankind? He cried out that all artificial and unjust hindrances should be swept away in one grand swoop. At the moment I discerned that a powerful inner flame was consuming the man, that a force of volcanic nature was gathering in the depths of his being.

This leader of small stature, but taller yet in vision and perspicacity, was no reed broken by the wind. In this respect he never hesitated, his convictions and beliefs were granite sure and firm. His master invocation was "Let my people go!" Already it was evident that Marcus considered himself the uncrowned emperor of a spiritual Africa of his own imagination; he believed that it was his destiny to lead all people of African descent towards a more glorious future.

When the glowing recital ended, I remained silent for a while. I wanted to be reassured that my feet were still on terra firma—solidly placed on the earth. I had heard so much in a short time that it had acted like heady wine. Such a deluge of dreams was overwhelming. I was disturbed, too, because Marcus was assuming that I, just as much as himself, was prepared to shoulder the herculean responsibilities of working for the uplifting of our race with all the implications of its formidable challenges.

As I sat in reverie, I saw the stern face of my mother uttering words of solemn maternal warnings. My mother was imbued with a strong sense of realism; the responsibilities of a family left her little time for flights of fancy, even had she been temperamentally so inclined. As for Marcus and his vision, they would have received scant sympathy from her. My doubts and hesitations did not deter the Black Moses. He must have read my mind, for he then addressed me in a much quieter voice and invited me to speak about my life and ambitions.

Before long I was relating how a sense of racial consciousness had been awakened in my own breast at the age of 12. It went back to an incident in my student days at Westwood.* My school had been collecting money for a mission fund, the Dorcas Society. Later I had visited Mrs. Webb, the wife of the Rev. William Webb, the founder of our school. I told her the amount we had collected for the fund. Her reply somewhat nettled and startled me. She said that it was a pity it was not going "to your people." I explained to Marcus that I had thought Mrs. Webb meant my own parents. The good lady, however, had noticed my confusion and then added that by my "people" she meant the people of Africa. When I asked her to explain she replied that the people of far-away Africa were living in heathen darkness and needed help from Christian missionaries. No one before had told me that I was of African descent. Being so young I was very puzzled by this bit of news and naturally I asked the lady many more questions about Africa.

At first her story of Africa had intrigued me; but when I was told that my forebears had been brought from Africa as slaves and sold to white plantation owners in the West Indies, I was horrified and frightened. I heard about slave ships and slave markets and cruel practices. I asked Mrs. Webb who had brought my ancestors from their land. I remember how she replied in a low voice that English traders had done this many years before. She then explained more fully what a great and thriving business the slave trade had been. By that time I was unable to listen further. I recoiled in horror as if from the presence of a newly-discovered enemy, and rushed out of the room.

It was this incident, I explained to Garvey, that had caused the birth of racial consciousness within me. Marcus, of course, was eager to learn what happened after that. Immediately I told him that I had written a long letter to my father. In it I had asked him, "Who are you? What is your name?" In his answer to my anguished queries my father seemed very puzzled as to what was troubling me. I did not find the reply satisfactory, despite the fact that he related the story of how an African King had proposed to Queen Victoria after the death of Albert. In my youthful agitation I hurriedly sent off another letter beseeching my father, "I want to know something about myself immediately! I am told that my ancestors were slaves right here in Jamaica!"

This time my father really was worried; so much so that he hurried back from Panama to Jamaica. His remedy for me was to take me to see my very old Grandmother. This old matriarch told me a very strange story. She had been born many years before in Jaubin the land of Ashanti,* then Gold Coast, now Ghana. When she had been still a girl of about sixteen, she had been kidnapped by a warring tribe along with her two sisters and sold into slavery. Along with many others she had been brought in a great ship across the ocean and sold again to a white master. In Ashanti her family name was Dabas, meaning iron or strong will; her first name was Boahimaa. The old lady was very proud of her lineage. She was very emphatic about the virility of her people and their prowess in war, producing the highest type of Ashanti. (In 1946 when the Asantehene, Sir Asi Agyeman Prempeh II, King of Ashanti, Custodian of Akan custom and culture, confirmed me an Ashanti and returned me to my family, I then learned that Amporte, one of Ashanti's greatest military generals, was my great, great-uncle).

Marcus still urged me to continue with my story. So I had to tell him that after the meeting with Grannie Dabas, I returned to school proud of my family and my people. I told him how this pride increased and how I often used to ask myself, "How shall I get back to Africa?" I explained how I felt impelled to be of use and service to my race in some positive way. I even told him that I had thought of becoming a missionary, but yet felt this was not the right road for me: I had yet to discover by what means my ambition to help Africa, and all her sons and daughters could be realised. Thus deep in my own heart I was in full sympathy with what Marcus had said concerning the future welfare of the African race.

In a short space of time, Marcus had already revealed his heart's secret to me. In response I had made my own confession of faith to him. Throughout my outpouring, he listened intently. He only rose when I had finished speaking, once again to astonish me with a sweeping and completely self-confident statement.

"Together," he said, "we can conquer the world; together we can help to educate our people; together we can help to awaken the Negro to his sense of racial insecurity! When I met you last night our fate was sealed. We are neither of us able to resist the other in this hour of need . . ." I was all the more astonished and thrilled because of the sincerity and old-world courtesy with which he addressed me.

This meeting of ours on a July morning a few days before the outbreak of the Great War was a wonderful event. It was a memorable occasion, not only for the two of us, but also, as later events proved, for the whole of our race. Neither Marcus, nor I, fully realised what had taken place, nevertheless we sensed that events of far-reaching consequences had been set afoot. As far as we were personally concerned, both of us felt that our private dreams were beginning to take tangible form. Hitherto, we had been groping in the dark. Now there was light and a way ahead. Each had helped the other to understand how better to serve the cause of Africa and her peoples.

Our joint love for Africa and our concern for the welfare of our race urged us on to immediate action. Together we talked over the possibility of founding an organisation to serve the needs of the peoples of African origin. We spent many hours deliberating what exactly our aims should be and what means we should employ to achieve those aims. Out of this lengthy tete-a-tete we finally improvised a policy and formulated a programme for our infant "organisation." In fact the two member movement was christened the Universal Negro Improvement Association and African Communities Imperial League. (The imperial was dropped later.)

The birth of what was to grow into a world-wide mass movement could not have been simpler or less pretentious. It began with a membership of two, but grew eventually, like a grain of mustard seed, into an organic whole of several millions. Doubtless, anyone who might have witnessed the foundation of the U.N.I.A. would have hooted with scorn and derision, dismissing its two founders as vague starry-eyed idealists. Certainly the vast majority of Afro-Americans at that time would have laughed loudly at our seemingly crazy notions.

Before the lengthy conference finally broke up for that day, it ended upon a most solemn note. Marcus Garvey stood before me and said in a very earnest voice, "Amy Ashwood, I appoint you secretary of the Universal Negro Improvement Association." I replied with an equal earnestness, "And Marcus Garvey, I appoint you president."

From *The Pan-African Connection: From Slavery to Garvey and Beyond* (Dover, MA: Majority Press, 1983). Reprinted by permission of the Majority Press.

Amy Jacques Garvey

Although history has unfairly relegated her to the status of simply wife number two of Marcus Garvey, the most prominent woman within the Garveyite movement was Amy Euphemia Jacques Garvey. She described her relationship with Garvey thus: "The value of a wife to him was like a gold coin—expendable, to get what he wanted, and hard enough to withstand rough usage in the process" (*Garvey and Garveyism* 169). Jacques Garvey withstood this treatment, tirelessly working on Garvey's behalf even after his death. She was, in fact, "the fuel that fed the powerful Garvey machine for so many years" (Reed 46).

Born in Kingston, Jamaica, on December 31, 1896, and raised by a middle-class family, Jacques Garvey suffered from bouts of malaria while growing up. The need for a more temperate climate to treat her illness led her to come to the United States in 1917. She began her affiliation with the UNIA in 1918, serving as Marcus Garvey's private secretary and office manager. Garvey and Amy Jacques were married in July 1922, shortly after his marriage to Amy Ashwood ended. Despite her husband's overwhelming presence and her devotion to the UNIA, Jacques Garvey never accepted a subordinate role to Marcus. When asked if she ever felt dominated by him, her reply was "Hell no, man! Never!" (qtd. in Reed 46). There was, of course, no reason for her to feel any sense of inferiority. Her support for Garvey's work dovetailed with her own beliefs in the struggle for Black nationalism. To Jacques Garvey the main objective was advancing the cause of "oppressed people of color . . . and it did not matter whether men or women took the lead in pursuing the goal" (Taylor, "Negro Women" 121). She contributed her substantial business and organizational skills to the UNIA, an effort that became particularly apparent after Garvey's incarceration in 1925 when Jacques Garvey was a dominant force in running the movement, making frequent speeches as well as serving as associate editor of the *Negro World* and overseeing administrative affairs.

Amy collected Marcus's writings in the *Philosophy and Opinions of Marcus Garvey* (1923), which was intended "as a personal record of the opinions and sayings of my husband." A second volume was completed in 1925 while Marcus was in prison in Atlanta. He requested her to mail out copies of the work to dozens of people who might help him to be released from prison. By the time she completed her Herculean effort, she "weighed 98 lbs., had low blood pressure and one eye was badly strained" (*Garvey and Garveyism* 168). The hectic pace of the Garveyite movement is readily apparent in Jacques Garvey's travel account of one barnstorming tour, "On a Trip from Coast to Coast." Incredibly, the grueling itinerary, described in six issues of the *Negro World*, is labeled by Amy as a "vacation."

Jacques Garvey's achievements do not, however, rest solely on her preservation of Garvey's message and on her organizational prowess. Jacques Garvey's writings reveal her as a significant figure in the struggles of both women and people of color generally. Her independent spirit is perhaps most in evidence in the essays she regularly wrote in her column "Our Women and What They Think" in the *Negro World* from 1924 to 1927. Unlike the women's pages of a number of other journals, which generally concentrated on fashion and domestic affairs, Jacques Garvey focused on myriad topics including Pan-Africanism and the need for resistance to racism, sexism, and imperialism. Three major themes emerge from Jacques Garvey's editorials: "the struggle towards self-determination, the importance of motherhood, and the importance of education to the emergence of the 'New Negro Woman'" (Taylor, "Veiled Garvey" 219). "The Hand That Rocks the Cradle," for example, stresses the role of mothers in advancing the Black nationalist cause. According to this editorial, it was the responsibility of Black women to procreate and to educate and care for children. Women's roles, however, were meant to extend beyond the home. In such pieces as "Women and World Peace," "Our

Women Getting into the Larger Life," and "Women as Leaders Nationally and Racially," Jacques Garvey expressed her belief that for the Black nationalist movement to be successful, it was necessary for women and men to work in tandem; however, when the Black man was not pulling his weight, then she felt that women should assume positions of leadership.[1]

Jacques Garvey had an international perspective, lamenting the lack of recognition race-conscious women received worldwide and praising them for often assuming the mantle of leadership in their cultures. She saw parallels between the oppression women often encountered at home and that of colonized peoples. Jacques Garvey, however, did not consider herself a feminist; in fact, she did not believe such a thing existed. She maintained that a woman's responsibility was "to help her man and make both of them great" (qtd. in I. Lewis 68). However, she attacked sexual injustice wherever she saw it, even within the UNIA. Her views were very much in keeping with those of community feminists, women whose "activism is focused on assisting the men and women in their lives . . . along with initiating and participating in activities to uplift their community" (Taylor, "Veiled Garvey" 194). Jacques Garvey came out of the tradition of the nineteenth-century Black club women, with one major difference: her emphasis was on nationalism, not integration. Her criticism of sexism and racism caused her to make some powerful enemies; however, she was up to the task of taking on such opponents unflinchingly.

After Marcus Garvey's release from prison in 1927, he was deported to Jamaica. In 1935, he moved to England, where he remained until his death in 1940. Amy remained in Jamaica except for a brief period from 1937–38, raising their two sons. Her involvement with the Black nationalist cause did not end with Marcus's death in 1940. Jacques Garvey wrote for a number of journals, including the *African*, and published two important works, *Garvey and Garveyism* (1963), a documentation of the movement, and *Black Power in America* (1968), a collection of articles on Garvey's impact. She remained a mentor to Black nationalists and a resource to scholars of Garveyism until her death in Jamaica on July 25, 1973. Her position is summed up best by her own words: "I thank God for the opportunity to serve my people, by standing besideor [*sic*] behind him [Garvey], and since his passing, by standing up for him" (qtd. in Collier-Thomas 247).[2]

NOTES

The bulk of Jacques Garvey's papers are in the Marcus Garvey Memorial Collection at Fisk University in Nashville, Tennessee.

1. Her frustration with the men of the race was doubtless triggered, in part, by her own quarrels with the leaders of the UNIA. For more on her view of Black men, see Taylor, "Negro Women" 115–20 and James 150–55.

2. Though both Amy Ashwood and Amy Jacques continued to advocate on Garvey's behalf after his death, their approach to the movement differed. Ashwood, who worked with integrationist groups such as the NAACP, maintained that Garvey would have adjusted his program to adapt to changing times. Jacques Garvey, on the other hand, believed that nothing in Garvey's Black nationalist message needed to be altered (Bennett 58).

Bennett, Lerone Jr. "The Ghost of Marcus Garvey: Interviews with Crusader's Two Wives." *Ebony* (March 1960): 53–61.

Collier-Thomas, Bettye. "Amy Jacques Garvey." *Notable Black American Women*. Book 2. Ed. Jessie Carney Smith. Detroit: Gale, 1996. 246–49.

Garvey, Marcus. *The Philosophy and Opinions of Marcus Garvey*. Comp. Amy Jacques Garvey. Dover, MA: Majority P, 1986.

Hill, Robert, ed. *The Marcus Garvey and Universal Negro Improvement Association Papers*. 9 vols. Berkeley: U of California P, 1983–.

Jacques Garvey, Amy. *Garvey and Garveyism*. 1963. London: Collier Books, 1970.

James, Winston. *Holding Aloft the Banner of Ethiopia: Caribbean Radicalism in Early Twentieth-Century America*. New York: Verso, 1998.

Lewis, Ida. "Mrs. Marcus Garvey Talks with Ida Lewis." *Encore* 2 (May 1973): 66–68.

Lewis, Rupert, and Maureen Warner-Lewis. "Amy Jacques Garvey." *Jamaica Journal* 20 (Aug.–Oct. 1987): 39–43.

Matthews, Mark D. "'Our Women and What They Think,' Amy Jacques Garvey and *The Negro World*." *Black Scholar* 10 (May–June 1979): 2–13.

Reed, Beverley. "Amy Jacques Garvey: Black, Beautiful & Free." *Ebony* 26 (June 1971): 45–54.

Taylor, Ula Yvette. "'Negro Women Are Great Thinkers as Well as Doers': Amy Jacques Garvey and Community Feminism in the United States, 1924–1927." *Journal of Women's History* 12 (Summer 2000): 104–26.

———. "The Veiled Garvey: The Life and Times of Amy Jacques Garvey." Diss. U of California, Santa Barbara, 1992. A revised edition of the dissertation was published under the same title by the University of North Carolina Press (2002).

Whither Goest Thou?

"I stole these things. For God's sake, send me away where I can get food to eat and a warm place to rest my head. Send me to Atlanta—anywhere," cried a Negro to the police lieutenant at a West Side precinct in New York City, at the same time depositing two packages on the lieutenant's desk.

Bill Jones, formerly of the South, now of nowhere, stood shivering in a suit of homespun tweed, a cap drawn tightly over his head. Surely Shakespeare* must have pictured such a man when he penned these lines:

> Famine is in thy cheeks,
> Need and oppression stareth in thy eyes,
> Contempt and beggary hangeth upon thy back;
> The world is not thy friend, nor the world's law.

But let us hear his tale. It runs thus:

"Two years ago I was a care-free and happy young man, working on a farm in Winona, Miss., where I was born. One Sunday night my pal and I, on leaving church, were attacked by a white mob. A white man pointed my pal out as having been seen with a white woman, and we were taken into the woods. My pal was lynched and burned and I was beaten into unconsciousness.

"When I regained consciousness I found myself on a train and a colored man bending over me. He read aloud a note pinned to my coat: 'Nigger, don't set foot back in Mississippi or you'll be a dead man.'

"'Never mind,' said the man, 'I will help you all I can.' He did. He took me to his home in Eldorado, Ark., and cared for me.

"After I got well I found work and for more than a year I tried to forget that horrible night.

"Passing through the main street of the town one night I saw quite a few colored folks gathered together; some crying, some talking excitedly. One old woman was on her knees praying aloud. 'What's the matter?' I asked, and someone said: 'Read,' pointing to a notice stuck up on the outer wall of a little shop: 'Niggers, clear out of town in 24 hours or else you will be as good as dead.'

"Not one of our group had expected such a thing. No trouble had ever occurred between the whites and the blacks in that town. Of course, quite a number of whites had come in and Negroes had become more prosperous since the war. I myself had hoped to be able to buy a home and settle down. What now? Stay and be tortured to death? A thousand times no! Whither, then? Anywhere.

"Next evening found me on a train bound for an Eastern city. Arriving in New York city with a little money I soon found lodgings, after which I set out to find work. I scanned the 'want' columns of the newspapers daily, made several applications for positions, but I was always greeted with the same answers: 'No colored help wanted,' or 'you must have experience.'

"One week passed without success and the second week I tried the employment agencies, but I was asked for recommendations. Should I have waited in Eldorado for recommendations? I tried to explain to an agency clerk why I had no recommendation. 'Why didn't you stay South from the start?' the impatient clerk asked.

"'Man,' I cried, unable to bear it any longer, 'have you ever seen one of your kind being roasted alive by a white mob? Have you ever smelled burning human flesh and heard the dying groans of your best pal? Have you ever been beaten almost to death and thrown into a dirty Jim Crow car? Man, go South!'

"Out in the street again. Back to my lodgings, only to meet an irate landlady at the door demanding either her rent or her room. She wanted rent and I wanted food.

"I retraced my steps downstairs to the street and as the keen winter air struck my cheeks, I buttoned up my overcoat and plunged my bare hands deep down in my pockets. My right hand touched something cold. I pulled it out—a nickel! My last nickel.

"I walked on for blocks until I came to the subway. I could at least think if I were warm, so I purchased my ticket and boarded the first train.

"Thoughts, countless thoughts, chased through my brain, but at the terminal I was in the same position, penniless and hungry. All my possessions—a couple of suits of underwear, shirts and socks—were in my suitcase at the room; the balance was on my back.

"I changed my coach for the return trip, and kept riding up and down for about two hours until a conductor found me out and ordered me off the train and a guard saw me to the street.

"My mouth felt hot and dry inside; my stomach almost kissed my back. Unable to bear it any longer, I went into the nearest pawn shop and left my overcoat. I came out, fifty cents in hand, and darted into a restaurant.

"Satisfying my hunger to the extent of fifty cents, I was again on the street. It was eight PM by the nearest clock; the snow commenced to fall. I dodged in and out of hallways until 12 o'clock, when they were all closed.

"I walked up and down for a couple of hours until my body was almost rigid with cold; my brain was on fire. I backed up against a shop door—visions of that last night in Winona, Mississippi, came before me. At intervals I heard the haunting cry of my dying pal—a mail wagon came—I felt the heavy lash of the whip—my stiff hands felt something—two mail bags."

The police lieutenant looked at Jones. "Hem," he said, "this is a federal case," and instructed his assistant to lock him up and trace the owners of the bags.

The owners of the bags were found, but refused to prosecute Jones once their property was returned. A detective at the station finally made a charge against him, and he was taken before a magistrate, who promptly dismissed the case.

Jones, summoning what little strength he had, appealed to the magistrate to send him to prison, but the police with a "This way out" led him toward the door. "Officer," said Jones, "you are sending me out into the streets again hungry and cold. I am going to commit one of the most fiendish robberies, for by hook or by crook I must have food and warm clothes."

The door closed behind him and the blizzard raged before him. Negro, whither goest thou?

From the *Negro World* March 31, 1923

On a Trip from Coast to Coast

Impressions of Mrs. Amy Jacques Garvey, Wife of President-General, on Vacation

SEEING THE WONDERS OF AMERICAN CIVILIZATION AS THEY FLASH UPON THE EYES OF THE TRAVELLER AS THE STEAM GIANT THUNDERS OVER THE MILES, AND AS SEEN IN CONTACT WITH GREAT, THRIVING CENTERS OF POPULATION

To the Editor of The Negro World:

In keeping with my promise to send you a weekly letter of my impressions while on my vacation, I send you the following as I am unable to write my numerous friends and well-wishers who would like to hear from me.

Sunday night, September 30. After an impressive and enthusiastic meeting at Liberty Hall, New York, we dashed off for the Pennsylvania Station, just in time to hear the familiar shout, "All aboard." It was midnight, and although we tried to observe the rules of the sleeper by being "Quiet, Quiet," our porter could not help breaking same on recognizing my husband, by exclaiming, "Mr. Garvey, himself—My, my. I never thought I would have seen you again. Yes indeed, the folks in Pittsburgh are looking out for you."

After being rocked in the cradle of a Pullman berth for half a night I woke up to see if I was all there, and, if not, to pull myself together. No sooner had I made my toilet and sat by the window to enjoy the feeble morning sun in its effort to penetrate the mist, than a waiter came along with dignified steps, and, as it were, chanting these words: "Last call for breakfast! Dining car in the rear."

At Pittsburgh

We went into the dining car and after having breakfasted, I said to myself the meal was worthy of that syncopated chant. Colored porters and waiters have certainly built up a reputation for Pullman cars. At about 10:30 we reached Pittsburgh. As usual Pittsburgh had all her furnaces lit, and her chimneys smoking, some belching forth flames. The smoke hung thick and low in the skies like rain clouds. This town controls the coal and steel mines of the outlying districts; it refines and moulds steel articles for local consumption and more particularly for export to all parts of the world. Negro laborers get from fifty to sixty cents per hour, working eight hour shifts. Some of the large plants employ [N]egro foremen. The influx of immigrants from the South has not affected the labor market, but it has affected to a great extent the housing conditions. Driving from the station, I noticed large placards with the inscription, "Prepare for the Ku Klux Klan." On enquiring, I learned that the Klan was expected any night to parade through the city.

In the afternoon the Local Division had a large parade, which was well attended by the uniformed ranks of the Organization, and members in automobiles and on foot.

At 8:30 we arrived at "The People's Tabernacle," where 2,000 people crowded the building, with hundreds on the outside who could not get in.***

My husband spoke for more than an hour. He described the two schools of thought in the race, and showed how the New Negro had evolved a philosophy of his own and refused to apply white men's philosophy to the needs, yearnings and ambitions of black men. He drew a vivid and realistic picture of two competitive races (black and white) living side by side in this country, and showed that the future boded ill for the weaker of the two if no provision is made now, as the weak and unprepared race is bound to starve and die, through economic pressure. In closing, he expressed his deep gratitude and appreciation to the members of the division, who in conjunction with the other members of the organization throughout the world made it possible for him to be released, by their splendid example of loyalty and devotion. Such conduct, he said, has caused the world to have a new estimate of the awakened spirit of the Negro, and made them realize that we are a force to be reckoned with in the future.

I was deeply impressed with the earnestness and devotion of the members and added my thanks to those of my husband's on introduction by the chairman.***

"Not the Same Garvey"

Two thirty PM found us boarding the train for Youngstown, Ohio. Arriving there at 4:55 PM, we were met at the station by Mr. W. Vaughn, the president of the local division, from whom I inquired the reason for the newspaper reports to the effect that the mayor of the city would prevent my husband from speaking there, and had called on the police to enforce his order. "Why," said Mr. Vaughn, smiling, "we got some cheap publicity. A preacher and some of his congregation, being jealous of our success, made representations to the mayor that Mr. Garvey was coming here to stir up race hatred and strife. When the mayor told them that he was present at the meeting at which Mr. Garvey spoke the last time he was in the city, and welcomed him to Youngstown, the preacher, without the least hesitation, told the mayor that it was not the same Garvey coming this time; it was another man. The mayor, to satisfy himself, sent for me, and when I explained it all to him, he was surprised at the hypocrisy practised on him and readily agreed to attend our meeting."

We had two hours to rest and eat supper, and then off to the meeting at the Oak Hill Auditorium. I learned that it was the first time that Negroes had held a meeting there. On our arrival the musical part of the program was gone through, and my husband was called on to speak. There were many white persons in the audience, and by the change of emotion on their faces one could easily see that they were deeply impressed with the seriousness of our program, and were perhaps a little surprised at the unvarnished truths leveled at them during my husband's speech. He made them see themselves as they really were in their contact with us, and exposed their future plan of slow extermination and further subjugation of our race. Then he pointed them to a true solution to the vexing problem of the races, to be achieved through following the divine apportionment of the earth: that is, each race to its native habitat—Europe for the Europeans, Asia for Asiatics, America for the white Americans, and Africa for the black peoples of the world. He felt sure that America, the greatest democracy in the world, would be large-minded enough to help us establish a national home of our own in Africa, even as we labored and worked in this country for over 300 years to help them build up this republic and make it what it is today.

At Farrell, Pa.

"Yours truly" was next introduced and I got off lightly with a few remarks, as we had to leave immediately for Farrell, Pa. ***

Dear friends, I must now close, hoping you are satisfied with my description of my first two days' vacation. My love to you all, and best wishes.

Yours truly,

AMY JACQUES GARVEY

From the *Negro World* October 20, 1923

The Hand That Rocks the Cradle

Napoleon Bonaparte once said that "the hand that rocks the cradle rules the world." Every man, every woman, who has achieved greatness, who has striven to make the world a safer and better place in which to live, could say as much, if he would. When women take the saying seriously they need not be accused of egotism; they should regard it as a high compliment and strive all the more earnestly to rear children who will be a credit to them and to the race.

The conceit that mere man is the whole thing in the making of good men and women has long been exploded, especially in Christian countries, where proper respect for motherhood and proper care of childhood have become among the most important matters for the attention of legislators and administrators, the medical profession, and the educators, all of whom are working industriously and along the most scientific lines for the safeguarding of child life.

Much needs to be done as yet before motherhood and childhood will be placed upon the scientific basis where the very best results can reasonably be expected in the production of the best and highest type of manhood and womanhood. This will be accelerated by the systematic education which young folks are now receiving in the home and the school; education in how to do things as they should be done, in proper deportment in the home and in public places, and in the development of character, shaping it in the proper way so that "as the twig is bent the tree will incline," so that when the child reaches the age when it must rely upon its own initiative it will go in the right and not in the wrong way. How important this is we all know. Much of sickness and death, much of running wild and getting into trouble out of which it is difficult to get, of young people is due to bad environment, lack of parental oversight and care, lack of proper education and reproof. "How shall the people know without a teacher?" asks the chief apostle to the Gentiles and which we may reasonably ask ourselves. And none of us ever grows too old to learn and none of us can begin too soon to learn the things necessary and worth while to know.

The obligation is upon the Negro to have progressively more care in the consideration and provision for his womanhood and childhood. Much has been gained in this respect in the past fifty years, but much is required, and there can be no let up in the good work. The world expects more of the Negro everywhere today than it did yesterday, and the Negro is expecting more of the world.

We have developed millions of homes in which the parents are educated and thoroughly alive to their obligation and duty to give the children the consideration, reproof and training that make most for strong adultage, for service in home and State and church, and for race, and we shall make greater progress in the same direction in the immediate years. But, however much progress we may make, we shall hardly be able to meet the growing need for a properly trained childhood, in order that we may have a properly trained manhood and womanhood, for many years to come. We need trained men and women everywhere; we need them, as other races need them, to do the larger work that has fallen to the lot of the race in these latter days.

The editor of The Woman's Page is proud of the splendid work our women have done in the home and school and church, and are doing, and are better prepared now to do than in other and more unfortunate days, and she has faith to hope that they will do better work in the coming days, as we tread always on the heels of them in the present, the present and the future being indissolubly lockstepped, and we should all keep constantly in mind the fact that "the hand that rocks the cradle rules the world."

From the *Negro World* July 5, 1924

Our Women Getting into the Larger Life

The world wide movement for the enlargement of woman's sphere of usefulness is one of the most remarkable of the ages. In all countries and in all ages men have arrogated to themselves the prerogative of regulating not only the domestic but the civic and economic life of women. In many countries women were subject entirely to the whims and legislation of men! It is that way now in most Asiatic countries and among some of the tribes of Africa.

The recent upheaval in Turkey has carried with it condemnation of the harem relations and the sanction of the family life as it has developed in Christian countries. Madam Kemal* is the leader of the Turkish women for larger freedom in the ordering of their lives, but the innovation, which is bound to work for the betterment of men as well as women, as the harem life is a blight on womanhood which degrades manhood as well, could only have been accomplished by the separation of Church and State, the Sultanate and the Caliphate, which amounts to negating the hitherto predominating influence of the Mohammedan religion in the affairs of State as of Church. However far the innovation will extend to other Moslem countries, and what influence, if any, it will have on the domestic life of the people of Asia and Africa, where the Mohammedan religion is strong, remains to be seen.

In Europe average womanhood has been held at a very low valuation until it got into the recently developed currents of modern innovation, and the average still remains low, peasant life for the man and the woman and their children being of the lowest and hardest. Only in Great Britain has the movement for the larger and better life for women, by allowing them reasonable voice in making and enforcing the laws, made any appreciable headway.

The United States has gone further than any other nation in giving woman a share in making and enforcing the laws and in regulating her economic life to her advantage and not entirely to the advantage of man. She is now given an equal part in political matters, and she is allowed a freedom in earning and controlling her earnings which is a great improvement upon the former of old things. In social and personal matters the American woman has attained to an independence and freedom which it will take centuries for the women of other nations to attain to.

Negro women of the United States share equally in the larger life which has come to women of other race groups, and she has met every test in the home, in bread winning, in church and social upbuilding, in charitable uplift work, and in the school room which could have been expected of her reasonably. She has yet to develop as active interest in political affairs as the women of other race groups, but she is bound to grow in this as in other matters in which her interests are involved.

The women of the Universal Negro Improvement Association have shown an interest and a helpfulness so far flung as to make it doubtful if the organization could have reached the high point of strength and effectiveness it has without them. To take woman and her sympathies and work out of the association would be like taking the wife out of the home of the husband. The women of the association are a tower of strength. They know it and glory in the fact, and their men are proud of them, and justly. The success of the Negro race thus far has been largely due to the sympathy and support which our women have given to the cause.

Our women are getting into the larger life which has the womanhood of the world in its sweep. We are sure they will be equal to all of the demands made upon them in the future as in the past, and the demands are going to increase in volume and importance as we go along. It stands to reason.

From the *Negro World* July 12, 1924

Women and World Peace

With the entry of women into politics and big business the next important factor that is engaging her attention is the problem of war. Should she bring children into the world, train them to the best of her ability, and when they arrive at an age of usefulness see them snatched from her and used as cannon-fodder or munition workers? The woman of today rebels against this ancient custom that robs her of her most precious gift—her children—and yet debars her from questioning the "whys and wherefores" or the justice or injustice of wars.

In some countries politics has given the sex a voice in the affairs of government which enables her to decide nationally the important question, "To war or not to war?" But her voice in politics in these countries is still young, therefore weak, while in others it is inaudible. Consequently she has divided her attention between politics and educating public opinion toward world peace.

Many women's conferences, national and international, have been held to discuss the cause and cure of war, but we believe that more stress has been made on the cure than on the real cause, which has been overlooked; hence the diagnosis is wrong and the cure when applied will not be effective.

"War," said a famous lecturer, "is the outgrowth of a state of mind." The state of mind of the powerful nations of the world is made up largely of selfishness, greed and avarice. They have no regard for the rights of weak peoples, and wage war on defenseless groups to fill the coffers of their treasuries, to expand their national boundaries, and to find an outlet for their surplus population. What matter if a few thousand Negroes are killed yearly mining diamonds to adorn the bodies of white women? Who cares if sixteen million Negroes are maimed and slaughtered in seven years in order to produce rubber for the Belgians? Does it matter at all if all the general wealth of Africa and India is robbed and exploited by the powerful white nations of the world to satisfy their greed? Is the small, wee voice of conscience stilled in the breasts of statesmen who administer the affair of those big nations? This is the age of force and power. "Might is right," is their cry, and who dares dispute their claim must fight it out or submit to oppression and exploitation.

Some organizations are agitating for international peace, but we believe that such an era will never dawn until nations learn to respect the rights and privileges of unorganized peoples. The same spirit of avarice that prompts the exploitation of weak peoples will cause strong nations to fight each other for the spoils of their pillage. There can be no peace among nations until there is peace in the whole world, and oppressed peoples everywhere, of every creed and race, are determined to get freedom or independence or die fighting for it. Powerful nations will always be kept busy stemming the tide of liberty and democracy, until they practice it among all humanity.

Women are playing a very important part in bringing about humane legislations, and it is hoped that they will use their influence and educate international opinion to the tenets of true christianity—which they profess—and which is embodied in these two scriptural injunctions, "Man, love thy brother," and, "Do unto others as you would that they should do to you."

From the *Negro World* January 31, 1925

The Tidal Wave of Oppressed Peoples Beats against the Color Line

The thoughtful of the white race are alive to the fact that the darker peoples of the world are taking the much discussed war pronouncement of the late Woodrow Wilson seriously, namely, "the principle of self-determination." This phrase has been echoing and re-echoing round the globe since it was uttered, the practical application of which would usher in a new era of political and economic freedom for the darker peoples, and peace to the world; but the avaricious, selfish white man sees in it a menace to the exploitation of the labor of his darker brother, a menace to his land grabbing activities in the East, and a menace to his overlordship.

The Eastern Giant is awakened, and in his consciousness he listens to the Christian teaching of the white missionary. "Do unto others, as ye would that they should do unto you." He watches them put this into practice, and he realizes that they preach what they do not, and never intend to, practice. He unmasks him, and behold! He sees a common land thief, whose sole purpose is to exploit and rule. The phrase, "the principle of self-determination" coming from the lips of the white man is applicable only to members of his race; but when it is spoken to men of other races it loses its original form, and in its application resembles "the principle of exploitation." The Eastern Giant is now exercising his muscles, and we notice a quiver in China, and an expansion in Morocco, but the day is fast approaching when he will have corralled all the strength of his scattered nerve power and stalk forth to sovereignty and to power.

The white man is too innately selfish to yield one inch of his ill-gotten power to another race. He refuses to be just and fair in his dealings with the other portion of humanity that does not look like him. Hence the Mohammedan has learned this—that as the white Christian preaches, "Thou shalt not kill," and yet he does, even so the Mohammedan teaches, "Thou shalt not kill," yet he must, or be wiped off the face of the globe by the white Christian.

Many white missionaries today are changing their tactics on the East, and instead of forcing the Bible and the rum bottle on the natives, are urging their religious home offices and nations to cooperate with them in an effort to apply a larger measure of fair play in their contact with the natives. They who are on the spot can better appreciate the necessity for this change of attitude, before the avenging hand of the Eastern Giant strikes his fatal blow at "white superiority."

***

The groans and entreaties of our forebears have gone up to high Heaven, and our supplications have been heard, and in God's good time he will bring to pass that happiness on earth that all downtrodden peoples pray for. Whether we be black Mohammedans or black Christians, we all believe in the same God, the Father of all. Our forms of worship may differ, but the basic principles are the same. We worship in spirit and in truth. Our racial interests are identical. We are all struggling under the same yoke, and by the help of God, Allah, the First Cause, or the omnipotent, we will join forces, and throw off the common oppressor, and live up to the high calling of our Creator, and in obedience to His injunction—"YE ARE THE LORDS OF CREATION!"

From the *Negro World* July 18, 1925

Imprison a Leader and You Boost His Cause

It is pleasing to note the awakened consciousness of Negroes every-where. Traveling as we are from State to State, and visiting the large cities of these United States, receiving letters and dispatches from the remotest parts of the world, we rejoice at the fact that the ideals of economic independence and nationalism expounded by Marcus Garvey have permeated the minds of men and women of African descent everywhere, and no human agency can stop them in their onward march to progress and to power.

The imprisonment of Marcus Garvey has not served the ene-mies' purposes. On the contrary it has intensified the determination and zeal of his followers, and roused to a sense of sympathetic under-standing the apathetic members of his race. White men who did not realize that a new type of Negro made up the membership of the Universal Negro Improvement Association are now alarmed at the growing proportions of the organization, and the large-hearted of them declare that such a splendid group of ambitious people ought to be helped and not persecuted. Yellow and brown men of Asia are reaching out the hand of fellowship to us, and saying, "Let us join forces and throw off the yoke of white oppression."

When a man can serve his people cheerfully and without materi-al gain, in spite of unjust and vicious attacks by his own people, and opposition and persecution by others, then he is truly a leader, and when he can go to prison and although suffering physically send out from week to week the most inspiring messages, surely his enemies are defeated in their plans, and the thoughtful are bound to admit the greatness of such a man and the righteousness of his cause. It is the suf-fering of martyrs that bring speedy success to any movement, and we are glad that the race at this time can produce one unselfish enough and courageous enough to bear imprisonment and even death for a free and redeemed Africa. His sacrifices are not being made in vain, and although his contemporaries are non-appreciative of him, yet posteri-ty of his own race will bless him, and other races respect him, because of his determined and unyielding stand for race and homeland.

The longer Marcus Garvey stays in prison, the bigger strides will the organization take. It may seem paradoxical to say this but it is true. His imprisonment is a blow aimed at independent Negro leadership, and knowing this Negroes are falling in line with the organization, as they never did before, and have pledged their lives to support their own leader, whether he be in New York, Atlanta, Timbuctoo or Liberia. Had Marcus Garvey been "picked" by the white people to lead Negroes, he would have had smooth sailing in his career, because he would have been the mouthpiece and tool of white oppression, hence only hearty co-operation would have come from the system in control, and Negroes would not have dared to oppose the white man's candidate who had financial and political backing. But when Marcus Garvey sounded the tocsin "Africa for the Africans, those at home and those abroad," he trod on the toes of greedy, exploiting European countries, who are tapping the economic resources of Africa, in order to feed their half starved population[;] when he stated that "Negroes should be governed by Negroes everywhere," he sounded the doom of the Colonial systems of exploitation and aggression by whites, and a strong independent Negro race loomed up on the horizon, which was termed "a black peril." When he declared that "Negroes should evolve a leadership of their own," the white man's candidates for leadership got busy and sought to destroy him, knowing that their salaries and "hands out" would cease, and they would have to lead on their own merits and racial achievements. So these combined forces succeeded in putting him in prison which, apart from affecting his health, has not worried him in the least, because Marcus Garvey has already spent eight years of ceaseless toil teaching his people, and the millions of converts he has gained and the territory that they have covered spreading the gospel of a redeemed Africa is bound to bring about the realization of his dreams in a shorter period of time than he anticipated.

No one can imprison the soul of a man. The mind will soar far beyond prison walls and iron rails. A brave man lives, even in confinement, when his beautiful thoughts are his boon companions, and any movement for the liberation of God's people will prosper if only because of the righteousness of its cause.

From the *Negro World* August 15, 1925

Women as Leaders Nationally and Racially

The exigencies of this present age require that women take their places beside their men. White women are rallying all their forces and uniting regardless of national boundaries to save their race from destruction and preserve its ideals for posterity. We see them in the law courts pleading as advocates; they preside as judges and administer laws; while in less numbers, yet they are to be seen in parliaments, congresses and council chambers legislating for their people. White men have begun to realize that as women are the backbone of the home, so can they, by their economic experience and their aptitude for details participate effectively in guiding the destiny of nation and race.

No line of endeavor remains closed for long to the modern woman. She agitates for equal opportunities and gets them; she makes good on the job and gains the respect of men who heretofore opposed her. She prefers to be a bread-winner than a half-starved wife. She is not afraid of hard work, and by being independent she gets more out of the present day husband than her grandmother did in the good old days.

The women of the East, both yellow and black, are slowly but surely imitating the women of the Western world, and as the white women are bolstering up a decaying white civilization, even so women of the darker races are sallying forth to help their men establish a civilization according to their own standards, and to strive for world leadership.

Women of all climes and races have as great a part to play in the development of their particular group as the men. Some readers may not agree with us on this issue, but do they not mould the minds of their children—the future men and women? Even before birth a mother can so direct her thoughts and conduct as to bring into the world either a genius or an idiot. Imagine the early years of contact between mother and child, when she directs his form of speech, and is responsible for his conduct and deportment. Many a man has risen from the depths of poverty and obscurity and made his mark in life because of the advices and councils of a good mother whose influence guided his footsteps throughout his life.

Women therefore are extending this holy influence outside the realms of the home, softening the ills of the world by their gracious and kindly contact.

Some men may argue that the home will be broken up and women will become coarse and lose their gentle appeal. We do not think so because everything can be done with moderation. Some women are good cooks, yet because of the call to the other duties they rarely ever cook a meal; but when the necessity presents itself they know how. Others are good business women, yet they would not neglect their children and homes to attend business with their husbands, but if hubby dies or becomes incapacitated, they can fit in his place and save a situation. The doll-baby type of woman is a thing of the past and the wide-awake woman is forging ahead, prepared for all emergencies and ready to answer any call, even if it be to face the cannons on the battlefields.

New York has a woman as secretary of state. Two States have women governors and we would not be surprised if within the next ten years a woman graces the White House in Washington, D. C. Women are also filling diplomatic positions, and from time immemorial women have been used as spies to get information for their country.

White women have greater opportunities to display their ability because of the standing of both races, and due to the fact that black men are less appreciative of their women than white men. The former will more readily sing the praises of white women than their own, and who is more deserving of admiration than the black woman, she who has borne the rigors of slavery, the deprivations consequent in a pauperized race and the indignities heaped upon a weak and defenseless people? Yet she has suffered all with fortitude, and stands ever ready to help in the onward march to freedom and power.

Be not discouraged black women of the world, but push forward, regardless of the lack of appreciation shown you. A race must be saved, a country must be redeemed, and unless you strengthen the leadership of vacillating Negro men, we will remain marking time until the yellow race gains the leadership of the world, and we be forced to subserviency under them, or extermination.

We are tired of hearing Negro men say, "There is a better day coming," while they do nothing to usher in the day. We are becoming so impatient that we are getting in the front ranks and serve notice to the world that we will brush aside the halting, cowardly Negro leaders and with prayer on our lips and arms prepared for any fray, we will press on and on until victory is ours.

Africa must be for Africans and Negroes everywhere must be independent, God being our helper and guide. Mr. Black Man, watch your step! Ethiopia's queens will reign again, and her Amazons protect her shores and people. Strengthen your shaking knees and move forward, or we will displace you and lead on to victory and to glory.

From the *Negro World* October 24, 1925

I Am a Negro—and Beautiful

Too much cannot be said in denouncing the class of "want-to-be-white" Negroes one finds everywhere. This race destroying group are dissatisfied with their mothers and with their creator—mother is too dark "to pass" and God made a mistake when he made black people. With this fallacy uppermost in their minds, they peel their skins off, and straighten their hair, in mad effort to look like their ideal type. To what end, one asks? To the end that they may be admitted to better jobs, moneyed circles, and, in short, share the blessings of the prosperous white race. They are too lazy to help build a prosperous Negro race, but choose the easier route—crossing the racial border. It is the way of the weakling, and in their ignorance and stupidity they advise others to do likewise. As if 400,000,000 Negroes could change their skins over night. And if they could, would they? Seeing that the bulk of Negroes are to be found on the great continent of Africa, and they, thank Heaven, are proud of their black skins and curly hair. The "would-be-white" few are fast disappearing in the Western world, as the entire race, through the preachments of Marcus Garvey, has found its soul, and is out to acquire for itself and its posterity all that makes other races honored and respected.

This urge for whiteness is not just a mental gesture. It is a slavish complex, the remnant of slavery, to look like "Massa," to speak like him, even to cuss and drink like him. In last week's issue of the Nation Magazine, Langston Hughes, a poet, wrote a splendid article* on the difficulties facing the Negro artist, in which he described the racial state of mind of a Philadelphia club woman, which is typical of the group under discussion. He states:

"The old subconscious 'white is best' runs through her mind. Years of study under white teachers, a lifetime of white books, pictures, and papers, and white manners, morals, and Puritan standards made her dislike the spirituals. And now she turns up her nose at jazz and all its manifestations—likewise almost everything else distinctly racial. She doesn't care for the Winold Reiss* portraits of Negroes because they are "too Negro." She does not want a true picture of herself from anybody. She wants the artist to flatter her, to make the white world believe that all Negroes are as smug and as near white in soul as she wants to be."

We are delighted with the frank statement of Mr. Hughes in a white magazine; we do not know if he is a registered member of the

Universal Negro Improvement Association; in any event his closing paragraph marks him as a keen student of Garveyism, and with stamina enough to express its ideals:

"To my mind, it is the duty of the younger Negro artist, if he accepts any duties at all from outsiders, to change through the force of his art that old whispering 'I want to be white,' hidden in the aspirations of his people, to 'Why should I want to be white? I am a Negro—and beautiful!' . . . We younger Negro artists who create now intend to express our individual dark-skinned selves without fear or shame. If white people are pleased we are glad. If they are not, it doesn't matter."

Bravo, Mr. Hughes! From now on under your leadership we expect our artists to express their real souls, and give us art, that is colorful, full of ecstacy, dulcent [*sic*] and even tragic; for has it not been admitted by those who would undervalue us that the Negro is a born artist. Then let the canvas come to life with dark faces; let poetry charm the muses with the hopes and aspirations of our race; let the musicians drown our sorrows with the merry jazz; while a race is in the making, and steadily moving on to nationhood and to power.

Play up, boys, and let the world know "we are Negroes and beautiful."

From the *Negro World* July 10, 1926

2
SOCIALISTS

Hubert H. Harrison

The "father of Harlem radicalism," Hubert Henry Harrison, was born in St. Croix, Virgin Islands, on April 27, 1883. He came to the United States in 1900 and quickly established himself as an authority on Black history and politics, writing articles, reviews, and letters on the condition of Blacks in America and abroad.[1] His writings were published in scores of periodicals, and many were collected in two books, *The Negro and the Nation* (1917) and *When Africa Awakes* (1920).

Believing that the ways of the old Black leaders were ineffective in advancing the cause of the Negro, Harrison published letters in the *New York Sun* chastising Booker T. Washington. The result, at the behest of Washington's allies, was Harrison's dismissal from the postal service, where he had been employed. This increased his involvement with the Socialist Party of America, which hired him as a lecturer. Harrison had joined the party around 1909, becoming one of its few Black members and the leading Black spokesperson. He soon became a fixture on street corners in Harlem and in the Wall Street and Madison Square Garden areas, preaching the socialist message. One person who witnessed Harrison's orations was the novelist Henry Miller, who commented that of all the street corner speakers no one could "hold a candle to Hubert Harrison" (qtd. in Samuels 58). Harrison also used his pen for the cause, publishing a series of articles on "The Negro and Socialism" in 1911–12 in the *New York Call* and the *International Socialist Review.* In "Socialism and the Negro" (reprinted with minor changes in *The Negro and the Nation*) Harrison laments the Socialist Party's lack of effort to make its cause understood to Black

Americans. He stresses that African Americans should receive special treatment from the party, since historically they have been "the most ruthlessly exploited working class group in America."

Rising within the socialist ranks, Harrison was recommended as a party organizer by W. E. B. Du Bois, at that time a socialist. Shortly after Harrison's articles appeared, the Colored Socialist Club was formed, though it was soon disbanded due to charges by members (including Du Bois) of racial segregation. Stung by the party's abandonment of the club and becoming increasingly convinced that the socialists were not fully committed to Black issues, Harrison began to turn more and more to the radical Industrial Workers of the World (IWW), becoming closely aligned with William "Big Bill" Haywood and Elizabeth Gurley Flynn. Harrison was brought up on "contempt" charges by the Socialist Party and suspended from it in 1914. He soon resigned from the party, albeit continuing to support many of its causes.

Harrison increased his speechmaking and in 1917 became president of the Liberty League, "a militant and independent, race-conscious, all-Black organization, fighting for equal rights, liberty, manhood and womanhood, and with an organizational and political voice—a newspaper [the *Voice*]" (Perry, "Hubert Henry Harrison" 466). "Launching the Liberty League" formulates the beginnings of the organization in the summer of 1917. Harrison saw the Liberty League as an early manifestation of the "new Negro Movement," which "represented a breaking away of the Negro masses from the grip of the old-time leaders." In the pioneering newspaper, the *Voice* (1917–19), and in another he would found, the *New Negro* (1919–20), Harrison spoke against the murder of Blacks in riots and lynchings breaking out across the nation. He believed that the New Negro had to be willing to fight back in order to be respected. He also advised Blacks not to align themselves with any one party and to keep independent politically. In "Two Negro Radicalisms" Harrison expounds that the determining factor in radicalizing the Negro is not so much class as it is race, and while the class line may be temporary, the color line is not. He argues that those who support socialism and Bolshevism do it out of race-consciousness since these movements help to undermine the structure established by the White world.

Harrison spoke out against Black organizations such as the NAACP and the National Urban League that he felt were elitist, conservative, and largely controlled by Whites. "The Descent of Du Bois" and "Just Crabs" (published in the *Negro World*) discuss Harrison's views on Black leadership. Harrison had known Du Bois since their early involvement with the Socialist Party. Harrison's excoriating essay "The Descent of Du Bois" criticized Du Bois for his support of the American war effort and helped prevent the NAACP leader from securing a post in the War Department.[2] "Just Crabs" is a humorous critique of Black leaders in the Socialist Party and the NAACP who, according to Harrison, spent more time criticizing other Black leaders than attempting to advance the cause of the race, thus playing into the hands of White officials.

Harrison also criticized the U.S. involvement in World War I as a means to spread capitalism and imperialism. He maintained that the First World War was fought not for democracy but rather over economics. In "The White War and the Colored World" Harrison, while condemning the devastation caused by the struggle, found some hope in the belief that Europe and America would be weakened by the cost of war, resulting in greater economic, social, and political freedom for people of color.

Despite the high circulation of the *Voice* (over ten thousand copies for most issues), the ranks of the Liberty League began to dwindle in 1918 because of internal squabbling, financial problems, and the extraordinary growth of Garvey's UNIA. Ironically, Harrison had been the facilitator for Garvey's first important speech, delivered in 1917. Harrison himself worked as an editor for the *Negro World* from 1920 to 1922, although he never actually became a member of the UNIA. Harrison reshaped the periodical, emphasizing race consciousness and expanding its cultural component. Harrison and Garvey had a number of differences, including a disagreement about whether, as Harrison believed, Negro Americans should devote their energies toward the racial struggle within the United States rather than invest in an overseas empire in Africa.[3] This belief was at the core of the International Colored Unity League (ICUL), founded in 1924, and its organ, *The Voice of the Negro*.

In his later years, in addition to his work with the ICUL, Harrison, who never received a university degree, was employed as a professor of embryology at the College of Chiropractics. Dubbed the Black Socrates, he also became a staff lecturer with the New York Board of Education and spoke at Columbia University and New York

University. He died in 1927 due to complications from an appendectomy. He was mourned by thousands and eulogized in numerous periodicals. The tributes by the common people, for whom Harrison had so long toiled, would have pleased him most.

Although Harrison influenced a generation of Black leaders, his candid challenges to those in power doubtless led to his undue critical neglect. His emphasis on Black history, racial pride, and the concept of "race first" certainly resonated with Garvey, who incorporated a number of Harrison's plans. His opposition to Black participation in World War I and his early socialist views impacted on A. Philip Randolph and Chandler Owen, editors of the *Messenger.* His emphasis on "Negro Manhood" and his writings on the "New Negro" influenced the younger, more radical members of the Harlem Renaissance. Harrison's New Negro had racial consciousness and was prepared to fight, with guns as well as words if necessary, for his or her rights. Perhaps his greatest influence was on radical political activists, including not only Randolph and Owen but particularly W. A. Domingo, Richard B. Moore, and Cyril Briggs. It has been only in recent years, however, that the importance of his contributions has begun to be recorded.

NOTES

Harrison's papers are in a private collection. See Perry, *Reader* xxvii, for further information.

1. What are now called the U.S. Virgin Islands were Danish possessions until the United States took ownership in 1917. A large number of anglophone Caribbean immigrants to the United States in the 1920s came from the Virgin Islands, in part because of the passage of the Volsted Act in 1919, enforcing the Eighteenth Amendment, which prohibited the manufacture and sale of alcohol. The economy of the islands, based largely on rum, was devastated by the act. Although people from the U.S. Virgin Islands were not part of the British colonial system, they were linked with British Caribbean territories culturally and linguistically. For example, 99 percent of Virgin Islanders were English-speaking at the time of Harrison's birth (Perry, "Hubert Henry Harrison" 14). For more on these islands, see Gordon K. Lewis, *The Virgin Islands: A Caribbean Lilliput* (Evanston, IL: Northwestern UP, 1972) and Geraldo Guirty, *Harlem's Danish-American West Indians, 1899–1964* (New York: Vantage, 1989).

2. Du Bois was being considered for a commission in military intelligence in Washington and some Black leaders felt Du Bois's "Close Ranks"

editorial (the *Crisis*, July 1918) was written to curry favor with the government. A member of the military opposed to Du Bois's appointment, Major Walter Howard Loving, requested that Harrison write this critique, which played a part in Du Bois's failure to attain the position (Perry, *Reader* 170–71).

3. It is interesting to note that the 1920 version of the article "Launching the Liberty League," unlike the original 1917 piece, titled "The Liberty League of Negro-Americans: How It Came to Be," mentions Garvey's presence at the League's founding. Perhaps this reflects Garvey's increasing popularity as well as Harrison's involvement with the UNIA in 1920 as editor of the *Negro World*. For more on Harrison's relationship with Garvey, see Perry, *Reader* 182–200.

BIBLIOGRAPHY

Foner, Philip S. *American Socialism and Black Americans: From the Age of Jackson to World War II*. Westport, CT: Greenwood P, 1977.

James, Portia. "Hubert H. Harrison and the New Negro Movement." *Western Journal of Black Studies* 13 (Summer 1989): 82–91.

James, Winston. *Holding Aloft the Banner of Ethiopia: Caribbean Radicalism in Early-Twentieth-Century America*. New York: Verso, 1998.

Perry, Jeffrey B., ed. *A Hubert Harrison Reader*. Middleton, CT: Wesleyan UP, 2001.

———. "Hubert Henry Harrison, 'The Father of Harlem Radicalism': The Early Years—1883 through the Founding of the Liberty League and 'The Voice' in 1917." Diss. Columbia U, 1986.

Rogers, J. A. *World's Great Men of Color*. Vol. 2. 1946. New York: Simon and Schuster, 1996. 432–42. 2 vols.

Samuels, Wilfred David. "Five Afro-Caribbean Voices in American Culture, 1917–1929; Hubert H. Harrison, Wilfred A. Domingo, Richard B. Moore, Cyril V. Briggs, and Claude McKay." Diss. U of Iowa, 1977.

Watkins-Owens, Irma. *Blood Relations: Caribbean Immigrants and the Harlem Renaissance*. Bloomington: Indiana UP, 1996.

Socialism and the Negro

1. Economic Status of the Negro

The ten million Negroes of America form a group that is more essentially proletarian than any other American group. In the first place the ancestors of this group were brought here with the very definite understanding that they were to be ruthlessly exploited. And they were not allowed any choice in the matter. Since they were brought here as chattels their social status was fixed by that fact. In every case that we know of where a group has lived by exploiting another group, it has despised that group which it has put under subjection. And the degree of contempt has always been in direct proportion to the degree of exploitation.

Inasmuch then, as the Negro was at one period the most thoroughly exploited of the American proletariat, he was the most thoroughly despised. That group which exploited and despised him, being the most powerful section of the ruling class, was able to diffuse its own necessary contempt of the Negro first among the other sections of the ruling class, and afterwards among all other classes of Americans. For the ruling class has always determined what the social ideals and moral ideas of society should be; and this explains how race prejudice was disseminated until all Americans are supposed to be saturated with it. Race prejudice, then, is the fruit of economic subjection and a fixed inferior economic status. It is the reflex of a social caste system. That caste system in America today is what we roughly refer to as the Race Problem, and it is thus seen that the Negro problem is essentially an economic problem with its roots in slavery past and present.

Notwithstanding the fact that it is usually kept out of public discussion, the bread-and-butter side of this problem is easily the most important. The Negro worker gets less for his work—thanks to exclusion from the craft unions—than any other worker; he works longer hours as a rule and under worse conditions than any other worker, and his rent in any large city is much higher than that which the white worker pays for the same tenement. In short, the exploitation of the Negro worker is keener than that of any group of white workers in America. Now, the mission of the Socialist Party is to free the working class from exploitation, and since the Negro is the most ruthlessly exploited working class group in America, the duty of the party to champion his cause is as clear as day. This is the crucial test of Socialism's sincerity and therein lies the value of this point of view—Socialism and the Negro.

2. The Need of Socialist Propaganda.

So far, no particular effort has been made to carry the message of Socialism to these people. All the rest of the poor have had the gospel preached to them, for the party has carried on special propaganda work among the Poles, Slovaks, Finns, Hungarians and Lithuanians. Here are ten million Americans, all proletarians, hanging on the ragged edge of the impending class conflict. Left to themselves they may become as great a menace to our advancing army as is the army of the unemployed, and for precisely the same reason: they can be used against us, as the craft unions have begun to find out. Surely we should make some effort to enlist them under our banner that they may swell our ranks and help to make us invincible. And we must do this for the same reason that is impelling organized labor to adopt an all-inclusive policy; because the other policy results in the artificial breeding of scabs. On grounds of common sense and enlightened self-interest it would be well for the Socialist party to begin to organize the Negroes of America in reference to the class struggle. The capitalists of America are not waiting. Already they have subsidized Negro leaders, Negro editors, Negro preachers and politicians to build up in the breasts of the black people those sentiments which will make them subservient to their will. For they recognize the value (to them) of cheap labor power and they know that if they can succeed in keeping one section of the working class down they can use that section to keep other sections down too.

3. The Negro's Attitude toward Socialism.

If the Socialist propaganda among Negroes is [to] be effectively carried on, the members and leaders of the party must first understand the Negro's attitude toward Socialism. That attitude finds its first expression in ignorance. The mass of the Negro people in America are ignorant of what Socialism means. For this they are not much to blame. Behind the veil of the color line none of the great world-movements for social betterment have been able to penetrate. Since it is not yet the easiest task to get the white American worker—with all his superior intellect—to see Socialism, it is but natural to expect that these darker workers to whom America denies knowledge should still be in ignorance as to its aims and objects.

Besides, the Negroes of America—those of them who think—are suspicious of Socialism as of everything that comes from the white people of America. They have seen that every movement for the extension of democracy here has broken down as soon as it reached the color line. Political democracy declared that "all men are created equal," meant only all white men. The Christian church found that the brotherhood of man did not include God's bastard children. The public school system proclaimed that the school house was the backbone of democracy—"for white people only," and the civil service says that Negroes must keep their place—at the bottom. So that they can hardly be blamed for looking askance at any new gospel of freedom. Freedom to them has been like one of

> "those juggling fiends*
> That palter with us in a double sense;
> That keep the word of promise to our ear,
> And break it to our hope."

In this connection, some explanation of the former political solidarity of those Negroes who were voters may be of service. Up to six years ago the one great obstacle to the political progress of the colored people was their sheep-like allegiance to the Republican party. They were taught to believe that God had raised up a peculiar race of men called Republicans who had loved the slaves so tenderly that they had taken guns in their hands and rushed on the ranks of the southern slaveholders to free the slaves; that this race of men was still in existence, marching under the banner of the Republican party and showing their great love for Negroes by appointing from six to sixteen near-Negroes to soft political snaps. Today that great political superstition is falling to pieces before the advance of intelligence among Negroes. They begin to realize that they were sold out by the Republican party in 1876; that in the last twenty-five years lynchings have increased, disfranchisement has spread all over the south and "jim-crow" cars run even into the national capital—with the continuing consent of a Republican congress, a Republican Supreme Court and Republican presidents.

Ever since the Brownsville affair,* but more clearly since Taft declared and put in force the policy of pushing out the few near-Negro officeholders, the rank and file have come to see that the Republican party is a great big sham. Many went over to the Democratic party because, as the *Amsterdam News* puts it, "they had nowhere else to go." Twenty years ago the colored men who joined that party were ostracized as scalawags and crooks—which they probably were. But today, the defection to the Democrats of such men as

Bishop Walters, Wood, Carr and Langston—whose uncle was a colored Republican congressman from Virginia—has made the colored democracy respectable and given quite a tone to political heterodoxy.

All this loosens the bonds of their allegiance and breaks the bigotry of the last forty years. But of this change in their political viewpoint the white world knows nothing. The two leading Negro newspapers are subsidized by the same political pirates who hold the title-deeds to the handful of hirelings holding office in the name of the Negro race. One of these papers* is an organ of Mr. Washington, the other pretends to be independent—that is, it must be "bought" on the installment plan, and both of them are in New York. Despite this "conspiracy of silence" the Negroes are waking up; are beginning to think for themselves; to look with more favor on "new doctrines." And herein lies the open opportunity of the Socialist party. If the work of spreading Socialist propaganda is taken to them now, their ignorance of it can be enlightened and their suspicions removed.

The Duty of the Socialist Party.

I think that we might embrace the opportunity of taking the matter up at the coming national convention. The time is ripe for taking a stand against the extensive disfranchisement of the Negro in violation of the plain provisions of the national constitution. In view of the fact that the last three amendments to the constitution contain the clause, "Congress shall have power to enforce this article by appropriate legislation," the party will not be guilty of proposing anything worse than asking the government to enforce its own "law and order." If the Negroes, or any other section of the working class in America, is to be deprived of the ballot, how can they participate with us in the class struggle? How can we pretend to be a political party if we fail to see the significance of this fact?

Besides, the recent dirty diatribes against the Negro in a Texas paper,* which is still on our national list of Socialist papers; the experiences of Mrs. Theresa Malkiel in Tennessee where she was prevented by certain people from addressing a meeting of Negroes on the subject of Socialism, and certain other exhibitions of the thing called southernism, constitute the challenge of caste. Can we ignore this challenge? I think not. We could hardly afford to have the taint of "trimming" on the garments of the Socialist party. It is dangerous—

doubly dangerous now, when the temper of the times is against such "trimming." Besides it would be futile. If it is not met now it must be met later when it shall have grown stronger. Now, when we can cope with it, we have the issue squarely presented: Southernism or Socialism—which? Is it to be the white half of the working class against the black half, or all the working class? Can we hope to triumph over capitalism with one-half of the working class against us? Let us settle these questions now—for settled they must be.

The Negro and Political Socialism.

The power of the voting proletariat can be made to express itself through the ballot. To do this they must have a political organization of their own to give form to their will. The direct object of such an organization is to help them to secure control of the powers of government, be able "to alter or abolish it, and to institute a new government, laying its foundation on such principles, and organizing its power in such form, as to them shall seem most likely to effect their safety and happiness"—in short, to work for the abolition of capitalism, by legislation—if that be permitted. And in all this, the Negro, who feels most fiercely the deep damnation of the capitalist system, can help.

The Negro and Industrial Socialism.

But even the voteless proletarian can in a measure help toward the final abolition of the capitalist system. For they too have labor power—which they can be taught to withhold. They can do this by organizing themselves at the point of production. By means of such organization they can work to shorten the hours of labor, to raise wages, to secure an ever-increasing share of the product of their toil. They can enact and enforce laws for the protection of labor and they can do this at the point of production, as was done by the Western Federation of Miners in the matter of the eight-hour law, which they established without the aid of the legislatures or the courts. All this involves a progressive control of the tools of production and a progressive expropriation of the capitalist class. And in all this the Negro can help. So far, they are unorganized on the industrial field, but industrial unionism beckons to them as to others, and the consequent program of the Socialist party for the Negro in the south can be based upon this fact.

From *The Negro and the Nation* (1917)

Launching the Liberty League

(From *The Voice* of July 4, 1917.)

The Liberty League of Negro-Americans, which was recently organized by the Negroes of New York, presents the most startling program of any organization of Negroes in the country today. This is nothing less than the demand that the Negroes of the United States be given a chance to enthuse over democracy for themselves in America before they are expected to enthuse over democracy in Europe. The League is composed of "Negro-Americans, loyal to their country in every respect, and obedient to her laws."

The League has an interesting history. It grew out of the labors of Mr. Hubert H. Harrison, who has been on the lecture platform for years and is well and favorably known to thousands of white New Yorkers from Wall Street to Washington Heights.

Two years ago Mr. Harrison withdrew from an international political organization, and, a little more than a year ago, gave up lecturing to white people, to devote himself to lecturing exclusively among his own people. He acquired so much influence among them that when he issued the first call for a mass-meeting "to protest against lynching in the land of liberty and disfranchisement in the home of democracy," although the call was not advertised in any newspaper, the church in which the meeting was held was packed from top to bottom. At this mass-meeting, which was held at Bethel Church on June 12, the organization was effected and funds were raised to sustain it and to extend its work all over the country.

Harrison was subsequently elected its president, with Edgar Grey* and James Harris as secretary and treasurer, respectively. At the close of this mass-meeting he hurriedly took the midnight train for Boston, where a call for a similar meeting had been issued by W. Monroe Trotter,* editor of *The Boston Guardian*. While there he delivered an address in Faneuil Hall, the cradle of American liberty, and told the Negroes of Boston what their brothers in New York had done and were doing. The result was the linking up of the New York and the Boston organizations, and Harrison was elected chairman of a national committee of arrangements to issue a call to every Negro organization in the country to send delegates to a great race-congress which is to meet in Washington in September or October and put their grievances before the country and Congress.

At the New York mass-meeting money was subscribed for the establishment of a newspaper to be known as *The Voice* and to serve as the medium of expression for the new demands and aspirations of the new Negro. It was made clear that this "New Negro Movement" represented a breaking away of the Negro masses from the grip of the old-time-leaders—none of whom was represented at the meeting. The audience rose to their feet with cheers when Harrison was introduced by the chairman. The most striking passages of his speech were those in which he demanded that Congress make lynching a Federal crime and take the Negro's life under national protection, and declared that since lynching was murder and a violation of Federal and State laws, it was incumbent upon the Negroes themselves to maintain the majesty of the law and put down the law-breakers by organizing all over the South to defend their own lives whenever their right to live was invaded by mobs which the local authorities were too weak or unwilling to suppress.

The meeting was also addressed by Mr. J. C. Thomas, Jr., a young Negro lawyer, who pointed out the weakness and subserviency of the old-time political leaders and insisted that Negroes stop begging for charity in the matter of their legal rights and demand justice instead.

Mr. Marcus Garvey, president of the Jamaica Improvement Association, was next introduced by Mr. Harrison. He spoke in enthusiastic approval of the new movement and pledged it his hearty support.

After the Rev. Dr. Cooper, the pastor of Bethel, had addressed the meeting, the following resolutions were adopted and a petition to Congress was prepared and circulated. In addition the meeting sent a telegram to the Jews of Russia, congratulating them upon the acquisition of full political and civil rights and expressing the hope that the United States might soon follow the democratic example of Russia.

From *When Africa Awakes* (1920)

The New Politics for the New Negro

The world of the future will look upon the world of today as an essentially new turning point in the path of human progress. All over the world the spirit of democratic striving is making itself felt. The new issues have brought forth new ideas of freedom, politics, industry and society at large. The new Negro living in this new world is just as responsive to these new impulses as other people are.

In the "good old days" it was quite easy to tell the Negro to follow in the footsteps of those who had gone before. The mere mention of the name Lincoln or the Republican party was sufficient to secure his allegiance to that party which had seen him stripped of all political power and of civil rights without protest—effective or otherwise.

Things are different now. The new Negro is demanding elective representation in Baltimore, Chicago and other places. He is demanding it in New York. The pith of the present occasion is, that he is no longer begging or asking. He is demanding as a right that which he is in position to enforce.

In the presence of this new demand the old political leaders are bewildered, and afraid; for the old idea of Negro leadership by virtue of the white man's selection has collapsed. The new Negro leader must be chosen by his fellows—by those whose strivings he is supposed to represent.

Any man today who aspires to lead the Negro race must set squarely before his face the idea of "Race First." Just as the white men of these and other lands are white men before they are Christians, Anglo-Saxons or Republicans; so the Negroes of this and other lands are intent upon being Negroes before they are Christians, Englishmen, or Republicans.

Sauce for the goose is sauce for the gander. Charity begins at home, and our first duty is to ourselves. It is not what we wish but what we must, that we are concerned with. The world, as it ought to be, is still for us, as for others, the world that does not exist. The world, as it is, is the real world, and it is to that real world that we address ourselves. Striving to be men, and finding no effective aid in government or in politics, the Negro of the Western world must follow the path of the Swadesha movement of India and the Sinn Fein movement of Ireland. The meaning of both these terms is "ourselves first." This is the mental background of the new politics of the New

Negro, and we commend it to the consideration of all the political parties. For it is upon this background that we predicate such policies as shall seem to us necessary and desirable.

In the British Parliament the Irish Home Rule party clubbed its full strength and devoted itself so exclusively to the cause of Free Ireland that it virtually dictated for a time the policies of Liberals and Conservatives alike.

The new Negro race in America will not achieve political self-respect until it is in a position to organize itself as a politically independent party and follow the example of the Irish Home Rulers. This is what will happen in American politics.—September, 1917.

From *When Africa Awakes* (1920)

The Descent of Du Bois

In a recent bulletin of the War Department it was declared that "justifiable grievances" were producing and had produced "not disloyalty, but an amount of unrest and bitterness which even the best efforts of their leaders may not be able always to guide." This is the simple truth. The essence of the present situation lies in the fact that the people whom our white masters have "recognized" as our leaders (without taking the trouble to consult us) and those who, by our own selection, had actually attained to leadership among us are being revaluated and, in most cases, rejected.

The most striking instance from the latter class is Dr. W. E. [B.] Du Bois, the editor of the *Crisis*. Du Bois's case is the more significant because his former services to his race have been undoubtedly of a high and courageous sort. Moreover, the act by which he has brought upon himself the stormy outburst of disapproval from his race is one which of itself, would seem to merit no such stern condemnation. To properly gauge the value and merit of this disapproval one must view it in the light of its attendant circumstances and of the situation in which it arose.

Dr. Du Bois first palpably sinned in his editorial "Close Ranks" in the July number of the *Crisis*. But this offense (apart from the trend and general tenor of the brief editorial) lies in a single sentence: "Let us, while this war lasts, *forget our special grievances* and close our ranks, shoulder to shoulder with our white fellow-citizens and the allied nations that are fighting for democracy." From the latter part of the sentence there is no dissent, so far as we know. The offense lies in that part of the sentence which ends with the italicized words. It is felt by all his critics, that Du Bois, of all Negroes, knows best that our "special grievances" which the War Department Bulletin describes as "justifiable" consist of lynching, segregation and disfranchisement, and that the Negroes of America can not preserve either their lives, their manhood or their vote (which is their political life and liberties) with these things in existence. The doctor's critics feel that America can not use the Negro people to any good effect unless they have life, liberty and manhood assured and guaranteed to them. Therefore, instead of the war for democracy making these things less necessary, it makes them more so.

"But," it may be asked, "why should not these few words be taken merely as a slip of the pen or a venial error in logic? Why all this hubbub?" It is because the so-called leaders of the first-mentioned class have already established an unsavory reputation by advocating this same surrender of life, liberty and manhood, masking their cowardice behind the pillars of war-time sacrifice? [*sic*] Du Bois's statement, then, is believed to mark his entrance into that class, and is accepted as a "surrender" of the principles which brought him into prominence—and which alone kept him there.

Later, when it was learned that Du Bois was being preened for a berth in the War Department as a captain-assistant (adjutant) to Major [Joel] Spingarn, the words used by him in the editorial acquired a darker and more sinister significance. The two things fitted too well together as motive and self-interest.

For these reasons Du Bois is regarded much in the same way as a knight in the middle ages who had had his armor stripped from him, his arms reversed and his spurs hacked off. This ruins him as an influential person among Negroes at this time, alike whether he becomes a captain or remains an editor.

But the case has its roots much further back than the editorial in July's *Crisis*. Some time ago when it was learned that the *Crisis* was being investigated by the government for an alleged seditious utterance a great clamor went up, although the expression of it was not open. Negroes who dared to express their thoughts seemed to think the action tantamount to a declaration that protests against lynching, segregation and disfranchisement were outlawed by the government.

But nothing was clearly understood until the conference of editors was called under the assumed auspices of Emmet[t] Scott* and Major Spingarn. Then it began to appear that these editors had not been called without a purpose. The desperate ambiguity of the language which they used in their report (in the War Department Bulletin), coupled with the fact that not one of them, upon his return would tell the people anything of the proceedings of the conference—all this made the Negroes feel less and less confidence in them and their leadership; made them (as leaders) less effective instruments for the influential control of the race's state of mind.

Now Du Bois was one of the most prominent of those editors "who were called." The responsibility, therefore, for a course of counsel which stresses the servile virtues of acquiescence and subservience falls squarely on his shoulders. The offer of a captaincy and Du Bois's flirtation with that offer following on the heels of these things seemed, even in the eyes of his associate members of the N. A. A. C. P. to afford clear proof of that which was only a suspicion before, viz: that the racial resolution of the leaders had been tampered with, and that Du Bois had been privy to something of the sort. The connection between the successive acts of the drama (May, June, July) was too clear to admit of any interpretation other than that of deliberate, cold-blooded, purposive planning. And the connection with Spingarn seemed to suggest that personal friendships and public faith were not good working team-mates.

For the sake of the larger usefulness of Dr. Du Bois we hope he will be able to show that he can remain as editor of the *Crisis;* but we fear that it will require a good deal of explaining. For, our leaders, like Caesar's wife, must be above suspicion.—July, 1918.

From *When Africa Awakes* (1920)

Just Crabs*

Once upon a time a Greedy Person went rummaging along the lagoon with a basket and a stick in quest of Crabs, which he needed for the Home Market. (Now, this was in the Beginning of Things, Best Beloved.) These were Land Crabs—which, you know, are more luscious than Sea Crabs, being more Primitive and more full of meat. He dug into their holes with his stick, routed them out, packed them on their backs in his basket and took them home. Several trips he made with his basket and his stick, and all the Crabs which he caught were dumped into a huge barrel. (But this time he didn't pack them on their backs.) And all the creatures stood around and watched. For this Greedy Person had put no cover on the barrel. (But this was in the Beginning of Things.)

He knew Crab nature, and was not at all worried about his Crabs. For as soon as any one Crab began to climb up on the side of the barrel to work his way toward the top the other Crabs would reach up, grab him by the legs, and down he would come, kerplunk! "If we can't get up," they would say—"if we can't get up, you shan't get up, either. We'll pull you down. Besides, you should wait until the barrel bursts. There are Kind Friends on the Outside who will burst the barrel if we only wait, and then, when the Great Day dawns, we will all be Emancipated and there'll be no need for Climbing. Come down, you fool!" (Because this was in the Beginning of Things, Best Beloved.) So the Greedy Person could always get as many Crabs as he needed for the Home Market, because they all depended on him for their food.

And all the creatures stood around and laughed. For this was very funny in the Beginning of Things. And all the creatures said that the Reason for this kink in Crab Nature was that when the Creator was giving out heads he didn't have enough to go around, so the poor Crabs didn't get any. And the Greedy Person thanked his lucky stars that Crabs had been made in that Peculiar way, since it made it unnecessary to put a cover on his barrel or to waste his precious time a-watching of them. (Now, all this happened long ago, Best Beloved, in the very Beginning of Things.)

The above is the first of our Just-So Stories*—with no apologies to Rudyard Kipling or any one else. We print it here because, just at this time the Crabs are at work in Harlem, and there is a tremendous clashing of claws as the Pull 'Em Down program goes forward. It's a great game, to be sure, but it doesn't seem to get them or us anywhere. The new day that has dawned for the Negroes of Harlem is a day of business accomplishment. People are going into business, saving their money and collectively putting it into enterprises which will mean roofs over their heads and an economic future for themselves and their little ones.

But the Subsidized Sixth* are sure that this is all wrong and that we have no right to move an inch until the Socialist millennium dawns, when we will all get "out of the barrel" together. It does not seem to have occurred to them that making an imperfect heaven now does not unfit any one for enjoying the perfect paradise which they promise us—if it ever comes. Truly it is said of them that "the power over a man's subsistence is the power over his will"—and over his "scientific radicalism,"* too. But we remember having translated this long ago into the less showy English of "Show me whose bread you eat, and I'll tell you whose songs you'll sing." Surely this applies to radicals overnight as well as to ordinary folk. And if not, why not?

But when the reek of the poison gas propaganda has cleared away and the smoke of the barrage has lifted it will be found that "White Men's Niggers" is a phrase that need not be restricted to old-line politicians and editors. Criticism pungent and insistent is due to every man in public life and to every movement which bids for public support. But the cowardly insinuator who from the safe shelter of nameless charges launches his poisoned arrows at other people's reputation is a contemptible character to have on any side of any movement. He is generally a liar who fears that he will be called to account for his lies if he should venture to name his foe. No man with the truth to tell indulges in this pastime of the skulker and the skunk. Let us, by all means, have clear, hard-hitting criticism, but none of this foul filth which lowers the thing that throws it. In the name of common sense and common decency, quit being Just Crabs.

From *When Africa Awakes* (1920)

Two Negro Radicalisms

Twenty years ago all Negroes known to the white publicists of America could be classed as conservatives on all the great questions on which thinkers differ. In matters of industry, commerce, politics, religion, they could be trusted to take the backward view. Only on the question of the Negro's "rights" could a small handful be found bold enough to be tagged as "radicals"—and they were howled down by both the white and colored adherents of the conservative point of view. Today Negroes differ on all those great questions on which white thinkers differ, and there are Negro radicals of every imaginary stripe—agnostics, atheists, I. W. W.'s, Socialists, Single Taxers, and even Bolshevists.

In the good old days white people derived their knowledge of what Negroes were doing from those Negroes who were nearest to them, generally their own selected exponents of Negro activity or of their white point of view. A classic illustration of this kind of knowledge was afforded by the Republican Party; but the Episcopal Church, the Urban League, or the U.S. Government would serve as well. Today the white world is vaguely, but disquietingly, aware that Negroes are awake, different and perplexingly uncertain. Yet the white world by which they are surrounded retains its traditional method of interpreting the mass by the Negro nearest to themselves in affiliation or contact. The Socialist party thinks that the "unrest" now apparent in the Negro masses is due to the propaganda which its adherents support, and believes that it will function largely along the lines of socialist political thought. The great dailies, concerned mainly with their chosen task of being the mental bellwethers of the mob, scream "Bolshevist propaganda" and flatter themselves that they have found the true cause; while the government's unreliable agents envisage it as "disloyalty." The truth, as usual, is to be found in the depths: but they are all prevented from going by mental laziness and that traditional off-handed, easy contempt with which white men in America, from scholars like Lester Ward to scavengers like Stevenson,* deign to consider the colored population of 12 millions.

In the first place the cause of the "radicalism" among American Negroes is international. But it is necessary to draw clear distinctions at the outset. The function of the Christian church is international. So is art, war, the family, rum and exploitation of labor. But none of these is entitled to extend the mantle of its own peculiar "internationalism" to cover the present case of the Negro discontent—although this has been attempted. The international Fact to which Negroes in America are now reacting is not the exploitation of laborers by capitalists; but the social, political and economic subjective of colored peoples by white. It is not the Class Line, but the Color Line, which is the incorrect but accepted expression for the Dead Line of racial inferiority. This fact is a fact of Negro consciousness as well as a fact of externals. The international Color Line is the practice and theory of that doctrine which holds that the best stocks of Africa, China, Egypt and the West Indies are inferior to the worst stocks of Belgium, England and Italy, and must hold their lives, lands and liberties upon such terms and conditions as the white races may choose to grant them.

On the part of the whites, the motive was originally economic; but it is no longer purely so. All the available facts go to prove that, whether in the United States or in Africa or China, the economic subjection is without exception keener and more brutal when the exploited are black, brown and yellow, than when they are white. And the fact that black, brown, and yellow also exploit each other brutally whenever Capitalism has created the economic classes of plutocrat and proletarian should suffice to put purely economic subjection out of court as the prime cause of racial unrest. For the similarity of suffering has produced in all lands where whites rule colored races a certain similarity of sentiment, viz.: a racial revulsion of racial feeling. The peoples of those lands begin to feel and realize that they are so subjected because they are members of races condemned as "inferior" by their Caucasian overlords. The fact presented to their minds is one of race, and in terms of race do they react to it. Put the case to any Negro by way of test and the answer will make this clear.

The great World War, by virtue of its great advertising campaign for democracy and the promises which were held out to subject peoples, fertilized the Race Consciousness of the Negro people into the stage of conflict with the dominant white idea of the Color Line. They took democracy at its face value—which is—Equality. So did the Hindus, Egyptians, and West Indians. This is what the hypocritical advertisers of democracy had not bargained for. The American Negroes, like the other darker peoples, are presenting their checques and trying to "cash in," and delays in that process, however unavoidable to the paying tellers, are bound to beget a plentiful lack of belief in either their intention or in their ability to pay. Hence the run on Democracy's bank—"the Negro unrest" of the newspaper paragraphers.

This Race Consciousness takes many forms, some negative, others positive. On the one hand we balk at Jim Crow, object to educational starvation, refuse to accept good-will for good deeds, and scornfully reject our conservative leaders. On the other hand, we are seeking racial independence in business and reaching out into new fields of endeavor. One of the most taking enterprises at present is the Black Star Line, a steamship enterprise being floated by Mr. Marcus Garvey of New York. Garvey's project (whatever may be its ultimate fate) has attracted tens of thousands of Negroes. Where Negro "radicals" of the type known to white radicals can scarce get a handful of people, Garvey fills the largest halls and the Negro people rain money on him. This is not to be explained by the argument of "superior brains," for the man's education and intelligence are markedly inferior to those of the brilliant "radicals" whose "internationalism" is drawn from other than racial sources. But this man holds up to the Negro masses those things which bloom in their hearts—racialism, race-consciousness, racial solidarity—things taught first in 1917 by THE VOICE and The Liberty League. That is the secret of his success so far.

All over this land and in the West Indies Negroes are responding to the call of battle against the white man's Color Line. And, so long as this remains, the international dogma of the white race, so long will the new Negro war against it. This is the very Ethiopianism which England has been combatting from Cairo to the Cape.

Undoubtedly some of these newly-awakened Negroes will take to Socialism and Bolshevism. But here again the reason is racial. Since they suffer racially from the world as at present organized by the white race, some of their ablest hold that it is "good play" to encourage and give aid to every subversive movement within that white world which makes for its destruction "as it is." For by its subversion they have much to gain and nothing to lose. But they build on their own foundations. Parallel with the dogma of Class-Consciousness they run the dogma of Race-Consciousness. And they dig deeper. For the roots of Class-consciousness inhere in a temporary economic order; whereas the roots of Race-consciousness must of necessity survive any and all changes in the economic order. Accepting biology as a fact, their view is the more fundamental. At any rate, it is that view with which the white world will have to deal.

From *New Negro* October 1919. Reprinted by permission of Wesleyan University Press from *A Hubert Harrison Reader*, edited by Jeffrey B. Perry. Copyright 2001 by the Estate of Hubert Henry Harrison.

The White War and the Colored World

The newspapers which we read every day inform us that the world is at war. Searching the pages of the statisticians, we find that the world is made up of 17 hundred million people of which 12 hundred million are colored—black and brown and yellow. This vast majority is at peace and remains at peace until the white minority determines otherwise. The war in Europe is a war of the white race wherein the stakes of conflict are the titles to possession of the lands and destinies of this colored majority in Asia, Africa and the islands of the sea.

There can be no doubt that the white race as it exists today, is the superior race of the world. And it is superior, not because it has better manners[,] more religion or a higher culture; these things are metaphysical and subject to dispute. The white race rests its claim to superiority on the frankly materialistic ground that it has the guns, soldiers, the money and resources to keep it in the position of the top-dog and to make its will go. This is what white men mean by civilization, disguise it how they may. This struggle is a conflict of wills and interests among the various nations which make up the white race, to determine whose will shall be accepted as the collective will of the white race; to decide, at least for this century, who shall be the inheritors of the lands of Africa and Asia and dictators of the lives and destinies of their colored inhabitants.

The peculiar feature of the conflict is that the white race in its fratricidal strife is burning up, eating up, consuming and destroying these very resources of ships, guns, men and money upon which its superiority is built. They are bent upon this form of self-destruction and nothing that we can say will stop them.

As representatives of one of the races constituting the colored majority of the world, we deplore the agony and blood-shed; but we find consolation in the hope that when this white world shall have been washed clean by its baptism of blood, the white race will be less able to thrust the strong hand of its sovereign will down the throats of the other races. We look for a free India and an independent Egypt; *for nationalities in Africa flying their own flags and dictating their own internal and foreign policies.* This is what we understand by "making the world safe for democracy." Anything less than this will fail to establish "peace on earth and good will toward men." For the majority races cannot be eternally coerced into accepting the sovereignty of the white race. They are willing to live in a world which is the equal possession of all peoples—white, black, brown and yellow. If the white race is willing, they will live at peace with it. But if it insists that freedom, democracy and equality are to exist only for white men, then, there will be such bloodshed later as this world has never seen. And there is no certainty that in such a conflict the white race will come out on top. Not the destinies of the world, but the destinies of the white race are in the hands of the white race.—1917.

From *When Africa Awakes* (1920)

Hands across the Sea

The most dangerous phase of developed capitalism is that of imperialism—when having subjugated its workers and exploited its natural resources at home, it turns with grim determination toward "undeveloped" races and areas to renew the same processes there. This is the phase in which militarism and navalism develop with dizzying speed with their accumulating burden of taxation for "preparedness" against the day when the capitalist class of the nation must use the final argument of force against its foreign competitors for markets. These markets change their character under the impact of international trade, and are no longer simply markets for the absorption of finished products, but become fields for the investment of accumulated surplus profits, in which process they are transformed into original sources for the production of surplus profits by the opening up of mines, railroads and other large-scale capitalist enterprises. It becomes necessary to take over the government of the selected area in order that the profits may be effectually guaranteed, and "spheres of influence," "protectorates," and "mandates" are set up.

Thus the lands of "backward" peoples are brought within the central influence of the capitalistic economic system and the subjection of black, brown and other colored workers to the rigors of "the white man's burden" comes as a consequence of the successful exploitation of white workers at home, and binds them both in an international opposition to the continuance of the capitalist regime. Most Americans who are able to see the process more or less clearly in the case of other nations are unable to see the same process implicit and explicit in the career of their own.

The case of Hayti and the present plight of the Haytian people helps us to see the aims of our own American imperialists in the white light of pitiless publicity. A people of African descent, scarcely seven hundred miles from our own shores, with a government of their own, have had their government suppressed and their liberties destroyed by the Navy Department of the United States without even the slight formality of a declaration of war by the United States Congress as required by the Constitution. In the presidential chair our "cracker" marines have installed a puppet in the person of Monsieur D'Artiguenave* to carry out their will; the legislative bodies of the erstwhile republic have been either suppressed or degraded; unoffending black citizens have been wantonly butchered in cold blood, and thousands have been forced into slavery to labor on the military roads without pay. Here is American imperialism in its stark, repulsive nakedness. And what are we going to do about it?

The fight which will soon be waged in Congress for the restoration of Haytian rights is receiving no help from the millions of Negroes who are presumably interested in the international movement for the practical advancement of people of Negro blood. It is high time that it should. This is an opportunity that lies ready to our hands. And if we would use our votes here in an intelligent, purposeful way we could at least make our voices heard and heeded in Washington on behalf of our brothers in black who are suffering seven hundred miles away. Pending this, we could inaugurate gigantic propaganda meetings in such places as Faneuil Hall, Madison Square Garden, and the Negro churches; we could in our newspapers and magazines agitate for the withdrawal of the forces of the American occupation, as the Irish did on behalf of Ireland; we could, at least, get up a gigantic petition with a million signatures and carry it to Congress. Even a "silent protest parade" would become us better than this slavish apathy and servile acquiescence in which we are now sunk.

Believe it or not as we will, the Negro American is now on trial before the eyes of the world and if he fails to act he may yet hear the God of opportunity utter those fateful words recorded in the third chapter of Revelations concerning the angel of the church of the Laodiceans.* For we may be sure that French, British and Belgian imperialism is a limb of the same tree of white domination on which our home-made branch grows.

From *Negro World* September 10, 1921

Race Consciousness

The general facts of the outside world reflect themselves not only in ideas but in our feelings. The facts that make up a general social condition are reflected in social states of mind. Thus the feeling of racial superiority which the white races so generally exhibit is produced by the external fact of their domination in most parts of the world. That same fact, by the way, produces in the minds of the masses of black, brown and yellow peoples in Africa, Asia and elsewhere what is called in psychology a protective reaction; and that is their race-consciousness. So that race-consciousness is like loyalty, neither an evil nor a good. The good or evil of it depends upon the uses to which it is put.

The recent World War has chiseled the channels of race-consciousness deeper among American Negroes than any previous external circumstances. For weal or woe that is a fact to be reckoned with. During the war we learnt that the Other People held race to be higher than patriotism when American army officers treated their Negro fellow soldiers worse than they did the German enemy. In times of peace we are taught that race is stronger than religion—as the existence of Negro churches prove. All of which need not mean that we have to hate white people. But it does mean that in sheer self-defense, we too must put race very high on our list of necessities. In fact if we hadn't been doing this all along there would have been no "Negro progress" to boast about as proof of our equal human possibilities. Negro churches, Negro newspapers, Negro life-insurance-companies, banks, fraternities, colleges and political appointees—all mean Negro race-consciousness.

So even if self-seekers have vilely exploited the thing that is no reason why we should condemn it as an evil. What is an evil is the ignorance and gullibility of those who let themselves be exploited. So long as the outer situation remains what it is we must evoke race-consciousness to furnish a background for our aspirations, readers for our writers, a clientele for our artists and professional people, and ideals for our future. For so long as a black boy may not aspire to be Governor of Massachusetts or President of the United States, like the son of an immigrant German or Russian, so long will we need race-consciousness.

From the *Boston Chronicle* March 15, 1924. Reprinted by permission of Wesleyan University Press from *A Hubert Harrison Reader*, edited by Jeffrey B. Perry. Copyright 2001 by the Estate of Hubert Henry Harrison.

Prejudice Growing Less and Co-operation More, Says Student of Question

Writer of Special Article for Courier Readers Says Immigrants are Becoming Americanized and Naturalized—Garveyism Has Had Little Effect On Mental Outlook.

New York, Jan. 27.—The destinies of the Negro-American and the Negro-West Indians have been tangled and twisted together from the very beginning in this Western world. Too many people forget that what Columbus discovered was the West Indies—long before anybody discovered America. And African slaves were first imported into the West Indian islands from which practice spread to the Spanish, Dutch, French and English colonies on the mainland. So that the West Indian Negro is an earlier product of Christian civilization than the American Negro.

Back and forth the currents of contact have flowed, now from this side, now from the other; sometimes Negro-American slaves who showed too stubborn a spirit were sold into the West Indies, and sometimes West Indian slaves were sold in southern slave-markets. And at one remove we have a black Santo Domingo regiment saving the white American patriots at the siege of Savannah in our Revolutionary war and hundreds of black American colonists who have settled in Hayti and elsewhere, and have been absorbed into the general West Indian population.

Individually the West Indian Negro has often played a great part in the drama of Negro development here in America. It is exactly one hundred years since the first Negro newspaper was published in America. This was "Freedom's Journal" which was domiciled in New York and edited by John Brown Russwurm, a West Indian, and the first Negro graduate of Dartmouth College. But before this time there was Alexander Hamilton who "passed for white" successfully after coming to America and became one of the Fathers of the country. At a later date there was Denmark Vesey, a Danish West Indian Negro, who, although a freeman and property holder, risked and lost freedom, property and life itself in a slave rebellion which he had organized in Charleston, S.C., in 1822. And more recently, West Indian Negro blood has flowed in the veins of at least one President of the United States.*

Today there are more than forty thousand West Indians in the United States of which about seven-tenths live in New York City alone. This concentration has resulted in intensifying the strains and problems of adjustment. The relations between them and their colored neighbors have changed and developed with the kinds and quantity of social contact and effective cooperation. In the first period of West India[n] immigration, when those who came here were mainly students and scholars seeking wider fields of usefulness, the Negroes of America drew from these samples some of their first and most favorable estimates of West Indian character. It was taken for granted that every West Indian immigrant was a paragon of intelligence and a man of birth and breeding.

Then came the slump in West Indian sugar, caused by German and American competition[,] and the impoverished islands began to decant upon the mainland their working population, laborers, mechanics, peasants, ambitious enough to be discontented with conditions at home and eager to improve their lot by seeking success in the land of Uncle Sam. At first they furnished the elevator operators, janitors, hall-boys and porters, maids and washerwomen of upper Manhattan almost exclusively, with a few tradesmen and skilled workers thrusting themselves forward into better positions and breaking the trail for the Negro-Americans to follow. But during the last two decades they have won their way in New York as business men, lawyers, doctors, school teachers, musicians and journalists. Besides, there is the significant fact that almost every important development originating in Negro Harlem—from the Negro Manhood Movement to political representation in public office, from collecting Negro books to speaking on the streets, from demanding Federal control over lynching to agitating for Negroes on the police force—every one of these has either been fathered by West Indians or can count them among its originators. And today the only Negro patron of art and letters in New York is Casper Holstein, a Negro from the Virgin Islands.

Of course, it has not always been easy sledding for the West Indian. There has been some prejudice. But that prejudice had worn so thin by 1917 that in the political campaign of that year West India[n] and American Negroes were pulling together like two horses in a team, working for the election of James C. Thomas, Jr., to the Aldermanic Board and for the principles of elective representation which has [sic] since been accepted by all political parties in Negro Harlem. It was the Liberty League under whose banner the West Indian and American Negroes first cooperated on anything like a large scale; although in St. Mark's and St. Benedict's lyceums in West 53rd street they effected a library combination some years before and in the Equity Congress such stalwarts as Captain Blount, Prof. Tobias, and Louis Leavelle could always count upon their support in that great movement which gave birth to the "Fighting Fifteenth."*

It may sound strange to outsiders, but it is my firm belief that, between the ordinary Negro American who lives by working and the ordinary West Indian in America there is not the least prejudice in the world. The working Negro American who lives by work gets that work from the white man, and, as he figures it, the white man has work enough for both. But with the Negro American who lives on prestige the case is different. It is to him a matter of life and death that the Negro masses should look up to him with reverence for the superiority vested in him by virtue of something called "education." He meets the West Indian similarly situated, and finds that whether that educated West Indian be Danish, Dutch, French, Spanish or English, he has been furnished by Denmark, Holland, France, Spain or England with a more thorough and competent intellectual equipment than race-prejudiced America has given to the Negro-American. Naturally, since it is to him a matter of life and death, we find that prejudices take shape in such a situation. But these prejudices seem restricted to the intelligen[t]sia on both sides. I speak, of course, of the men. The cause of the West Indian woman is one which I shall not touch upon just now.

In the meanwhile West Indian men are marrying Negro-American women in ever-increasing numbers and rearing children who are American Negroes. These are indistinguishable from other Negro-Americans. I presume that most Negro-Americans know of the West Indian ancestry of such well known Negro-Americans as W. E. B. Du Bois, Charles W. Anderson, collector of Internal Revenue in New York City; of George E. Wibecan of Brooklyn and William Stanley Braithwaite (pronounced in English, "Braf-fit").*

Despite the general belief, British West Indians are becoming naturalized Negro Americans at a fairly rapid rate. But, whether naturalized or not they certainly do become Americanized—even despite the Garvey movement. They grow into spiritual participation with Negro-America and exchange cultural gifts with increasing facility. If the West Indian brings to the market a certain out-spoken and downright courage, he gains there a certain flexibility and tact which is necessary both for survival and success in the American atmosphere. And when the years bring their harvest it will be found that the mingling of West Indian with American Negro has been highly beneficial to Harlem—and to America at large.

From the *Pittsburgh Courier* January 29, 1927

"No Negro Literary Renaissance,"
Says Well Known Writer

New York, March 10.—Doubtless you who now read these lines are "genuinely interested" in the Negro as he has been exhibited in recent or contemporary literature by white and Negro writers. Perhaps you are even one of the intelligentsia (the "g" is hard as in "get"), or one of the "new" Negroes. Of course, you know who wrote "The American Cavalryman," "The Leopard's Claw," "Veiled Aristocrats" or "The Vengeance of the Gods."* No? Really? Dear me! But we will let that pass. These things are fiction and are not perhaps important. Though I did think that since you have bought and read "Nigger Heaven" you might have also read Miss Sanborn's book wherein a white author does try to hold your race up.

Well, then—But, surely, you know who is Alrutheus Ambush Taylor, and are acquainted with that fine sonnet on "The Mulatto"; have read Ferris' book, or at least know it by name? What! "Sidelights on Negro Soldiers," then? Or, "Two Colored Women With the A. E. F." or that immortal poem by the Baltimore poet entitled "Lenox Avenue?"* No? Then, exactly what do you mean when you talk about a Negro literature renaissance?

Seriously, the matter of a Negro literary renaissance is like that of the snakes of Ireland—there isn't any. Those who think that there are usually people who are blissfully ignorant of the stream of literary and artistic products which have flowed uninterruptedly from Negro writers from 1850 to the present. If you ask them about the historical works of Major Wilson, George Williams, William C. Neill, William Wells Brown, Rufus L. Perry, Atticus G. Haygood; the essays of T. Thomas Fortune,* the fictional writings of Negroes from Frances E. Watkins to Pauline Hopkins, Dunbar and Chesnutt, they stammer and evade to cover up their confusion. And if anyone thinks that this is true only of casual colored people, I beg him to consider the following case:

In the year 1905 Professor W. E. B. Du Bois of Atlanta University was hailed by black and white people as pre-eminently, the "scholar" of the race. If anyone was an authority on the Negro American he was assuredly "it." In that same year the learned litterateur brought forth under the auspices of Atlanta University a work which was meant to be authoritative. It was entitled "A Select Bibliography of the Negro American." Now, when this family album was assembled Charles W. Chesnutt, the greatest Negro-American novelist, had already published "The Conjure Woman," "The Wife of His Youth," The House Behind the Cedars" "and "The Marrow of Tradition." Yet you will search Dr. Du Bois' bibliography of 1905 in vain for any mention of Chesnutt. But that is nothing unusual for Dr. Du Bois. In his family magazine for February, 1927, he lists under "The Looking Glass" an unusual article by a black West Indian author in a white magazine called "The Modern Quarterly"—but he studiously refrains from mentioning the writer's name, although it was and is perfectly well known to him.* He did something similar to Mr. George S. Schuyler recently. The significant thing is that this is not peculiar to Dr. Du Bois, but is a common trait of all our "guardians of the gate." No one can name a single Negro author or artist whom any one of them "discovered." They blissfully wait until some white person stumbles on him (as was the case with Dunbar, William Lonsdale Brown,* Charles Gilpin and Countee Cullen) before they venture to acknowledge him; with the result that each such casual discoverer thinks that the stream of Negro literary production bubbled up at the precise point where he discovered it. And, so long as through the niggardly narrowness or the cowardly critical defect of such people the white man (who doesn't know our literary history) remains our only vendor of values in Negro writings, so long will we be cursed with Jejune Jazz artists who must have managed to hop over both Burns and Dunbar in their wild gyrations.

For, let it be said once for all, that if the hysteria of uneducated kiddies with which we are being deluged at this time is poetry, then the writings of Milton, Keats, Lowell, Dunbar, Hawkins* and Claude McKay must be something else. At the moment of writing this I learn that one of these kiddies who has perpetrated two books of alleged "poems" is engaged in studying at school, for the first time, Milton's "Paradise Lost." One does insist that a violinist should have studied the violin and what has been done on it before venturing to ask people to pay for his performances. The same applies to a washerwoman with clothes—and to the entire range of art that links the two. One doesn't object to youth: Byron, Shelley, Keats and Tennyson were all youths when they mastered the technique of verse. But they mastered it first. And, after all, literature is the expression of life-values in terms of word-values. How, then, can we get literature from those who haven't lived, who haven't even read?

Over the Van Vechten matter* Chicago, Pittsburgh and even Charleston have begun to sneer at this mushroom mentality, product of that enfeeblement which follows whenever the more sturdy types of mankind ape the more sophisticated and neurotic without understanding what they ape. The Negro has something to give to American literature; but that something will follow the line of "The Chipwoman's Fortune" rather than those as "Salome" or "Lulu Belle."* It will root itself in the abler work of Walter White (his first novel [*The Fire in the Flint* 1924]). In scholarship it will build on Brawley, Taylor, Sinclair, Cromwell and Woodson—that is, something more solid than the mere showing of their names! It will see in McKay and Watkins* the only capable poets of our race today—as Dunbar was two decades ago—and will recognize in Countee Cullen (who is NOT a minister's son!) the one youngster marked out by Nature for a poet, with a fine development ahead of him rather than adequate achievement behind him. It will discover the virile short stories of William Pickens and the reason why no white critic praises them. It will pounce on the early work of Kelly Miller and Du Bois (before the one began to talk twaddle in print and the other to imitate himself, like an ancient and animated dowager). But in that day the Negro writer will be going for his authority on race-values, not to Mr. Reuter (who lists Kelly Miller as a mulatto!) nor to Mr. Herskovits (who in a review of Talbot's* recent work on Nigeria shows a woeful ignorance of that author's earlier studies), but to the place where he should go—to the broad bosom of his own people.

This "Negro literary renaissance" has its existence at present only in the noxious night life of Greenwich Village neurotics who invented it, not for the black brothers' profit but their own. Nor do their darker dupes stand on any safer ground. If anyone, in public, should care to pick any decade between 1850 and 1910 I will undertake to present from among the Negroes of that decade as many writers and (with Schomburg to back me) as many lines of literary and artistic endeavor as he can show for this decade. And I go further! I will also undertake to show (with perhaps three exceptions) more able Negro writers for any decade in that period than can be found today. The challenge is open to anyone—but I do suggest that they read some of the things referred to before they take up the gage.

And now, a word in closing about this Negro Harlem which the neurotics of the New Jerusalem have discovered. It has brains: I say this because I know, having lived in it for twenty years. I can walk a mile from the place where this is written and converse with the ablest economist (I used to teach economics to whites) of our race. A few blocks north I can shake hands with our best biologist (barring Ernest Just).* I am acquainted with a journalist who slings niftier prose than anyone else whom I know, and a scholar whose book reveals a wider historic knowledge of racial contacts than any other scholar, white or black.* Their names? Well, you would not recognize them if I gave them here. For Harlem doesn't "boost" Harlem.

Some time soon there will be a genuine literary renaissance, a release of creative energy which will face the task of expressing the life-values of our people in prose-forms redolent with the tang of great literature, with poetry that bubbles up honestly and spontaneously out of the wide experience and understanding of the Head: out of the warm intuitions of the Heart. But, depend upon it, there will be nothing in that Real Renaissance for neurotics to exploit. The men and women who create it will have to stand crucifixion upon the publishers' calvarys; they will not care to publish their writings. (For so long as the Negro plays the mountebank or the coward so long will his Boys' Brigades be worth playing with). None of the white experts on "Negro" literature today seem to have heard of Taylor, Browne [sic] or Rogers, while they are tying ribbons on the little tabby-kittens whose reputations will be as dead as David's sow* a short ten years from now. Even so, in that day to come, will they ignore all those who will be doing the good work in which neurotics find no bait for their perverted self-esteem.

From the *Pittsburgh Courier* March 12, 1927

W. A. Domingo

Wilfred Adolphus Domingo was a steadfast supporter of socialism for much of his life. Although he was asked by Marcus Garvey, his longtime friend, to become the first editor of the *Negro World*, their different political perspectives quickly caused them to break ranks. Thereafter, Domingo became one of Garvey's fiercest foes, joining the editorial staff of the anti-Garvey *Messenger* and becoming a member of the African Blood Brotherhood (ABB).

Domingo was born in Kingston, Jamaica, on November 26, 1889, the son of a Spanish father and a Jamaican mother. He was orphaned at an early age and was raised by his maternal uncle in St. Ann's parish, Garvey's home. He did not meet Garvey, however, until taking a job in Kingston. The two collaborated on a pamphlet, *The Struggling Mass* (1910), dealing with the plight of Jamaica's hard-pressed peasants.

Leaving Jamaica in 1910, Domingo arrived shortly thereafter in Boston, where he hoped to study medicine. He soon abandoned this plan, however, and in 1912 moved to New York, where he established a business importing food from Jamaica. Domingo's interest in the struggles of the Black masses continued after his arrival in the United States. He encountered a number of Black political figures and introduced Garvey to them after he came to New York in 1916. Domingo met A. Philip Randolph and Chandler Owen in 1917, becoming a member of the Twenty-First Assembly District Socialist Club and working for the mayoral campaign of Morris Hillquit. Garvey called on his friend to become the editor of the *Negro World* in August 1918. Domingo, however, opposed what he considered to be Garvey's racialism. His decidedly socialist stance, evident in his editorials, led to his forced resignation in July 1919 (unfortunately, few copies of the *Negro World* from that time period have survived). Domingo's departure from the *Negro World* was no doubt hastened by his long piece titled "Socialism Imperilled, or the Negro—A Potential Menace to American Radicalism." The pamphlet, seized by the Lusk Committee in its raid on the Rand School in 1919, aroused the type of government scrutiny that Garvey wished to avoid.

After his break with Garvey, Domingo re-established his relationship with the *Messenger* group. He was a contributing editor to the magazine from 1919 to 1923. Here he freely aired his socialist beliefs in numerous articles, including "Socialism the Negroes' Hope." In this piece, Domingo expresses his concern that so few Negroes have adhered to socialism and posits that worldwide "the foremost exponents of socialism in Europe and America are characterized by the broadness of their vision towards all oppressed humanity." In "A New Negro and a New Day," he criticizes the capitalist system, which he feels benefits only the "favored few" while abusing all others, particularly Blacks. He equates Blacks with colonized peoples and states, "If Negroes would be free then they must unite with others who are struggling with freedom." His militancy is evident in "If We Must Die," taking its spirit from McKay's poem of the same name. Praising the new fighting attitude of Blacks, he maintains that the "New Negro has arrived with stiffened back bone, dauntless manhood, defiant eye, steady hand and a will of iron." It was such bold assertions that caused the government to consider the *Messenger* to be "the most dangerous of all the Negro publications" (qtd. in Kornweibel, *"Seeing Red"* 76).

In March 1920, Domingo founded a weekly newspaper, the *Emancipator,* with contributing editors including Richard B. Moore, Cyril Briggs, Randolph, and Owen. Though it lasted for only ten issues (many of which have not survived), the paper was important for its support of Marxism and its anti-Garveyite fervor. The paper expressed the belief that the darker races would rise up against their enslavers. Domingo also blistered Garvey for his "execrable exaggerations, staggering stupidities, blundering bombasts, and abominable asininities" (qtd. in Samuels 87).

Even while working on the *Emancipator* Domingo was involved with the *Messenger* group and with the ABB (for which he was director of publicity and propaganda). The *Messenger*, the *Emancipator*, and the *Crusader* all were venues for his Marxist, anti-Garvey positions. He was deeply involved with the *Messenger*'s Garvey Must Go campaign. It has been said that when Garvey was arrested, Domingo wired the government prosecutor, commending him for "Bagging the Tiger." As a result, Domingo has often been said to have betrayed Garvey, who accused him of being "a mischief maker and a barber shop and tailor shop philosopher who recently drifted into Communism" (qtd. in Hill and Bair 101). Harold Cruse went so far as to charge Domingo with being "a revolutionary Marxist first, a West Indian second, and a Negro last" (130). These accusations, however, are not fair to Domingo, who was, as he said, "not afraid to speak my mind" (Hill and Bair 113). He was a socialist and when he saw others were leaning in different directions, such as Black nationalism or communism, Domingo disagreed with them. Those with whom he disagreed included his ABB friends Moore and Briggs. Domingo often espoused unpopular positions, even when it would cost him dearly. He wrote articles favorable toward socialism in the *Negro World* even though such views were antithetical to Garvey. He broke with Garvey because of their differing views of race and class. However, when he felt the editors of the *Messenger* displayed anti–West Indian sentiments in their zeal to deport Garvey, he publicly disagreed and resigned his position (*Messenger* March 1923).[1]

After Domingo's resignation from the *Messenger*, he became an importer of West Indian foods. Yet even then, his contributions were considerable. As Irma Watkins-Owens points out, "By distributing his products to black retailers, he expanded race enterprise. His independent income allowed him to pursue his political views more freely" (130). These political interests increasingly focused less on American politics and more on the affairs of his native land. In 1936 he helped establish the Jamaica Progressive League, a group demanding self-government for the island. He also was involved in the formation of what was to become the People's National Party (PNP). His involvement with this nationalistic group led to his arrest and internment in 1941 in Jamaica. After more than a year in prison, he was released but was forced to remain in Jamaica an additional four years because the United States refused to grant him a visa. In 1947 he returned to America, where he resumed his fight for Jamaican independence. He broke with the PNP in the 1950s, when he criticized the planned

West Indian Federation, preferring instead an independent Jamaica. After suffering a debilitating stroke in 1964, Domingo died in New York City on February 14, 1968.

NOTES

The bulk of Domingo's papers are in private collections.
1. For more on the *Messenger*'s West Indian position, see Kornweibel, *No Crystal Stair* 132–75.

BIBLIOGRAPHY

Cruse, Harold. *The Crisis of the Negro Intellectual.* 1967. New York: Quill, 1984.

Foner, Philip S. *American Socialism and Black Americans: From the Age of Jackson to World War II.* Westport, CT: Greenwood P, 1977.

Hill, Robert, ed. *The Marcus Garvey and Universal Negro Improvement Association Papers.* 9 vols. Berkeley: U of California P, 1983–.

Hill, Robert, and Barbara Bair, eds. *Marcus Garvey: Life and Lessons.* Berkeley: U of California P, 1987.

James, Winston. *Holding Aloft the Banner of Ethiopia: Caribbean Radicalism in Early Twentieth-Century America.* New York: Verso, 1998.

Kornweibel, Theodore, Jr. *No Crystal Stair: Black Life and the "Messenger," 1917–1928.* Westport, CT: Greenwood P, 1975.

———. "Seeing Red": Federal Campaign against Black Militancy, 1919–1925. Bloomington: Indiana UP, 1998.

Samuels, Wilfred David. "Five Afro-Caribbean Voices in American Culture, 1917–1929: Hubert H. Harrison, Wilfred A. Domingo, Richard B. Moore, Cyril V. Briggs, and Claude McKay." Diss. U of Iowa, 1977.

Watkins-Owens, Irma. *Blood Relations: Caribbean Immigrants and the Harlem Renaissance.* Bloomington: Indiana UP, 1996.

Socialism the Negroes' Hope

It is a regrettable and disconcerting anomaly that, despite their situation as the economic, political and social door mat of the world, Negroes do not embrace the philosophy of socialism, and in greater numbers than they now do. It is an anomaly because it is reasonable to expect those who are lowest down to be the ones who would most quickly comprehend the need for a change in their status and welcome any doctrine which holds forth any hope of human elevation. In matters of religion they respond and react logically and naturally enough, for to them, the religion of Christ, the lowly Nazarene, brings definite assurance of surcease from earthly pains and the hope of celestial readjustment of mundane equalities. Their acceptance of the Christian religion with its present day emphasis upon an after-life enjoyment of the good things denied them on the earth is conclusive proof of their dissatisfaction with their present lot, and is an earnest [*sic*] of their susceptibility to Socialism, which intends to do for human beings what Christianity promises to do for them in less material regions.

That they and all oppressed dark peoples will be the greatest beneficiaries in a socialist world has not been sufficiently emphasized by Socialist propaganda among Negroes.

Perhaps this is not clearly understood, but a little examination of the facts will prove this to be the case.

Throughout the world Negroes occupy a position of absolute inferiority to the white race. This is true whether they are black Frenchmen, black Englishmen, black Belgians or black Americans.

As between themselves and the masses of white proletarians their lives are more circumscribed, their ambitions more limited and their opportunities for the enjoyment of liberty and happiness more restricted. White workingmen of England who are Socialists are immeasurably the political and social superiors of the average Negro in the West Indies or Africa; white workingmen of France who are Socialists are unquestionably the political and social superiors of Senegalese and Madagascan Negroes; white workingmen of the United States who are Socialists are indisputably the social and political superiors of the millions of Negroes below the Mason and Dixon line; yet despite their relative and absolute superiority these white workers are fighting for a world freed from oppression and exploitation, whilst Negroes who are oppressed cling to past and present economic ideals with the desperation of a drowning man.

Socialism as an economic doctrine is merely the pure Christianity preached by Jesus, and practiced by the early Christians adapted to the more complex conditions of modern life. It makes no distinction as to race, nationality or creed, but like Jesus it says "Come unto me all ye who are weary and heavy laden and I will give you rest."* It is to procure that rest that millions of oppressed peoples are flocking to the scarlet banner of international Socialism.

So far, although having greater need for its equalizing principles than white workingmen, Negroes have been slow to realize what has already dawned upon nearly every other oppressed people: That Socialism is their only hope.

The 384,000,000 natives of India groaning under the exploitation of the handful of English manufacturers, merchants and officials who profit out of their labor are turning from Lloyd George and the capitalistic Liberal Party to Robert Smillie, the Socialist and the Independent Labor Party. The 4,000,000 Irish who suffer national strangulation at the hands of British industrialists and militarists have turned to the Socialists of England for relief besides becoming Socialists themselves. The Egyptians who are of Negro admixture being convinced that their only hope for freedom from British exploitation is in international Socialism are uniting forces with British Socialists and organized labor. In fact, every oppressed group of the world is today turning from Clemenceau, Lloyd George and Wilson to the citadel of Socialism, Moscow. In this they are all in advance of Western Negroes with the exception of little groups in the United States and a relatively well-organized group in the Island of Trinidad, British West Indies.

Because of ignorant and unscrupulous leadership, Negroes are influenced to give their support to those institutions which oppress them, but if they would only do a little independent thinking without the aid of preacher, politician or press they would quickly realize that the very men like Thomas Dixon, author of "The Clansman," Senators Hoke Smith of Georgia and Overman of North Carolina,* who are fighting Socialism or as they maliciously call it Bolshevism, are the same men who exhaust every unfair means to villify [sic], oppress and oppose Negroes. If anything should commend Socialism to Negroes, nothing can do so more eloquently than the attitude and opinions of its most influential opponents toward people who are not white.

On the other hand, the foremost exponents of Socialism in Europe and America are characterized by the broadness of their vision towards all oppressed humanity. It was the Socialist Vendervelde* of Belgium, who protested against the Congo atrocities practiced upon

Negroes; it was the late Keir Hardie and Philip Snowdon* of England, who condemned British rule in Egypt; and in the United States it was the Socialist, Eugene V. Debs, who refused to speak in Southern halls from which Negroes were excluded. Today, it is the revolutionary Socialist Lenin, who analyzed the infamous League of Nations and exposed its true character; it is he as leader of the Communist Congress at Moscow, who sent out the proclamation: "Slaves of the colonies in Africa and Asia! The hour of proletarian dictatorship in Europe will be the hour of your release!"

From the *Messenger* July 1919

"If We Must Die"

America won the war that was alleged to be fought for the purpose of making the world safe for democracy, but in the light of recent happenings in Washington, the Capital city, and Chicago, it would seem as though the United States is not a part of the world. In order to win the war President Wilson employed "force, unstinted force," and those who expect to bring any similar desirable termination to a just cause can do no less than follow the splendid example set them by the reputed spokesman of humanity. That the lesson did not take long to penetrate the minds of Negroes is demonstrated by the change that has taken place in their demeanor and tactics. No longer are Negroes willing to be shot down or hunted from place to place like wild beasts; no longer will they flee from their homes and leave their property to the tender mercies of the howling and cowardly mob. They have changed, and now they intend to give men's account of themselves. If death is to be their portion, New Negroes are determined to make their dying a costly investment for all concerned. If they must die they are determined that they shall not travel through the valley of the shadow of death alone, but that some of their oppressors shall be their companions.*

This new spirit is but a reflex of the great war, and it is largely due to the insistent and vigorous agitation carried on by younger men of the race. The demand is uncompromisingly made for either liberty or death, and since death is likely to be a two-edged sword it will be to the advantage of those in a position to do so to give the race its long-denied liberty.

The new spirit animating Negroes is not confined to the United States, where it is most acutely manifested, but is simmering beneath the surface in every country where the race is oppressed. The Washington and Chicago outbreaks should be regarded as symptoms of a great pandemic, and the Negroes as courageous surgeons who performed the necessary though painful operation. That the remedy is efficacious is beyond question. It has brought results, for as a consequence the eyes of the entire world are focused upon the racial situation in the United States. The world knows now that the New Negroes are determined to observe the primal law of self-preservation whenever civil laws break down; to assist the authorities to preserve order and prevent themselves and families from being murdered in cold blood. Surely, no one can sincerely object to this new and laudable determination. Justification for this course is not lacking, for it is the white man's own Bible that says "Those who live by the sword shall perish by the sword,"* and since white men believe in force, Negroes who have mimicked them for nearly three centuries must copy them in that respect. Since fire must be fought with hell fire, and diamond alone can cut diamond, Negroes realize that force alone is an effective medium to counteract force. Counter irritants are useful in curing diseases, and Negroes are being driven by their white fellow citizens to investigate the curative values inherent in mass action, revolvers and other lethal devices when applied to social diseases.

The New Negro has arrived with stiffened back bone, dauntless manhood, defiant eye, steady hand and a will of iron. His creed is admirably summed up in the poem of Claude McKay ["If We Must Die"], the black Jamaican poet, who is carving out for himself a niche in the Hall of Fame[.] [The article concludes with a copy of "If We Must Die," omitted here but reprinted on page 283 in this anthology.]

From the *Messenger* September 1919

A New Negro and a New Day

A new spirit is abroad in the world. Ancient wrongs and oppressions are melting before the rising wrath of the masses of the entire world. This new spirit is a direct result of the war which destroyed millions of lives and enormous quantities of the products of labor, besides intensifying the sufferings of toilers everywhere. Just as the world war embraced all the races of mankind so have its consequences, typified by the new spirit, permeated all peoples. None is free from its influence; all are making demands for the democracy and justice that were eloquently mouthed by those who had and still have the power to make those words living realities. For the first time in human history have the lowly workers of the world asserted themselves and given intelligent expression to their needs. Subject races, small nationalities and oppressed workers are realizing their kinship. The white workers of Russia, the yellow coolies of Korea, the brown ryots* of India and the black toilers of Africa, the West Indies and the United States are making similar demands upon their oppressors, although they and their masters in many instances are alike in race, color, language and religion. The former speak the language of the oppressed; the latter the language of the oppressor. Labor is the common denominator of the working class of the world. Exploitation is the common denominator of oppressors everywhere.

Many oppress because they profit from it, or think they do. There is a community of interests between oppressors. The real beneficiaries of exploitation are a small minority. They maintain their position because they control the machinery of government and the vehicles of public information—the school, church, stage, press and platform. These agencies support similar institutions. They defend present economic conditions, defame the working class, white and black, and abuse the Negro race as a whole.

As a considerable part of the American working class, Negroes have grievances against those who profit from the present system which operates against the interest of all workers. As Negroes they have specific reasons for desiring the downfall of those who manipulate public opinion for the creation of race prejudice which in turn divides the black and white workers of the country into warring camps. The workers of both races suffer from this vicious propaganda and it is to their interest to change conditions which make it possible. The reason for this propaganda and its resultant division of the working class is to rob them of the product of their labor. And the robbery of the workers of the product of their toil is sanctioned by our present system of government. Even if the black and white workers unite industrially, as they are slowly but surely doing, they will still be robbed of some of the product of their toil unless they unite for working-class political action. To stop present robbery and remove the cause of most of our racial friction it is necessary to change the system which legalizes the robbery.

In our present society most human being[s] must work to live. They must have access to a job. The private owners of land, factories, railroads, mines and machinery have in their power to deny their fellows work. And without work a man and his family must suffer. Because of the developments brought about by inventions a man can produce more than is necessary for the consumption of himself and his family. But because the things produced do not belong to the producer but to the owner of his job the former finds wages, which represent a small portion of the things he has produced, insufficient to keep himself and his family in a reasonable degree of comfort. The owners of jobs have common interests and pay only as much wages as they are forced to pay. Their interests are opposed to those of their employees. And color or race makes no difference. Jews underpay Jews, and Negro employers rob their employees regardless of race or color. The interests of all workers are alike. Many workers do not realize this and work against their own interests. They refuse to join labor unions or exclude some workers because of their color. They also vote to strengthen the political chains which enslave them.

This is true of the Negro worker who votes for the Republican party which is frankly the party of Big Business. It is the party of the landlord and banker, black and white, Jew or Gentile. But most Negroes vote for the Republican party because it was the party of Lincoln and because he had freed their fathers. Whatever debt Negroes owed the Republican party has been paid long ago. Besides, it is the Republican party that delivered the Negro into the hands of the South in 1876 when Hayes was seated on condition that he withdraw federal troops from the South. For nearly fifty years the Republican party has been in power, controlling the Army, Navy and Supreme Court and during that period the oppression of Negroes has been cumulatively increased.

The only party that can make any appeal to Negroes that is based upon mutual interests is the Socialist Party. It is composed of enlightened workers who repudiate the Du Bois-Gompers tactics of "rewarding friends and punishing enemies." These workers realize that the chain of labor is as strong as its weakest link and from the standpoint of class consciousness Negroes are, through no fault of theirs, the weakest link.

If Negroes would be free then they must unite with others who are struggling for freedom. And it is the Socialists who are striving to free America from the throes of wage slavery. The slogan "those who would be free must themselves strike the first blow" gains added importance in the present political struggle. If Negroes think themselves freer than white workingmen then let them vote for Mr. Harding and the Republican party which represent the forces of reaction; if they feel themselves less free than white working men then let them vote with their fellow workers of all colors who repudiate both the Democratic and Republican tickets and vote for Eugene V. Debs, freedom and progress on November 2.

From the *Messenger* November 1920

[Everywhere Bolshevism brings terror to the heart of Imperialism]

Everywhere Bolshevism brings terror to the heart of Imperialism, secret diplomacy, hypocrisy and oppression, and yet, the chieftains of this liberating doctrine are afraid of some of the very races whom they would free.

This is the great paradox—the great tragedy, some of the very Indians and negroes are the potential hangmen of their only disinterested friend,—Soviet Russia.

It is not idle fear that Trotzky voices. It is easy for propaganda to reach a literate people; but it is a tremendously more difficult task for it to reach an illiterate people. Poland and Roumania illustrate this.

However, there are signs of negro awakening. All over the West Indies there are strikes and unrest; in South Africa, benighted and oppressed land, 40,000 natives are on strike, and two colored delegates to a labor conference in Johannesburg have been hailed as comrades and brothers. One of them even seconded a motion to support Soviet Russia to the limit. Social equality was also recognized as a prerequisite to industrial unity and racial harmony. The dawn is breaking in Negrodom.

Black soldiers from the West Indies, South Africa and a certain self-righteous republic, imbued with the spirit of the New Negro will not be willing tools of those who now rule Egypt, India, the West

Indies, Africa and Arkansas with machine guns in the destruction of the people's non-imperialist government of Russia.

We appreciate Trotzky's fear, but feel that it is a little over-drawn. The war has opened the eyes of the darker races a little. They will no longer be their own enslavers. On the Comrades of Trotzky in other lands devolves the duty of paying attention to the "needs" of the black masses whom the Russian war minister sees as the only possible material in the hands of the imperialists of the world.

From *Revolutionary Radicalism: Its History, Purpose and Tactics* (1920). Originally published in the *Emancipator* March 13, 1920

Socialism Imperilled, or the Negro— A Potential Menace to American Radicalism

[F]ailure to make negroes class conscious is the greatest potential menace to the establishment of socialism in America whether by means of the ballot or through a dictatorship of the proletariat, and in this must all Socialists and radicals, whether Right or Left Wingers, see their danger. For the sake of their cause, if not for the sake of negro workers, must they confront this problem squarely and firmly. How can the disaster portrayed be escaped, is the task of this booklet to point out. In the first place danger must not be ignored by a gesture or met by a theory. It must be removed. To do this it is necessary for American radicals to do the following:

First.—They must unequivocally condemn all forms of injustice practiced against negroes and encouch same in their declarations of principles and platforms, and Socialist officials and legislators must embrace every opportunity to make public denouncements of lynch-ings, etc.

Second.—They must give the negro more prominence in their discussions whether by speech or in their publications relative to injus-tices done in America.

Third.—They must seek to attract negroes to their meetings and to induce them to become members of their organizations.

Fourth.—Those who are members of labor unions must work for the repeal of all racially discriminatory practices in their organiza-tions and endeavor to gain the admission of negroes into them on terms of equality.

Fifth.—They must have specially prepared propaganda showing negroes how they as a group are likely to benefit and improve their social and economic status by any radical change in the present economic system.

Sixth.—Radical negro publications must be supported financially even if subventions are to be made to them.

Seventh.—Radical white speakers must be instructed to try and reach negro audiences while competent paid negro speakers must be kept touring the country spreading radical propaganda. So far, the Socialist Party has taken a definite position on the 14th and 15th Amendments, but this fact is not known to the majority of negroes. It is only known to a few Northern negroes in districts where their votes were catered for. This, and even stronger pronouncements on the negro, should be distributed among the race in the South, because it is the Southern negroes who are most likely to be used as mercenary White Guards. Giving the negro more publicity would induce them to read more radical literature. Already many negroes read the "Call," the "Liberator" and "Pearson's"* for that reason. The same will, no doubt, be true of radical lectures. Induce intelligent negroes to attend radical meetings and to become members of radical organizations and radical propaganda will spread among them. Most negroes avoid these meetings at present because they fear social discrimination. More social contact carries great potential propaganda value. It has healing in its wings. If it becomes known among negroes that Socialists are fighting discrimination in labor unions they will soon learn that Socialists are their friends. At present, as a result of persistent capitalistic misrepresentation negroes identify Socialists with the discriminatory practices of the American Federation of Labor.***

> Excerpt from "Socialism Imperilled, or the Negro—A Potential Menace to American Radicalism." Reprinted in *Revolutionary Radicalism: Its History, Purpose and Tactics* (1920).

Gift of the Black Tropics

Almost unobserved, America plays her usual rôle in the meeting, mixing and welding of the colored peoples of the earth. A dusky tribe of destiny seekers, these brown and black and yellow folk, eyes filled with visions of an alien heritage—palm-fringed seashores, murmuring streams, luxuriant hills and vales—have made an epical march from the far corners of the earth to the Port of New York and America. They bring the gift of the black tropics to America and to their kinsmen. With them come vestiges of a quaint folk life, other social traditions, and as for the first time in their lives, colored people of Spanish, French, Dutch, Arabian, Danish, Portuguese, British and native African ancestry meet and move together, there comes into Negro life the stir and leavening that is uniquely American. Despite his inconsiderable numbers, the black foreigner is a considerable factor and figure. It is not merely his picturesqueness that he brings, his lean, sun-burnt features, quaint manners and speech, his tropical incongruities, these as with all folkways rub off in less than a generation— it is his spirit that counts and has counted in the interplay of his life with the native population.

According to the census for 1920 there were in the United States 73,803 foreign-born Negroes; of that number 36,613, or approximately 50 per cent, lived in New York City, 28,184 of them in the Borough of Manhattan. They formed slightly less than 20 per cent of the total Negro population of New York.

Here they have their first contact with each other, with large numbers of American Negroes, and with the American brand of race prejudice. Divided by tradition, culture, historical background and group perspective, these diverse peoples are gradually hammered into a loose unit by the impersonal force of congested residential segregation. Unlike others of the foreign-born, black immigrants find it impossible to segregate themselves into colonies; too dark of complexion to pose as Cubans or some other Negroid but alien-tongued foreigners, they are inevitably swallowed up in black Harlem. Their situation requires an adjustment unlike that of any other class of the immigrant population; and but for the assistance of their kinfolk they would be capsized almost on the very shores of their haven.

For 1920 to 1923 the foreign-born Negro population of the United States was increased nearly 40 per cent through the entry of 30,849 Africans (black). In 1921 the high-water mark of 9,873 was registered. This increase was not permanent, for in 1923 there was an exit of 1,525 against an entry of 7,554. If the 20 per cent that left that year is an index of the proportion leaving annually, it is safe to estimate a net increase of about 24,000 between 1920 and 1923. If the newcomers are distributed throughout the country in the same proportion as their predecessors, the present foreign-born Negro population of Harlem is about 35,000. These people are, therefore, a formidable minority whose presence cannot be ignored or discounted. It is this large body of foreign-born who contribute those qualities that make New York so unlike Pittsburgh, Washington, Chicago and other cities with large aggregations of American Negroes.

The largest number come from the British West Indies and are attracted to America mainly by economic reasons: though considerable numbers of the younger generation come for the purposes of education. The next largest group consists of Spanish-speaking Negroes from Latin America. Distinct because of their language, and sufficiently numerous to maintain themselves as a cultural unit, the Spanish element has but little contact with the English-speaking majority. For the most part they keep to themselves and follow in the main certain definite occupational lines. A smaller group, French-speaking, have emigrated from Haiti and the French West Indies. There are also a few Africans, a batch of voluntary pilgrims over the old track of the slave-traders.

Among the English-speaking West Indian population of Harlem are some 8,000 natives of the American Virgin Islands. A considerable part of these people were forced to migrate to the mainland as a consequence of the operation of the Volstead [sic] Act which destroyed the lucrative rum industry and helped to reduce the number of foreign vessels that used to call at the former free port of Charlotte Amelia for various stores. Despite their long Danish connection these people are culturally and linguistically English, rather than Danish. Unlike the British Negroes in New York, the Virgin Islanders take an intelligent and aggressive interest in the affairs of their former home, and are organized to co-operate with their brothers there who are valiantly struggling to substitute civil government for the present naval administration of the islands.

To the average American Negro, all English-speaking black foreigners are West Indians, and by that is usually meant British subjects. There is a general assumption that there is everything in common among West Indians, though nothing can be further from the truth. West Indians regard themselves as Antiguans or Jamaicans as the case might be, and a glance at the map will quickly reveal the physical obstacles that militate against homogeneity of population; separations of many sorts, geographical, political and cultural tend everywhere to make and crystallize local characteristics.

This undiscriminating attitude on the part of native Negroes, as well as the friction generated from contact between the two groups, has created an artificial and defensive unity among the islanders which reveals itself in an instinctive closing of their ranks when attacked by outsiders; but among themselves organization along insular lines is the general rule. Their social grouping, however, does not follow insular precedents. Social gradation is determined in the islands by family connections, education, wealth and position. As each island is a complete society in itself, Negroes occupy from the lowliest to the most exalted positions. The barrier separating the colored aristocrat from the laboring class of the same color is as difficult to surmount as a similar barrier between Englishmen. Most of the islanders in New York are from the middle, artisan and laboring classes. Arriving in a country whose every influence is calculated to democratize their race and destroy the distinctions they had been accustomed to, even those West Indians whose stations in life have been of the lowest soon lose whatever servility they brought with them. In its place they substitute all of the self-assertiveness of the classes they formerly paid deference to.

West Indians have been coming to the United States for over a century. The part they have played in Negro progress is conceded to be important. As early as 1827 a Jamaican, John Brown Russwurm, one of the founders of Liberia, was the first colored man to be graduated from an American college and to publish a newspaper in this country;* sixteen years later his fellow countryman, Peter Ogden, organized in New York City the first Odd-Fellows Lodge for Negroes. Prior to the Civil War, West Indian contribution to American Negro life was so great that Dr. W. E. B. Du Bois, in his *Souls of Black Folk*, credits them with main responsibility for the manhood program presented by the race in the early decades of the last century. Indicative of their tendency to blaze new paths is the achievement of John W. A. Shaw of Antigua who, in the early '90's of the last century, passed the civil service tests and became deputy commissioner of taxes for the County of Queens.

It is probably not realized, indeed, to what extent West Indian Negroes have contributed to the wealth, power and prestige of the United States. Major-General Goethals, chief engineer and builder of the Panama Canal, has testified in glowing language to the fact that when all other labor was tried and failed it was the black men of the

Caribbean whose intelligence, skill, muscle and endurance made the union of the Pacific and the Atlantic a reality.

Coming to the United States from countries in which they had experienced no legalized social or occupational disabilities, West Indians very naturally found it difficult to adapt themselves to the tasks that are, by custom, reserved for Negroes in the North. Skilled at various trades and having a contempt for body service and menial work, many of the immigrants apply for positions that the average American Negro has been schooled to regard as restricted to white men only, with the result that through their persistence and dogged-ness in fighting white labor, West Indians have in many cases been pioneers and shock troops to open a way for Negroes into new fields of employment.

This freedom from spiritual inertia characterizes the women no less than the men, for it is largely through them that the occupational field has been broadened for colored women in New York. By their determination, sometimes reinforced by a dexterous use of their hat-pins, these women have made it possible for members of their race to enter the needle trades freely.

It is safe to say that West Indian representation in the skilled trades is relatively large; this is also true of the professions, especially medicine and dentistry. Like the Jew, they are forever launching out in business, and such retail businesses as are in the hands of Negroes in Harlem are largely in the control of the foreign-born. While American Negroes predominate in forms of business like barber shops and pool rooms in which there is no competition from white men, West Indians turn their efforts almost invariably to fields like grocery stores, tailor shops, jewelry stores and fruit vending in which they meet the fiercest kind of competition. In some of these fields they are the pioneers or the only surviving competitors of white business concerns. In more ambitious business enterprises like real estate and insurance they are relatively numerous. The only Casino and moving picture theatre operated by Negroes in Harlem is in the hands of a native of one of the small islands. On Seventh Avenue a West Indian woman conducts a millinery store that would be a credit to Fifth Avenue.

The analogy between the West Indian and the Jew may be carried farther; they are both ambitious, eager for education, willing to engage in business, argumentative, aggressive and possessed of great proselytizing zeal for any cause they espouse. West Indians are great contenders for their rights and because of their respect for law are inclined to be litigious. In addition, they are, as a whole, home loving, hard-working and frugal. Like their English exemplars they are fond of sport, lack a sense of humor (yet the greatest black comedian of America, Bert Williams, was from the Bahamas) and are very serious and intense in their attitude toward life. They save their earnings and are mindful of their folk in the homeland, as the volume of business of the Money Order and Postal Savings Departments of College Station Post Office will attest.

Ten years ago it was possible to distinguish the West Indian in Harlem, especially during the summer months. Accustomed to wearing cool, light-colored garments in the tropics, he would stroll along Lenox Avenue on a hot day resplendent in white shoes and flannel pants, the butt of many a jest from his American brothers who, to-day, have adopted the styles that they formerly derided. This trait of non-conformity manifested by the foreign-born has irritated American Negroes, who resent the implied self-sufficiency, and as a result there is a considerable amount of prejudice against West Indians. It is claimed that they are proud and arrogant; that they think themselves superior to the natives. And although educated Negroes of New York are loudest in publicly decrying the hostility between the two groups, it is nevertheless true that feelings against West Indians is strongest among members of that class. This is explainable on the ground of professional jealousy and competition for leadership. As the islanders press forward and upward they meet the same kind of opposition from the native Negro that the Jew and other ambitious white aliens receive from white Americans. Naturalized West Indians have found from experience that American Negroes are reluctant to concede them the right to political leadership even when qualified intellectually. Unlike their American brothers, the islanders are free from those traditions that bind them to any party and, as a consequence, are independent to the point of being radical. Indeed, it is they who largely compose the few political and economic radicals in Harlem; without them the genuinely radical movement among New York Negroes would be unworthy of attention.

There is a diametrical difference between American and West Indian Negroes in their worship. While large sections of the former are inclined to indulge in displays of emotionalism that border on hysteria, the latter, in their Wesleyan Methodist and Baptist churches maintain in the face of the assumption that people from the tropics are necessarily emotional, all the punctilious emotional restraint characteristic of their English background. In religious radicalism the foreign-born are again pioneers and propagandists. The only modernist church among the thousands of Negroes in New York (and perhaps the country) is led by a West Indian, Rev. E. Ethelred Brown,* an ordained Unitarian minister, and is largely supported by his fellow islanders.

In facing the problem of race prejudice, foreign-born Negroes, and West Indians in particular, are forced to undergo considerable adjustment. Forming a racial majority in their own countries and not being accustomed to discrimination expressly felt as racial, they rebel against the "color line" as they find it in America. For while color and caste lines tend to converge in the islands, it is nevertheless true that because of the ratio in population, historical background and traditions of rebellions before and since their emancipation, West Indians of color do not have their activities, social, occupational and otherwise, determined by their race. Color plays a part but it is not the prime determinant of advancement; hence, the deep feeling of resentment when the "color line," legal or customary, is met and found to be a barrier to individual progress. For this reason the West Indian has thrown himself whole-heartedly into the fight against lynching, discrimination and the other disabilities from which Negroes in America suffer.

It must be remembered that the foreign-born black men and women, more so even than other groups of immigrants, are the hardiest and most venturesome of their folk. They were dissatisfied at home, and it is to be expected that they would not be altogether satisfied with limitation of opportunity here when they have staked so much to gain enlargement of opportunity. They do not suffer from the local anesthesia of custom and pride which makes otherwise intolerable situations bearable for the home-staying majorities.

Just as the West Indian has been a sort of leaven in the American loaf, so the American Negro is beginning to play a reciprocal rôle in the life of the foreign Negro communities, as for instance, the recent championing of the rights of Haiti and Liberia and the Virgin Islands, as well as the growing resentment at the treatment of natives in the

African colonial dependencies. This world-wide reaction of the darker races to their common as well as local grievances is one of the most significant facts of recent development. Exchange of views and sympathy, extension and co-operation of race organizations beyond American boundaries, principally in terms of economic and educational projects, but also to a limited extent in political affairs, are bound to develop on a considerable scale in the near future. Formerly, ties have been almost solely through the medium of church missionary enterprises.

It has been asserted that the movement headed by the most-advertised of all West Indians, Marcus Garvey, absentee "president" of the continent of Africa, represents the attempt of West Indian peasants to solve the American race problem. This is no more true than it would be to say that the editorial attitude of *The Crisis* during the war reflected the spirit of American Negroes respecting their grievances or that the late Booker T. Washington successfully delimited the educational aspirations of his people. The support given Garvey by a certain type of his countrymen is partly explained by their group reaction to attacks made upon him because of his nationality. On the other hand, the earliest and most persistent exposures of Garvey's multitudinous schemes were initiated by West Indians in New York like Cyril Briggs and the writer.

Prejudice against West Indians is in direct ratio to their number; hence its strength in New York where they are heavily concentrated. It is not unlike the hostility between Englishmen and Americans of the same racial stock. It is to be expected that the feeling will always be more or less present between the immigrant and the native born. However it does not extend to the children of the two groups, as they are subject to the same environment and develop identity of speech and psychology. Then, too, there has been an appreciable amount of intermarriage, especially between foreign-born men and native women. Not to be ignored is the fact that congestion in Harlem has forced both groups to be less discriminating in accepting lodgers, thus making for reconciling contacts.

The outstanding contribution of West Indians to American Negro life is the insistent assertion of their manhood in an environment that demands too much servility and unprotesting acquiescence from men of African blood. This unwillingness to conform and be standardized, to accept tamely an inferior status and abdicate their humanity, finds an open expression in the activities of the foreign-born Negro in America.

Their dominant characteristic is that of blazing new paths, breaking the bonds that would fetter the feet of a virile people—a spirit eloquently expressed in the defiant lines of the Jamaican poet, Claude McKay:

> Like men we'll face the murderous, cowardly pack,
> Pressed to the wall, dying, but fighting back.

From *The New Negro* (New York: Albert & Charles Boni, 1925)

Frank R. Crosswaith

The work of Frank Rudolph Crosswaith centered on the need for Blacks and Whites to unite against common foes. With this goal, he worked for a number of organizations intending to initiate Blacks into the labor movement while persuading White workers to accept them into their ranks. He was, therefore, adamantly opposed to any groups, from Black nationalists to communists, that he felt disrupted racial integration.[1]

Crosswaith was born in Fredericksted, St. Croix, Virgin Islands, on July 16, 1892. A product of mixed race, Crosswaith was educated at the University Preparatory School in Fredericksted before immigrating to the United States about 1907.

After he had spent several years in the United States Navy, the socialist cause attracted Crosswaith's attention. He was awarded a scholarship to the Rand School in New York City while working as an elevator operator. Upon his graduation, Crosswaith taught economics and sociology at the school for five years. He also proved to be a skilled speaker and was frequently assigned by the Socialist Party to address various groups on labor issues.

By 1925, Crosswaith had founded the Trade Union Committee for Organizing Negro Workers. He helped to unionize motion picture operators, barbers, elevator operators, and laundry workers. The organization had limited success, however, in integrating the unions because of White labor resistance, and insufficient funding resulted in its dissolution in 1926.

Crosswaith then became a leading organizer for A. Philip Randolph's Brotherhood of Sleeping Car Porters (BSCP). Randolph and other leaders of the BSCP, including Virgin Islander Ashley Totten, aided the twelve thousand porters and maids who worked for the Pullman Company, long known for its abusive treatment of Black workers. Crosswaith hoped that the success of the Brotherhood would have a galvanizing effect on Black workers, causing them to see trade unionism as their best chance for economic salvation. Toward this end, he wrote a series of articles for the *Messenger* advocating the BSCP. "Toward the Home Stretch" extols the success of the Brotherhood, urging organized labor to remove the color barrier and warning organized capital that the days of the unorganized and powerless Black worker were over.

Crosswaith remained committed to socialism even as many Black radicals were turning to communism. Throughout his life, Crosswaith maintained that communists were using Blacks merely to advance their own cause. He wrote regularly for the *New Leader*, a socialist paper with a largely White readership, and for the *Chicago Defender*, becoming the first Black socialist to receive a byline in a major Black newspaper. A lead article written for the *New Leader*, "Black Man's Burden: Harlem Doubly Enslaved by Color and Capitalism," provides Crosswaith's insights into the workings of the capital of Black America. Largely ignoring the cultural aspects of the Harlem Renaissance, Crosswaith saw Harlem as an exploited community, one taken advantage of by White businessmen, "the capitalist-minded Negro," organized labor with its White chauvinism, landlords, and mainstream politicians. Not surprisingly, he felt that the only way to improve the situation was for Blacks and Whites to come together and embrace the socialist message (Seabrook 42–50).

Crosswaith's chief accomplishment was likely his organization of the Negro Labor Committee (NLC) in 1935. The group, created by the International Ladies Garment Workers Union, with which Crosswaith had a long affiliation, attempted to integrate the American Federation of Labor unions. The NLC not only "assisted Black workers into unions, but more importantly . . . it did, indeed, bring about the beginning of continued solidarity and cooperation between Black and white trade unionists in New York City" (Walter 43). He expounded upon these views in the sixty-page pamphlet that he wrote with Alfred Baker Lewis, *True Freedom for Negro and White Labor* (1935).

During the 1920s and 1930s Crosswaith sought office frequently (and unsuccessfully) on the Socialist Party line. Several factors hampered his runs for office. First, he seldom had time to mount an organized campaign, as he was often away on speaking engagements. Furthermore, his virulent attacks on communists and his less strident but still biting barbs at White unionists guilty of chauvinism made for some powerful enemies.

By the 1940s, Crosswaith had distanced himself from the Socialist Party. He did remain committed, however, to the labor movement and the need for improved housing for lower-income people. He worked for the American Labor Party and as a member of the New York City Housing Authority in addition to helping to organize Randolph's proposed march on Washington in 1941. Crosswaith continued to advance these causes through his role as a well-recognized public figure until his death in Chicago on June 17, 1965.

NOTES

Crosswaith's papers are at the Schomburg Center in New York City.

1. Crosswaith did, however, have an early flirtation with Garveyism from 1917 to 1920.

BIBLIOGRAPHY

Foner, Philip S. *American Socialism and Black Americans: From the Age of Jackson to World War II.* Westport, CT: Greenwood P, 1977.

Jones, James T. "Crosswaith, Frank Rudolph." *Dictionary of Negro Biography.* Ed. Rayford W. Logan and Michael R. Winston. New York: Norton, 1982. 142–44.

Kornweibel, Theodore, Jr. *No Crystal Stair: Black Life and the "Messenger," 1917–1928.* Westport, CT: Greenwood P, 1975.

Marcus, Irwin. "Frank Crosswaith: Black Scholar, Labor Leader, & Reformer." *Negro History Bulletin* 37 (Aug.–Sept. 1974): 287–88.

Opdycke, Sandra. "Crosswaith, Frank Rudolph." *American National Biography.* Ed. John A. Garraty and Mark C. Carnes. Vol. 5. New York: Oxford UP, 1999. 793–95.

Pfeffer, Paula F. "Crosswaith, Frank Rudolph." *Encyclopedia of African American Culture and History.* Ed. Jack Salzman, David Lionel Smith, and Cornel West (New York: Macmillan, 1996): 697–98.

Seabrook, John H. "Black and White Unite: The Career of Frank R. Crosswaith." Diss. Rutgers U, 1980.

Walter, John C. "Frank R. Crosswaith and the Negro Labor Committee in Harlem, 1925–1939." *Afro-Americans in New York Life and History* 3 (July 1979): 35–49.

Watkins-Owens, Irma. *Blood Relations: Caribbean Immigrants and the Harlem Renaissance.* Bloomington: Indiana UP, 1996.

Black Man's Burden: Harlem Doubly Enslaved by Color and Capitalism

To the enterprising young hunter of literary laurels and the profit propelled publishers of modern journalism, Negro Harlem has suddenly loomed upon the journalistic horizon as the Klondike appeared to the gold seekers a generation or so ago.

From near and far they come, pen in hand, to uncover before a gasping and gullible world the hidden secrets of black Harlem. They assume—these scribes—the pose of a Howard Carter or a Lord Carnarvon* about to unearth Tutankhamen's buried treasures and tickle the flickering fancy of their readers. Most of what they write about Harlem is misleading and much is false. Many of them approach Harlem with a sympathetic attitude. They mean well, but they come expecting to find countless curios of cave-dwelling days; they hope to discover that long-looked-for, but never-found "thing" which makes the Negro in one instance the victim of savage hostility and again the object of sympathy and benevolence; in other words, they enter this "city in itself" to prove the old claim that the Negro is "different"; that he reacts differently, lives differently, worships differently, and that there is a great "difference" and "distance" between life in Negro Harlem and life in the rest of New York City, all of which is not true.

Negro Harlem Typically American

Negro Harlem is a typical American industrial community containing all of the evidences of such a community. In Harlem one finds—as one finds in other working-class centers—a plethora of churches; some of them are attractive and compelling, others are repelling and grotesque. One is tempted to say that every known religious faith has its faithful followers in Harlem. Here, as elsewhere, religion is a lucrative profession for the leaders. Many who fail in other callings finally claim the Bible is a means to secure an easy and profitable existence; these are usually without the necessary training to fit them as competent expounders of that much expounded book. There are some cultured and educated preachers in Harlem.

Harlem is superstitious and patriotic; Babbittry* is rampant here. On national holidays, Harlem, like any other working-class section, celebrates with its unfurled flags, the parades, dances and picnics. In war-time, Harlem, too, hates the "enemy" and subscribes willingly to war loans. It supports the Red Cross, it furnishes its quota of volunteers; it has its "uplift organizations," its Y. M. C. A. and Y. W. C. A. There is a local Chamber of Commerce and a home for fallen girls. Harlem is honeycombed with secret societies—not of a subversive nature—which hold tightly to "long ago" and are dedicated to "yesterday"; any intelligent consideration of "today" and "tomorrow" is firmly opposed by them.

"Intense and Pathetic" Gullibility

Not unlike the average working-class community, Harlem's gullibility is intense and pathetic. Proof of this is plainly evidenced by the response to movements such as the Garvey movement and Sister Harrell's spectacular campaign of "healing."

Garvey holds, in common with the Knights of the Ku Klux Klan, that this is a white man's country; he opposes the election of Negroes to high political office and accepts as true the assertion that Negroes are inferior to white men; he justifies Jim Crowism on the railroads on the grounds that Negroes have never built any roads and do not own any. Nevertheless, Garvey is reported to have collected over $2,000,000 from Negroes for the purpose of building an Empire in Africa, with himself as Emperor, President or Potentate—whichever title suits his particular fancy at the time he is speaking—and transporting all Negroes thereto.

Sister Harrell (white), with a Negro spokesman, came to Harlem. Of course, she came at the command of God to "heal" the crippled, the halt and the blind—the three dominant types found today in every industrial center—at one dollar or more per "heal." Business was exceptionally good. She "healed" them going and coming, right and left (departed). Of course, all who desired could not be "healed." Some did not have the price, which was of prime importance in one's being "healed," and besides, her mandate from God was to "heal" only Jews and Negroes. Having witnessed the remarkable process (financially) of these two movements, one confidently awaits the day when Harlem will be honored by a "raiser up," i.e., one who will raise up the dead; what a fortune awaits such a thrifty genius!

Main Street Papers

There are published in Harlem four weekly newspapers. These are truly Main Street; the news that they see "fit to print" mainly considers murders, divorces, fights, court decisions, scandals, etc. Naturally, they are all successful and some of them even exercise political influence. There are four or five monthly magazines which are concerned, in the main, with chronicling Negro achievements in the field of literature and business.

Negro Harlem differs from any other industrial center in two aspects only. Firstly, it is a veritable human rainbow; every possible shade of color between the extremes of white and black is represented; thereby giving the concrete negative answer to the late President Harding's assertion that there is "a fundamental, eternal and inescapable difference between the races." There are some Negroes here who can pass the Nordic's rigid inspection and qualify for the Ku Klux Klan. One only regards these as Negroes because they themselves insist upon being so classified, at least, while they are in Harlem. And the second difference is, the degree of exploitation to which Harlem is subjected.

The Economic Lever

The overwhelming majority of Negroes in Harlem are workers, and during the period of industrial activity Harlem reflects this fact in a large number of weddings, gorgeous social functions, theater parties, elaborate and costly funerals and the spontaneous rise of petty business, etc. When the industrial pace slackens, bringing with it inevitable unemployment, poverty and hard times, Harlem again registers this change by contributing its share of holdup men, beggars, schemers, bootleggers, business failures, employment agencies and installment peddlers.

When unemployment sets in, Negro workers suffer longest and severest; it is unfortunately too true that they are the last to be hired and the first to be fired. This is due partly to the race prejudice evidenced in every walk of life in the United States, whether it be in the church, the school or in the factory; and partly to the fact that Negro workers are largely unorganized. Contrary to common belief, the absence of any large numbers of Negroes in the unions of the industries in which they work is due not to the Negro's failure to grasp the significance and importance of Unionism in the life of the modern worker, but to the failure of organized labor generally to realize that the Negro is simply a worker whose skin is black.

Unions and Race Prejudice

Most of the trade unions are saturated through and through with race prejudice; many of them covertly bar the Negro from their ranks, others openly deny him entrance; all of them show practically no desire to unionize the Negro worker except during the period of a strike when he is used by the employers against the union. Wherever he has been able to force his way into the trade union movement, we find that he is not accorded all of the rights and privileges exercised by other union men; in some cases, the union is fearful of the Negro. They dread the thought that if permitted in the union in large numbers he will dominate the organization and perhaps monopolize the jobs. As a result of this attitude, there is a growing conviction among Negroes to believe that, while they deplore the necessity for such action, the only way of escape is for Negro workers to form a colored Federation of Labor. Some Negroes oppose this idea and hope that organized Labor will soon see the folly of its ways and change its attitude before the Negro worker is driven to this extreme, perhaps to the mutual hurt of both black and white labor in the United States.

The lot of the Negro worker in New York City is a harder one, perhaps, than it is in any other industrial and financial center. New York boasts of no basic industry like the packing industry in Chicago or the automobile industry in Detroit[;] consequently, the great bulk of Negro labor is unskilled, and we find him employed here today, there tomorrow, and God knows where the next day.

"The Profiteer's Paradise"

Negro Harlem is the profiteer's paradise. Due to segregation, the Negro worker is the victim of a savage and double-edged exploitation.

Like all workers, he is exploited generally by the white industrial masters, and in addition to these, he is gouged by the capitalist-minded Negro, who makes his appeal on the basis of race.

In the kingdom of the profiteers, a Harlem landlord is king. The shortage of homes in Negro Harlem is an ever present and serious matter; owing to the restrictions placed upon the Negro tenant, and being unable to move where he can find a vacancy, he is compelled to remain within the pale. The landlords of Harlem take advantage of this condition to bleed him most mercilessly. The practice usually is to replace white tenants with colored ones and in the process increase the rent of the latter anywhere from 50 to 100 per cent.

The supreme tragedy of this is better grasped when we bear in mind the fact that the Negro worker receives far less in wages than his white brother. There are any number of Negroes whose rent far exceeds their wages. Having to choose between paying the high rent or be without a home, they decide to pay; to do so they resort to the established custom of taking in "lodgers"; in most cases these "lodgers" are total strangers to the family with whom they lodge; a lodger's character may be shady and low and his habits loose, vulgar and harmful to the morals of the children in the home. This matters not, however. All that counts is to get the big rent for the landlord.

The Vicious Circle

But while the morals of the children in the home may be corrupted, while the home itself may be broken up through clandestine love affairs, in the final analysis it is the lodgers who pay most of the rent; for whenever the landlord increases the rent of a tenant, say, $10 per month, said tenant in turn distributes this increase on the weekly rental of the lodgers—lodgers pay rent not monthly like tenants, but weekly—and by so doing realizes in most instances much more than the additional $10 per month. One may find a family today occupying the status of a tenant, tomorrow that same tenant becomes a lodger, and so the vicious circle goes on and on.

There is an old tradition which still survives, to the effect that whenever Negroes move into a community the property value decreases; like many another fable, this one is not true. Negroes maintain that when the assured and steady income from ownership in a certain piece of property is greatest it is then that the value should be high. But, say those who hold the former opinion, "while we are receiving more income from the property when occupied by Negro tenants, we find, when compelled to secure loans, that the lenders of money demand a higher percentage of interest and more security than when the property is occupied by white tenants, because the former do not take as good care of property as do the latter."

To which Negroes make this reply: "Granting as true what is said about loans, the question thereupon comes down to a class basis. A Negro worker has as much or as little appreciation of property as his white brother in the same class. The reverse is also true; a white person of leisure, culture and refinement will treat property in the same manner as does the colored brother with similar culture and refinement."

Merciless Exploitation

Nevertheless, the Negro tenant is the victim of a brutal and merciless exploitation by both black and white landlords, and the tragedy of the situation lies in the fact that there is no escape for him. White tenants may move unhampered from one end of the city to the other. Not so the colored tenant; while segregation continues, Negro tenants will continue to be offered up on the altar of greed and profit, to the glory of gold and the benefit of real estate sharks.

Politically, Negro Harlem is reactionary. Until very recently Harlem "en masse" went to the polls and voted as "my grand-daddy did." The old tradition of the Negro in politics as voiced by Frederick Douglass, viz., that "the Republican party is the ship and all else the sea," was for a long time accepted by Negroes here and elsewhere as "Gospel truth." Of late, however, a decided change has taken place in the political life of Negro Harlem. Negroes no longer blindly follow the Republican party, but have gone over to Tammany Hall. Last year Harlem was represented both in the State Legislature and in the Board of Aldermen by Negro Democrats.

Radicals Make Progress

The Negro radicals in Harlem have done splendid work, which can hardly be realized and appreciated by those out of touch with conditions within the black belt. From the day the Negro radical began his agitation in Harlem he was made to realize that between the great mass of white workers and the bulk of Negro workers, in so far as understanding and serving their own interest was concerned, there was absolutely no difference. The two groups are alike in their opposition to anything new; they glorify the past and are fearful of any departure therefrom.

Encouraged by a reactionary leadership, they have set their faces stubbornly against radicalism and change; whether it be in religion, politics, economics or in any other field. The general attitude of Negro Harlem towards a change in our economic system was tersely voiced by a recognized leader of the race who said: "The Negro, just out of slavery, cannot afford to agitate for the abolition of capitalism; he must protect and prolong capitalism until he has had a chance to taste the sweets of private property."

Meetings Broken Up

The street meetings of Negro Socialists have on numerous occasions been interrupted and broken up; their speakers assaulted, just as white Socialist meetings have been broken up, and their speakers assaulted in other sections of the city and country. Nevertheless, it is safe to say that the amicable relationship observed between the races in Harlem is due largely to the influence of the persistent propaganda of Negro Socialists. Of all the groups propagandizing in Harlem, none have done as much to remove suspicion and hatred and to foster the spirit of tolerance and mutual good-will among the two races as have the Socialists; even their most bitter enemies pay them this tribute.

In spite of many obstacles, however, and with a firm determination that is at once admirable and commendable, the Negro radicals have kept up the fight, until today one can say with pride that Harlem has more Negro Socialists, organized and unorganized, than anywhere else in the Untied States, and one is even tempted to predict that the first Negro Socialist to be elected in the United States will come from black Harlem.

From the *New Leader* April 11, 1925

Toward the Home Stretch

With the eyes of the Nation turned upon it, and the hearts of a race beating with mingled hope and prayer for its victory, the Brotherhood of Sleeping Car Porters turns its head, figuratively speaking, toward the home stretch. Seldom, if ever before, has a group of workers in their struggle to rid themselves of some of the cob webs of industrial oligarchy succeeded in attracting as much attention and gained such widespread sympathy as in the case of the 12,000 Negroes employed as Porters and Maids by the Pullman Company. Students of labor history, experienced labor leaders, aged preachers and politicians all have marvelled at the picturesque figure cast upon the American industrial stage by the Brotherhood of Sleeping Car Porters, for, the Brotherhood's success has shattered many of the beliefs and left over ideas about the Negro worker and his capacity to function in the industrial realm; it has also given fresh courage to our friends who believe in the humanhood of the Negro race.

In the success of the Brotherhood of Sleeping Car Porters there lies a lesson of deep import both to organized labor and organized capital. To the former it sounds the advanced note of the arrival of the Negro worker into the ranks of the organized labor movement to play its part in tearing down the color bar which has so long divided labor. To the latter, it is a warning that the end of the day is at hand when the unorganized Negro worker can be so handily used by capital in its struggle with labor. In the world of thinking men and women, the above truths are clearly recognized. The Nation Magazine, in its issue of June 9th carried an editorial on "The Pullman Porter" in which appears this significant paragraph: "These men who punch our pillows and shine our shoes and stow our bags under the seat bear in their black hands no little responsibility for the industrial future of their race."

Already unorganized Negro workers in almost every industry are beginning to look with inquiring eyes to the Brotherhood for council and leadership in their endeavor to organize and equip themselves the better to grapple with the problem of making a living. That Negro workers have been systematically kept out of the labor movement will not be denied by any honest and fair-minded person familiar with the story of American labor. The story is a long and gruesome one tempered only with a few saving instances which need not be mentioned here. It is quite apropos to say, however—and it is now generally admitted—that labor, by bending before the color line did much to weaken itself in its struggle with capital and to justify the antagonism evinced up to but recently by Negro workers toward the cause of labor. On the other hand such tragedies as East St. Louis, Chicago, Cartharet, etc., tell more eloquently than words can how organized capital has profited from the rift made by color prejudices in the ranks of labor.

With the onward sweep of our industrial developments and their attendant social evils and advantages it was inevitable that the Negro worker would be drawn more fully into the conflict between our industrial masters and the working class. That he would enter the struggle so defiantly enthusiastic, was not expected by even those who had given some serious thought to the perplexing questions of labor and capital. But, contrary to calculations he not only proudly entered the list, but with lightning rapidity broke down some of the traditions falsely attributed to his race, and established a new record in the history of workers organizing in the United States; he also brings with him those admirable attributes for which the race is noted. The spiritual zest and fervor carefully cultivated during the days of slavery; his courage, so often attested to by all who know the military and pioneer history of the United States, his devotion and faithfulness to a cause in which he believes, and above all, his soul sweetening music which has given America a place high in the musical world. All of these he brings to the organized workers of the United States, as can be observed at the meetings of the Brotherhood of Sleeping Car Porters.

When one recalls some of the stories that have gone the rounds of this country and the world anent* the eternal, inescapable and fundamental difference (*sic*) between the Negro and white man, it is not such a hard matter to understand the general interest and surprise which the spectacular growth and expansion of the Brotherhood has caused. To have expected that 12,000 Negroes would continue to accept unquestioningly a condition of employment which denied them a living wage, which subjected them to inhumanly long hours of work and which demanded of them the submersion of their manhood by making public beggars of them, is to evince a sort of juvenile optimism that is deserving of the utmost pity.

In spite of the deplorable conditions attendant upon the porter's employment, however, it might safely be said that the rapid progress and success of the Brotherhood is due to the resourcefulness and courage of the General Organizer. This young Negro, with a social vision, brought to the Pullman Porters' movement a rich experience and thorough training in labor problems, economics, sociology, history, etc. It can be stated that seldom has a leader of any group assumed active leadership so thoroughly prepared as is the case with A. Philip Randolph. For over ten years this pioneer Negro labor leader struggled against the organized ignorance of his group and the wide-spread prejudice of the whites in an effort to bring the liberating message of industrial freedom to Negro workers. We quite vividly recall the apathy, the open and subtle hostility and fear which greeted him and his colleagues in the early morn of their crusading days.

Now, however, the Brotherhood of Sleeping Car Porters is an established fact, its roots are sunk deep in the life of the American people. As the days roll into weeks and months, and the months into years, its influence will spread wider and deeper until all the workers of the Nation realize that the fate of the whole working class is inextricably bound up with that of every other section of the working class. When this truth is accepted by the tortured toilers of the land, it will mean the dawning of a new day, and a realization of the prophetic advice, uttered by one of the world's great benefactors: "*Workers of the World Unite!* You have nothing to lose but your chains, you have a world to gain"; and, in that day, the Brotherhood of Sleeping Car Porters will sink its identity into a bigger and nobler Brotherhood.

From the *Messenger* July 1926

3
COMMUNISTS

Cyril V. Briggs

Perhaps the most militant of the Caribbean communist contingent was Cyril Valentine Briggs, who was born on May 28, 1888, on Nevis, though he was educated and grew up on the neighboring island of St. Kitts before immigrating to the United States on July 4, 1905. Briggs, of mixed race, was light-complexioned enough that he described himself as the "angry, blond Negro." Although he had a speech impediment that rendered it difficult to engage in a conversation with him, Briggs more than made up for this handicap with his writing ability. Utilizing his experience as a reporter in the Caribbean, Briggs gained employment with the *Amsterdam News* in 1912. After the United States entered World War I, Briggs penned increasingly militant pieces, including one arguing for "the right of self-determination" for Blacks, leading to his eventual break with the paper in 1919 (unfortunately, no copies of the paper have survived from the time of Briggs's editorship).

Briggs's frustration at the *Amsterdam News* and a donation from Caribbean importer J. Anthony Crawford led to his establishment of the *Crusader*, a magazine espousing "race patriotism." Briggs's philosophy, that Blacks should be proud of their race and be prepared to make any sacrifice for it, is summed up in "Race Catechism," from the initial issue of the periodical. Briggs attacked those still advocating accommodation (e.g., "The Old Negro Goes: Let Him Go in Peace"). He also castigated W. E. B. Du Bois in "Dr. Du Bois Misrepresents Negrodom" for urging Blacks to fight in World War I and for not pressing for African self-determination.

Although Briggs would continue to stress the idea of race patriotism, after the "Red Summer" of 1919, the *Crusader* grew increasingly anti-capitalist and anti-imperialist, as evidenced by such essays as "Bolshevism's Menace: To Whom and to What?" The periodical also become the voice of the African Blood Brotherhood (ABB). This group's objectives are exemplified in the "Programme of the African Blood Brotherhood." Inspired by nationalist movements such as the Irish Republican Brotherhood and by the growth of communism, the Brotherhood's aims included "Absolute Race Equality . . . The Fostering of Racial Self-Respect . . . Organized and Uncompromising Opposition to the Ku Klux Klan . . . Higher Wages for Negro Labor, Shorter Hours and Better Living Conditions . . . Co-operation With Other Darker Races and With the Class-Conscious White Workers" (qtd. in Hill 1:xxviii). The semi-secret organization was an attempt to blend Black nationalism with an interracial working-class program. The editorial "The Salvation of the Negro" encapsulates Briggs's plan for saving the race: by creating an autonomous Black state "in Africa or elsewhere" and by establishing "a Universal Socialist Co-operative Commonwealth."

Briggs increasingly became convinced that the aims of Black liberation worldwide would necessitate bloodshed. This militancy reached its apex after the Tulsa riot in 1921, triggered when a Black man was accused of raping a White girl. Fifty Whites and more than 150 Blacks died in the rioting. Accusations were raised in the New York *Times* on June 3 and 4, 1921, that the ABB was involved. Although Briggs never admitted any Brotherhood involvement in the riot, he praised the use of force by Blacks in essays such as "The Tulsa Riot and the African Blood Brotherhood." One *Crusader* editorial read: "BETTER A THOUSAND RACE RIOTS THAN A SINGLE LYNCHING." The notoriety generated by such editorials gave the organization much-needed publicity, leading to more open recruitment, which increased their numbers.

If the perceived involvement of the ABB in the Tulsa riot was disturbing to the government, the attempt by the ABB to infiltrate the UNIA, with its many followers, must have been truly frightening. After abandoning his initial support of a Black homeland in America because of the intractability of American racism, Briggs made unsuccessful overtures to Garvey in an attempt to work with the UNIA at their convention in 1921. Briggs hoped to form a federation uniting all Black organizations. After being rebuffed by Garvey, Briggs became one of his sharpest critics, using the *Crusader* to wage a strong anti-Garvey campaign.

After the demise of the *Crusader* in 1922 (in part because of increasing government pressure), Briggs headed the Crusader News Agency, which disseminated radical news items to over two hundred newspapers. Briggs also published pieces in various forums for Marxist thought, including the *Daily Worker* and the *Communist*, on many of his long-term concerns. He would ruminate, for example on his long-time nemesis in "The Decline of the Garvey Movement."

Briggs strove to create another radical Black journal. He edited the *Negro Champion*, the house organ of the communist-backed American Negro Labor Congress (ANLC), and the *Liberator*, which was the voice of the League of Struggle for Negro Rights (LSNR). Both the ANLC and the LSNR were attempts by the party to appeal to Black nationalists. In them, for the first time, the party began to emphasize the importance of race, not just class, in the attempt to improve Blacks' living conditions. The Communists' most radical proposal regarding the Negro question came at the Sixth World Congress, held in Moscow in 1928, when the Comintern declared that Blacks in the American South had the right of self-determination as "a subject nation." Briggs was at the forefront of this controversial movement toward Black self-determination, which he expounds on in "For Self-Determination in the Black Belt."

By 1939, after quarrels with James W. Ford, the leading Black member of the Communist Party, Briggs was expelled from the party because of his support of Black nationalism. He moved to Los Angeles in 1944 and rejoined the Communist Party in 1948. During the late 1950s he worked as an editor with the *Los Angeles Herald-Dispatch* and the communist *People's World*. Briggs also became involved with younger Black radicals in the 1960s, continuing his association with them until his death of a heart attack on October 18, 1966.

The largest collections of Briggs's papers are located at the University of California at Los Angeles and Emory University in Atlanta.

BIBLIOGRAPHY

Draper, Theodore. *American Communism and Soviet Russia.* 1960. New York: Vintage, 1986.

Foner, Philip S., and James S. Allen, eds. *American Communism and Black Americans: A Documentary History, 1919–1929.* Philadelphia: Temple UP, 1987.

202 Part 3. Communists

Foner, Philip S., and Herbert Shapiro, eds. *American Communism and Black Americans: A Documentary History, 1930–1934.* Philadelphia: Temple UP, 1991.

Hill, Robert A., intro. and ed. *The Crusader.* 3 vols. New York: Kraus, 1987.

James, Winston. *Holding Aloft the Banner of Ethiopia: Caribbean Radicalism in Early Twentieth-Century America.* New York: Verso, 1998.

Kornweibel, Theodore, Jr. *"Seeing Red": Federal Campaign against Black Militancy, 1919–1925.* Bloomington: Indiana UP, 1998.

Solomon, Mark. *The Cry Was Unity: Communists and African Americans, 1917–1936.* Jackson: UP of Mississippi, 1998.

Thomas, Theman. "Cyril Briggs and the African Blood Brotherhood: Another Radical View of Race and Class during the 1920s." Diss. U of California, Santa Barbara, 1981.

Vincent, Theodore G. *Black Power and the Garvey Movement.* Rev. ed. San Francisco: Ramparts P, 1972.

Watkins-Owens, Irma. *Blood Relations: Caribbean Immigrants and the Harlem Renaissance.* Bloomington: Indiana UP, 1996.

Race Catechism

(Teach it to the little ones, learn and practise it yourself)

Question: How do you consider yourself in relation to your Race?

Answer: I consider myself bound to it by a sentiment which unites all.

Question: What is it?

Answer: The sentiment that the Negro Race is of all races the most favored by the Muses of Music, Poetry and Art, and is possessed of those qualities of courage, honor and intelligence necessary to the making of the best manhood and womanhood and the most brilliant development of the human species.

Question: What are one's duties to the Race?

Answer: To love one's Race above one's self and to further the common interests of all above the private interests of one. To cheerfully sacrifice wealth[,] ease, luxuries, necessities and, if need be, life itself to attain for the Race that greatness in arms, in commerce, in art, the three combined without which there is neither respect, honor nor security.

Question: How can you further the interests of the Race?

Answer: By spreading Race Patriotism among my fellows; by unfolding the annals of our glorious deeds and the facts of the noble origin, splendid achievements and ancient cultures of the Negro Race to those whom Alien Education has kept in ignorance of these things; by combatting the insidious, mischievous and false teachings of school histories that exalt the white man and debase the Negro, that tell of the white man's achievements but not of his ignominy while relating only that part of the Negro's story that pertains to his temporary enslavement and partial decadence; by helping Race industries in preference to all others; by encouraging Race enterprise and business to the ends of an ultimate creation of wealth, employment and financial strength within the Race; by so carrying myself as to demand honor and respect for my Race.

Question: Why are you proud of your race?

Answer: Because in the veins of no human being does there flow more generous blood than in our own; in the annals of the world the history of no race is more resplendent with honest, worthy glory than that of the Negro Race, members of which founded the first beginning of civilization upon the banks of the Nile, developing it and extending it southward to Ethiopia and westward over the smiling Sudan to the distant Atlantic, so that the Greeks who came to learn from our fathers declared that they were "the most just of men, the favorites of the gods."

From the *Crusader* September 1918

Dr. Du Bois Misrepresents Negrodom

This publication desires to register an emphatic protest against the compromising tactics of Dr. William Edward Burghardt Du Bois at Paris.

When Dr. Du Bois, taking advantage of a public sentiment worked up by others than himself, jumped out of the very hot pot in which he had found himself as a result of his cringing, compromising editorial on "Close Ranks" and his willingness to accept a post in the Intelligence Department of the government, and placed himself (in the estimation of himself and friends, at the head of a movement in which until his departure for Paris he had shown little interest), indignant as we were at the fraud we held our peace in the hope that, having gotten to Paris, he would aid in bringing about the fulfillment of the aspirations of the African race everywhere for a free Africa. But Du Bois at Paris has been the same compromiser and traitor to the Negro's legitimate aspirations as Du Bois in America during the war. It is now easy to understand why he was allowed to go to Paris when passports were refused to other Negroes—these others elected by popular will to present the aspirations of the Negro to the peoples of the Allies and, if possible to the Peace Conference.

Du Bois, the unelected, was granted the passport privileges refused to the Negro's elected delegates! And Du Bois sailed in the brave company of Moton!* In spirit he has apparently been in the same company ever since. His "exposure" of the ill-treatment of the Negro soldiers was a mild farce. Knowing much he told little. With facts and information easy to hand he assiduously refrained from using anything that might embarrass the government or get his publication in bad with Bourbon Burleson.*

And the work of the Pan-African Conference of which we are told Du Bois is "founder and secretary" is along the same line of compromise and genuflection. While hundreds of colored men died in Nyassaland* in 1914 and thousands are today dying in Egypt, Morocco and Nigeria for the African's right to govern himself this Du Bois' "Pan-African Conference" makes a mockery of the sacrifices of these Africans by presenting the Peace Conference with a set of resolutions calling merely for "better" white government of the black man.

How is a thing that is rotten to the core to be made better? Government without the consent of the governed is iniquitous and there are no two ways about it. European super-imposed rule has brought more suffering than anything to the African. The African is heartily sick of it. Native uprisings are the rule and not the exception. The entire continent of Africa is seething with dissatisfaction of alien rule. President Wilson and the rest of the Allied leaders have from time to time declared for the "self-determination of peoples." What reasons can Du Bois have for not seeking to apply this principle of "self-determination" to the case of Africans? Does he believe them incapable of governing themselves? Any people is more capable of governing themselves than is someone else of governing that people. Super-imposed rule may annihilate a people—it usually does!—but it can never elevate them. The African peoples got along fairly well before the advent of the cultured barbarians. They gave birth to civilization and erected such time-defying monuments as the Sphinx and pyramids. They can get along again without the white man. Better, in fact, without him than with him! And that Africa ardently desires her freedom is to be seen in the revolts taking place today in Egypt and Morocco and the uprising in Nigeria and other parts of Africa. What are Dr. Du Bois' reasons for misrepresenting Africa?

From the *Crusader* May 1919

The Old Negro Goes: Let Him Go in Peace

The old Negro and his futile methods must go. After fifty years of him and his methods the Race still suffers from lynching, disfranchisement, jim-crowism, segregation and a hundred other ills. His abject crawling and pleading have availed the Cause nothing. He has sold his life and his people for vapid promises tinged with traitor gold. His race is done. Let him go.

The New Negro now takes the helm. It is now OUR future at stake. Not his. His future is in the grave. And if the New Negro, imbibing the spirit of Liberty, is willing to suffer martyrdom for the Cause, then certainly the very least that the Old Negro can do is to stay in the background for his remaining years of life or to die a natural death without in his death struggles attempting to hamper those who take new means to effect ends which the Old Leaders throughout fifty years were not able to effect.

Can the Old Leaders deny that there is more wholesome respect for the Negro following the race riots in Washington, Chicago, Knoxville and other places than there was before those riots and when there were only lynchings and burnings of scared Negroes and none of the fear in the white man's heart that comes from the New Negro fighting back? They cannot deny it, so let them go their way. The future is the New Negro's. It should have come to us safeguarded. But the Old Leaders have failed ignobly. Ours now is the task of safeguarding that future and of giving it to our children secured for all time. For us the future and all the great tasks that lie ahead. For the Old Leaders *Requiescat en Pace!**

From the *Crusader* October 1919

Bolshevism's Menace: To Whom and to What?

Of a truth, Bolshevism is a menace. That much is conceded alike by friend, foe and neutral. That is the chief motif of the tune that is constantly dinned into the ears of the Negro and the world in general.

But just whom and what does Bolshevism menace? Is it not vital that we should know exactly against whom and what is directed this alleged threat of Bolshevism? Against the Negro and the rest of the workers, or against those who are exploiting the workers of the world and robbing the Negro group both of its labor and of its fatherland? If against us, should we not fight it, and if against the imperialist thieves of Europe, who are our foes, should we not be glad of its spread?

England and France and the rest of the piratical crew claim that Bolshevism is a menace to "democracy." What "democracy"? The "democracy" in which an autocratic minority living in France and England rule and oppress "subject peoples" against their known wishes and legitimate aspirations and solely for the benefit of home industries and manufactures? The "democracy" which imposes its will upon weaker peoples by force and murders them when this alien superimposed will is questioned, as "democratic" England is doing today in Egypt, India, Persia, Mesopotamia, the West Indies and many other unfortunate countries, as "democratic" France is now doing in Morocco, West Africa and Indo-China? The "democracy" which exploits, under the murderous capitalistic system, its own people, its weak women and young children? Is this the "democracy" to which the spread of Bolshevism is a menace? Then may God advance the spread of Bolshevism throughout Europe, Asia and Africa, and in every country where oppression stalks!

On the other hand, what is Bolshevism? Regarding it there are myriad lies, tales and rumors, but from what one can deduct from the testimony of impartial witnesses like Col. Robins and Mr. Bullitt* it appears to be a system of government of the people, by the people and for the people, and under which the resources of the country, like the mines, the coal fields and water power, are owned and operated, as they ought to be, by the State. Under Bolshevism all persons are producers. There are no classes. All are workers. We are told that Bolshevism's success in forcing the parasites to work lies in the fact that preference in rationing is given, and rightly, to those who produce, after, of course, the wants of the mothers, children and sick have been attended to. But this is the domestic side of Bolshevism and while a study of this side will do much to explain the phenomena now taking place in Russia, it is in the international side in which we are especially interested. What is Russian Bolshevism's attitude toward the people of other countries, especially oppressed people like the Africans, Indians, and Irish?

Bolshevism in its international phase is feared by the capitalist-imperialist powers even more than they fear Bolshevism in its domestic operations.

Bolshevism, from the international standpoint, is totally different from, and wholly opposed to imperialism. In fact, one of the first acts of Soviet Russia was the renunciation of the imperialistic claims of Czarist Russia on the territory and destiny of the people of Persia, thus repudiating the part played by old Russia with Great Britain in the strangling of Persia. Soviet Russia has gladly and promptly recognized the right of self-determination of the peoples of Finland, Poland, the Ukraine and other parts of the former Russian Empire. The right to self-determination of even certain weak and so-called "backward" peoples in Asiatic Russia has been recognized by the Bolshevists.

Bolshevism so far, then, is in direct opposition and contradiction of the "principles" of "democracy" as those principles are applied by England in India, Africa, Ireland, and elsewhere, and by France in Africa and Indo-China. And it is to these "principles," to this "democracy," that Bolshevism is a menace. Like Wilson's mistake in talking about the rights of "peoples great and small," Bolshevism is setting a bad example to the enslaved populations under British and French rule. It is putting ideas extremely injurious to the masters in the heads of the African, Indian and Irish peoples. That Bolshevism is a direct menace (and is seen as such) to the lying wickedness of *European eminent domain* under guise of carrying "the white man's burden," is demonstrated by the following statement from a capitalist source: "and the triumph of Russian Bolshevism, as now constituted, means the victory of the doctrine of their allies, the I. W. W. in America, and the destruction of Great Britain's power in India, in all other parts of Asia and in the Dark Continent."

If Bolshevism will free the "subject races," what should be the attitude of these races towards Bolshevism?

The *New York Sun,* in an editorial comment on the overwhelming defeat of Kolchak, Denikine* and other anti-Bolshevists, also lets the cat out of the bag in these two paragraphs:

> And so now Lenine [*sic*] and his disciples are turning their faces eastward as to the land of promise. Mohammedan hostility against the European rulers that hold so much of Islam in bondage is to be the great means of spreading Bolshevism throughout Asia.
>
> Already Great Britain becomes anxious. She realizes that the new Russia offers a menace to her power in the East not less than that of the former Czar. But what means she will take to prevent the threatened overflow of radicalism from the north into Persia and India remains to be seen. That she must act at once, however, is becoming evident to all.

And in these confessions and indiscreet comments of the capitalist press, in this anxiety of the chief enslaving powers, we have the answer and the truth as to who and what Bolshevism menaces.

From the *Crusader* February 1920

The Salvation of the Negro

As the Negro's position, even in America, is not utterly hopeless there must be at least several *possibilities* of achieving his salvation.

The important thing, then, would be to sift these *possibilities* with a view to picking out the fairest *probabilities.* One may argue that it is possible for black and white men to live together in peace and equality without fear of refutation on the point of *possibility.* But history has shown it is highly *improbable* that they would so live together. At least, history shows that they would not so live together *under the Capitalist System.* Replace the Capitalist System with the Socialist Co-operative Commonwealth and they *might* live together in peace and equality. Anyway there is this much to say in favor of the Socialist Co-operative Commonwealth, i.e.: while the oppression of one group by another is a necessary and ever present feature of Capitalism, such a thing in the Socialist Co-operative Commonwealth would be impossible, since were one group to exert even the mildest form of oppression toward another group that would be the signal for the disintegration of the Socialist Co-operative Commonwealth, and for the return of Capitalism. Just as today the democratic state can be destroyed as such and its citizens' rights annulled by imperialistic tendencies outward, so in the Socialist Co-operative Commonwealth freedom from exploitation would be lost for all the moment it were lost for one.

It is clear then that it is *possible* to achieve the Negro's salvation through the destruction of the present system and the substitution for it of the Socialist Co-operative Commonwealth. This, always a *possibility*, has become, since the destruction of Czarist Capitalism in Russia and the establishment of a Communist Co-operative Commonwealth, a *probability*. The Russian Jews have found their salvation—of course, that salvation can be no more permanent than the Communist State through which it was achieved—in the destruction of Capitalism in Russia. Along with Capitalism went Jew-baiting.

That the Negro can *possibly*—even *probably*—achieve his salvation through the Socialist Co-operative Commonwealth, does not mean, however, that he can achieve it *only through that means*. Other groups have saved themselves in the past without engaging in a death struggle with Capitalism. World-wide substitution of the Socialist Co-operative Commonwealth for the vicious Capitalist System is only one way whereby oppressed *races* may save themselves from the oppression engendered by the functioning of imperialist capitalism. Of course, it has the virtue of offering the most complete salvation since saving not only from alien political expression but from capitalistic exploitation by members of its own group as well. It has the advantage for the Negro race of being along the lines of our own race genius as evidenced by the existence of Communist States in Central Africa and our leaning towards Communism wherever the race genius has had free play. It is supposed to have the advantage, too, of making unnecessary a general Exodus. But it has not that advantage exclusively. That advantage is also held by the proposition of a strong, stable and independent Negro state, whether in Africa, South America, the Island of Hispaniola or elsewhere. The establishment of such a state would not necessarily require a wholesale exodus of American Negroes, though it is not altogether inconceivable that American Negroes would rather build up a state of their own for themselves, under governments of the Negro, by the Negro and for the Negro, in preference to helping build up a state in which the vast majority are white and in which the rights of minorities would always be dependent upon *the state of mind* of the majority.

From the point of view of "humanity" it would be much more preferable to gain our rights through the Socialist Co-operative

Commonwealth. But the Negro has been treated so brutally in the past by the rest of humanity that he may be pardoned for now looking at the matter more from the viewpoint of the Negro than from that of a humanity that is not humane. And again, he may prefer that his rights and immunity from oppression be based upon his own power rather than upon the problematical continued existence of the Socialist Co-operative Commonwealth. To the writer it is inconceivable that the Socialist Co-operative Commonwealth once established would ever be abolished, but then the oppressive Capitalist System was also inconceivable to our Communist African forefathers, as was also the European dictum latterly flung in the face of Asiatics and Africans that "might makes right."

The surest and quickest way, then, in our opinion, to achieve the salvation of the Negro is to combine the two most likely and feasible propositions, viz.: salvation for all Negroes through the establishment of a strong, stable, independent Negro State (along lines of our own race genius) in Africa or elsewhere; and salvation for all Negroes (as well as other oppressed peoples) through the establishment of a Universal Socialist Co-operative Commonwealth. To us it seems that one working for the first proposition would also be working for the second proposition. We invite discussion, and offer the free use of our columns for the purpose.

From the *Crusader* April 1921

The Tulsa Riot and the African Blood Brotherhood

The African Blood Brotherhood has been accused by the Oklahoma State and military authorities of having "fomented and directed the Tulsa riot" and of being a "highly aggressive" organization "seeking to foment unrest among Negroes."

As pretty nearly everybody knows that the Tulsa riot was fomented by the malicious misrepresentation by the Tulsa white press as an attack, with the implication of rape, an exchange of words between a Negro man and a white woman, there is no need to answer the charge that the A. B. B. fomented the riot.

As to whether the Tulsa Post of the A. B. B. had any part in *organizing and directing* Negro defense once the riot had started—that is another matter, and something that the Oklahoma authorities can find out for themselves.

The accusation that the A. B. B. seeks to foment unrest among Negroes is false, and the white authorities of Oklahoma and all of their cracker brethren in other southern states know it to be such. The A. B. B. is organized not for aggression, but for protection of otherwise defenceless Negroes. We do not have to foment unrest among Negroes when unrest already exists among them. Agitation is not needed, since the white man's many acts of injustice and malicious cruelty serve the purpose all too effectively. The trouble with the white man is that he forgets that the Negro is human and will accordingly react in much the same manner as other humans to wrongs and injustices. Cruelty and kindness need no interpretation, but are their own interpreters. It is not necessary, as the white man seems to believe, for Negro "agitators" to interpret and explain to the Negro masses the white man's acts of injustice against them. Negroes do not have to be told that lynchings and mob murders are barbarous acts of injustice. Where there is injustice, what need to seek for other agitational causes?

As a matter of fact, however, the accusation against the A. B. B. comes not of an honest belief on the part of the Oklahoma authorities that this organization had any part in fomenting or starting the recent riot, but rather from a belief that we are responsible for the organization and tactics which enabled the attacked Negroes to defend themselves so effectively and eliminate the easy massacre of leaderless Negroes which in earlier years regularly featured the so-called race riots of that time. As to that, we neither deny nor affirm. We merely hope that all Negroes in the United States will be wise enough to emulate the national policies of the United States and prepare in event of wanton attack to sell their lives dearly. For this defensive and essentially non-aggressive purpose we call upon all Negro men and women to enroll with the African Blood Brotherhood, a peace-loving but protective organization of red-blooded Negroes.

THE AFRICAN BLOOD BROTHERHOOD,

Cyril V. Briggs, *Executive Head*

From the *Crusader* July 1921

Programme of the African Blood Brotherhood*

A race without a programme is like a ship at sea without a rudder. It is absolutely at the mercy of the elements. It is buffeted hither and thither and in a storm is bound to flounder. It is in such a plight as this that the Negro race has drifted for the past fifty years and more. Rarely ever did it know exactly what it was seeking and never once did it formulate any intelligent and workable plan of getting what it was seeking, even in the rare instances when it did know what it wanted. It is to meet this unfortunate condition and to supply a rudder for the Negro ship of State—a definite directive force—that the following programme adopted by the African Blood Brotherhood is herewith offered for the consideration of other Negro organisations and of the race in general.

There is nothing illusory or impractical about this programme. Every point is based upon the historic experience of some section or other of the great human family. Those who formulated the programme recognised (1) the economic nature of the struggle (not wholly economic, but nearly so); (2) that it is essential to know from whom our oppression comes: that is, who are our enemies; and to make common cause with all forces and movements that are working against our enemies; (3) that it is not necessary for Negroes to be able to endorse the programme of these other movements before they can make common cause with them against the common enemy; that the important thing about Soviet Russia, for example, is not the merits or demerits of the Soviet form of Government, but the outstanding fact that Soviet Russia is opposing the imperialist robbers who have partitioned our motherland and subjugated our kindred, and that Soviet Russia is feared by those imperialist nations and by all the capitalist plunder-bunds of the earth, from whose covetousness and murderous inhumanity we at present suffer in many lands.

Africa

Our Motherland, Africa, is divided by the Big Capitalist Powers into so-called "colonies."

The colonies in turn are parcelled out to white planters and capitalists, some of them colonists, others absentee landlords. To this end the free life of the African peoples have been broken up and the natives deprived of their lands in order to force them to work, at starvation wages, on the lands of these white capitalists. These planter-capitalists have settled down in our country to exploit the riches of the land as well as the labour of our people.

But our people were not tamely submissive and had to be subjugated. They refused to be exploited and rebelled and fought the invader in an unequal struggle. The invaders, armed with weapons of modern technique, and precision, as against the primitive and old weapons of our forefathers, were finally able to subdue our people. But not until many a "British square" had been broken and many a sudden disaster suffered by the forces of all of the invading capitalist Powers.

How We Were Enslaved

And the fight is not yet over. A people living in oppression may be compared to a volcano. At any moment it may rise like a giant and run its enemies into the sea. To prevent this eventuality the capitalist planters, with the aid of their home governments, have organised "Colonial Armies," formed and equipped according to methods of modern technique. And to conquer our militant spirit and win us to slavish acceptance of their dominance they brought in the white man's religion, Christianity, and with it whisky. By the white man's religion our people's militant spirit was drugged; with his whisky they were debauched. The white man's treachery, the white man's religion and whisky had as great a part in bringing about our enslavement as the white man's guns.

But in order to more intensively exploit our rich motherland and the cheap labour power of an enslaved people, it was necessary to bring into our land certain machine industries and certain material improvements, like railroads, etc., and to-day we may witness, especially in the coast cities of Africa, the steady growth of modern enterprise. With the introduction of industrial equipment the African has learned to wield the white man's machines, his guns, his methods, and with the possession of this knowledge has grown a new hope and determination to achieve his freedom and become the master of his own motherland.

Hope Never More Justified

Indeed, the hope of the Negro people to free themselves from the imperialist enslavers was never more justified than at present. The home governments of the planter-capitalists are weakening day by day, and are trembling under the menace of the Proletarian Revolution. The oppressed colonies and small nations are in constant rebellion, as witness the Irish, Turks, Persians, Indians, Arabs, Egyptians, etc.

While the Interior of Africa is as yet barely touched by predatory Capitalism, the tribes fully realise the danger they would be subjected to should the enslavers penetrate more into the interior. Under the leadership of the more able and developed Negroes in the coast district, the tremendous power of the Negro race in Africa could be organised. Towards this end we propose that every effort shall be bent to organise the Negroes in the coast districts, and bring all Negro organisations in each of the African countries into a world-wide Negro Federation. The various sections of the Federation to have their own Executive Committees, etc., and to get in touch with the tribes in the interior, with a view of common action. The Supreme Executive Committee to get in touch with all other peoples on the African continent, the Arabs, Egyptians, etc., as well as the revolutionists of Europe and America, for the purpose of effecting co-ordination of action.

Labour organisations should be formed in the industrial sections in order to protect and improve the conditions of the Negro workers.

No opportunity should be lost for propagandising the native soldiers in the "colonial armies" and for organising secretly a great Pan-African army in the same way as the Sinn Fein* built up the Irish Army under the very nose of England.

Modern arms must be smuggled into Africa. Men sent into Africa in the guise of missionaries, etc., to establish relations with the Senussi,* the various tribes of the interior, and to study the topography of the country. The Senussi already have an "army in existence," a fact that is keeping European capitalist statesmen awake o'nights.

Every effort and every dollar should be spent to effect the organisation of a Pan-African army, whose very existence would drive respect and terror into the hearts of the white capitalist-planters, and protect our people against their abuses. Remember: MIGHT MAKES RIGHT—ALWAYS DID AND ALWAYS WILL.

America

Whatever interest the capitalist displayed in the Negro was always motivised by considerations of cheap labour power.

It was early recognised that the Negro people were the most endurant in the world, and when the New World was discovered the rich exploiters organised expeditions to enslave our people and forcibly carry them into New World lands, there to build empires and create wealth where otherwise none would have been possible. This is the history of most of the Negro populations in foreign lands.

THE CAUSE OF THE CIVIL WAR

In the United States, as is well known, the Negroes but a few decades ago were exploited according to the most crude and primitive system of exploitation; chattel slavery. This chattel slavery prevailed in the South, while in the North the modern capitalist method of exploitation (wage slavery) prevailed. The two systems could not exist side by side and therefore the so-called war of liberation, in which Northern Capitalists and their retinue, in a smoke of idealist camouflage, went to war against feudal capitalists in the South in order to decide supremacy between the two systems in the Americas. Northern Capitalists won and chattel slavery in the South was abolished with lurid speeches and glamour about Liberty, Democracy, etc.

But the Negroes were not to have even the comparative liberty which the great Capitalist Czars tolerate under the wage-slavery system. They were scrupulously disarmed, while their former owners with their henchmen remained armed. To repress all Negro aspirations for real freedom and suppress all desires to better their condition, secret murder societies like the Ku Klux Klan were organised by the former owner class who tortured and murdered secretly in cold blood thousands of defenceless Negroes and many whites wherever the humanitarian instincts prompted them to champion the Negroes' cause. And the victorious Capitalist "Liberators" of the North not only did not move a finger to enforce justice but suppressed the facts of this terrible persecution of the Negro and his few white friends. Through years of terror exercised by these white cracker societies the Negro again became totally subjugated, and Peonage is the lot of many to-day in the Southern States, while many are lynched or massacred each year. Lately the New Negro has come upon the scene and in response to his rebellious spirit and that of the exploited in general, we see the resurrection of the Ku Klux Klan.

NEGRO MIGRATION

As a result of continued oppression and maltreatment in the South, many thousands of Negroes have managed to escape to the North, and to-day every big Northern city has a large Negro population.

The comparative freedom of the North is propitious for great organisations and cultural activities, and it is here that the vanguard and general staff of the Negro race must be developed.

A Great Negro Federation

In order to build a strong and effective Movement on the platform of Liberation for the Negro People and protection of their rights to "life, liberty, and the pursuit of happiness," etc., all Negro organisations should get together on a Federation basis, thus creating a united centralised movement. Such a movement could be carried on openly in the North, but would have to be built up secretly in the South in order to protect those members living in the South and to safeguard the organisation from premature attack. Within this Federation a secret protective organisation should be developed—the real Power—to the membership of which should be admitted only the best and most courageous of the race. The Protective organisation would have to function under strict military discipline, ready to act at a moment's notice whenever defence and protection are necessary.

Labour and Economic Organisations

Millions of Negroes have come North and are employed as labourers and mechanics, etc., in the various industries and capitalist enterprises of the North. Being unorganised, they are compelled to work at the meanest jobs and under the worst conditions. When depression in industry appears they are the first to suffer. The white workers, through their labour organisations, have not only compelled the capitalists to give them more money and a shorter workday, but also partial employment during slack times. And when better times arrive, the white workers, through their organisation, are ready to take full advantage of the situation. Negro workers, whenever organised in Labour Unions, have improved their living conditions, won shorter hours, more money and steadier employment, as witness the sleeping car conditions, the Negro Longshoremen in Philadelphia, etc. And since the strength of a people depends upon the degree of well-living by that people, we must by all means strive to substantially improve the standard of living, etc. All worth-while Negro organisations and all New Negroes must therefore interest themselves in the organising of Negro workers into Labour Unions for the betterment of their economic condition and to act in close co-operation with the class-conscious white workers for the benefit of both.

NEGRO FARMER ORGANISATION

The same principle applies to the small Negro farmers and farm labourers. They must get together to resist exploitation as well as to protect themselves against peonage and other injustices. Wherever co-operation with white farmers is possible it is of course desirable.

CO-OPERATIVE ORGANISATIONS

There has developed among our people the naive belief that permanent employment, better conditions, and our salvation as a race can be accomplished through the medium of Negro factories, steamship lines, and similar enterprises. We wish to warn against putting too great dependence along this line, as sudden financial collapse of such enterprises may break the whole morale of the Liberation Movement. Until the Negro controls the rich natural resources of some country of his own he cannot hope to compete in industry with the great financial magnates of the capitalist nations on a scale large enough to supply jobs for any number of Negro workers, on substantial dividends for Negro investors. Let those who have invested in such propositions tell you whether they have obtained either jobs or dividends by such investment.

The only effective way to secure better conditions and steady employment in America is to organise the Negro's Labour Power as indicated before into labour organisations. Every big organisation develops certain property in the shape of buildings, vacations farms, etc. In prosperous times they may even develop co-operative enterprises such as stores, etc., but such enterprises must be co-operative property of all members of the organisation, and administered by members elected for the purpose. Under no circumstances should such property be operated under corporation titles written over to a few individuals to be disposed of at their pleasure. But experience has proven that such enterprises can only exist when the oppressed class is well organised. Without adequate organisation an industrial crisis like the present would sweep them off their feet. But where backed by adequate organisation the co-operative idea can be worked to advantage. Unlike the corporation, which lifts a few men on the shoulders and life-savings of the many, the co-operative is of equal benefit to all.

Alliances

There can be only one sort of alliance with other peoples and that is an alliance to fight our enemies, in which case our allies must have the same purpose as we have. Our allies may be actual or potential, just as our enemies may be actual or potential. The small oppressed nations who are struggling against the capitalist exploiters and oppressors must be considered as actual allies. The class-conscious white workers who have spoken out in favour of African liberation and have a willingness to back with action their expressed sentiments, must also be considered as actual allies and their friendship further cultivated. The non-class conscious white workers who have not yet realised that all workers regardless of race or colour have a common interest, must be considered as only potential allies at present and everything possible done to awaken their class-consciousness toward the end of obtaining their co-operation in our struggle. The revolutionary element which is undermining the imperialist powers that oppress us must be given every encouragement by Negroes who really seek liberation. This element is led and represented by the Third International which has its sections in all countries. We should immediately establish contact with the Third International and its millions of followers in all countries of the world. To pledge loyalty to the flags of our murderers and oppressors, to speak about alliances with the servants and representatives of our enemies, to prate about first hearing our proven enemies before endorsing our proven friends is nothing less than cowardice and the blackest treason to the Negro race and our sacred cause of liberation.

It is the Negroes resident in America—whether native or foreign born—who are destined to assume the leadership of our people in a powerful world movement for Negro liberation. The American Negro by virtue of being a part of the population of a great empire, has acquired certain knowledge in the waging of modern warfare, the operation of industries, etc. This country is the base for easy contact with the whole world, and the United States is destined, until the Negro race is liberated, to become the centre of the Negro World Movement. It is in this country, especially, that the Negro must be strong. It is from here that most of the leaders and pioneers who carry the message across the world will go forth. But our strength cannot be organised by vain indulgence in mock-heroics, empty phrases, unearned decorations and titles, and other tomfoolery. It can only be done by the use of proper tactics, by determination and sacrifice upon the part of our leaders and by intelligent preparatory organisation and education.

To be kidded along with the idea that because a few hundreds of us assemble once in a while in a convention that therefore we are free to legislate for ourselves; to fall for the bunk that before having made any serious effort to free our country, before having crossed swords on the field of battle with the oppressors, we can have a government of our own, with presidents, potentates, royalties and other queer mixtures; to speak about wasting our energies and money in propositions like Bureaus of Passports and Identification, diplomatic representatives, etc., is to indulge in pure moonshine, and supply free amusement for our enemies. Surely, intelligent, grown-up individuals will not stand for such childish nonsense if at all they are serious about fighting for Negro liberation! We must come down to earth, to actual practical facts and realities, and build our strength upon solid foundations—and not upon titled and decorated tomfoolery.*

From the *Communist Review* (London) April 1922

The Decline of the Garvey Movement

Garveyism, or Negro Zionism, rose on the crest of the wave of discontent and revolutionary ferment which swept the capitalist world as a result of the post-war crisis.

Increased national oppression of the Negroes, arising out of the post-war crisis, together with the democratic slogans thrown out by the liberal-imperialist demagogues during the World War (right of self-determination for all nations, etc.) served to bring to the surface the latent national aspirations of the Negro masses. These aspirations were considerably strengthened with the return of the Negro workers and poor farmers who had been conscripted to "save the world for democracy." These returned with a wider horizon, new perspectives of human rights and a new confidence in themselves as a result of their experiences and disillusionment in the war. Their return strengthened the morale of the Negro masses and stiffened their resistance. So-called race riots took the place of lynching bees and massacres. The Negro masses were fighting back. In addition, many of the more politically advanced of the Negro workers were looking to the example of the victorious Russian proletariat as the way out of their oppression. The conviction was growing that the proletarian revolution in Russia was the beginning of a world-wide *united* movement of downtrodden classes and oppressed peoples. Even larger numbers of the Negro masses were becoming more favorable toward the revolutionary labor movement.

Distortion of National Revolutionary Movement by the Reformists

This growing national revolutionary sentiment was seized upon by the Negro petty bourgeoisie, under the leadership of the demagogue, Marcus Garvey, and diverted into utopian, reactionary, "Back to Africa" channels. There were various other reformist attempts to formulate the demands of the Negro masses and to create a program of action which would appeal to all elements of the dissatisfied Negro people. None of these met with even the partial and temporary success which greeted the Garvey movement.

The leadership of the Garvey movement consisted of the poorest stratum of the Negro intellectuals—declassed elements, struggling business men and preachers, lawyers without a brief, etc.—who stood more or less close to the Negro masses and felt sharply the effects of the crisis. The movement represented a split-away from the official Negro bourgeois leadership of the National Association for the Advancement of Colored People which even then was linked up with the imperialists.

The main social base of the movement was the Negro agricultural workers and the farming masses groaning under the terrific oppression of peonage and share cropper slavery, and the backward sections of the Negro industrial workers, for the most part recent migrants from the plantations into the industrial centers of the North and South. These saw in the movement an escape from national oppression, a struggle for Negro rights throughout the world, including freedom from the oppression of the southern landlords and for ownership of the land. To the small advanced industrial Negro proletariat, who were experienced in the class struggle, the Garvey movement had little appeal.

While the movement never had the millions organizationally enrolled that its leaders claimed, it did have in 1921, at the time of its second congress, nearly 100,000 members on its books, as revealed in an analysis made by W. A. Domingo* of the deliberately confused financial statement given by the leadership to the delegates at the Second Congress. Moreover, the movement exercised a tremendous ideological influence over millions of Negroes outside its ranks.

Reflected Militancy of the Masses in Its Early Stages

The movement began as a radical petty bourgeois national movement, reflecting to a great extent in its early stages the militancy of the toiling masses, and in its demands expressing their readiness for struggle against oppression in the United States. From the very beginning there were two sides inherent to the movement: a democratic side and a reactionary side. In the early stage the democratic side dominated. To get the masses into the movement, the national reformist leaders were forced to resort to demagogy. The pressure of the militant masses in the movement further forced them to adopt progressive slogans. The program of the first congress was full of militant demands expressing the readiness for struggle in the United States.

A Negro mass movement with such perspectives was correctly construed by the imperialists as a direct threat to imperialism, and pressure began to be put on the leadership. A threat of the imperialists, inspired and backed by the leadership of the N.A.A.C.P., to exclude Garvey from the country on his return from a tour of the West Indies brought about the complete and abject capitulation of the national reformist leaders. Crawling on his knees before the imperialists, Garvey enunciated the infamous doctrine that "the Negro must be loyal to all flags under which he lives." This was a complete negation of the Negro liberation struggle. It was followed by an agreement with the Ku Klux Klan, in which the reformists catered for* the support of the southern senators in an attempt to secure the "repatriation" of the Negro masses by deportation to Liberia.

The objective difficulties and subjective weakness of the movement, arising out of reformist leadership and its attempt to harmonize the demands of all the dissatisfied elements among the Negro people, inevitably led to the betrayal of the toiling masses.

Surrendered Right of Self-Determination of Negro Majorities of U.S. and West Indies

While never actually waging a real struggle for national liberation the movement did make some militant demands in the beginning. However, these demands were soon thrown overboard as the reactionary side of the movement gained dominance. There followed a complete and shameful abandonment and betrayal of the struggles of the Negro masses of the United States and the West Indies. The right of the Negro majorities in the West Indies and in the Black Belt of the United States to determine and control their own government was as completely negated by the Garvey national reformists as by the imperialists. The Garvey movement became a tool of the imperialists. Even its struggle slogans for the liberation of African peoples, which had always been given main stress, were abandoned and the movement began to peddle the illusion of a *peaceful return to Africa*.

At first giving expression to the disgust which the Negro masses felt for the religious illusions of liberation through "divine" intervention, etc., the Garvey movement became one of the main social carriers of these illusions among the masses, with Marcus Garvey taking on the role of High Priest after the resignation and defection of the Chaplain-General, Bishop McGuire.* Feudal orders, high sounding titles and various commercial adventures were substituted for the struggle demands of the earlier stages.

How completely the reactionary side came to dominate the movement is shown in (1) its acceptance of the Ku Klux Klan viewpoint that the United States is a white man's country and that the Negro masses living here are rightfully denied all democratic rights; (2) the rejection by the leaders at the 1929 convention in Jamaica, B.W.I., of a resolution condemning imperialism.

In both cases the betrayals just noted were carried to their logical conclusion, in Garvey's bid for an alliance with the Ku Klux Klan, and in an article he wrote in the *Black Man* (Jamaica organ of the movement) shortly after the 1929 convention in which he attacked the Jamaica workers for organizing into unions of the T.U.U.L.* to better their conditions. In this article he attacked Communism as a menace to the imperialists and warned the Negro masses of Jamaica that they "would not dare accept and foster something tabooed by the mother country." So complete was the counterrevolutionary degeneration of the national reformists that the oppressing imperialism was openly accepted by them as their "mother country!" The imperialist oppressors were presented to the masses as "friends who have treated him (the Negro) if not fairly, with some kind of consideration!"

The decline of the movement synchronized with the subsiding of the post war crisis. As a result both of the lessening of the economic pressure on the masses and the awakening of the most militant sections of the membership to the betrayals being carried out by the national reformist behind the gesture of struggle phrases and demagogy, the masses began to drop away from the movement. Relieved of the pressure of the militant masses the movement began to assert more and more its reactionary and anti-democratic side.

Already at the Second Congress it was evident that the national reformists were losing their grip on the masses. As a result of the widespread exposures carried on by the Negro radicals* against the dishonest business schemes and consistent betrayals of the national Negro liberation movement by the Garvey reformists, the sympathetic masses outside of the organization were becoming more and more critical of the national reformists. Within the organization itself there was such wide-spread dissatisfaction that the top leadership was forced to make sacrificial goats of several rubber-stamp lieutenants. Within a few months of the closing of the Second Congress, the first big mass defections occurred (California, Philadelphia). These revolts, however, were led by reformists and were significant only from the point of view of the growing disintegration of the movement. From 1921, the movement has undergone a continuous process of deterioration and break-up, as the masses increasingly came to realize the treacherous character of the national reformist leaders.

The recent decision of Garvey to sell the Jamaica properties of the organization (pocketing the proceeds) and take up his residence in Europe (far from the masses he has plundered and betrayed), denotes a high stage in the collapse of this reactionary movement, whose dangerous ideology, as pointed out by the C. I. [Communist International],* bears not a single democratic trait.

Historically however the movement has certain progressive achievements. It undoubtedly helped to crystalyze the national aspirations of the Negro masses. Moreover, the Negro masses achieved a certain political ripening as a result of their experience and disillusionment with this movement.

New Negro Liberation Movement Goes Forward under the Hegemony of the Negro Proletariat

The betrayal of these aspirations and the national liberation struggle by the Garvey national reformists was facilitated by (1) the immaturity of the Negro working-class; (2) the weakness both in theoretical and in organizational strength of the revolutionary labor movement in the United States at that time.

To-day as the result of large-scale migrations into the industrial centers of large numbers of Negroes from the plantations, a strong Negro proletariat has come into being, developing in the class struggle and freeing themselves of petty bourgeois influences and reformist illusions. Further, as the result of the present crisis and the correct application by the Communist Party of the U. S. A. of the C. I. line on the Negro question, the Negro liberation movement again goes forward, this time under the sign of proletarian hegemony, and wages a relentless fight against imperialism and for unconditional Negro equality, including the right of self-determination of the Negro majorities in the Black Belt of the South, in the West Indies and the Negro peoples of Africa.

Before concluding, it is necessary to emphasize here that the Garvey movement, while in decline and on the verge of collapse, still represents a most dangerous reactionary force, exercising considerable ideological influence over large masses of Negroes. It will not do to ignore this movement which is most dangerous in its disintegration because of the desperate attempts being made by the national reformist leaders to maintain their influence over the Negro masses, either by saving the movement as it is or by luring the dissatisfied masses into other organizations under the control of the national reformists.

The situation affords considerable opportunity for the winning of the Negro masses away from the influence of the reformists and in another article I will deal with the tasks of the Party in relation to the disintegration and decline of the Garvey Movement.

From the *Communist* June 1931

"For Self-Determination in the Black Belt"

In an immense territory of the South, a territory commonly known as the Black Belt, live millions of Negro workers and farmers. These

Negroes build and man the factories of this territory. The Negro farmers and tenants till the land of this territory. They produce the wealth of this territory.

But the rulers of this territory are not Negroes. The factories that the Negroes man, belong to white owners. The land that the Negroes till, and water with their sweat, belongs to white landlords. The officials of the territory, from the governors of states down to the holders of the lowest local offices, are white men. The courts of this territory are presided over by white judges. The police and the sheriffs of this territory are white.

A handful of white bankers and landlords have imposed upon the millions of Negroes a foreign bondage. And in order to maintain this bondage, Negroes are held in slavery on the land, starved on the farms, whipped on the chain-gangs, hanged from trees, or legally lynched in the courts.

The land of the Black Belt rightfully belongs to the millions of Negroes who till it. These Negroes should own the land in this territory; they should rule its territory and make its laws and sit in judgment in its courts. They should have the right to determine what form of government they desire; and should they decide upon a government separate from the United States, they must be free to act upon their decision.

This is, briefly, what is meant by the demand raised by the Communist Party: the right of self-determination in the Black Belt. The demand is part and parcel of the demand of the working class Party for equal rights. Without the right of self-determination in the Black Belt, all talk of equal rights is empty and futile.

But this slogan horrifies, not only the white bosses and landlords who grow fat by keeping the Negroes in subjection, but likewise the supporters, open and concealed, of these bosses and landlords. And one of those who cry out against the right of self-determination is Heywood Broun,* mouthpiece of the Socialist Party.

To Broun, the idea of a handful of white bosses ruling millions of Negroes is entirely acceptable. But when the proposition is made that the Negroes of this territory shall govern this territory in which they are a majority, and govern the handful of white men who live there—then Broun and all his fellow-faker[s] are alarmed.

"It means a new form of Jim-Crowism," says Broun. Broun does not cry out against Norman Thomas,* Socialist candidate for President, who regularly segregates Negroes in his meetings in the South.

And although he has frankly stated that he is opposed to enforcement of the fourteenth and fifteenth amendments,* Broun is much "concerned" over "Jim-Crowism" in the Black Belt.

Does the right of self-determination mean Jim-Crowism? It means the opposite—freedom from bondage and inequality. The rule of Negroes in the Black Belt does not mean the setting aside of this territory for the Negroes alone, and forcing Negroes to live there. Equal rights for the Negroes in every part of the United States, with freedom to come and go as they wish—this is one of the main aims of the Communists. But the demand for equal rights is a hollow mockery unless the Negroes can throw off their backs this handful of white rulers who keep them in bondage. That is the meaning of the demand of the Communists: Equal rights for Negroes, self-determination for the Black Belt.

From the *Liberator* August 1, 1932

Richard B. Moore

Richard Benjamin Moore was a lecturer, political organizer, and book dealer. He was a leading African American member of the Workers' (Communist) Party and the African Blood Brotherhood (ABB). A lifelong activist, his principal concerns included housing, education, and labor issues.

Born in Hastings, Christ Church, Barbados, on August 9, 1893, Moore immigrated to New York on July 4, 1909. Raised by an evangelical Christian father who taught him the values of brotherly love, Moore was shocked when he saw Black Christians in New York segregated in church. He immediately tried to educate himself about conditions of Blacks in the United States and was drawn to the socialist cause after hearing Hubert Harrison speak.

By 1918 he had joined the Twenty-First Assembly branch of the Socialist Party in Harlem. This included such radicals as Frank Crosswaith, A. Philip Randolph, Chandler Owen, Otto Huiswoud, W. A. Domingo, and Grace Campbell. Largely because of his oratorical abilities, Moore was generally assigned to make speeches rather than write articles. His speeches were bold enough that one government informant called him "the most outspoken, daring and radical among all the other negro 'Reds' in Harlem" (qtd. in Kornweibel, "*Seeing Red*" 141). In his speeches and writings he railed against race riots (or as he called them, "wholesale massacres"), causing him to be under government surveillance, which would continue throughout his life, from as early as 1920. While working with the socialists, he helped form the People's Educational Forum with Domingo. He also was involved with Domingo and others in editing the *Emancipator* in 1920. Despite the strong anti-Garveyite tone of the journal, Moore steadfastly refused to sign any appeals pressuring the government to deport Garvey.[1]

Like many African Americans, Moore became disenchanted with the Socialist Party and broke from it in 1921. He had already joined the more radical ABB about 1919. He, along with Briggs, represented the ABB at the Negro Sanhedrin, a meeting of sixty-one Black organizations, in 1924. Intended to promote intraracial harmony, the Sanhedrin, presided over by Kelly Miller, was far too conservative for the ABB members.

About that time he joined the Workers' (Communist) Party because he believed it "to be the most militant in acting against the conditions which were quite distressing" (qtd. in Turner 51). Moore's affiliation with the party would last some twenty years.

Moore was elected to the general executive board of the American Negro Labor Congress (ANLC) in 1925 and was a contributing editor to its organ, the *Negro Champion*. He represented the ANLC in Brussels at the International Congress against Colonial Oppression and Imperialism and for National Independence in 1927. The Common Resolution of the Negro Question that he drafted was unanimously adopted. Perhaps most striking is the list of demands made "[f]or the emancipation of the Negro peoples of the world" and the measures necessary "[t]o accomplish these ends," which include an end to colonialism, complete equality for Blacks, and solidarity between workers.

A lifelong advocate of workers' rights, Moore was often in contention with organized labor, which he felt was weighted with White chauvinism. This put him in conflict not only with the American Federation of Labor (AFL) but also with many of his one-time socialist colleagues, such as A. Philip Randolph. The article "An Open Letter to Mr. A. Philip Randolph, General Organizer of the Brotherhood of Sleeping Car Porters" "exposes not only the problems confronting Afro-American workers and the great breach separating Afro-American leaders but also the sharp animosities generally within the labor movement" (Turner 139). Randolph essentially ignored the challenge to debate put forth by Moore in his letter.

One of Moore's chief concerns was housing. While working for the ANLC, he organized the Harlem Tenants League, formed in

1928, which was successful in limiting rental fees and generally raising the level of housing available in Harlem. His essay "Housing and the Negro Masses" reflects this interest in tenants' rights.

In 1931, he was appointed defense counsel in the trial of August Yokinin, a member of the Finnish Workers' Club in Harlem who was accused of White chauvinism for helping to exclude three Black members from a social event in the club. Moore argued that although Yokinin was guilty of chauvinism, he was actually just a vessel of "the chief criminal," the "vicious capitalist system." The trial became a landmark case in the party's attempt to purge itself of racism.[2]

Moore was also vice president of the International Defense League. Much of his attention while in the IDL went to the Scottsboro case. Moore, spokesman of the Scottsboro Mothers Delegation, helped compile a pamphlet, *Mr. President: Free the Scottsboro Boys!* (1934), an eloquent plea on behalf of the nine young Black youths falsely accused of raping two southern White women. Moore went on four cross-country tours on the boys' behalf. In one span of seventy-two days, he made appearances in fifty-five cities in twenty-three different states (Turner and Turner 60–61, 155–60).

By the mid-1930s Moore felt the party had lost its impetus. He was expelled in 1942 largely because of his continued emphasis on Black nationalism. He remained active, however, in Harlem and Caribbean politics. In 1940 he founded the Frederick Douglass Historical and Cultural League and published the *Life and Times of Frederick Douglass*, which had been long out of print. In addition, in 1942 he opened the Frederick Douglass Book Center, containing material on the African diaspora. It would remain a Harlem landmark until 1968, when it was razed. He also lobbied to replace the term "Negro" with "Afro-American" and published the pamphlet *The Name Negro— Its Origin and Evil Use* (1960). In addition, Moore was a strong advocate for West Indian federation. He was involved in these and other activities until his death in Barbados on August 18, 1978.

NOTES

Moore's papers are located at the Schomburg Center in New York City.

1. See his article "The Critics and Opponents of Marcus Garvey," in *Marcus Garvey and the Vision of Africa*, ed. John Henrik Clarke with the assistance of Amy Jacques Garvey (New York: Vintage, 1974), 210–35.

2. Despite Moore's defense, Yokinin was expelled. For more on the trial and a copy of Moore's speech, see Philip Foner and Herbert Shapiro, *American Communism and Black Americans: A Documentary History, 1930–1934* (Philadelphia: Temple UP, 1991), 147–81.

BIBLIOGRAPHY

Hutchinson, Earl Ofari. *Blacks and Reds: Race and Class in Conflict 1919–1990.* East Lansing: Michigan State UP, 1985.

James, Winston. *Holding Aloft the Banner of Ethiopia: Caribbean Radicalism in Early Twentieth-Century America.* New York: Verso, 1998.

Kornweibel, Theodore, Jr. *"Seeing Red": Federal Campaign against Black Militancy, 1919–1925.* Bloomington: Indiana UP, 1998.

McNeill, Lydia. "Moore, Richard Benjamin." *Encyclopedia of African American Culture and History.* Ed. Jack Salzman, David Lionel Smith, and Cornel West. New York: Macmillan, 1996. 1848–49.

Samuels, Wilfred David. "Five Afro-Caribbean Voices in American Culture, 1917–1929: Hubert H. Harrison, Wilfred A. Domingo, Richard B. Moore, Cyril V. Briggs, and Claude McKay." Diss. U of Iowa, 1977.

Solomon, Mark. *The Cry Was Unity: Communists and African Americans, 1917–1936.* Jackson: UP of Mississippi, 1998.

Turner, W. Burghardt, and Joyce Moore Turner, eds. *Richard B. Moore, Caribbean Militant in Harlem.* Bloomington: Indiana UP, 1988.

Vincent, Theodore G. *Black Power and the Garvey Movement.* Rev. ed. San Francisco: Ramparts P, 1972.

Watkins-Owens, Irma. *Blood Relations: Caribbean Immigrants and the Harlem Renaissance.* Bloomington: Indiana UP, 1996.

The Colonial Congress and the Negro*

The International Congress against Colonial Oppression and Imperialism held in Brussels last February passed a strong set of resolutions on the Negro problem, from which we publish an abstract:

General Resolution on the Negro Question

For five hundred years the Negro Peoples of the World have been the victims of a most terrible and ruthless oppression. The institution of the slave trade, as a consequence of the commercial revolution and expansion of Europe was the beginning of a regime of terror and robbery that is one of the most horrible in the history of mankind. As a result of this traffic, Africa lost a hundred million of her people. Four out of every five of these were killed in the bloody business of capture and transport, the survivors being consigned to a most cruel slavery in the New World.

The immense wealth derived from this gruesome trade was the foundation of the wealth and development of European merchants and states. But the development of the African peoples was thereby abruptly arrested and their civilization, which in many areas had reached a high state of advancement, was almost completely destroyed. These peoples henceforward were declared to be heathen and savage, an inferior race, ordained by the Christian God to be slaves of the superior Europeans, without any rights that a white man is bound to respect. And a bitter and hostile prejudice arose against the Negro race which has dominated the feeling of almost all Europeans towards them, causing them to be subjected to numerous unequal, degrading and pernicious prescriptions.

The abolition of chattel slavery freed the Negro peoples only from the thralldom of being legally held as personal property; the enslavement, exploitation and extermination of these peoples continue until the present moment. The process of subjugation was greatly accelerated by the mad scramble of European Powers for African territory between 1880 and 1890. This was due to the desire that financial capital had to put its reserves into the production of raw material, far from those areas of the industries of transformation which had just begun to develop in Europe. Afterwards, for the sake of its own development, industrial capitalism is joined to financial capitalism in the colonial robbery. By force and fraud the independent African states were subjected, their lands and possessions almost all forcibly expropriated and distributed among European corporations and persons, and their peoples driven by a most brutal and inhuman system to produce immense wealth for their oppressors. Virulent diseases were introduced among the people and devastation can be realized from the fact that despite the great virility and fecundity of the African peoples, Africa is now the least populous of the continents of the world.

Thus were the blessings of Christianity and civilization brought to the Africans. So that to-day in that vast continent of 11,500,000 square miles only two small states, Abyssinia and Liberia, are accounted independent. The former is now threatened by the Anglo-Italian pact,* and the latter with its customs and constabulary in the hands of American officials, and a great concession granted to a Wall Street corporation,* can no longer by considered free. The expropriation of the lands and extermination of the people proceeds grimly in Kenya and the Sudan, a suitable reward from the imperialists to the Africans whom they sacrificed in the great World War which was heralded as a war "to make the world safe for democracy and for the rights of weaker peoples."

Similarly the Union of South Africa has recently enacted a Color Bar Bill which prohibits the native from working with machinery and from employment in the civil services, which adds new burdens to these people already oppressed by Pass Laws, Hut Taxes and the like, and who are herded into miserable reservations and compounds and terribly exploited on the farms and in the mines. Everywhere also in Africa, excepting a small area on the West Coast where the lands and customs of the natives have been maintained by them, there exists a rigorous repression of the people under the yoke of foreign imperialists. The productivity of this area which is 8 times greater than that of neighboring areas of European owned plantations, is an irrefutable proof of the utterly wanton and vicious nature of this system of modern slavery.

In the United States, the 12 million "Negroes" though guaranteed equal rights under the Constitution, are denied the full and equal participation in the life of the Nation. This oppression is greatest in the Southern States where the spirit of chattel slavery still predominates. Segregation, disfranchisement, legal injustice, debt and convict slavery, and lynching and mob violence degrade and crush these peoples. This vicious system of suppression operates to reduce this race to an inferior servile caste, exploited and abused by all other classes of society. Haiti, established by Toussaint l'Ouverture and his fellow-slaves, the first successful Slave revolution in history, is now crushed and subjugated by the marines of that very power which proclaimed "the war for democracy." More than 3,000 Haitians have been murdered and large numbers are enslaved for the building of military roads under [the] corvee system.* They have been despoiled of their lands and liberties, and imprisonment and torture is the lot of all who dare to speak for their freedom. In the Caribbean colonies, the Negro peoples are subjected under varying forms of imperialist rule. Limited franchise and oppressive plantation systems reduce these masses to a permanent condition of serfdom and penury. In Latin America, Negroes suffer no special suppression. The cordial relations resulting from the social and political equality in the races in these countries prove that there is no inherent antagonism between them.

For the Republic of Haiti, Cuba, Santo Domingo and for the peoples of Porto Rico and the Virgin Islands, we must demand complete political and economic independence and the immediate withdrawal of all imperialist troops. For the other Caribbean colonies, we must likewise demand and obtain self-government. The Confederation of the British West Indies should be achieved and the Union of all these peoples accomplished.

For the emancipation of the Negro peoples of the world, we must wage a resolute and unyielding struggle to achieve:

1. Complete freedom of the peoples of Africa and of African origin;

2. Complete equality between the Negro race and all other races;

3. Control of the land and governments of Africa by the Africans;

4. Immediate abolition of all compulsory labor and unjust taxation;

5. Immediate abolition of all racial restrictions, social, political and economic;

6. Immediate abolition of military conscription and recruiting;

7. Freedom of movement within Africa and elsewhere;

8. Freedom of speech, press and assembly;

9. The right of education in all branches;

10. The right to organize trade-Unions.

To accomplish these ends we must prosecute the following measures:

1. The organization of the economic and political power of the people;

(a) Unionization of Negro workers

(b) Organization of cooperatives

2. Organization and coordination of the Negro liberation movements:

3. Prosecution of the fight against imperialist ideology: Chauvinism, fascism, kukluxism and race prejudice;

4. Admission of the workers of all races into all unions on the basis of equality;

5. Unity with all other suppressed peoples and classes for the fight against world imperialism.

Wayne State University Press wishes to thank the Crisis Publishing Co., Inc., the publisher of the magazine of the National Association for the Advancement of Colored People, for the use of this material first published in the July 1927 issue of *Crisis*.

An Open Letter to Mr. A. Philip Randolph, General Organizer of the Brotherhood of Sleeping Car Porters

July 31, 1928

Dear Mr. Randolph:

You have time and again declared that the fight of the Pullman Porters is not only their struggle, but the concern of the entire Negro race, since it is a basic struggle for the economic well-being of the Negro Race. In this you are entirely correct, and it is because we realize the importance of this struggle for the oppressed Negro masses and for the exploited workers that we are addressing you [in] this open letter.

It is our duty to declare to you that the policy which you have followed, and in which you still persist, is a policy which can only bring disaster and ruin to the cause of the Porters and Maids. This policy of trailing behind the labor aristocrats who betray the interest of the workers, who follow a policy of co-operation with the employers, of refusal to strike, and of narrow craft segregation, has been proved to be a policy which weakens and divides the workers, which surrenders their interests to the bosses who exploit them.

That you have completely fallen for this ruinous policy was proved by your "postponement" of the strike at the instance of Wm. Green* of the American Federation of Labor, and by your further statement that the strike orders now in the hands of the Regional Supervisors will only be opened "after the consultation of the Pullman Porters' leaders with Mr. Green."

Now we submit, Mr. Randolph, that Mr. Green did not organize the Pullman Porters, that his very failure to do so is evidence of his lack of interest in these workers. We submit that the Porters Union was organized because the Porters themselves rebelled against the miserable wage and the inhuman treatment to which they were subjected by the Pullman Company. And we say that to turn the organization of the Porters, built up by their sacrifice and struggle, into the hands of this misleader of labor, is to doom this organization to defeat.

It is now over seven weeks since the strike was "postponed." Immediately we issued a statement warning against the danger which threatened to these workers from this backdown. We clearly warned against the misleadership of the prejudiced labor aristocrats of the A. F. L. and the narrow craft monopolists of the railroad brotherhoods. We called for a united front with the progressive rank and file of these unions, to overcome the isolation of the Porters and to strengthen their union. We called for a new policy of militant struggle against the oppressive Pullman Company and against the agents of these oppressors in the labor movement. We demanded action to save the Porters Union, to strengthen the position of the Porters and Maids whose livelihood and status are at stake.

The Bulletin which you issued, explaining why the strike was postponed, clearly shows your subservience to Mr. Green. You say: "Gossip about Mr. Green being insincere is the veriest nonsense and silliest tommy-rot which could only emanate from crack-brained fanatics and low-grade morons." This abuse does not answer the criticisms of your mistaken policy, nor does it white-wash the known record of Mr. Green, as a labor misleader who consistently refuses to lead the workers in active struggle for the improvement of their conditions but who on the contrary aids the employers in schemes, plans, and moves for binding the workers more securely to their lot of oppression and exploitation.

In this Bulletin, you further betray your complete failure to understand what strike strategy really is, what is really necessary to bring the oppressors of labor to book. You say: "We have done almost as much damage to the company by threatening a strike as we would have done by striking." Perhaps this is what you wished to do, but seriously, Mr. Randolph, do you think that the Pullman Company has been in the least disturbed by an empty threat of strike which failed to materialize? No indeed! One does not need to be a labor expert to know that the Pullman Company has merely used that threat to perfect a strike machinery, which it can now use to damaging effect against the Porters. And this very fact, that you did not have the courage to go through with the strike, means only one thing for the company, that you lack the power and the spirit actually to strike.

But the Porters had the courage and the spirit. According to your own statement, "85 percent of the men would not only have walked off but would have prevented any others from walking on." And you revealed that you were not at all prepared for this when you stated: "I myself was amazed at the spirit of the men for the strike."

Why should you be amazed, Mr. Randolph? When you yourself issued a call to action in which you declared to the Porters: "The WAR is on! We must fearlessly face the fight to the finish for freedom. Our task now is to stand firm, steadfast and immovable, and prepare to go on with the fight TO THE FINISH, regardless of cost. Now, men, this is the time for ACTION, MORE ACTION, and STILL MORE ACTION."

The men responded like men to this appeal. They were "weighed in the balance and not found wanting." But you were not prepared for action. You were not ready to lead the men forward into the struggle, into the action, which was absolutely necessary to protect their interests.

You have further declared, Mr. Randolph, "We are certain that we could win the strike alone, without the cooperation of any other labor organization." Now this is rather doubtful, but it is remotely possible. The question which this raises, which you will have to answer if you can, is: "Why did you, then, 'postpone' the strike? Why did you, then, submit to Mr. Green's 'advice'? Why do you still trail meekly and supinely behind the American Federation of Labor?["] Obviously there is no need for this if you are assured that you are sufficiently powerful to win your struggle without their aid.

Moreover, Mr. Randolph, are you blind to what is happening under your very eyes in the labor movement? Do you not see that Wm. Green, John L. Lewis,* etc. have aided the employers in wrecking the United Mine Workers of America, in defeating the strike of the miners of Pennsylvania and Ohio, thousands of whom are Negro workers? Do you not see that this same reactionary officialdom is playing the role of betrayal in the strike of the textile workers of New Bedford? And are you not aware of the complete disaster brought to the workers of the Interborough Rapid Transit Company by these very labor misleaders?

A. F. of L. officialdom took control of the traction workers' strike. They assumed the leadership of the old union, of the Consolidated Traction Workers Union. What did they do? They ditched the former leaders who had built up the union and they dallied with Mayor Walker and the Tammany Hall politicians* and completely betrayed the struggle of these workers. Their union was smashed, their strike defeated, and their interests completely betrayed into the hands of the Interborough. Today the company union of the Interborough flourishes and the condition of the workers of this company is miserable indeed.

Should not this be a warning to the Porters? Should not this keep them from giving over the leadership and control of the union, which they have sacrificed to build up, into the hands of these same labor betrayers and union-wreckers?

This struggle of the Porters is too important a matter to be passed over lightly. It is too significant for the struggle of all the oppressed Negro workers against their exploiters to permit its weakening by mistaken policies or its betrayal by treacherous labor misleaders.

And so we must insist, Mr. Randolph, that this matter be openly threshed out in order that a correct policy, and an efficient and courageous leadership, shall be assured these struggling workers, who are groaning under the burden of capitalist exploitation. We must ask you to debate this question with us. We feel that this is a duty which we cannot escape. We will meet you at any time and at any place that you will mention to discuss this question which is so vital to the economic well-being of the Negro masses. We will maintain that the present policy of the leadership of the Porters' union of non-strike, of co-operation with the employers, and of trailing behind the prejudiced and treacherous labor aristocrats, is a policy which threatens destruction and defeat of this great movement for the advancement of the Negro workers.

We trust that you will accept this invitation to debate in the spirit in which it is made, the spirit of sincere devotion to the cause of the workers, and we await your reply.

Yours for militant struggle in the interests of the workers,

AMERICAN NEGRO LABOR CONGRESS,

RICHARD B. MOORE, *National Organizer.*

From the *Negro Champion* August 8, 1928

Housing and the Negro Masses

One of the most vital problems which the Negro masses face is the problem of Housing. How very vital, in fact, how actually menacing this problem now is, will be realized when it is known that the record of the death rate in cities shows that Negro children are dying from two to eight times faster than the children of other races. This frightful mortality, this slaughter of the innocents, is due directly to the terrible housing conditions imposed upon the Negro masses under the present oppressive system which is based upon RENT, INTEREST, and PROFIT.

Rent profiteering, overcrowding, unsanitary and beastly conditions are at their worst in the segregated districts where Negroes are compelled to live. Unable to move out of these miserable Ghettoes, the Negro masses are forced to pay the most exorbitant and outrageous rents for houses in every state of dilapidation and lack of sanitation. They are the prey of the greedy landlords and grasping capitalists who literally suck the life blood out of them.

Exploited at the point of production where they are paid the lowest wages for the most taxing and menial labor, Negro workers are set upon at the point of consumption by rent hogs and landlord sharks who take advantage of their segregated situation to gouge and bleed them to death. Terrible indeed is the plight of our people caught in the meshes of this vicious and lethal system of profit-making and rent-gouging. Impoverishment, degradation, disease and death—this is the terrible toll which we are forced to pay under this evil system which yields ill-gotten gain and blood-money to a few capitalist and landlord parasites.

It is a fact of special note and full of great significance that Negro landlords and real estate agents are ready participants in and active supporters of this system which pauperizes, degrades, and crushes the masses of the Negro race. It is an undeniable and weighty fact that Negro landlords and agents are no more considerate of the purse, safety, health and lives of Negro tenants than white landlords.

Indeed, it is to be observed that Negro real estate agents have been a very active class in increasing rent. They are exceedingly active and skillful in the business of persuading landlords to put in colored tenants at *doubled* rentals. What does it matter to them what these tenants do or how they live in order to pay these oppressive rents? What does it matter to these Negro agents whether black babies live or die?

Only one thing matters with them as with all landlords and capitalists of whatever race, and that is—PROFIT.

The higher the rent, the greater the commission, the larger the gain. And again, the less coal burned, the fewer repairs made, the greater the profit. So rents are raised, steam heat and hot water are hardly to be obtained, and repairs and sanitation are neglected by black as well as by white landlords and agents. With results for the masses of our people that are terrible to contemplate. Destitution, degeneration, disease, and death, these are the tragic results.

When measures are introduced for the protection of tenants or for the improvement of housing conditions, such as the extension of the Emergency Rent Laws and the Dwellings Law Bill which were brought before the New York legislature this year, it is to be noted that black and white landlords are united in the fight to defeat them. They line up together to kill laws which would help to abolish fire-traps and disease breeding slums and which would improve standards of safety and health in the homes of the masses. They fight as one to erase from the statute books laws which afford tenants and workers some protection against "unjust, unreasonable, and oppressive rents." The Negro landlords and agents protect their class interests, their profits, not the interests of the oppressed Negro masses who are being driven to the wall.

It is the workers and tenants organizations that are found fighting for the protection of the masses of our people. The AMERICAN NEGRO LABOR CONGRESS sent telegrams to the governor and legislature of New York State and HARLEM TENANTS LEAGUE sent resolutions and delegates along with the representatives of other tenants leagues, labor bodies and social agencies to fight for these measures for the protection of the welfare and lives of the masses of the people.

The lesson of this situation is plain and pointed. It is clear before our eyes. The fight to reduce high rents and to clean up the housing conditions which menace the health and survival of the Negro race will have to be waged against the bitter opposition of both black and white landlords who fatten upon these vile and murderous conditions. The Negro tenants and workers, united with the tenants and workers of other races, will have to carry on this necessary struggle for the salvation of the race.*

They must build strong tenants leagues and powerful labor unions as their essential instruments for this vital struggle. They must organize politically to defeat the parties of the capitalists and the landlords, the Republican and Democratic parties. They must build and support the party of the workers, farmers, and tenants which fights militantly against the system of rent profiteering and capitalist exploitation.

Only thus can this vital problem of Housing be solved. Only thus will we be able to meet and master this deadly menace to the welfare, safety, and survival of the oppressed Negro race.

From the *Negro Champion* September 8, 1928

Free the Scottsboro Boys!

In the name of hundreds of thousands of members of our organization and affiliated bodies, and in the name of millions of toilers and other people in the United States and throughout the world, who support the struggle for the freedom of the nine innocent Scottsboro boys, we protest vehemently against this statement of yours to the Scottsboro mothers. This statement gives direct aid and support to the Alabama ruling-class lynch terrorists in their attempt to burn the Scottsboro boys and also to the fascist suppressors of the Negro people and the entire working class throughout the whole country, and indeed, throughout the world.

We protest further against your refusal to receive and to hear the Scottsboro mothers and their entire delegation and against the humiliating and hostile treatment accorded them. We protest also against your similar action toward the delegation of 5,000 Negro and white workers and other people who marched to Washington on May 8 last year with a petition signed by hundreds of thousands, demanding the freedom of the Scottsboro boys and the adoption of the Bill of Civil Rights for Negroes, presented by them for the enforcement of the thirteenth,* fourteenth and fifteenth amendments to the Constitution.

Your action in these and other instances compel us to recall the following statement among the catalog of oppressive acts set forth in the Declaration of Independence as the occasion and the necessity for the revolution of 1776. "In every stage of these Oppressions, We have petitioned for Redress in most humble terms. Our repeated Petitions have been answered only by repeated injury.

We demand that you act as chief executive of the United States government to secure the immediate, unconditional and safe release of the nine, innocent Scottsboro boys. We demand that you act to enforce all the democratic rights of the Negro people and the working class enumerated in the Constitution. We demand full equal rights, economic, political and social, for Negroes, and the right of self-determination for the Negro people in the Black Belt of the South. We further demand the release of Angelo Herndon, Tom Mooney,* and all victims of class oppression. We demand that you take steps to stop the lynching and oppression of the Negro people, the murder of striking workers, and the increasing brutal attacks upon the masses of impoverished and unemployed workers and poor farmers and their organizations.

INTERNATIONAL LABOR DEFENSE

WILLIAM L. PATTERSON,* *National Secretary*

RICHARD B. MOORE, *Spokesman of the Scottsboro Mothers Delegation*

> Excerpt from *Mr. President: Free the Scottsboro Boys** (New York: International Labor Defense, 1934)

Otto E. Huiswoud

tto Eduard Huiswoud, the first Black member of the American Communist Party, was born in Paramaribo, Dutch Guiana (now Suriname), on October 28, 1893.[1] He came to the United States illegally on January 17, 1910, jumping ship in Brooklyn. Huiswoud joined the Socialist Party about 1916 and studied agriculture for two years at Cornell University before accepting a fellowship from the Socialist Party to attend the Rand School in New York. He soon became a member of the Harlem Twenty-First District Club of the Socialist Party and worked on the editorial board of the *Messenger*. When the Socialist Party divided in 1919, Huiswoud joined the newly formed Communist wing (Solomon 10–11).

Huiswoud attended the Fourth Congress of the Communist International as an official delegate of the Workers' Party of America in 1922, using the name J. Billings. Huiswoud, in speaking before the full congress on November 25, 1922, argued that although the Negro problem was primarily one of economics, it was exacerbated by racial tensions. Huiswoud "emphasized the exclusion of Negroes from the trade unions and the situation in the South—'when you come there, you imagine yourself to be in Dante's Inferno'" (qtd. in Draper 327). He was one of the members of a newly formed Negro Commission, which was the first serious effort by the Comintern to express its views regarding Blacks.[2]

He returned to the United States in 1923 and was appointed to the Central Executive Committee of the party in 1929. In addition, he helped integrate the African Blood Brotherhood, of which he also became a member, into the Workers' Party of America (James 177). He was often sent on recruiting trips to left-wing labor unions, and was said by W. A. Domingo to be highly effective as both an organizer and a speaker (cited in Kornweibel 153). Huiswoud also helped organize the American Negro Labor Congress (ANLC). In 1929 he attended the UNIA convention in Kingston, Jamaica, as a representative of the ANCL, engaging Garvey in a debate on the working class and capitalism. In addition, Huiswoud published regularly in several key radical periodicals. In "The Negro Problem Is Important" he puts the burden on the communists to reach out to the Negro masses, who because of their exploitation by the capitalist system are ripe to join the class struggle. "It is the duty of the revolutionists to turn this race consciousness [of Blacks] into class-consciousness."

Huiswoud was not afraid to take a stand contrary to the party. This was most evident in his position against the decision voted in at the Comintern's Sixth Congress in 1928 regarding "the Right of Self-Determination for Negroes." Huiswoud agreed that American Blacks were "'racially persecuted,' but [he felt] they were not 'colonially exploited'" (Hutchinson 53). Thus, he maintained there was no justification for establishing a separate nation for Blacks in the American South as the party proposed. Huiswoud's unorthodox opinion aroused controversy, but he continued to work for the party until 1937.

Huiswoud examines the conditions of Blacks in Africa, the West Indies, and in the United States in his article "World Aspects of the Negro Question." While he believes that Blacks are universally "a subject race," he argues that their condition varies under different situations (for example, whether or not they are a majority where they are living) and each situation must be treated accordingly. Though one may certainly question his contention that Black Americans have "no distinct language and culture from the dominant racial group," Huiswoud is generally perceptive in his evaluation of the differences between Blacks internationally.[3]

In the 1930s Huiswoud traveled throughout Europe, writing, speaking, and organizing for the Communist cause. He became head of the International Trade Union Committee of Negro Workers, editing their organ, the *Negro Worker*, in 1933 and, under the name Charles Woodson, from 1934 to 1937 (Hill 220). Huiswoud returned to Dutch Guiana in 1941 but was immediately interned for almost two years because of his radical politics. Upon his release, he never returned to the United States. In 1947, Huiswoud moved to Holland, where he remained until his death on February 20, 1961.

NOTES

While there are no repositories of Huiswoud's papers, the Tamiment Library at New York University has useful materials including a biographical memo from his wife, Hermina.

1. Huiswoud's name was occasionally given as Huiswood. Huiswoud, of Black and Dutch ancestry, was not from an English-speaking territory. However, Dutch Guiana had large Creole and maroon populations that retained traditional African languages and culture. It is to these Black diasporic communities that Huiswood felt his cultural allegiance, and he is generally included in studies on Black and Caribbean radical politics.

2. Claude McKay, an unofficial delegate at the Congress, essentially dismissed Huiswoud in his autobiography, *A Long Way from Home*. McKay, in a speech before the Congress, harshly criticized the American socialists and communists for White chauvinism. Huiswoud was decidedly less critical of his comrades. For the text of the speeches by Huiswoud and McKay see the *International Press Correspondence* 3 (Jan. 5, 1923): 14–17. For more on McKay and Huiswoud see Wayne Cooper, *Claude McKay* 176–80.

3. For a response to Huiswoud, see Harry Haywood's "Against Bourgeois-Liberal Distortions of Leninism on the Negro Question in the United States," *Communist* August 1930: 694–712.

BIBLIOGRAPHY

Briggs, Cyril. "Otto Huiswoud." *Worker* (Dec. 16, 1961): 8.

Draper, Theodore. *American Communism and Soviet Russia.* 1960 New York: Vintage, 1986.

Haywood, Harry. *Black Bolshevik: Autobiography of an Afro-American Communist.* Chicago: Liberator P, 1978.

Hill, Robert A. "Huiswoud, Otto." *Biographical Dictionary of the American Left.* Ed. Bernard K. Johnpoll and Harvey Klehr. New York: Greenwood P, 1986. 219–21.

Hutchinson, Earl Ofari. *Blacks and Reds: Race and Class in Conflict 1919–1990.* East Lansing: Michigan State UP, 1985.

James, Winston. *Holding Aloft the Banner of Ethiopia: Caribbean Radicalism in Early Twentieth-Century America.* New York: Verso, 1998.

Kornweibel, Theodore, Jr. *"Seeing Red": Federal Campaign against Black Militancy, 1919–1925.* Bloomington: Indiana UP, 1998.

Solomon, Mark. *The Cry Was Unity: Communists and African Americans,*
    1917–1936. Jackson: UP of Mississippi, 1998.

Turner, Joyce Moore, with the assistance of W. Burghhart Turner. *Caribbean*
    Crusaders and the Harlem Renaissance. U of Illinois P, 2005.

The Negro Problem Is Important

The Negro Problem is one of the most important problems facing the
Workers Party. Fundamentally an economic problem but intensified by
racial antagonism it demands our special attention and careful study.

The Negro population constitutes one-tenth of the population
of the country and is a most important factor for the success or failure
of any working-class movement. It is overwhelmingly a proletarian
mass. It is the most ruthlessly exploited of any working class group.

Eighty per cent of the Negroes live in the South. Here is where
the class struggle rages in its most brutal form. Oppressed and
exploited beyond description in order to pile up huge profits for the
land owning class the Negro can barely eke out a miserable existence.
Peonage is rampant. He is disfranchised and segregated. Lynching
and burning at the stake has become a famous American pastime.

That gigantic butchery—the World War—shook the very foundation of Capitalist Society and destroyed its equilibrium. It has also
shattered the apathy of the Negro workers; they are now sharply conscious of their wrongs as Negroes. One may reflect upon the part
played by the Negro in the Washington and Chicago Race Riots.
They did not let themselves be shot down as dogs. Instead, they put
up an effective and organized resistance. There is also developing a
revolutionary element among the Negroes. This element recognizes
clearly the source of their exploitation and the reasons for their
oppression.

Disappointed and disillusioned by the constant failures of the
political reformers to secure any redress of their wrongs, many
Negroes are turning to radical movements and are acting as a leaven
for the Masses. They are at present race conscious. It is the duty of
the revolutionists to turn this race consciousness into class-consciousness. But it requires persistency and tact. It is the duty of the Workers
Party to attract this section of the American Working class. And the
Party must in all seriousness undertake to win the support of the
Negro workers. Just as they are used by the ruling class to-day as strike

breakers, so will they be used in the future to crush any revolutionary attempt on the part of the white workers. And the capitalist class is preparing for this event. They are building a new Armory in the Negro district—what for? Well, you may guess.

Comrades, it is your duty to aid these masses in their struggle against peonage, and against economic exploitation. It is your duty to rally the Negro workers under the revolutionary banner of the Working Class Movement. Comrades, go to the Negro Masses!

From the *Daily Worker* April 28, 1923

World Aspects of the Negro Question

Until recent years the Negro question and its relationship to the revolutionary working class movement was practically unnoticed, almost completely ignored. Little attention was paid to the Negro masses in their struggles against imperialist exploitation and subjection, no thought given to their revolutionary potentialities—to the role they are destined to play in the movement for the emancipation of the working class from capitalist domination and enslavement. As a result, little or no attempts were made to draw the Negro workers in the struggle against world imperialism.

Our approach to the Negro question has not only been largely sectional rather than international, but our concept and interpretation of the Negro question was narrow and incorrect. The old Social Democratic notion that the Negro question is only a class question, prevailed with us for a considerable time. We are only now beginning to realize that the Negro question is not only a class question but also a race question. We are beginning to understand that the Negro masses are not only subjected to the ordinary forms of exploitation as other workers, but that they are also the victims of a brutal caste system which holds them as an inferior servile class; that lynching, segregation, peonage, etc., are some of the means utilized to keep them the underdog in capitalist society—social outcasts.

In order to maintain its policy of repression, violence and exploitation of the Negro, the bourgeoisie creates a false racial ideology among the whites and fosters contempt and hatred for the Negro. The idea of "superior" and "inferior" races is the theoretical justification for their policy of super-exploitation of the Negro race.

The situation of the Negro masses varies in the different countries and therefore requires investigation and analysis. The concrete application of the policies and tasks of the Communist Parties are dependent upon the prevailing conditions in the various countries. It is of utmost importance that we note the differences that characterize the position of the Negroes in the different parts of the world. The following territorial divisions based upon population and certain general common features should be considered:

A) The United States and some Latin American countries, in which the Negro population is a minority.

B) Africa and the West Indies, where the Negro population is the majority in relation to the white population.

C) The "independent" Negro nations (Haiti and Liberia) which are in reality semi-colonies of American imperialism.

While the Negro race everywhere is a subject race and there exists a common bond of interest based upon racial oppression, nevertheless, the conditions of the Negroes are not similar in the above mentioned territorial divisions. It is essential that we distinguish the situation of the Negro masses in the colonies—Africa and the West Indies; the semi-colonies—Haiti and Liberia, who suffer from colonial exploitation, from that of the Negro in America, a racial minority, subjected to racial persecution and exploitation. We must take into consideration the National-colonial character of the Negro question in Africa and the West Indies and the racial character of this question in the United States.

We must take note of the fact that the Negro question in Africa has all the characteristic features of the national-colonial question. Some of these features are:

1. Majority of population and organized communities.

2. A common language and culture. In contrast to this the Negro in America has

a) no distinct language and culture from the dominant racial group;

b) it is a minority of the population;

c) its only distinguishing feature is its racial origin.

It is therefore imperative that the concrete policies and tasks of the Communist Parties be based on the foregoing considerations. Only with a clear understanding of these conditions can we apply the correct policies and tactics.

Conditions of the Negro in Africa

What we are mostly concerned with in this article is the present epoch of imperialism which is marked by the complete division of Africa and the complete subjection and enslavement of its population. This period is especially marked by the de-tribalizing of the native population, robbing them of their land and forcing them into the industries as the main source of cheap labor supply. Imperialism in its function as colonial exploiter utilizes Africa for the subtraction of super-profits in the sale of its industrial products, as an outlet for its accumulated surplus capital and for an important source of its raw material. But, at the same time, capitalism purposely retards the industrial development of the colonies except in-so-far as it is to the interest of the preservation of its colonial monopoly and furthers the economic dependence of these colonies.***

The Central African colonies exemplify the most cruel and barbaric methods of capitalist exploitation and subjection. In this section of Africa, colonial exploitation assumes the very worst forms in the combination of feudal and slave-owning methods of exploitation. The profit-hunters have employed the most fiendish methods of torture to coin profits out of the blood of these natives. The deliberate murder and extermination of the natives by the imperialists in Belgian Congo in their quest for rubber is one of the blackest pages in colonial history. In the post-war period there has been a tremendous flow of capital into Africa, resulting in the concentration of large masses of expropriated natives in the huge plantations and industries.

The "independent" nations, Abyssinia and Liberia, are the constant prey of the imperialist powers. Through various treaties they seek to partition Abyssinia and reduce her to a complete vassal. Liberia is now completely under the domination of the United States. The Firestone Rubber Co., in its determination to break the British rubber monopoly, has secured thousands of acres of fertile land in Liberia, employing more than 10,000 natives for the miserable pittance of 30 cents per day. The Negro bourgeoisie in Liberia has completely "sold out" to Firestone & Co. and gives effective aid in the enslavement of the native population.

In South Africa the Negro masses are practically a landless peasantry. They are being expropriated from the land by the white colonists under the direct protection and aid of the government. They are disfranchised, their freedom of movement curtailed, and they are the victims of one of the most brutal forms of race and class oppression. The policy of the exploiters has been to take possession of the fertile land, ousting the natives therefrom, and to have these landless natives a source of cheap labor supply. As a result of this policy the six million natives are herded like cattle into what are known as reservations, the least fertile and usable land, comprising one-eighth of the total area. On the other hand, seven-eights of the land, the most fertile section, is placed at the disposal of 1,500,000 whites.***

The West Indian Islands

The West Indian Islands are controlled by England, France, Holland and the United States. England is the dominant power in the Caribbean and possesses the most valuable colonies. We shall only take into consideration here the islands predominantly populated by Negroes and which are completely under the domination of the imperialist powers.***

The natives of these islands are the victims of a most vicious colonial policy and are subjected to pre-capitalist forms of exploitation. The great mass of pauperized peasants live under the most primitive and poverty-stricken conditions. In most of these islands a semi-slave condition exists on the huge banana and sugar plantations, largely owned and controlled by big foreign corporations and absentee landlords. Working long hours under a broiling sun, housed in company-owned shacks, the mass of agricultural workers are paid a miserable pittance for their toil. The small farmers and tenant farmers are compelled to dispose of their products for little pay to the big corporations who exercise absolute power and control. The paltry sum received by the peasants must be supplemented by women and children who are forced to toil long hours on the plantations.***

Alive to their own interests, fighting for political and economic control of the islands, the native bourgeoisie and their political representatives have launched a campaign for the Federation of British

Islands with dominion status. This nationalist ideology is rapidly taking shape. Under the slogan of a "Federated West Indies," as symbolizing native rule, the native bourgeoisie is able to influence the masses, who are clamoring for native (non-white) representation in the Legislative Councils. Though restricted in the franchise by taxation qualifications and other bourgeois devices, the masses are rapidly developing political consciousness, as reflected in the increasing number of natives elected to the Legislatures.

Unlike the United States, there are no racial problems to speak of. Garvey's racial propaganda is artificially stimulated. Though he has considerable influence among the masses, their allegiance to his movement is based primarily upon the expectation of immediate economic relief. While there is no racial question in the West Indies, there is a rigid caste system based on color. The white ruling class, in order to divide the workers and rule them more effectively inculcates the idea of superiority over the blacks among the mulatto element.

Due to the fact that the bourgeoisie and petty-bourgeoisie are largely colored, and the working class entirely native, the class, rather than the race, issues are to the forefront. In fact, the class lines within the native population are quite rigid and short. Operating under such conditions, Marcus Garvey, who has transferred his main activities now to the islands, particularly Jamaica, was forced to come out more openly in support of capitalism, while using liberal and racial slogans to befuddle the masses.***

The Negro in the United States

In the United States the Negro is an oppressed racial minority. The exploitation of the Negro masses in America is of a twofold character—racial and class exploitation. The twelve million Negroes in the United States are the special victims of capitalist exploitation and subjection. Members of a racial minority, they are singled out for the severest attacks and persecution by the employing class.

The development of America required cheap labor for the southern cotton and tobacco plantations. Africa became the source of supply of the much needed man-power. The slave trade, while resulting in the death of millions of Africans, the depopulation on a wholesale scale of the African Continent, and in the most horrible violence and atrocities against the African natives, produced millions in profits for the slave traders and their bankers.

Chained to the land for over 300 years through the system of chattel slavery, Negro labor produced the basis of the wealth of the United States. Driven with the lash, subjected to the most horrible forms of torture and brutality, the Negro slaves produced untold riches for the ruling class. The many revolts of the slaves against this monstrous system of enslavement and exploitation were brutally suppressed by the wealthy landowners and the State. Following the Civil War, the primitive mode of production of chattel slavery was replaced with that of wage slavery.

However, while the Negroes in the North became wage slaves during the period of reconstruction, the Southern Negro was practically completely re-enslaved on the plantations. The courts enacted innumerable laws which served to keep the Negro under the complete domination of the landowners. Every instrument at its disposal was used by the ruling class to shackle the Negro workers and bind them to the plantations.

The South

The Negro population is not only concentrated in the South, but the bulk is concentrated in the rural sections. Out of the nearly 9,000,000 Negroes living in sixteen Southern states, about 6,000,000 or two-thirds live in the rural areas. In a number of states the Negro masses form a large part of the population. In Alabama and Louisiana, they constitute (1920 census) 38%, in Georgia, 42% and in Mississippi and South Carolina 51% of the total population.

In the South the millions of Negro workers and farmers are largely concentrated within certain areas known as the "Blackbelt," due primarily to the plantation type of agriculture. The Negro tenant farmer share cropper, and farm workers are virtually slaves on the land. The poor farmer and share cropper can never hope to own the land he tills, due to a credit and mortgage system which chains him to the land and makes him the serf of the merchants, landholders and bankers. Not only the land, but even the implements, crops— everything is mortgaged, placing them under complete domination of the white ruling class. The Negro farm workers are compelled to toil long hours under the most revolting conditions and for a miserable pittance as wages, receiving in some instances, as in Georgia, as little as $19 per month. Peonage, debt and convict slavery, vagrancy laws, disfranchisements, segregation, lynching and mob violence are the methods used to mercilessly exploit and oppress the Negroes in the South. These are the methods of double exploitation of the Negro used by the capitalist class in order to extract super profits from their labor.***

Segregated into the worst sections, compelled to live in flimsy, dirty shanties, jim-crowed at every turn, the Negro masses are bitterly exploited and live in the most abject poverty. They are disfranchised and subjected to violence if they dare assert their rights to vote in elections. Intimidated and brutally lynched by the Ku Klux Klan, the Night Riders and various other terroristic agencies of the capitalist class, the Negro masses in the South are unable to resist their oppression and exploitation, because of the lack of organization and the prejudiced attitude, not only of the employers, but also of the white workers who are saturated with the idea of race "superiority." Blinded by race hatred, deliberately fostered by the capitalist class, the mass of white workers fail to see the common interest between them and the Negro workers. Despite this racial antagonism, the worsening of the conditions of the white workers practically to the level of that of the Negroes, and the organizing and propaganda activities of the left wing unions and the Communist Party are laying the basis for the united action on the part of black and white against their common enemy—the exploiters.

The North

Soon after the Civil War, a slow but steady migration of Negroes from the South to the North began. Thousands of Negro peasants abandoned the plantations for the Northern cities. The demand for labor in the war industries and the check on foreign immigration provided the basis for a huge mass movement from the South to the North, involving hundreds of thousands of Negroes. The Negro population of the North increased tremendously.***

Turning their backs to the oppressive conditions of the South, with its intense exploitation, low wages and long hours, peonage and terrorism, the migrants flocked into the North. In his efforts to escape the open terrorism, jim-crowism and serfdom in the South, the Negro soon discovered that the conditions in the North are only little better than those from which he has escaped. In the North he is the special object of intense exploitation and proscription. He is confronted with discrimination and jim-crowism in restaurants, theatres and other public places. He is the special prey of the landlords and real estate sharks. The segregation of Negroes into restricted areas, forcing them to pay rents forty to fifty per cent higher than white tenants pay for similar accommodations, is one of the methods of double exploitation utilized by the bourgeoisie against the Negro. Both white and Negro landlords reap a harvest of profits through this system of segregating Negroes into districts notorious for their unsanitary conditions, thereby causing a shockingly high death rate of the Negro workers. Racial separation, through segregation, is an effective means of reducing the Negro to a social outcast.

The Negro farmhand of yesterday has become an industrial worker in the North. Absorbed into the various industries, the two million Negro workers are an important factor in the basic industries, such as steel, coal, iron, automobile, railroad, etc.***

Taking his place side by side with the white workers in the gigantic factories, mills and mines, subjected to capitalist rationalization, wage cuts, speed-up and unemployment, with its consequent radicalization of the masses, the role the Negro proletariat will play in the sharpening class struggles can no longer be ignored.

The Negro workers are largely unorganized as a result of the A. F. of L. policy of outright refusal to organize the mass of semi-skilled and unskilled workers. The reactionary bureaucracy in control of the craft unions bar Negroes outright or practice gross discrimination against them. With their policy of racial separation and hostility, they play the game of the employers. The A. F. of L. and socialist leaders constantly betray the Negro workers in their struggle, as in the waiters' strike in Chicago in 1922, the calling off of the scheduled Pullman porters' strike and the issuing of a "Federal Charter" to the Brotherhood of Sleeping Car Porters, thereby jim-crowing and weakening the organization, leaving the workers at the mercy of the Pullman Company. In spite of the treacherous policy of these labor "leaders" there are nearly 200,000 Negro workers organized in the trade unions.

The sharpening class differentiation within the Negro population must no longer be ignored. The segregation of the Negro masses creates the basis for the development of a group of real estate brokers, merchants and bankers. Under the deceptive slogan of "race loyalty" the Negro bourgeoisie has been able to establish an ideological influence over the Negro masses.

The Garvey movement and the N. A. A. C. P. are classic examples of the reformist movements exerting considerable ideological influence over the Negro, diverting his militancy into reformist channels, betraying the Negro workers in their struggle against capitalist exploitation.

A basic task before the Communist Parties and the revolutionary unions is the winning over of the Negro masses in America and in the colonies for the struggle against world imperialism, under the leadership of the Communist International.

The recent revolts of the natives throughout Africa are indicative of the readiness of the African workers to fight against the brutal exploitation and oppression of world imperialism. The colonial slaves in Africa and the West Indies must be organized and drawn into the world-wide revolutionary movement for the overthrow of world capitalism.

In the United States the proletarianization and the growing radicalization of the Negro masses provide us the basis for organizing the Negro industrial workers in the new revolutionary trade unions under the leadership of the Trade Union Unity League. The attendance and active participation of sixty-four Negro delegates at the Cleveland Convention of the T. U. U. L. is a sign of the awakening of the Negro workers and their readiness for joint struggle with the white workers against capitalist rationalization and enslavement.

The Communist Party must throw all its energy, mobilize all its forces for the winning of the millions of Negro workers and farmers for the revolution. The peculiar forms of racial exploitation of the Negro masses provide the basis for a race liberation movement which must be actively supported by the Communist Party. Our slogan of race equality as well as political and social equality must be translated into action and the Party become the champion and the active organizer of the oppressed Negro race for full emancipation. Gastonia* proves to us the possibilities of smashing the age-old Southern traditions and prejudices, mobilizing the white and black workers for common struggle against exploitation and oppression.

The danger of another imperialist war and of a war against the Soviet Union, into which thousands of Negroes will be drawn and sacrificed to appease the greed of world imperialism in their scheme for the re-division of the world, must be utilized to mobilize the Negro workers for struggle against world capitalism.

It is the duty of our Party to mobilize and rally the masses of white workers in defense of the Negro workers, linking up the struggles of the white with that of the black workers through all of its campaigns and activities.

A determined fight must be waged against every manifestation of white chauvinism among the broad masses of white workers and a campaign to stamp out all neglect and indifference among our white comrades toward Negro work.

The Party must intensify its work among the Negro masses, drawing them into the Party, aiding in the strengthening and building up of the American Negro Labor Congress and mobilizing the Negro workers under our leadership.

From the *Communist* February 1930

George Padmore

eorge Padmore, a noted exponent of Pan-Africanism and a leader of international communism, was born Malcolm Ivan Meredith Nurse on June 28, 1902, in Arouca District, Tacarigua, in Trinidad.[1] He said of his early background, "I never suffered economically. I was never hungry. I entered socialism and communism because the Communists were in the forefront of the struggle for racial equality in the United States." This interest in improving the conditions for Blacks was the driving force in his life.

Padmore immigrated to the United States to study medicine at Fisk University in 1924 and enrolled at the school the next year. He switched, however, to law. He then matriculated at New York University Law School in 1927 but never attended classes. Soon after, he enrolled at Howard Law School at the urging of the Communist Party, which he had joined earlier, taking the name George Padmore as a means to disguise his communist identity. The plan was successful enough that one of his Howard professors, Ralph Bunche, did not know for years that Padmore and Nurse were the same person.

In 1928–29 Padmore commuted between New York and Washington, D.C., helping to establish the *Negro Champion* (later the *Liberator*). He also began working with labor unions toward interracial unity. He helped promote the American Negro Labor Congress (ANLC), giving numerous speeches and writing extensively for communist periodicals. His article on the strike at the Gastonia, North Carolina, textile mills offers his cautious optimism about organizing Black and White labor and his recommendations for future action.

Padmore was invited by the Comintern to visit the Soviet Union in 1929 and was given a one-way ticket to Moscow, as they expected him to remain in the Soviet Union. In Russia he traveled in important circles and was elected secretary of the International Trade Union Committee of Negro Workers (ITUC-NW) though he spoke no Russian. He withdrew from Howard in March 1930 and never returned to the United States, which would deny his repeated requests for a visa.

In Europe, he helped plan the First International Conference of Negro Workers in Hamburg in 1930 and edited the *Negro Worker*, the organ of the ITUC-NW. During this time he wrote several pamphlets, including *The Life and Struggles of Negro Toilers* (1931), "a classic of the antiimperialist canon" (Hill 306). It was radical enough to be banned by most colonial governments. "Revolutionary Perspectives," one section of the pamphlet, discusses the function of the Red International of Labour Unions (Profintern) in the radical struggle. Padmore argues that Blacks and Whites must both do better in the fight against capitalism. Whites must purge themselves of racial chauvinism, and Blacks must shed themselves of "petty bourgeois reformists," including Du Bois, and "trade union lackeys," such as Randolph and Crosswaith. They also must struggle against Garveyism, "a dangerous ideology which bears not a single democratic trait, and which toys with the aristocratic attributes of a non-existent 'Negro Kingdom.'"[2]

In 1933, the German government, which had searched the ITUC-NW office in Hamburg, imprisoned Padmore for several months before deporting him to England, where he would spend the bulk of the next twenty years working with fellow Trinidadian émigrés C. L. R. James and Eric Williams. In England, he increasingly clashed with the communist hierarchy on several issues. He was expelled from the party in 1934, "for contacts with a provocateur, for contacts with bourgeois organisations on the question of Liberia, for an incorrect attitude to the national question (instead of class unity striving towards race unity)" ("Expulsion" 14). His real "offense," however, was likely his denouncement of the Soviet Union for its alignment with Britain and France to oppose the expanding Fascist presence in Europe, which he felt weakened anti-imperialism.[3]

During this time, Padmore facilitated contributors for Nancy Cunard's anthology *Negro* (1934) in addition to supplying four essays himself and co-writing a pamphlet with her, *White Man's Duty* (1942). He also published several pieces in the *Crisis*, the journal of his one-time foe, Du Bois. In addition, he published several works, including *Africa and World Peace* (1937), an analysis of the crisis in Ethiopia; *Africa: Britain's Third Empire* (1949), a condemnation of imperialism; and *The Gold Coast Revolution* (1953), a study of the African colony's struggle for independence. One of his best-known works, *Pan-Africanism or Communism?* (1956), examines Black nationalism, Pan-Africanism, and communism and attempts "to devise a coherent political strategy for the African independent struggle that would deny the West the excuse of intervening against its forward march on the pretext of stopping the spread of communism in Africa" (Hill 307).

Padmore founded the Pan-African Federation and formed close ties with Kwame Nkrumah while the two organized the Fifth Pan-African Congress in Manchester, England, in 1945. When Ghana achieved its independence in 1957, Padmore moved to Accra to serve as Prime Minister Nkrumah's adviser on African affairs. Padmore continued to promote Pan-Africanism until contracting dysentery in 1959. He sought medical treatment in London, and died there on September 23, 1959. His ashes were buried in Ghana.

NOTES

Padmore's papers are largely located in private collections.

1. This date is given by James R. Hooker (2). Some sources list the year as 1900 or 1903.

2. As Padmore shifted toward Pan-Africanism, he would later modify his views of Du Bois and Garvey. For his changing attitudes toward Garvey, see Tony Martin, *Race First: The Ideological and Organizational Struggles of Marcus Garvey and the Universal Negro Improvement Association* (1976; Dover, MA: Majority P, 1986), 261–65.

3. The "provocateur" was Padmore's friend Garan Kouyaté of the French colony Soudan (now part of Mali). Kouyaté, a Bambara school teacher fluent in French, was expelled from the party for embezzlement. He was eventually executed in Germany. Padmore had long been interested in Liberia, having written several pieces on the United States' presence there (e.g., "American Imperialism Enslaves Liberia," *Communist*, February 1931; "Hands off Liberia!" *Negro Worker*, October 4, 1929). By the time of his expulsion from the party, Padmore had been accused of supporting bourgeois interests in Liberia (Hooker 33).

BIBLIOGRAPHY

Davis, Helen [Hermina Huiswoud]. "The Rise and Fall of George Padmore as a Revolutionary Fighter." *Negro Worker* Aug. 1934: 15–17, 21.

Du Bois, W. E. B. "George Padmore's Life." *National Guardian* Oct. 12, 1959: 12.

"Expulsion of George Padmore from the Revolutionary Movement." *Negro Worker* June 1934: 14–15.

Hill, Robert A. *Biographical Dictionary of the American Left.* Ed. Bernard K. Johnpoll and Harvey Klehr. New York: Greenwood P, 1986. 305–08.

Hooker, James R. *Black Revolutionary: George Padmore's Path from Communism to Pan-Africanism.* New York: Praeger, 1967.

James, C. L. R. "George Padmore." *Radical America* 2 (July–Aug. 1968): 18–29.

Langley, J. Ayodele. *Pan-Africanism and Nationalism in West Africa, 1900–1945: A Study in Ideology and Social Classes.* New York: Oxford UP, 1973.

Martin, Tony. "George Padmore as a Prototype of the Black Historian in the Age of Militancy." *The Pan-African Connection: From Slavery to Garvey and Beyond.* Dover, MA: Majority P, 1983. 155–63.

Murapa, Rukudzo. "Padmore's Role in the African Liberation Movement." Diss. Northern Illinois U, 1974.

Gastonia: Its Significance to Negro Labor

The acute conflict centered around Gastonia does not simply express another phase of the class struggle on the American battle front of world capitalism, but also symbolizes in a far reaching and significant form events making for the emancipation of millions of oppressed and brutally persecuted Negroes in the South.

Gastonia is merely the beginning of a series of class battles which are destined to take place throughout the newly industrialized South. We have already seen the workers in action in New Orleans; Elizabethton, Tennessee; Marion, North Carolina; and the various mining sections of West Virginia. Sharper and more bitterly fought out struggles will occur as the class consciousness of the black and white workers of Dixie become aroused by the very nature of the intensive process of capitalist rationalization which means the worsening of their present horrible standard of living. The condition of these southern workers represent[s] the very lowest among the American working class. The primitive life which both the Negroes and poor whites are reduced to, can only be compared with that of the colonial and semi-colonial toilers in China, India, Africa, the West Indies and Latin America.

It is out of these class conflicts which will sweep over the South with greater rapidity than most of us anticipate, that the Negro and white workers will come to realize their class relations in the present social order. In proportion as they recognize that despite their racial differences, they are both members of the proletariat, will they be able to fight effectively in the common struggles of the working class against the capitalist overlords. This unity of purpose will be the most powerful force in breaking through the age long prejudices between the workers of both races. Herein lies the greatest hopes of the Negro masses in their struggles for self-determination. Let us not deceive ourselves that the eradication of race prejudice will take place over night, but on the other hand, it must come about as a result of the social forces propelling both groups in the same direction and throwing them in the struggle against their class enemy—capitalism.

For years the capitalist oppressors of the South have used the race issue as their most effective instrument to maintain their privileged position. Like the capitalist class of czarist Russia, the white ruling class of Dixie have been able until now to inflame the poor whites against the blacks and in this way withdraw the attention of the workers from the class nature of society. In the czar's days, the Russian workers and peasants were always made to believe that the Jewish masses were the cause for their poverty, and in this way led to carry out bloody pogroms against a helpless minority. Similarly, the Southern capitalists and their hangers-on—the preachers, politicians, editors and teachers—have taught the white workers that their poverty is caused by the Negroes. With this belief inculcated in the minds of the workers it was therefore easy to incite them into lynching mobs.

Gastonia shows that the workers will no longer be fooled by the deceptive propaganda of their oppressors. Present events indicate the fighting spirit of the masses.

Gastonia has already thrown to the forefront several burning issues. Chief among these, it has dramatized in the boldest aspect the viciousness of the ruling class and the role of the capitalist state during strikes. Thousands of these southern workers who only yesterday suffered from the illusion that the government was their "protector," today are able to see for themselves that the police, the state militia, and other defenders of "law and order," are the chief agents of the bosses and mill owners.

Early in 1929, the National Textile Workers' Union, a left wing organization which grew out of the betrayals of the United Textile Workers' Union affiliated with the A. F. of L., and controlled by a group of labor fakers who style themselves the Muste "progressives," invaded the South under the leadership of Fred Beal, a stalwart trade unionist and Communist. After a few months of preliminary work among the workers in the Loray Mill of Gastonia a strike was called. Despite the betrayals of the A. F. of L. unions in the past, the workers goaded by the "stretch out" system, long hours and starvation wages—which hardly exceeded $12 for adults and $5 for children per week of 69 hours—responded to the appeal of the new left-wing union leaders and came out on strike. No sooner had the workers left the mills and organized their picket lines were they confronted with the state militia called in to break the strike by Governor Max Gardner, a mill owner and one of the richest men in the state.

These Anglo-Saxon workers, who for generations have been taught by the ruling class to consider the militia as a special force to keep the "niggers" in their place, for the first time realized that whenever they dared to demand better conditions that they too would be shot down like dogs alongside of the black workers.

During the course of the strike it became necessary for the union to also organize some Negro workers employed in the mills around Gastonia and Bessemer City. Loyal to their program of full social, political and economic equality for the Negroes, the organizers immediately began to tackle what has always been considered the most delicate problem in the South—the organization of Negro and white workers into the same union. The A. F. of L. has never attempted to undertake this task. Rather, they have always pursued the line of least resistance by leaving the black workers unorganized, and in the few instances where they did organize them they set them apart in Jim-Crow locals. These militant trade unionists, despite their knowledge of the slave traditions of the South, and fully aware of the fact that the business men and their lackeys would exploit the stand taken on behalf of the Negroes, nevertheless refused to surrender their positions. Their heroism in the face of mob law and the lynching appeals of the press will never be forgotten by the American workers. Their courage surpassed that of the abolitionists. Theirs was a mission to emancipate not only Negroes but white workers as well from the fetters of wage slavery.

"The Gastonia Gazette," owned by the mill bosses, issued appeal after appeal to lynch Beal and the other organizers. This paper tried its best to play up race prejudice against these men and women who openly championed the rights of Negroes in North Carolina.

In keeping with its policy, the "Gazette" carried news that the union was controlled by Communists who hated "god" and loved "niggers."

The business men and the preachers—a class that can always be found on the side of reaction—called upon the workers to forget the fact that they and their families were being shot down by the gunmen of the mill owners, and to unite with the "respectable" citizens to rid the town of the dirty "foreigners." Realizing that the appeals were in vain, that the workers refused to be stampeded into a lynching mob, the reactionary forces organized a fascist battalion called the "committee of one hundred" and set out to take the lives of the strike leaders themselves.

During the raid on the strike headquarters by the "committee of one hundred" headed by the police, a very significant thing happened which in itself shows the tremendous spirit of class solidarity between the white and the black workers which Gastonia has already brought into being. This new attitude of class alliance was also reflected in the speeches made by the southern delegates of the recent T.U.U.L. convention in Cleveland.

Otto Hall,* a Negro organizer for the textile union, was on his way from Bessemer City to Gastonia on the night of the raid in question. The white workers realizing the grave danger to which Hall was exposed if he happened to get into Gastonia that night, formed a body guard and went out to meet Hall and warned him to keep away. They met Hall two miles out of town and took him in a motor car to Charlotte where they collected enough money among themselves to pay his railroad fare to New York. No sooner had Hall embarked on the train a mob broke into the house where he hid before his departure. It was only the timely and prompt action of these white workers that saved the life of their Negro comrade.

One can easily imagine why these fascists were so anxious to get hold of Hall. As a Negro it would have been very easy to accuse him of some alleged crime and thereby "justify" their action of lynching him. After that, the class nature of the Gastonia struggle would have been diverted into one of a racial issue leading to the wholesale lynchings of the white Communists, the champions of equality for the blacks.

The Negro workers, together with the white workers of America, must answer this challenge of the capitalist class by mass protest action until the revolutionary fighters now on trial at Charlotte are freed from the clutches of the mill barons.

We can already deduct [sic] several valuable lessons from Gastonia in relation to the working class in general and the Negro in particular.

(1) The struggle immediately brings on the order of the day the right of the workers to defend themselves. This must be the central issue for us, for as indicated the workers will engage in more and more such class battles in the near future, during which fascist elements such as the "committee of one hundred" would be mobilized against the strikers. We cannot surrender the right of self defense, otherwise we will be simply inviting wholesale massacre of the working class.

(2) Race prejudice is not a geographical feature of American capitalist society. It is everywhere, although more bitterly entrenched in the South, because of its semi-feudal remnants. As the process of industrialization proceeds and the Negroes and poor whites are drawn from the rural communities into the industrial centers they will be forced to discard the ideology of the past and to orientate themselves to their new environment. This process of urbanization will bring them together and out of these contacts they will learn to recognize that both groups are the slaves of the bosses. They will further learn through their everyday experiences that the employers foster race prejudice in order to keep them apart and thereby exploit them more easily.

(3) The new class battles which will increasingly break out will necessitate the application of new methods of class warfare. We have already realized that the antiquated Jim Crow craft unions fostered by the A. F. of L. must be displaced by new industrial unions under the militant leadership of the Communists and the left wing

T.U.E.L. Every battle will present us with new lessons in class tactics and methods of struggle. We must therefore be always on the alert to recognize our weak and strong points. Rigid self-criticism must be indulged in, in order to immediately correct our mistakes and steel our fighting forces so that all advantageous positions gained by the workers will be consolidated.

(4) A systematic ideological campaign against white chauvinism must be carried on among the workers as well as within the Party ranks. There is still a tremendous underestimation of Negro work among some of our comrades. Up till now too little serious attention has been given to this phase of our activities. The T.U.U.L. convention marks a new effort, which, however, must now end merely in resolutions. The large Negro delegation shows the two are capable of winning the black workers to our banner if we ourselves carry on systematic work among them. These Negro workers, as pointed out by the Comintern over and over again, represent revolutionary potentialities which it will be criminal for us to neglect for the social revolution. We must therefore intensify our work among them, and draw them not only into the new unions but also into the ranks of the Party.

(5) We must popularize our slogans of full social, political, and economic equality for Negroes more than we have done in the past. The most effective means of doing this is through our press, especially the "Negro Champion," which should be developed into the mass organ of the Negro workers. In districts and centers where large groups of Negroes are employed especially in the centers of the basic industries special leaflets and bulletins dealing in a concrete way with their everyday problems should be distributed at regular intervals. The Negro press can also be utilized to a greater extent than some of our comrades recognize. In order to do this the Crusader News Service should be subsidized.

Because of the peculiar position of the Negro petty-bourgeoisie and intellectuals, they too, are compelled to support our slogans of equality for the Negro workers or else expose their reactionary role before the masses. Experience has taught that those slogans of equality mean more to the Negro working class than to the black bourgeoisie and the middle class hangers-on, because they already enjoy a certain privileged position in Afro-American society, by playing second fiddle to the powers that be.

As the struggle assumes sharper class lines the so-called Negro leaders who still befuddle the black workers and peasants with radical propaganda such as Garvey's "Back to Africa" slogan—a form of black Zionism—will be compelled to show their true colors and in this way expose their counter-revolutionary position before the Negro working class.

From the *Daily Worker* October 4, 1929

Revolutionary Perspectives

The Role of the R.I.L.U. in the Struggles of the Negro Workers

The Red International of Labour Unions (Profintern) celebrated its Tenth Anniversary in 1930. Having been organised in the very heat of the acute post-war economic and political crisis in the most important European countries, the Profintern came to be the militant revolutionary headquarters of the world trade union movement, rallying to its banner all the class-conscious proletarian elements of the whole world.

To-day the Profintern is in the thick of its struggle for winning over the working class. In spite of its fine successes in extending its influence the Profintern cannot yet say that it embraces the majority of the working class. The Profintern is still obliged to wage a relentless struggle for freeing the workers from the influence of the bourgeoisie, the reformists and anarcho-syndicalists*.***

The Profintern is the first real International of Trade Unions, because the workers of all nationalities and races, regardless of colour or creed, have rallied to its banner. The Profintern has its sections in practically all countries in the world, in the form of independent trade unions and opposition groups and minorities inside the reformist trade unions. Besides these trade unions, which are organisationally connected with the Profintern, there are a whole number of trade union federations which adhere to the ideological leadership of the Profintern. Two very powerful organisations are among these—the

Pan-Pacific Trade Union Secretariat and the Latin-American Confederation of Labour.

The Red International of Labour Unions is the first Trade Union International which furthered the development of the trade union movement among the colonial peoples, and succeeded in rallying a great part of them to its banner. It is the only international which conducts a consistent and permanent struggle against white chauvinism, for equal rights and the labour movement in the colonial and semi-colonial countries, for the correct solution of the national-race problem. This struggle has only just begun. The problem of national equality has not been sufficiently appraised even by many of the Profintern supporters, while in the ranks of those sections of the working class which still follow the reformist and the reactionary leadership the "race struggle" in most cases, we regret to say, overshadows the class struggle. The Profintern has, however, mapped out a correct line for solving the national-race problem. It has indicated the path for waging the struggle against race chauvinism, against all colour bars, for uniting the workers of all races and nations.

A very vivid example of the national-race policy of the Profintern is its fight for strengthening and extending the trade union movement among the Negro workers. The Negro workers are the most exploited, the most oppressed in the world. It was the fate of the Negro workers to pay the horrible tribute to slavery, which served to destroy millions upon millions of black toilers. The Negro workers even now are actually slave-bound to their white conquerors. Different forms of forced labour, peonage, expropriation of their lands, extraordinary laws and unbearably heavy taxes, lynchings, segregation, etc., etc., are up till now the fate of the Negro toiling masses languishing under the yoke of imperialism. Tens of thousands of Negro workers are still groaning under the lash of their enslavers.

The Negro workers, however, exploited and oppressed by the imperialists, have not received the necessary support of the organised labour movement. The white worker, in many cases even to-day, still regards the Negro as a pariah, and scornfully refuses to stretch out a helping hand to his black brother. Even in the ranks of the revolutionary workers numerous examples of white chauvinism can be recorded. A long and bitter struggle has been waged by the Profintern against this psychology of "white superiority." Day in and day out, year after year, the Profintern has raised the Negro problem before its affiliated sections in the U.S.A., South Africa, England, France, Belgium, Portugal, etc., sharply condemning any and all manifestations of white chauvinism and underestimation of winning the black workers for the class struggle, pointing out the necessity of paying the most serious attention to the organisation of the Negro workers into revolutionary trade unions together with the white workers.

In order to strengthen and stimulate trade union activities among the Negro masses, the Profintern finally established a Negro Trade Union Committee composed of Negro workers from the United States, South, East, West and Equatorial Africa, the British and French West Indies and Latin America.

Since the establishment of the Committee, the Profintern has to some extent succeeded in overcoming white chauvinism in its ranks, and has corrected the mistakes of its American section, which formerly ignored work among the Negroes. The Profintern will continue its fight until it completely eradicates all traces of white chauvinism from its ranks and unites all workers—white, black, yellow, brown—in one revolutionary trade union movement.

What Must Be Done?

In order to help the Profintern and its revolutionary trade union sections in the United States and South Africa to carry out the task of building up strong unions by strengthening the bonds of solidarity between the white and black workers, two things must be done.

(1) The class-conscious white workers must take the initiative of drawing the Negro workers into the revolutionary unions and the movement of the unemployed, guaranteeing to them every opportunity of actively participating in shaping the policies of the workers' organisations and leading the united front struggles of the working class against the offensive of the capitalists.

In this connection it is the special task of the revolutionary unions to bring the white workers into the struggle on behalf of the Negro demands. It must be borne in mind that the Negro masses will not be won for the revolutionary struggles until such time as the most conscious section of the white workers show, by action, that they are fighting with the Negroes against all racial discrimination and persecution. Every class-conscious worker must bear in mind that the age-long oppression of the colonial and weak nation-alities by the imperialist powers has given rise to a feeling of bitter-ness among the masses of the enslaved countries, as well as a feeling of distrust toward the oppressing nation in general and toward the proletariat of those nations. This point was particularly emphasised in the resolution of the Communist International on the Negro Question in U.S.A.

It is absolutely necessary to pursue this policy. No retreat before white chauvinism must be tolerated, for only by *deeds and not words* will we be able to dispel the distrust which the more backward sections of the Negro toiling masses have towards the whites, a sus-picion which has developed among them as a result of the tradi-tional policy of the white reformist trade union leaders (Green, Matthew Woll,* John L. Lewis, etc.). These A.F. of L. fakers not only refuse to organise the Negroes, but, when compelled to do so in order to safeguard the privileged position of the white labor aris-tocrats, invariably "Jim-Crow" the Negroes into separate unions and leave them at the mercy of the capitalists.

Furthermore, the white workers must realise that in the present condition of world capitalism one of the aims of the imperialists is to find a way out of their difficulties by using the Negro workers, especially in the colonies, to worsen the already low standard of the white workers. Because of this the struggles of the Negro workers against the capitalist offensive must be made part and parcel of the common struggle against imperialism.

The emancipation of the white workers from the yoke of capi-talism can only be achieved by making a decisive break with all reformist tendencies, which are the ideologies of the bourgeoisie within the ranks of the working class. They must come forward boldly in support of the programme of the Communist Interna-tional and the R.I.L.U., which alone struggle for the overthrow of capitalism and the liberation of the toiling masses of all races and colour.

The workers of the imperialist countries must not forget the memorable words of Marx that "labour in the white skin cannot free itself while labour in the black is enslaved."

(2) The Negro workers must also take a more active part in the revolutionary struggles of the working class as a whole. They must make a decisive break with all bourgeois and petty-bourgeois

reformist movements. They must not permit themselves to be mis-led by the "left" phrases of the American Negro petty-bourgeois reformists, such as Du Bois, Moton, Depriest,* etc., etc., who are merely office-seekers and demagogues paid by the ruling class to befuddle the Negro masses in order to direct their attention away from revolutionary struggle into reformist channels.

The Negro workers must also conduct a more relentless struggle against the Negro trade lackeys of the reformists, whose chief task is to betray the struggles of the Negroes on the economic front. This has been glaringly revealed both in the U.S.A. and in South Africa. For example, A. Phillip Randolph and his henchman, Frank Croswaith [sic], "leaders" of the Pullman Porters' Union and members of the Socialist Party, are the most outstanding examples of Negro reformists. Some years ago the Pullman Porters' Union was the biggest mass organisation among Negro workers, but thanks to the opportunist policies pursued by Randolph and his supporters, the organisation is almost bankrupt. To-day it is largely a dues-paying organization and sick and death benefit society, completely under the domination of the bureaucrats of the A.F. of L., whose last act of betrayal of the Negro workers was openly to sabotage their struggles against the Pullman Company in 1928.***

The struggle against Garveyism represents one of the major tasks of the Negro toilers in America and the African and West Indian colonies.

Why must we struggle against Garveyism? As the "Programme of the Communist International" correctly states: "Garveyism is a dangerous ideology which bears not a single democratic trait, and which toys with the aristocratic attributes of a non-existent 'Negro Kingdom'! It must be strongly resisted, for it is not a help but a hindrance to the mass Negro struggle for liberation against American imperialism."

Garvey is more than a dishonest demagogue who, taking advantage of the revolutionary wave of protest of the Negro toilers against imperialist oppression and exploitation, was able to crystallise a mass movement in America in the years immediately after the war. His dishonesty and fraudulent business schemes, such as the *Black Star Line*, through which he extorted millions and millions of dollars out of the sweat of the Negro working class, soon led to his imprisonment. After his release Garvey was deported back to Jamaica, his native country. Isolated from the main body of the organisation, Garvey has been unable to maintain his former autocratic control over the movement, as a result of which there has been a complete disintegration of the organisation, which is now under the control of a number of warring factional leaders. Garvey, who was formerly in the service of American imperialism, has now switched his allegiance to the British, who are utilising him in order to keep the Negro toilers in the British colonies under submission. With this object in view the imperial Government has permitted Garvey to open his headquarters in London.

Despite the bankruptcy of the Garvey movement the ideology of Garveyism, which is the most reactionary expression in Negro bourgeois nationalism, still continues to exert some influence among *certain* sections of the Negro masses. The black landlords and capitalists who support Garveyism are merely trying to mobilise the Negro workers and peasants to support them in establishing a Negro Republic in Africa, where they would be able to set themselves up as the rulers in order to continue the exploitation of the toilers of their race, free from white imperialist competition. In its class content Garveyism is alien to the interests of the Negro toilers. Like *Zionism* and *Gandhism*, it is merely out to utilise racial and national consciousness for the purpose of promoting the class interests of the black bourgeoisie and landlords. In order to further their own aims, the leaders of Garveyism have attempted to utilise the same demagogic methods of appeal used by the leaders of Zionism. For example, they promise to "free" the black workers from all forms of oppression in reward for supporting the utopian programme of "Back to Africa," behind which slogan Garvey attempts to conceal the truly imperialist aims of the Negro bourgeoisie.

The Negro workers must not be deceived by the demagogic gestures of Garvey and his supporters. They must realise that the only way in which they can win their freedom and emancipation is by organising their forces millions strong, and in alliance with the class-conscious white workers in the imperialist countries, as well as the oppressed masses of China, India, Latin American and other colonial and semi-colonial countries, deliver a final blow to world imperialism.

From *The Life and Struggles of Negro Toilers* (London: Red International of Labour Unions, 1931)

4
LITERARY FIGURES

Claude McKay

Born to a middle-class family in the hills of Jamaica on September 15, 1889, Festus Claudius McKay became one of the leading literary figures of the Harlem Renaissance. McKay, the youngest child in a large family, was influenced by both his parents, who instilled in him a sense of Black pride. His deeply felt love for his mother is evident in such poems as "My Mother." Though he felt no such strong affection for his father, who told him folk stories about Africa, Claude always harbored a respect for him. The family's influence continued through his eldest brother, Uriah Theodore (known as U. Theo), an elementary school teacher, who was responsible for the boy's early education.

McKay was further educated by Walter Jekyll, a wealthy Englishman who had written a book on Jamaican folk song and literature, *Jamaican Song and Story* (1907). Jekyll encouraged McKay to write Jamaican dialect poetry. The result, in 1912, was *Songs of Jamaica* and *Constab Ballads* (McKay had been employed for a time in the constabulary). In these volumes, McKay wrote of the simple beauties of Jamaica and the vibrancy of the common people, who often overcame oppressive economic and political conditions. In these poems, as Winston James points out, "McKay's lifelong concern with race, color, class, justice and injustice, oppression and revolt are all given expression" (56).[1]

Having begun to establish himself as a poet, McKay felt he had to escape the narrow confines of his rural home and strike out elsewhere. The budding author came to study agronomy at Tuskegee Institute in 1912 and later at Kansas State University; however, soon,

273

as he said, "[t]he spirit of the vagabond, the daemon of some poets, had got hold of me" (*Long Way from Home* 4). He knew that he had literary rather than agrarian ambitions and came to New York City in 1914. Though he was forced into a number of menial jobs, he reveled in the excitement of Harlem. Despite fondly remembering his days in the hills of Jamaica, McKay was fascinated by the city, saying, "I gave myself entirely up to getting deep down into . . . [the] rhythm of Harlem life which still remains one of the most pleasurable sensations of my blood" (qtd. in Cooper 72).

Not all of these early experiences, however, were so pleasant. McKay was unprepared for the racism he encountered in America, which contributed to his involvement in radical political movements, particularly after meeting Hubert Harrison. McKay published extensively in Max Eastman's Marxist magazine the *Liberator* between 1919 and 1923.[2] Despite his frequent use of stilted language and his reliance on traditional form, he was innovative in his use of the sonnet to treat political issues. It was in the *Liberator* that he published "If We Must Die." The poem, with its message of defiance, became a paean to many oppressed groups and established McKay as a well-known figure in radical circles. Though the sonnet does not state directly that it deals with White/Black relationships, as Nathan Huggins maintains, "no one could doubt that the author was a black man and the 'we' of the poem black people too" (72). Because of such writings, McKay was cast in the role of "race poet," one with which he was not entirely comfortable, preferring that his work be valued for its literary merit rather than its political content. This would be one of the central tensions in McKay's life and work.

At the end of 1919, McKay journeyed to England, working on Sylvia Pankhurst's socialist weekly the *Workers' Dreadnought*. He was likely the first Black Marxist to write for a British periodical. While in England, McKay also learned a painful lesson in race relations. He had been brought up to believe Jamaicans were black Britons, but by the time he left England, McKay was convinced prejudice against Blacks was "almost congenital" with the British (*Long Way from Home* 76).[3]

After his return to the United States in 1921, McKay wrote for a number of periodicals, including briefly for Garvey's the *Negro World*. McKay had been an early supporter of Garvey, but in the essay "Garvey as a Negro Moses," while admiring Garvey's ability to inspire the masses and his "very energetic and quick-witted mind," McKay presents him as someone completely out of touch with reality, an almost comic figure possessed of little knowledge of Africa or business. The piece on Garvey was published in the *Liberator* while McKay was a co-editor of the magazine. McKay's quarrels with the other editors (particularly the more orthodox communist Michael Gold) over the amount of Black material to be included in the periodical may have contributed to his resignation as an executive officer in June 1922.[4]

That year also saw the publication of *Harlem Shadows*, generally considered McKay's most significant poetic contribution and often thought of as the first major work of the Harlem Renaissance. The volume was an expanded version of *Springtime in New Hampshire* (published while McKay was in England in 1920) but included several pieces, such as "If We Must Die," dealing with racial issues excluded from the earlier volume. McKay had been advised to omit these politically charged poems, but he regretted his initial temerity. The volume's combination of highly charged political poems and romantic ones such as "The Tropics in New York" and "Flame-Heart," dreamily nostalgic remembrances of Jamaica, demonstrate the two conflicting strains in McKay's writing: one political and urban and the other romantic and pastoral. These two sides often co-exist in an uneasy tension in McKay's work.

The political aspects of McKay's philosophy are demonstrated in his interest in the Russian Revolution. Although he denied ever having been a member of the Communist Party, McKay clearly had connections with it, even helping to move the African Blood Brotherhood, a group to which he briefly belonged, into its affiliation with the Communist Party. McKay visited the Soviet Union in 1922–23. As he said in his autobiography, *A Long Way from Home*: "Russia signaled. A vast upheaval and a grand experiment. What could I understand there? What could I learn for my life, for my work? Go and see, was the command" (150). He was one of two Blacks, with Otto Huiswoud, at the Fourth Congress of the Comintern in Moscow in 1922. McKay angered the majority members of the American Communist Party, who favored remaining underground; instead, he sided with the open Workers' Party of America. Despite attempts by the American Communist Party to expel him, McKay generally was feted throughout his visit, meeting Leon Trotsky, giving readings of his work, and having a May Day poem published in *Pravda*. The articles he wrote for the Soviet press were collected in *Negry v Amerika* [*The Negroes in America*] and he published several essays, including "Soviet Russia and the Negro," in the *Crisis*. Although he was impressed by the effects of communism in the Soviet Union, McKay was appalled by racism within the Communist Party in America. As with other issues, McKay's outspokenness on this issue caused him to make enemies, and in later years he became vehemently anti-communist although often loosely advocating Marxist beliefs.[5]

After leaving Russia, McKay began a series of travels throughout Europe and North Africa marked by illness (including lung infection and syphilis) and persistent financial problems but also periods of literary productivity. During this time, McKay worked on a proposed novel of Harlem Life, "Color Scheme." Unable to find a publisher for the work because of its graphic nature, McKay destroyed the manuscript in frustration. Some of the material for this novel, however, undoubtedly went into the making of his bestselling novel *Home to Harlem* (1928). The story of Jake, an earthy young AWOL soldier, and Ray, a Haitian intellectual, reflects the two sides of McKay's psyche. The novel brought on a firestorm of conflicting views. Many Blacks, particularly those in the middle class, still smarting from White author Carl Van Vechten's novel of the sordid side of Harlem life, *Nigger Heaven* (1926), felt that McKay was contributing to the negative stereotyping of Blacks with his gritty portrayal of Harlem life. *Home to Harlem* is rife with abusive relationships, drugs and alcohol, violence, loose sex (both heterosexual and homosexual), and color complexes. Many of the incidents, no doubt, were taken from McKay's own experiences. There is little sense of family, and Ray is the sole representative of Black middle-class life in the novel. In short, the novel horrified much of the Black bourgeoisie. What the critics failed to see was that McKay used his imaginative skills "to evoke a sense of Harlem's authentic inner life, frame black selfhood in positive terms, and elevate personal, cultural, and ethnic self-esteem" (De Jongh 32). It is a celebration of the common Black, a novel that is, in Langston Hughes's words, "the flower of the Negro Renaissance, even if it is no lovely lily" (qtd. in Tillery 88) An early chapter, "Arrival," details Ray's excitement at returning to the vitality of Harlem and his first encounter with and separation from "the little brown." Ray's quest to find his mysterious love would be at the center of the novel.[6]

McKay tried to capitalize on the financial success of *Home to Harlem*. His next novel, *Banjo* (1929), is set on the docks of Marseilles.

Ray reappears in this novel and the title character, Lincoln Agrippa Daily (Banjo), is similar to Jake. *Gingertown*, a collection of short stories set largely in Jamaica (such as "Crazy Mary") or New York ("Mattie and Her Sweetman"), followed in 1932. *Banana Bottom* (1933), the story of a young girl, Bita Plant, returns to the Jamaica of McKay's youth. It is a celebration of folklife despite the hardships Bita must endure. Despite the high literary quality of his fiction, particularly *Banana Bottom*, McKay's work sold poorly, in part as a result of the Great Depression.

By the time McKay returned to America in 1934, he was largely forgotten, as is reflected by the poor sales of *A Long Way from Home* (1937) and a collection of essays, *Harlem: Negro Metropolis* (1940). In an early essay, McKay had written that "each soul must save itself." Yet despite his fierce individualism and skepticism of organizations, McKay seemed compelled to join groups. After his return to America, McKay joined one final organization, the Catholic Church, in 1944. Perhaps his decision to become an American citizen in his later years was also an attempt to belong, at last, instead of continuing a life of ceaseless wandering. He died in Chicago on May 22, 1948, and is buried in New York.[7]

NOTES

The largest collection of McKay materials is located in the James Weldon Johnson Collection at Yale University.

1. Although McKay's Jamaican dialect poetry goes outside the chronological and geographic scope of this anthology, its importance must be recognized. Unfortunately, because of its difficulty for non-Jamaicans, it has not been given its proper due. For further discussion, see Cooper and especially James. For more on McKay's years in Jamaica see his *A Long Way from Home* and *My Green Hills of Jamaica and Five Jamaican Short Stories*, ed. Mervyn Morris (Kingston: Heinemann Education Books, 1979). See also Cooper 1–62; Tillery 3–37; and Rupert Lewis and Maureen Lewis, "Claude McKay's Jamaica," *Caribbean Quarterly* 13 (1977): 38–53.

2. This was not the same periodical that was edited by Cyril Briggs.

3. For more on McKay and England see Cooper 103–33; Cooper and Robert C. Reinders, "A Black Briton Comes Home: Claude McKay in England," *Race* 9 (1967): 67–83; and Tillery 42–48.

4. McKay would provide differing views on Garveyism throughout his life. "If We Must Die" was a favorite at Garvey rallies, and in 1919, at the invitation of Hubert Harrison, then editor, McKay published several articles

in the *Negro World*. Unfortunately, none of the copies have survived. McKay and Garvey have several obvious similarities, including their upbringing in rural, middle-class Jamaican families. Their devotion to their mothers and more ambivalent relationships with their fathers is also evident. Furthermore, both felt a strong admiration for the common people. They had been drawn to America, in part, through an initial interest in the philosophy of Booker T. Washington. Although he continued to support many of the beliefs that Garvey espoused, McKay, like many Black leaders, could not abide by Garvey's autocratic tendencies and eventually abandoned the movement. Over the years, McKay discussed Garvey in several venues. He is described in *A Long Way from Home* as "a West Indian charlatan . . . full of antiquated social ideas; yet within a decade he raised the social consciousness of the Negro masses more than any leader ever did" (354). In a lengthy overview of Garvey's life in *Harlem: Negro Metropolis* (New York: E. P. Dutton, 1940) McKay recognized Garvey's enormous charisma and his role in raising "a finer feeling of racial consciousness," but noted that his demagoguery blinded him, causing his movement to be a failure. The article, written shortly after Garvey's death, has the feel almost of a eulogy: "Garvey was no violator of the flower of the human spirit; he was more obsessed with the idea that the spirit of humanity should flower more universally" (179). McKay wrote a laudatory sonnet about Garvey in his posthumously published series of poems "The Cycle," circa 1943 (McKay, "Complete Poems" 268). See also Tony Martin, *Literary Garveyism: Garvey, Black Arts and the Harlem Renaissance* (Dover, MA: Majority P, 1983), 132–38 and Garvey's critique on *Home to Harlem* on pages 94–96 of this volume.

  5. While McKay was in Russia, he published *Negry v Amerika* (1923), later translated by Robert J. Winter as *The Negroes in America*, ed. Alan L. McLeod (Port Washington, NY: Kennikat P, 1979). *Harlem: Negro Metropolis* reveals McKay's anti-communist sentiments clearly. For more on McKay in Russia, see *A Long Way from Home* 153–234; Cooper 171–92; and Tillery 62–75. Also see William Maxwell, *New Negro, Old Left* (New York: Columbia UP, 1999), 63–93.

  6. For contemporary reviews of McKay's work see John E. Bassett's *Harlem in Review: Critical Reactions to Black American Writers, 1917–39* (Selinsgrove, PA: Susquehanna UP, 1992). McKay wrote his own review of the book in James Clarke, conductor, "Significant Books Reviewed by Their Own Authors," *McClure's* 60 (June 1928): 81.

  7. For more on this period, see McKay's essays "On Becoming a Roman Catholic," *Epistle* 2 (Spring 1945): 43–45 and "Why I Became a Catholic," *Ebony* 1 (March 1946): 32. See also Tillery 165–83 and Cooper 347–69.

BIBLIOGRAPHY

Bone, Robert A. *The Negro Novel in America*. New Haven, CT: Yale UP, 1958.

Cooper, Wayne F. *Claude McKay: Rebel Sojourner in the Harlem Renaissance, A Biography*. Baton Rouge: Louisiana UP, 1987.

Giles, James R. *Claude McKay*. Boston: G. K. Hall, 1976.

Hathaway, Heather. *Caribbean Waves: Relocating Claude McKay and Paule Marshall*. Bloomington: Indiana UP, 1999.

Helbling, Mark Irving. *The Harlem Renaissance: The One and the Many*. Westport, CT: Greenwood, 1999.

Huggins, Nathan Irvin. *Harlem Renaissance*. New York: Oxford, 1971.

James, Winston. *A Fierce Hatred of Injustice: Claude McKay's Jamaica and His Poetry of Rebellion*. London: Verso, 2000.

Kent, George. *Blackness and the Adventure of Western Culture*. Chicago: Third World P, 1972.

Lowney, John. "Haiti and Black Transnationalism: Remapping the Migrant Geography of *Home to Harlem*." *African American Review* 34 (2000): 413–19.

McKay, Claude. *Complete Poems*. Ed. and intro. by William J. Maxwell. Urbana: U of Illinois P, 2004.

———. *A Long Way from Home*. 1937. San Diego: Harcourt Brace, 1970.

McLeod, A. L., ed. *Claude McKay: Centennial Studies*. New Delhi: Sterling, 1992.

Ramchand, Kenneth. *The West Indian Novel and Its Background*. New York: Barnes and Noble, 1970.

Singh, Amritjit, ed. *The Novels of the Harlem Renaissance: Twelve Black Writers, 1923–1933*. University Park: Pennsylvania State UP, 1976.

Tillery, Tyrone. *Claude McKay: A Black Poet's Struggle for Identity*. Amherst: U of Massachusetts P, 1992.

Wagner, Jean. *Black Poets of the United States: From Paul Laurence Dunbar to Langston Hughes*. Trans. Kenneth Douglas. Urbana: U of Illinois P, 1973.

The Harlem Dancer

Applauding youths laughed with young prostitutes
And watched her perfect, half-clothed body sway;
Her voice was like the sound of blended flutes
Blown by black players upon a picnic day.

She sang and danced on gracefully and calm,
The light gauze hanging loose about her form;
To me she seemed a proudly-swaying palm
Grown lovelier for passing through a storm.
Upon her swarthy neck black shiny curls
Luxuriant fell; and tossing coins in praise,
The wine-flushed, bold-eyed boys, and even the girls,
Devoured her shape with eager, passionate gaze;
But looking at her falsely-smiling face,
I knew her self was not in that strange place.

From *Harlem Shadows* 1922

The Tired Worker

O whisper, O my soul! The afternoon
Is waning into evening, whisper soft!
Peace, O my rebel heart!* for soon the moon
From out its misty veil will swing aloft!
Be patient, weary body, soon the night
Will wrap thee gently in her sable sheet,
And with a leaden sigh thou wilt invite
To rest thy tired hands and aching feet.
The wretched day was theirs, the night is mine;
Come tender sleep, and fold me to thy breast.
But what steals out the gray clouds red like wine?
O dawn! O dreaded dawn! O let me rest!
Weary my veins, my brain, my life! Have pity!
No! Once again the harsh, the ugly city.

From *Harlem Shadows* 1922

My Mother

I

Reg* wished me to go with him to the field,
I paused because I did not want to go;
But in her quiet way she made me yield
Reluctantly, for she was breathing low.
Her hand she slowly lifted from her lap

And, smiling sadly in the old sweet way,
She pointed to the nail where hung my cap.
Her eyes said: I shall last another day.
But scarcely had we reached the distant place,
When o'er the hills we heard a faint bell ringing;
A boy came running up with frightened face;
We knew the fatal news that he was bringing.
I heard him listlessly, without a moan,
Although the only one I loved was gone.

II
The dawn departs, the morning is begun,
The trades* come whispering from off the seas,
The fields of corn are golden in the sun,
The dark-brown tassels fluttering in the breeze;
The bell is sounding and the children pass,
Frog-leaping, skipping, shouting, laughing shrill,
Down the red road, over the pasture-grass,
Up to the school-house crumbling on the hill.
The older folk are at their peaceful toil,
Some pulling up the weeds, some plucking corn,
And others breaking up the sun-baked soil.
Float, faintly-scented breeze, at early morn
Over the earth where mortals sow and reap—
Beneath its breast my mother lies asleep.

From *Harlem Shadows* 1922

Flame-Heart

So much have I forgotten in ten years,
So much in ten brief years! I have forgot
What time the purple apples* come to juice,
And what month brings the shy forget-me-not.
I have forgot the special, startling season
Of the pimento's flowering* and fruiting;
What time of year the ground doves brown the fields
And fill the noonday with their curious fluting.
I have forgotten much, but still remember
The poinsettia's red, blood-red in warm December.

I still recall the honey-fever grass,*
But cannot recollect the high days when
We rooted them out of the ping-wing* path
To stop the mad bees in the rabbit pen.
I often try to think in what sweet month
The languid painted ladies* used to dapple
The yellow by-road mazing from the main,
Sweet with the golden threads of the rose-apple.*
I have forgotten—strange—but quite remember
The poinsettia's red, blood-red in warm December.

What weeks, what months, what time of the mild year
We cheated school to have our fling at tops?
What days our wine-thrilled bodies pulsed with joy
Feasting upon blackberries in the copse?
Oh some I know! I have embalmed the days,
Even the sacred moments when we played,
All innocent of passion, uncorrupt,
At noon and evening in the flame-heart's shade.
We were so happy, happy, I remember,
Beneath the poinsettia's red in warm December.

From *Harlem Shadows* 1922

The Tropics in New York

Bananas ripe and green, and ginger-root,
    Cocoa in pods and alligator pears,*
And tangerines and mangoes and grape fruit,
    Fit for the highest prize at parish fairs,

Set in the window, bringing memories
    Of fruit-trees laden by low-singing rills,
And dewy dawns, and mystical blue skies
    In benediction over nun-like hills.

My eyes grew dim, and I could no more gaze;
    A wave of longing through my body swept,
And hungry for the old, familiar ways,

I turned aside and bowed my head and wept.

From *Harlem Shadows* 1922

If We Must Die

If we must die, let it not be like hogs
Hunted and penned in an inglorious spot,
While round us bark the mad and hungry dogs,
Making their mock at our accursèd lot.
If we must die, O let us nobly die,
So that our precious blood may not be shed
In vain; then even the monsters we defy
Shall be constrained to honor us though dead!
O kinsmen! we must meet the common foe!
Though far outnumbered let us show us brave,
And for their thousand blows deal one deathblow!
What though before us lies the open grave?
Like men we'll face the murderous, cowardly pack,
Pressed to the wall, dying, but fighting back!

From *Harlem Shadows* 1922

America

Although she feeds me bread of bitterness,
And sinks into my throat her tiger's tooth,
Stealing my breath of life, I will confess
I love this cultured hell that tests my youth!
Her vigor flows like tides into my blood,
Giving me strength erect against her hate.
Her bigness sweeps my being like a flood.
Yet as a rebel fronts a king in state,
I stand within her walls with not a shred
Of terror, malice, not a word of jeer.
Darkly I gaze into the days ahead,
And see her might and granite wonders there,
Beneath the touch of Time's unerring hand,
Like priceless treasures sinking in the sand.

From *Harlem Shadows* 1922

Baptism*

Into the furnace let me go alone;
Stay you without in terror of the heat.
I will go naked in—for thus 'tis sweet—
Into the weird depths of the hottest zone.
I will not quiver in the frailest bone,
You will not note a flicker of defeat;
My heart shall tremble not its fate to meet,
My mouth give utterance to any moan.
The yawning oven spits forth fiery spears;
Red aspish tongues shout wordlessly my name.
Desire destroys, consumes my mortal fears,
Transforming me into a shape of flame.
I will come out, back to your world of tears,
A stronger soul within a finer frame.

From *Harlem Shadows* 1922

Exhortation: Summer, 1919*

Through the pregnant universe rumbles life's terrific thunder,
And Earth's bowels quake with terror; strange and terrible storms
    break,
Lightning-torches flame the heavens, kindling souls of men, there-
    under:
Africa! long ages sleeping, O my motherland, awake!

In the East the clouds glow crimson with the new dawn that is
    breaking,
And its golden glory fills the western skies.
O my brothers and my sisters, wake! arise!
For the new birth rends the old earth and the very dead are waking,
Ghosts are turned flesh, throwing off the grave's disguise,
And the foolish, even children, are made wise;
For the big earth groans in travail for the strong, new world in
    making—
O my brothers, dreaming for dim centuries,
Wake from sleeping: to the East turn, turn your eyes!

Oh the night is sweet for sleeping, but the shining day's work for
    working;
Sons of the seductive night, for your children's children's sake,
From the deep primeval forests where the crouching leopard's
    lurking,
Lift up your heavy-lidded eyes, Ethiopia! awake!

In the East the clouds glow crimson with the new dawn that is
    breaking,
And its golden glory fills the western skies.
O my brothers and my sisters, wake! arise!
For the new birth rends the old earth and the very dead are waking,
Ghosts are turned flesh, throwing off the grave's disguise,
And the foolish, even children, are made wise;
For the big earth groans in travail for the strong, new world in
    making—
O my brothers, dreaming for long centuries,
Wake from sleeping; to the East turn, turn your eyes!

From *Harlem Shadows* 1922

The White House*

Your door is shut against my tightened face,
And I am sharp as steel with discontent;
But I possess the courage and the grace
To bear my anger proudly and unbent.
The pavement slabs burn loose beneath my feet,
And passion rends my vitals as I pass,
A chafing savage, down the decent street;
Where boldly shines your shuttered door of glass.
Oh I must search for wisdom every hour,
Deep in my wrathful bosom sore and raw,
And find in it the superhuman power
To hold me to the letter of your law!
Oh I must keep my heart inviolate,
Against the poison of your deadly hate.

From the *Liberator* May 1921

A Negro Poet

I am a black man, born in Jamaica, B. W. I., and have been living in America for the last six years. During my first year's residence in America I wrote the following group of poems. It was the first time I had ever come face to face with such manifest, implacable hate of my race, and my feelings were indescribable. I sent them so that you may see what my state of mind was at the time. I have written nothing similar to them since and don't think I ever shall again.

The whites at home constitute about 14 percent of the population only and they generally conform to the standard of English respectability. The few poor ones accept their fate resignedly and live at peace with the natives. The government is tolerant, somewhat benevolent, based on the principle of equal justice to all. I had heard of prejudice in America but never dreamed of it being so intensely bitter; for at home there is also prejudice of the English sort, subtle and dignified, rooted in class distinction—color and race being hardly taken into account.

It was such an atmosphere I left for America to find here strong white men, splendid types, of better physique than any I had ever seen, exhibiting the most primitive animal hatred towards their weaker black brothers. In the South daily murders of a nature most hideous and revolting, in the North silent acquiescence, deep hate half-hidden under a puritan respectability, oft flaming up into an occasional lynching—this ugly raw sore in the body of a great nation. At first I was horrified, my spirit revolted against the ignoble cruelty and blindness of it all. Then I soon found myself hating in return but this feeling couldn't last long for to hate is to be miserable.

Looking about me with bigger and clearer eyes I saw that this cruelty in different ways was going on all over the world. Whites were exploiting and oppressing whites even as they exploited and oppressed the yellows and blacks. And the oppressed, groaning under the lash, evinced the same despicable hate and harshness towards their weaker fellows. I ceased to think of people and things in the mass—why should I fight with mad dogs only to be bitten and probably transformed into a mad dog myself? I turned to the individual soul, the spiritual leaders, for comfort and consolation. I felt and still feel that one must seek for the noblest and best in the individual life only: each soul must save itself.

And now this great catastrophe [World War I] has come upon the world proving the real hollowness of nationhood, patriotism, racial pride and most of the things which one was taught to respect and reverence.

There is very little to tell of my uneventful career. I was born in the heart of the little island of Jamaica on the 15th of September, 1889. My grandparents were slaves, my parents free-born. My mother was very sweet-natured, fond of books; my father, honest, stern even to harshness, hard working, beginning empty-handed he coaxed a good living from the soil, bought land, and grew to be a comparatively prosperous small settler. A firm believer in education, he tried to give all his eight children the best he could afford.

I was the last child and when I was nine years old my mother sent me to my eldest brother who was a schoolmaster in the northwestern part of the island.

From that time on I became interested in books. The school building, to which was attached the teacher's cottage, was an old slave house, plain, substantial and comfortable. My brother, an amateur journalist, country correspondent for the city papers, was fond of good books and possessed a nice library—all the great English masters and a few translations from the ancients. Not caring very much for play and having plenty of leisure I spent nearly all my time out of school reading. I read whatever pleased my fancy, secretly scribbling in prose and verse at the same time, novels, history, Bible literature, tales in verse like Scott's I read, and nearly all Shakespeare's plays for the absorbing story interest. As yet I couldn't perceive the truths. Now, looking back, I can see that that was a great formative period of my life—a time of perfect freedom to play, read and think as I liked.

I finished elementary school with my brother and helped him to teach while studying further under him. In 1906 I passed an examination for the Government Trade Scholarship and was apprenticed to a wheelwright and cabinet maker. But I couldn't learn a trade.

At this time I began writing verses of Jamaican peasant life in Negro dialect. I met an Englishman who loved good books and their makers more than anything else. He opened up a new world to my view, introduced me to a greater, deeper literature—to Buddha, Schopenhauer and Goethe, Carlyle and Browning, Wilde, Carpenter,* Whitman, Hugo, Verlaine, Baudelaire, Shaw and the different writers of the Rationalist Press—more than I had time to read, but nearly all my spare time I spent listening to his reading choice bits from them, discussing the greatness of their minds, and telling of their lives, which I must confess I sometimes found even more interesting than their works.

Trade proved a failure. I gave it up, joined the Jamaican Constabulary 1910–11, despised it and left. With Mr. [Walter] Jekyll's help, the Englishman mentioned before, my *Songs of Jamaica* was published at this time. I went home and farmed rather half-heartedly. The government was then encouraging the younger men to acquire a scientific agricultural education so that it could employ them to teach the peasantry modern ways of farming. I came to America in 1912 to study agriculture, went to Tuskegee, but not liking the semi-military, machinelike existence there, I left for the Kansas State College where I stayed two years.

In the summer of 1914 I came to New York with a friend. We opened a little restaurant* among our people which also proved a failure because I didn't put all my time and energy into it.

After a while I got married,* but my wife wearied of the life in six months and went back to Jamaica. I hated to go back after having failed at nearly everything so I just stayed here and worked desultorily—porter, houseman, janitor, butler, waiter—anything that came handy. The life was different and fascinating and one can do menial work here and feel like a man sometimes, so I didn't mind it.

I am a waiter on the railroad now. Here are a few of my poems.*

From *Pearson's Magazine* September 1918

Garvey as a Negro Moses

Garveyism is a well-worn word in Negro New York.

And it is known among all the Negroes of America, and throughout the world, wherever there are race-conscious Negro groups. But while Garvey is a sort of magic name among the ignorant black masses, the Negro intelligentsia thinks by his spectacular antics—words big with bombast, colorful robes, Anglo-Saxon titles of nobility (Sir William Ferris, K. C. O. N., for instance, his editor, and Lady Henrietta Vinton Davis, his international organizer), his stream-roller-like mass meetings and parades and lamentable business ventures—Garvey has muddied the waters of the Negro movement for freedom and put the race back for many years. But the followers of Marcus Garvey, who are legion and noisy as a tambourine yard party, give him the crown of Negro leadership. Garvey, they assert, with his Universal Negro Improvement Association and the Black Star Line, has given the Negro problem a universal advertisement and made it as popular as Negro minstrelsy. Where men like Booker T. Washington, Dr. Du Bois of the National Association for the Advancement of Colored People, and William Monroe Trotter of the Equal Rights League had but little success, Garvey succeeded in bringing the Associated Press to its knees every time he bellowed. And his words were trumpeted round the degenerate pale-face world trembling with fear of the new Negro.

To those who know Jamaica, the homeland of Marcus Garvey, Garveyism inevitably suggests the name of Bedwardism.* Bedwardism is the name of a religious sect there, purely native in its emotional and external features and patterned after the Baptists. It is the true religion of thousands of natives, calling themselves Bedwardites. It was founded by an illiterate black giant named Bedward about 25 years ago, who claimed medical and healing properties for a sandy little hole beside a quiet river that flowed calmly to the sea through the eastern part of Jamaica. In the beginning prophet Bedward was a stock newspaper joke; but when thousands began flocking to hear the gigantic white-robed servant of God at his quarterly baptism, and the police were hard put to handle the crowds, the British Government in Jamaica became irritated. Bedward was warned and threatened and even persecuted a little, but his thousands of followers stood more firmly by him and made him rich with great presents of food, clothing, jewelry and money. So Bedward waxed fat in body and spirit. He began a great building of stone to the God of Bedwardism which he declared could not be finished until the Second Coming of Christ. And in the plenitude of his powers he sat in his large yard under an orange tree, his wife and grown children, all good Bedwardites, around him, and gave out words of wisdom on his religion and upon topical questions to the pilgrims who went daily to worship and to obtain a bottle of water from the holy hole. The most recent news of the prophet was his recent arrest by the government for causing hundreds of his followers to sell all their possessions and come together at his home in August Town to witness his annunciation; for on a certain day at noon, he had said, he would ascend into heaven upon a crescent moon. The devout sold and gave away all their property and flocked to August Town, and the hour of the certain day came and passed with Bedward waiting in his white robes, and days followed and weeks after. Then his flock of sheep, now turned into a hungry, destitute, despairing mob, howled like hyenas and fought each other until the Government interfered.

It may be that the notorious career of Bedward, the prophet, worked unconsciously upon Marcus Garvey's mind and made him work out his plans along similar spectacular lines. But between the mentality of both men there is no comparison. While Bedward was a huge inflated bag of bombast loaded with ignorance and superstition, Garvey's is beyond doubt a very energetic and quick-witted mind, barb-wired by the imperial traditions of nineteenth-century England. His spirit is revolutionary, but his intellect does not understand the significance of modern revolutionary developments. Maybe he chose not to understand[,] he may have realized that a resolute facing of facts would make puerile his beautiful schemes for the redemption of the continent of Africa.

It is rather strange that Garvey's political ideas should be so curiously bourgeois-obsolete and fantastically utopian. For he is not of the school of Negro leader that has existed solely on the pecuniary crumbs of Republican politics and democratic philanthropy, and who is absolutely incapable of understanding the Negro-proletarian point of view and the philosophy of the working class movement. On the contrary, Garvey's background is very industrial, for in the West Indies the Negro problem is peculiarly economic, and prejudice is, Englishwise, more of class than of race. The flame of revolt must have stirred in Garvey in his early youth when he found the doors to higher education barred against him through economic pressure. For when he became a printer by trade in Kingston he was active in organizing the compositors, and he was the leader of the printers' strike there, 10 years ago, during which time he brought out a special propaganda sheet for the strikers. The strike failed and Garvey went to Europe, returning to Jamaica after a few months' stay abroad, to start his Universal Negro Society. He failed at this in Jamaica, where a tropical laziness settles like a warm fog over the island. Coming to New York in 1917, he struck the black belt like a cyclone, and there lay the foundation of the Universal Negro Improvement Association and the Black Star Line.

At that time the World War had opened up a new field for colored workers. There was less race discrimination in the ranks of labor and the factory gates swung open to the Negro worker. There was plenty of money to spare. Garvey began his "Back to Africa" propaganda in the streets of Harlem, and in a few months he had made his organ, "the Negro World," the best edited colored weekly in New York. The launching of the Black Star Line project was the grand event of the movement among all Garveyites, and it had an electrifying effect upon all the Negro peoples of the world—even the black intelligentsia. It landed on the front page of the white press and made good copy for the liberal weeklies and the incorruptible monthlies. The "Negro World" circulated 60,000 copies, and a perusal of its correspondence page showed letters breathing an intense love for Africa from the farthest ends of the world. The movement for African redemption had taken definite form in the minds of Western Negroes, and the respectable Negro uplift organizations were shaken up to realize the significance of "Back to Africa." The money for shares of the Black Star Line poured in in hundreds and thousands of dollars, some brilliant Negro leaders were drawn to the organization, and the little Negro press barked at Garvey from every part of the country, questioning his integrity and impugning his motives. And Garvey, Hearst-like, thundered back his threats at the critics through the "Negro World" and was soon involved in a net of law suits.

The most puzzling thing about the "Back to Africa" propaganda is the leader's repudiation of all the fundamentals of the black worker's economic struggle. No intelligent Negro dare deny the almost miraculous effect and the world-wide breadth and sweep of Garvey's propaganda methods. But all those who think broadly on social conditions are amazed at Garvey's ignorance and his intolerance of modern social ideas. To him Queen Victoria and Lincoln are the greatest figures in history because they both freed the slaves, and the Negro race will never reach the heights of greatness until it has produced such types. He talks of Africa as if it were a little island in the Caribbean Sea. Ignoring all geographical and political divisions, he gives his followers the idea that that vast continent of diverse tribes consists of a large homogeneous nation of natives struggling for freedom and waiting for the Western Negroes to come and help them drive out the European exploiters. He has never urged Negroes to organize in industrial unions.

He only exhorted them to get money, buy shares in his African steamship line, and join his Universal Association. And thousands of American and West Indian Negroes responded with eagerness.

He denounced the Socialists and Bolshevists for plotting to demoralize the Negro workers and bring them under the control of white labor. And in the same breath he attacked the National Association for the Advancement of Colored People, and its founder, Dr. Du Bois, for including white leaders and members. In the face of his very capable mulatto and octoroon colleagues, he advocated an all-sable nation of Negroes to be governed strictly after the English plan with Marcus Garvey as supreme head.

He organized a Negro Legion and a Negro Red Cross in the heart of Harlem. The Black Star line consisted of two unseaworthy boats and the Negro Factories Corporation was mainly existent on paper. But it seems that Garvey's sole satisfaction in his business venture was the presenting of grandiose visions to his crowd.

Garvey's arrest by the Federal authorities after five years of stupendous vaudeville is a fitting climax. He should feel now an ultimate satisfaction in the fact that he was a universal advertising manager. He was the biggest popularizer of the Negro problem, especially among Negroes, since "Uncle Tom's Cabin." He attained the sublime. During the last days he waxed more falsely eloquent in his tall talks on the Negro Conquest of Africa, and when the clansmen yelled their approval and clamored for more, in his gorgeous robes, he lifted his hands to the low ceiling in a weird pose, his huge ugly bulk cowing the crowd, and told how the mysteries of African magic had been revealed to him, and how he would use them to put the white man to confusion and drive him out of Africa.

From the *Liberator* April 1922

Soviet Russia and the Negro (Part 2)*

Russia, in broad terms, is a country where all the races of Europe and of Asia meet and mix. The fact is that under the repressive power of the Czarist bureaucracy the different races preserved a degree of kindly tolerance towards each other. The fierce racial hatreds that flame in the Balkans never existed in Russia. Where in the South no Negro might approach a *"cracker"* as a man for friendly offices, a Jewish pilgrim in old Russia could find rest and sustenance in the home of an orthodox peasant. It is a problem to define the Russian type by features. The Hindu, the Mongolian, the Prussian, the Arab, the West

European—all these types may be traced woven into the distinctive polyglot population of Moscow. And so, to the Russian, I was merely another type, but stranger, with which they were not yet familiar. They were curious with me, all and sundry, young and old, in a friendly, refreshing manner. Their curiosity had none of the intolerable impertinence and often downright affront that any very dark colored man, be he Negro, Indian or Arab, would experience in Germany and England.

In 1920, while I was trying to get out a volume of my poems in London, I had a visit with Bernard Shaw who remarked that it must be tragic for a sensitive Negro to be an artist. Shaw was right. Some of the English reviews of my book touched the very bottom of journalistic muck. The English reviewer outdid his American cousin (except the South, of course, which could not surprise any white person much less a black) in sprinkling criticism with racial prejudice. The sedate, copperhead *Spectator* as much as said: no "cultured" white man could read a Negro's poetry without prejudice, that instinctively he must search for that "something" that must make him antagonistic to it. But fortunately Mr. McKay did not offend our susceptibilities! The English people from the lowest to the highest, cannot think of a black man as being anything but an entertainer, boxer, a Baptist preacher or a menial. The Germans are just a little worse. Any healthy looking black coon of an adventurous streak can have a wonderful time palming himself off as another Siki* or a buck dancer. When an American writer introduced me as a poet to a very cultured German, a lover of all the arts, he could not believe it, and I don't think he does yet. An American student tells his middle class landlady that he is having a black friend to lunch: "But are you sure that he is not a cannibal?" she asks, without a flicker of a humorous smile!

But in Petrograd and Moscow, I could not detect a trace of this ignorant snobbishness among the educated classes, and the attitude of the common workers, the soldiers and sailors was still more remarkable. It was so beautifully naive; for them I was only a black member of the world of humanity. It may be urged that the fine feelings of the Russians towards a Negro was the effect of Bolshevist pressure and propaganda. The fact is that I spent most of my lecture time in nonpartisan and anti-bolshevist circles. In Moscow I found the Luxe Hotel where I put up extremely depressing, the dining room was anathema to me and I grew tired to death of meeting the proletarian ambassadors from foreign lands, some of whom bore themselves as if they were the holy messengers of Jesus, Prince of Heaven, instead of working-class representatives. And so I spent many of my free evenings at the Domino Café, a notorious den of the dilettante poets and writers. There came the young anarchists and menshevists* and all the young aspiring fry to read and discuss their poetry and prose. Sometimes a group of the older men came too. One evening I noticed Pilnyak, the novelist, Okonoff the critic, Feodor* the translator of Poe, an editor, a theatre manager and their young disciples, beer-drinking through a very interesting literary discussion. There was always music, good folk-singing and bad fiddling, the place was more like a second rate cabaret than a poets' club, but nevertheless much to be enjoyed, with amiable chats and light banter through which the evening wore pleasantly away. This was the meeting place of the frivolous set with whom I eased my mind after writing all day.

The evenings of the proletarian poets held in the Arbot were much more serious affairs. The leadership was communist, the audience working class and attentive like diligent, elementary school children. To these meetings also came some of the keener intellects from the Domino Café. One of these young women told me that she wanted to keep in touch with all the phases of the new culture. In Petrograd the meetings of the intelligentzia seemed more formal and inclusive. There were such notable men there as Chukovsky the critic, Eugene Zamiatan the celebrated novelist and Maishack* the poet and translator of Kipling. The artist and theatre world were also represented. There was no communist spirit in evidence at these intelligentzia gatherings. Frankly there was an undercurrent of hostility to the bolshevists. But I was invited to speak and read my poems whenever I appeared at any of them and treated with every courtesy and consideration as a writer. Among those sophisticated and cultured Russians, many of them speaking from two to four languages, there was no overdoing of the correct thing, no vulgar wonderment and bounderish superiority over a Negro's being a poet. I was a poet, that was all, and their keen questions showed that they were much more interested in the technique of my poetry, my views on and my position regarding the modern literary movements than in the difference of my color. Although I will not presume that there was no attraction at all in that little difference!

On my last visit to Petrograd I stayed in the Palace of the Grand Duke Vladimir Alexander, the brother of Czar Nicholas the Second. His old, kindly steward who looked after my comfort wanders round like a ghost through the great rooms. The house is now the headquarters of the Petrograd intellectuals. A fine painting of the Duke stands curtained in the dining room. I was told that he was liberal minded, a patron of the arts, and much liked by the Russian intelligentzia. The atmosphere of the house was theoretically non-political, but I quickly scented a strong hostility to bolshevist authority. But even here I had only pleasant encounters and illuminating conversations with the inmates and visitors, who freely expressed their views against the Soviet Government, although they knew me to be very sympathetic to it.

During the first days of my visit I felt that the great demonstration of friendliness was somehow expressive of the enthusiastic spirit of the glad anniversary days, that after the month was ended I could calmly settle down to finish the book about the American Negro that the State Publishing Department of Moscow had commissioned me to write, and in the meantime quietly go about making interesting contacts. But my days in Russia were a progression of affectionate enthusiasm of the people towards me. Among the factory workers, the red-starred and chevroned soldiers and sailors, the proletarian students and children, I could not get off as lightly as I did with the intelligentzia. At every meeting I was received with boisterous acclaim, mobbed with friendly demonstration. The women workers of the great bank in Moscow insisted on hearing about the working conditions of the colored women of America and after a brief outline I was asked the most exacting questions concerning the positions that were most available to colored women, their wages and general relationship with the white women workers. The details I could not give; but when I got through, the Russian women passed a resolution sending greetings to the colored women workers of America, exhorting them to organize their forces and send a woman representative to Russia. I received a similar message from the Propaganda Department of the Petrograd Soviet which is managed by Nicoleva, a very energetic woman. There I was shown the new status of the Russian women gained through the revolution of 1917. Capable women can fit themselves for any position; equal pay with men for equal work; full pay during the period of pregnancy and no work for the mother two months before and two months after the confinement. Getting a divorce is comparatively easy and not influenced by money power, detective chicanery and wire pulling. A special department looks into the problems of joint personal property and the guardianship and support of the children. There is no penalty for legal abortion and no legal stigma of illegitimacy attaching to children born out of wedlock.

There were no problems of the submerged lower classes and the suppressed national minorities of the old Russia that could not bear comparison with the grievous position of the millions of Negroes in the United States to-day. Just as Negroes are barred from the American Navy and the higher ranks of the Army, so were the Jews and the sons of the peasantry and proletariat discriminated against in the Russian Empire. It is needless repetition of the obvious to say that Soviet Russia does not tolerate such discriminations, for the actual government of the country is now in the hands of the combined national minorities, the peasantry and the proletariat. By the permission of Leon Trotsky, Commissar-in-chief of the military and naval forces of Soviet Russia, I visited the highest military schools in the Kremlin and environs of Moscow. And there I saw the new material, the sons of the working people in training as cadets by the old officers of the upper classes. For two weeks I was a guest of the Red Navy in Petrograd with the same eager proletarian youth of new Russia, who conducted me through the intricate machinery of submarines, took me over aeroplanes captured from the British during the counter-revolutionary war around Petrograd and showed me the making of a warship ready for action. And even of greater interest was the life of the men and the officers, the simplified discipline that was strictly enforced, the food that was served for each and all alike, the extra political educational classes and the extreme tactfulness and elasticity of the political commissars, all communists, who act as advisers and arbitrators between the men and students and the officers. Twice or thrice I was given some of the *kasha* which is sometimes served with the meals. In Moscow I grew to like this food very much, but it was always difficult to get. I had always imagined that it was quite unwholesome and unpalatable and eaten by the Russian peasant only on account of extreme poverty. But on the contrary I found it very rare and sustaining when cooked right with a bit of meat and served with butter—a grain food very much like the common but very delicious West Indian rice-and-peas.

The red cadets are seen in the best light at their gymnasium exercises and at the political assemblies when discipline is set aside. Especially at the latter where a visitor feels that he is in the midst of the early revolutionary days, so hortatory are the speeches, so intense the enthusiasm of the men. At all these meetings I had to speak and the students asked me general questions about the Negro in the American Army and Navy, and when I gave them the common information, known to all American Negroes, students, officers and commissars were unanimous in wishing that a group of young American Negroes would take up training to become officers in the Army and Navy of Soviet Russia.

The proletarian students of Moscow were eager to learn of the life and work of Negro students. They sent messages of encouragement and good will to the Negro students of America and, with a fine gesture of fellowship, elected the Negro delegate of the American Communist party and myself to honorary membership in the Moscow Soviet.

Those Russian days remain the most memorable of my life. The intellectual Communists and the intelligentzia were interested to know that America had produced a formidable body of Negro intelligentzia and professionals, possessing a distinctive literature and cultural and business interests alien to the white man's. And they think naturally, that the militant leaders of the intelligentzia must feel and express the spirit of revolt that is slumbering in the inarticulate Negro masses, precisely as the emancipation movement of the Russian masses had passed through similar phases.

Russia is prepared and waiting to receive couriers and heralds of good will and international understanding from the Negro race. Her demonstration of friendliness and equality for Negroes may not conduce to promote healthy relations between Soviet Russia and democratic America[;] the anthropologists of 100 per cent pure white Americanism may soon invoke Science to prove that the Russians are not at all God's white people. I even caught a little of American anti-Negro propaganda in Russia. A friend of mine, a member of the Moscow intelligentzia repeated to me the remarks of the lady correspondent of a Danish newspaper: that I should not be taken as a representative Negro for she had lived in America and found all Negroes lazy, bad and vicious, a terror to white women. In Petrograd I got a like story from Chukovsky, the critic, who was on intimate terms with a high worker of the American Relief Administration and his southern wife. Chukovsky is himself an intellectual "westerner," the term applied to those Russians who put Western-European civilization before Russian culture and believe that Russia's salvation lies in becoming completely westernized. He had spent an impressionable part of his youth in London and adores all things English, and during the world war was very pro-English. For the American democracy, also, he expresses unfeigned admiration. He has more Anglo-American books than Russian in his fine library and considers the literary section of the New York Times a journal of a very high standard. He is really a maniac of Anglo-Saxon American culture. Chukovsky was quite incredulous when I gave him the facts of the Negro's status in American civilization.

"The Americans are a people of such great energy and ability," he said, "how could they act so petty towards a racial minority?" And then he related an experience of his in London that bore a strong smell of *cracker* breath. However, I record it here in the belief that it is authentic for Chukovsky is a man of integrity: About the beginning of the century, he was sent to England as correspondent of a newspaper in Odessa, but in London he was more given to poetic dreaming and studying English literature in the British Museum and rarely sent any news home. So he lost his job and had to find cheap, furnished rooms. A few weeks later, after he had taken up his residence in new quarters, a black guest arrived, an American gentleman of the cloth. The preacher procured a room on the top floor and used the dining and sitting room with the other guests among whom was a white American family. The latter protested the presence of the Negro in the house and especially in the guest room. The landlady was in a dilemma, she could not lose her American boarders and the clergyman's money was not to be despised. At last she compromised by getting the white Americans to agree to the Negro's staying without being allowed the privilege of the guest room, and Chukovsky was asked to tell the Negro the truth. Chukovsky strode upstairs to give the unpleasant facts to the preacher and to offer a little consolation, but the black man was not unduly offended:

"The white guests have the right to object to me," he explained, anticipating Garvey, "they belong to a superior race."

"But," said Chukovsky, "*I* do not object to you. *I* don't feel any difference; we don't understand color prejudice in Russia."

"Well," philosophized the preacher, "you are very kind, but taking the scriptures as authority, I don't consider the Russians to be white people."

From the *Crisis* January 1924

Courtesy of the Literary Representatives for the Works of Claude McKay, Schomburg Center for Research in Black Culture, the New York Public Library, Astor, Lenox and Tilden Foundations.

A Negro to His Critics

When the work of a Negro writer wins recognition it creates two widely separate bodies of opinion, one easily recognizable by the average reader as general and the other limited to Negroes and therefore racial.

Although this racial opinion may seem negligible to the general reader, it is a formidable thing to the Negro writer. He may pretend to ignore it without really succeeding or being able to escape its influence, for very likely he has his social contacts with the class of Negroes who create and express this opinion in their conversation and through the hundreds of weekly Negro newspapers and the monthly magazines.

This peculiar racial opinion constitutes a kind of censorship of what is printed about the Negro. No doubt it had its origin in the laudable efforts of intelligent Negro groups to protect their race from the slander of its detractors after Emancipation, and grew until it crystallized into racial consciousness. The pity is that these leaders of racial opinion should also be in the position of sole arbiters of intellectual and artistic things within the Negro world. For although they may be excellent persons worthy of all respect and eminently right in their purpose, they often do not distinguish between the task of propaganda and the work of art.

I myself have lived a great deal in the atmosphere of this opinion in America, in sympathy with and in contact with leaders and groups expressing it and am aware of their limitations.

A Negro writer feeling the urge to write faithfully about the people he knows from real experience and impartial observation is caught in a dilemma (unless he possesses a very strong sense of esthetic values) between the opinion of this group and his own artistic conscientiousness. I have read pages upon pages of denunciation of young Negro poets and story-tellers who were trying to grasp and render the significance of the background, the fundamental rhythm of Aframerican life. But not a line of critical encouragement for the artistic exploitation of the homely things—of Maundy's wash tub, Aunt Jemima's white folks, Miss Ann's old clothes for work-and-wages, George's Yessah-boss, dining car and Pullman services, barber and shoe shine shop, chittling and corn pone joints—all the lowly things that go to the formation of the Aframerican soil in which the best, the most pretentious of Aframerican society still has its roots.

My own experience has been amazing. Before I published *Home to Harlem* I was known to the Negro public as the writer of the hortatory poem, "If We Must Die." This poem was written during the time of the Chicago race riots. I was then a train waiter in the service of the Pennsylvania Railroad. Our dining car was running between New York, Philadelphia and Pittsburgh, Harrisburg and Washington and I remember we waiters and cooks carried revolvers in secret and always kept together going from our quarters to the railroad yards, as a precaution against a sudden attack.

The poem was an outgrowth of the intense emotional experience I was living through (no doubt with thousands of other Negroes) in those days. It appeared in the radical magazine "The Liberator," and was widely reprinted in the Negro press. Later it was included in my book of poetry, "Harlem Shadows." At the time I was writing a great deal of lyric poetry and none of my colleagues on "The Liberator" considered me a propaganda poet who could reel off revolutionary poetry like an automatic machine cutting fixed patterns. If we were a rebel group because we had faith that human life might be richer, by the same token we believed in the highest standards of creative work.

"If We Must Die" immediately won popularity among Aframericans, but the tone of the Negro critics was apologetic. To them a poem that voiced the deep-rooted instinct of self-preservation seemed merely a daring piece of impertinence. The dean of Negro critics denounced me as a "violent and angry propagandist, using his natural poetic gifts to clothe angry and defiant thoughts."* A young disciple characterized me as "rebellious and vituperative."

Thus it seems that respectable Negro opinion and criticism are not ready for artistic or other iconoclasm in Negroes. Between them they would emasculate the colored literary aspirant. Because Aframerican group life is possible only on a neutral and negative level our critics are apparently under the delusion that an Aframerican literature and art may be created out of evasion and insincerity.

They seem afraid of the revelation of bitterness in Negro life. But it may as well be owned, and frankly by those who know the inside and heart of Negro life, that the Negro, and especially the American, has bitterness in him in spite of his joyous exterior. And the more educated he is in these times the more he is likely to have.

The spirituals and the blues were not created out of sweet deceit. There is as much sublimated bitterness in them as there is humility, pathos and bewilderment. And if the Negro is a little bitter, the white man should be the last person in the world to accuse him of bitterness. For the feeling of bitterness is a natural part of the black man's birthright as the feeling of superiority is of the white man's. It matters not so much that one has had an experience of bitterness, but rather how one has developed out of it. To ask the Negro to render up his bitterness is asking him to part with his soul. For out of his bitterness he has bloomed and created his spirituals and blues and conserved his racial attributes—his humor and ripe laughter and particular rhythm of life.

However, with the publication of "Home to Harlem" the Aframerican elite realized that there was another side to me and changed their tune accordingly. If my poetry had been too daring, my prose was too dirty. The first had alarmed, the second had gassed them. And as soon as they recovered from the last shock, they did not bite their tongues in damning me as a hog rooting in Harlem, a buzzard hovering over the Black Belt scouting for carcasses and altogether a filthy beast.

If my brethren had taken the trouble to look a little into my obscure life they would have discovered that years before I had recaptured the spirit of the Jamaican peasants in verse, rendering their primitive joys, their loves and hates, their work and play, their dialect. And what I did in prose for Harlem was very similar to what I had done for Jamaica in verse.

The colored elite thought that if animal joy and sin and sorrow and dirt existed in the Belt as they did in ghettos, slums, tenderloins and such like places all over the world, they had no place in literature, and therefore my book was a deliberate slander against Aframerica.

From being too much of a rebel I was now a traitor who should be suppressed. . . .

Here I may well protest publicly that my affection for Aframerica is profound. During my first couple of years in the States as a student I had a real admiration for the many colored students I came to know and the refined colored society I was introduced into at Tuskegee, Manhattan (Kansas), Kansas City, Wichita, Denver and later for the smart set of musicians and theatrical persons I met in New York.

But it was not until I was forced down among the rough body of the great serving class of Negroes that I got to know my Aframerica. I was perhaps then at the most impressionable adult age and the warm contact with my workmates, boys and girls, their spontaneous ways of acting on and living for the moment, the physical and sensuous delights, the loose freedom in contrast to the definite peasant patterns by which I had been raised—all served to feed the riotous sentiments smoldering in me and cut me finally adrift from the fixed moorings my mind had been led to respect, but to which my heart had never held. During the first years among these Negroes my only object in working was to possess the means to live as they did. I forgot poetry.

I did not grow up in the fear of skeletons in the closet, whether they were family, national or racial, sacred cows and the washing of dirty clothes in public. And I have often wondered why many subjects that seemed to me most beautiful and suitable for literature and by which art might have done better than society—subjects that intellectual persons of both sexes discuss over the dinner table and in the salon and that people in the street gossip about should be publicly shocking in print and taboo in art.

What does it matter that the superior class of Negroes are all aware of the existence of the Jakes and Strawberry Lips and Billy Biasses, the Congo Roses, Susies and Madam Lauras* of the race; that they sometimes get up round robins for the white landlord to put them out of the nice Black Belt streets when they flaunt themselves too boldly in the face of Colored Respectability. The best Negroes will gossip and joke about such people in their drawing rooms, but as soon as they are captured as characters between the covers of a book and made to live in black and white, these same people set up a howl of protest, and all their organs from the littlest newspaper in Alabama to the heaviest magazine in New York burst forth in denunciation of the writer as a traitor to his race.

Their idea is that Negroes in literature and art should be decorous and decorative. These nice Negroes think that the white public, reading about the doings of the common Negroes, will judge them by the same standards. I should be the last person to defend the intelligence of any public simply because it read. However, the whites may know more about the blacks on the inside than the blacks think. Who knows that there may not be a potential writer among the young men of the vice squad doing the Belts who is making careful use of his eyes and ears while chasing a job? Or that there may not be an intellectual among the white bohemians who are privileged guests at exclusive Negro speakeasies and in the homes of the colored smart sets? . . . Negro apprentices to the craft of writing may be quite raw in dealing with the material to their hand, but their work will have that authentic ring of one who has lived familiarly and freely in the atmosphere of his creation. And if they sin a little on the side of crude realism—why, no people more than a suppressed minority needs self-criticism to save itself from the miserable soul-stifling pit of self-pity. If aspiring Negro writers are made afraid and artistically inarticulate from fear and pressure within their own circles, the truth may come from without, perhaps in unpleasant and inartistic form.

On the "broader" side (literally at least) my work has been approached by some discriminating critics as if I were a primitive savage and altogether a stranger to civilization. Perhaps I myself unconsciously gave that impression. However, I should not think it was unnatural for a man to have a predilection for a civilization or culture other than that he was born unto. Whatever may be the criticism implied in my writing of Western civilization I do not regard myself as a stranger but as a child of it, even though I may have become so by the comparatively recent process of grafting. I am as conscious of my new-world birthright as of my African origin, being aware of the one and its significance in my development as much as I feel the other emotionally.

One of my most considerate critics suggested that I might make a trip to Africa and there write about Negro life in its pure state. But I don't believe that any such place exists anywhere upon the earth today, since modern civilization has touched and stirred the remotest corners. I cherish no Utopian illusions about any state of human society. Poets may dream, but dreams are ferment of the stuff of experience. The poet of a subject people may sing for the day of deliverance without being afflicted by fanciful visions of any society of people in which the eternal problems of existence would not still exist. A Negro poet living in a purely Negro community would automatically become free of the special problems of race and color, of foreign arrogance insisting upon an aristocracy of color or stock and that a man of parts was inferior because the group of people he belonged to was suppressed by brute power.

But I can see no reason why an Aframerican intellectual should go to any part of Africa to undertake an experiment in living unless he felt irresistibly forced to do so. Negroid Africa will produce in time its own modern poets and artists peculiar to its soil. The Aframerican may gain spiritual benefits by returning in *spirit* to this African origin, but as an artist he will remain a unique product of Western civilization, with something of himself to give that will be very different from anything that may come out of a purely African community.

I don't know if I ever suggested the superiority of pure-black over pure-white virtues, although I will confess that I do prefer virtues that are colorful to the sepulchral kinds. Some sympathetic critics have rebuked me for making my black drifters finer than the white, when I thought I was being specially impartial. I may have sinned in my book "Banjo" by being too photographic, too much under the fetid atmosphere of the bottoms of Marseilles.

But there was factually a remarkable difference between the attitude of the white and the black drifters. Most of the black[s], and especially the Aframericans, were virtually taking a holiday away from the United States—a country where they had less freedom of movement and contact with white people than in Europe. They could return when they wanted to, but preferred to exist as they could on the beach because Europe was new-found land to them.

But the whites were Europeans who had been rounded up in America to be dumped upon the shores from which they had been trying to escape. Some of them came from unimaginably poor and austere regions, others from countries ruled by dictatorships under which they dreaded to return and had been mercifully set down upon the more hospitable shores of Provence. One sees at once why these men were despondent and lacking in the irresponsible holiday spirit of the blacks.

From all this I should say that we are all floundering in a mass of race, color, national consciousness and all the correlative consciousnesses. Besides, many of us who are trying to see and live tolerantly and temperately are worried by a guilty conscience. White and colored. In spite of our professions we become very self-conscious and rather uneasy as soon as we open a book in which there are white and colored characters in action or in conflict. We are prone to put too much stress on the identity of the characters, having an automatic reaction to them not just as people but rather as types representative of our separate divisions. And we are quick to pounce upon exaggerated types that we think were presented with bias, forgetting that bias may be in our own minds. But as one finds this trait even among the great major groups of people who own and inherit the earth—to a despairing extent to any one who puts the artistic record of life above patriotism and prejudice—it may be forgiven among the poor minorities, especially the colored, who often find it rubbed into them that their state is due to their lack of "white" virtues.

In a tale some characters will almost always be finer than others. One may have the highest ideals of human brotherhood, but the fact under our ideals is that humanity is actually divided into races and nations and classes. And individuals do bear the marks of their special group.

A sincere artist can represent characters only as they seem to him. And he *will* see characters through his predilections and prejudices, unless he sets himself deliberately to present those cinema-type figures that are produced to offend no unit of persons whose protest may involve financial loss. The time when a writer will stick only to the safe old ground of his own class of people is undoubtedly passing. Especially in America, where all the peoples of the world are scrambling side by side and modern machines and the ramifications of international commerce are steadily breaking down the ethnological barriers that separate the peoples of the world.

From the *New York Herald-Tribune* March 6, 1932

Courtesy of the Literary Representatives for the Works of Claude McKay, Schomburg Center for Research in Black Culture, the New York Public Library, Astor, Lenox and Tilden Foundations.

Arrival (from Home to Harlem)

Jake was paid off. He changed a pound note he had brought with him. He had fifty-nine dollars. From South Ferry he took an express subway train for Harlem.

Jake drank three Martini cocktails with cherries in them. The price, he noticed, had gone up from ten to twenty-five cents. He went to Bank's and had a Maryland fried-chicken feed—a big one with candied sweet potatoes.

He left his suitcase behind the counter of a saloon on Lenox Avenue. He went for a promenade on Seventh Avenue between One Hundred and Thirty-fifth and One Hundred and Fortieth Streets. He thrilled to Harlem. His blood was hot. His eyes were alert as he sniffed the street like a hound. Seventh Avenue was nice, a little too nice that night.

Jake turned off on Lenox Avenue. He stopped before an ice-cream parlor to admire girls sipping ice-cream soda through straws. He went into a cabaret. . . .

A little brown girl aimed the arrow of her eye at him as he entered. Jake was wearing a steel-gray English suit. It fitted him loosely and well, perfectly suited his presence. She knew at once that Jake must have just landed. She rested her chin on the back of her hands and smiled at him. There was something in his attitude, in his hungry wolf's eyes, that went warmly to her. She was brown, but she had tinted her leaf-like face to a ravishing chestnut. She had on an orange scarf over a green frock, which was way above her knees, giving an adequate view of legs lovely in fine champagne-colored stockings. . . .

Her shaft hit home. . . . Jake crossed over to her table. He ordered Scotch and soda.

"Scotch is better with soda or even water," he said. "English folks don't take whisky straight, as we do."

But she preferred ginger ale in place of soda. The cabaret singer, seeing that they were making up to each other, came expressly over to their table and sang. Jake gave the singer fifty cents. . . .

Her left hand was on the table. Jake covered it with his right.

"Is it clear sailing between us, sweetie?" he asked.

"Sure thing. . . . You just landed from over there?"

"Just today!"

"But there wasn't no boat in with soldiers today, daddy."

"I made it in a special one."

"Why, you lucky baby! . . . I'd like to go to another place, though. What about you?"

"Anything you say, I'm game," responded Jake.

They walked along Lenox Avenue. He held her arm. His flesh tingled. He felt as if his whole body was a flaming wave. She was intoxicated, blinded under the overwhelming force.

But nevertheless she did not forget her business.

"How much is it going to be, daddy?" she demanded.

"How much? *How* much? Five?"

"Aw, no, daddy. . . ."

"Ten?"

She shook her head.

"Twenty, sweety!" he said, gallantly.

"Daddy," she answered, "I wants fifty."

"Good," he agreed. He was satisfied. She was responsive. She was beautiful. He loved the curious color on her cheek.

They went to a buffet flat on One Hundred and Thirty-seventh Street. The proprietress opened the door without removing the chain and peeked out. She was a matronly mulatto woman. She recognized the girl, who had put herself in front of Jake, and she slid back the chain and said, "Come right in."

The windows were heavily and carefully shaded. There was beer and wine, and there was plenty of hard liquor. Black and brown men sat at two tables in one room, playing poker. In the other room a phonograph was grinding out a "blues," and some couples were dancing, thick as maggots in a vat of sweet liquor, and as wriggling.

Jake danced with the girl. They shuffled warmly, gloriously about the room. He encircled her waist with both hands, and she put both of hers up to his shoulders and laid her head against his breast. And they shuffled around.

"Harlem! Harlem!" thought Jake. "Where else could I have all this life but Harlem? Good old Harlem! Chocolate Harlem! Sweet Harlem! Harlem, I've got you' number down. Lenox Avenue, you're a bear, I know it. And, baby honey, sure enough youse a pippin for your pappy. Oh boy!" . . .

After Jake had paid for his drinks, that fifty-dollar note was all he had left in the world. He gave it to the girl. . . .

"Is we going now, honey?" he asked her.

"Sure, daddy. Let's beat it." . . .

Oh, to be in Harlem again after two years away. The deep-dyed color, the thickness, the closeness of it. The noises of Harlem. The sugared laughter. The honey-talk on its streets. And all night long, ragtime and "blues" playing somewhere, . . . singing somewhere, dancing somewhere! Oh, the contagious fever of Harlem. Burning everywhere in dark-eyed Harlem. . . . Burning now in Jake's sweet blood. . . .

He woke up in the morning in a state of perfect peace. She brought him hot coffee and cream and doughnuts. He yawned. He sighed. He was satisfied. He breakfasted. He washed. He dressed. The sun was shining. He sniffed the fine dry air. Happy, familiar Harlem.

"I ain't got a cent to my name," mused Jake, "but ahm as happy as a prince, all the same. Yes, I is."

He loitered down Lenox Avenue. He shoved his hand in his pocked—pulled out the fifty-dollar note. A piece of paper was pinned to it on which was scrawled in pencil:

"Just a little gift from a baby girl to a honey boy!"

Excerpt from *Home to Harlem* (1928)

Courtesy of the Literary Representatives for the Works of Claude McKay, Schomburg Center for Research in Black Culture, the New York Public Library, Astor, Lenox and Tilden Foundations.

Mattie and Her Sweetman*

In the neighborhood of 135th Street and Lenox Avenue a parlor social was taking place in the flat of a grass widow* called Rosie.

Rosie had sent out invitations to a number of chambermaids, bellhops, waiters, 'longshoremen, and railroad men whom she knew personally. She asked them to bring their friends and to tell their friends to bring their friends.

The price of admission was twenty-five cents. Soda pop and hard drinks were sold at prices a little more than what was paid in the saloon. At ten o'clock Rosie's place began filling up with guests.

It was that type of apartment called railroad flat. The guests put their wraps in Rosie's bedroom and danced in the dining-room and parlor.

Rosie kept the soda pop and beer cold in the ice-box in the kitchen. Whisky, wine, and gin were locked up in a cabinet whose key was secured by a red ribbon suspended from her waist.

The parlor social was good company. There was a fascinating melange of color: chocolate, cocoa, chestnut, ginger, yellow, and cream. The people for whom these parlor maids and chambermaids worked would have gazed wonder-eyed at them now. Aprons and caps set aside, the maids were radiant in soft shimmering chiffon, crêpe de Chine and satin stuff. How do they do it? those people would have commented, wearing the things they do on their wages?

In that merry crowd was one strange person—a black woman in her fifties. She wore a white dress, long white gloves, black stockings and black shoes, and a deep-fringed purple shawl. She was of average height and very thin. Her neck was extraordinary; it was such a long, excessively skinny neck, a pathetic neck. Her face was much finer than her neck, thin also, but marked by a quiet, dark determination.

She danced with a codfish-complexioned strutter wearing a dress suit. He was tall with a trim ready-to-wear appearance and his hair was plastered down, glistening with brilliantine.* His mouth wore a perpetual sneer. The woman danced badly. Her partner was a good dancer and tried to make her look as awkward as he could. The music stopped and they found seats near the piano.

"What youse gwina drink, Jay?" she asked.

"Gin," he said, casually.

"Rosie!" the woman called.

Rosie bustled over, a marvel of duck-chested amiability. Rosie's complexion was a flat café-au-lait, giving the impression of a bad mixture, coffee over-parched, or burned with skimmed milk, and the generous amount of powder she used did not make the effect any pleasanter.

"Whaz you two agwine to hev, Mattie?" She knew, of course, that Jay was Mattie's sweetman and Mattie did the paying.

"One gin and one beer," said Mattie.

"Gwine to treat the pianist to something?" Rosie knew how to tease her guests into making her parlor socials things worth giving.

"You throw me a good ball a whisky, sistah," said the pianist, a slight-built, sharp-featured black, whose eyes were intense, the whites appearing inflamed. . . .

Hands waved at Rosie from a group seated at a small table wedged against the mantlepiece, and an impatient young man called:

"Seven whiskies, Rosie, and four bottles a ginger ale jest that cold as you c'n makem."

"Right away, right away, mah chilluns." Rosie started a quick-time duck step to the cabinet.

Two girls pushed their way through a jam of men blocking the way between the dining-room and the parlor. The smaller was a satin-skinned chocolate; the other, attractive in a red frock, was cocoa. The cocoa girl saw Jay with Mattie and cried: "Hello, Jay! Howse you?"

"Hello, you Marita!" said Jay.

"Having a good time?"

"Kinder," he sneered.

Marita was the waitress at Aunt Hattie's pigs'-feet-and-chittlings joint. Jay went there to eat sometimes. Marita rather liked him, put more food than ordinary in his dish, and chatted with him. She would have liked to keep company with Jay, but he made her realize that he had no desire to go with a girl in the regular way. He never felt that sort of feeling that would urge a fellow on to rent a room for two and live, a good elevator boy, in the Black Belt. For it was easier going with the Matties and grass-widows of Harlem. Marita couldn't imagine herself down to the level of Jay's women. Not yet—when she was young and strong and pretty. But she rather admired his casual way of getting along and felt a romantic fascination for the sneer that sharp living had marked him by.

The pianist turned his inflamed eyes to the ceiling and banged the piano. Jay left Mattie alone to jazz with Marita.

"What a scary way she's dressed up!" said Marita as they wiggled past Mattie.

Jay grinned. Marita went liltingly with his movement. He disliked toting a middle-aged black hen round the room. Not that he minded being Mattie's sweetman. He was very proud of his new job. For three months before he met her he had been dogged by hard luck. The bottom had been eaten out of his nigger-brown pants. A flashy silk shirt, the gift of his last lady, had given way around the neck and at the cuffs. For thirteen weeks it had not seen the washtub, and when it did it went all to pieces. The toes of his ultra-pointed shoes were turned pathetically heavenward and the pavement had gnawed through his rubber heels down to the base of the leather.

Meeting Mattie at a parlor social in the Belt's Fifth Avenue had materially changed Jay's condition. He had been taken to 125th Street and fitted to a good pair of shoes. Mattie chose also a decent shirt for him. But it was not silk. He hadn't achieved a new suit yet. The choice was between that and an overcoat. Mattie's resources could not cover both at once. One would have to wait until she could put by enough out of their daily living to get it. And so she decided that a heavy, warm overcoat was more necessary, for it was mid-January and in his ruined summer suit Jay had been freezing along the streets of Harlem.

It was not quite a month since Mattie and Jay had come together, and docile as she seemed, she was well worn in experience and carried a smoldering fire in her ugly black body. Years ago she had had a baby for a white man in South Carolina. But being one black woman who did not feel proud having a yellow pickaninny at any price, she had got rid of the thing, strangling it at birth and, quitting relatives and prayer-meeting sisters, made her way up North.

Marita's girl pal discovered friends and went to drink with them. Marita followed, and Jay danced after her and got in with the gang. They were making rapid time with Old Crow whisky. They sent Rosie over to the pianist with a double drink of whisky to spur him on.

"Play that theah 'Baby Blues,'" she said. "Them good spenders ovah theah done buys you this drink and ask foh it."

The pianist tossed off his whisky, turned his eyes to the ceiling, and banged, "Baby blues, Baby blues."

Mattie stood up and went over to Jay. "Le's dance," she said. She loved dancing as a pastime, but it wasn't in her blood, and so she was a bad dancer.

"Not now," Jay said, angrily. "Ahm chinning with the gang."

He was putting away a lot of the boys' good liquor and it was working on him in a bad way for Mattie. Disappointed, she looked round for Rosie. Rosie was bustling about in the kitchen getting new glasses. Mattie gulped down two stiff drinks of gin and returned to her seat by the piano. . . .

Baby Blues! Baby Blues!

"Le's do this heah sweet strut, gal." And before Jay, Marita was on her feet and poised for movement. Her pal was jigging with one of the chocolate boys. The space was filled thick and warm with dancers just shuffling round and round. Hot cheeks, yellow, chestnut, chocolate, each perspiring against each.

"Is that theah thing you' lady now?" Marita asked.

"She ain't a bad ole mammy as she looks," said Jay. "She's good giving. Fixed *me* up all right."

"Did she buy you this heah dress suit? Youse the only one here all dressed up so swell."

Jay grinned for the compliment.

"No. I hired this off a ole Greenbaum. The other was so bad. But she got me these heah shoes and a swell overcoat. And she's gwine get me a nifty suit."

"But youse kinder rough on her, though. You ain't treating her right, is you?"

Young and pretty, Marita disapproved of Mattie, old and ugly, having Jay; but she also resented with feminine feeling Jay's nastiness to the older woman.

"I ain't soft and sissified with no womens," said Jay. "Them's all cats, always mewing or clawing. The harder a man is with them the better."

"Think so?" Marita said. Her resentment rose to anger and she wanted to stop wriggling, but Jay's casual manner (which said, I don't care whether you dance or quit) held her tethered to him.

Mattie, sitting alone, had swallowed her sixth glass of gin. Rosie, feeling sympathetic, went and gossiped with her for a while.

"Ain't dancing, honey?"

"No, but I guess I'll take the next one."

"Don't you sit heah and get too lonely drinking all by you'se'f and that yaller strutter a yourn having such a wicked time."

"I don't mind him fooling with his own crowd when we goes to a pahty, 'causen Ise pass their age."

Finished "Baby Blues."

Jay went back to the waiters' table. One of his poolroom pals came in and joined the group, greeting Jay with enthusiasm and praising his rig-out.

In the poolroom where Jay loafed and played, he had become the hero of the place since his new affair. Colored boys who washed water-closets and cleaned spittoons for a living, with no hope of ever doing better, envied the way Jay could always get on to some woman to do everything for him. They wished they had Jay's magic. Jay might have his bad days getting by sometimes, but his luck never deserted him. He toted a charm.

The pianist turned his face to the ceiling and began a plaintive "Blues." He cast down his eyes for a moment and said to Mattie, "Ain't you gwina dance, sistah?"

Mattie essayed a smile. "Guess I will."

She crossed over to Jay and asked, "Wanta dance this with me?"

Jay glared at her, "Wha's scratching you? I don't wanta dance. Ahm having a good time heah."

The sneer deepened under the influence of the mixed drinks working on his temper. Mattie lingered near the table, but nobody asked her to sit down. Turning to go, she said to Jay hesitatingly, "Well—any time you feels like dancing with me Ise ready."

"Oh, foh Gawd's sake," he exclaimed, "gimme a chance! Shake a leg, black woman."

Everybody within hearing turned to look at Mattie, some with suppressed giggling, others with pity. Marita and her pal were ashamed and could not look at Mattie. For there is no greater insult among Aframericans than calling a black person black. That is never done. In Aframerican literature, perhaps, but never in social life. A black person may be called "nigger" as a joke in Aframerica, but never "black," which is considered a term of reproach in the mouths of colored people quite as contemptuous as "nigger" in the mouths of whites. And so Aframericans have invented pretty names such as low-brown, seal-skin brown, chocolate, and even prune as substitutes for black.

Oh, Blues, Blues, Brown-skin Blues: the piano wailed.

"That was a mean one," said Marita.

"Oh, mean hell. I guess the ole mug likes when you handle her rough. Don't she, Jay?" said his pal.

"Ain't nobody wanting their bad points thrown up to them as nasty as that," declared Marita.

Her pal agreed. The girls imagined themselves growing old some day and ridden by a special passion like Mattie.

And Mattie by the piano, thinking that everybody was laughing at her, called for another gin. She wanted not to care. She knew she did not belong to a fast parlor-social set where everybody was young or acting young. Rosie with her hostess's tricks looked like a vampire beside her. But although she was ugly and unadjustable, she loved amusement and was always ready to pay for it.

Mattie worked hard doing half-time and piecework, washing and ironing and mending for white people. Her work was finely done and her patrons recommended her to their friends. She earned twenty to thirty and forty dollars a week.

Living for Mattie was harder than working. Having an irresistible penchant for the yellow daddy-boys of the Black Belt, she had realized, when she was much younger, that because she was ugly she would have to pay for them.

She occupied a large rear room on the second floor of a private house, situated in the cheapest section of the Belt. The price was moderate and she was allowed the use of the kitchen and the spacious back yard for laundry work.

Mattie's coming and going quietly through the block was remarked by the good and churchy neighbors of the African Methodist, the Colored Methodist, and the Abyssinian and Cyrenian churches. And they marveled at her, a steady, reliable worker, refusing to be persuaded into membership in a church. . . .

Mattie brooded. Nevah befoh I been slapped like that by an insult so public. Slam in the face: Black woman! Black woman! Didn't I know I was that and old and no beauty?

Oh, mamma, sweet papa. Blues, Blues, seal-skin, brown-skin Blues. The pianist was gone on a wailing Blues.

Mattie got up to go home. She looked round for Jay. He had hurt her, but her pride had fallen, humbled and broken, under desire. Jay was not in the room. Mattie found him in the kitchen with his pool-room pal and a boozy gang over a bottle of gin.

"I'm gwine along home, Jay," she said. "Youse coming?"

Jay was going drunk. "Why you nosing and smelling after a fellah like that foh?" he demanded.

"Don't get mad, Jay. I ain't bothering you. If you wanta stay—"

"Oh, beat it outa here, you no-'count black bitch."

Mattie slunk off to Rosie's bedroom and put on her coat. She saw Jay's overcoat and felt it and after a slight hesitation slipped it on over hers. Outside it was snowing. She dove her hands into the deep pockets and said: "A man's clothes is that much more solid and protecting than a woman's is." She went home, southward, along Lenox Avenue.

The gang finished the gin. Jay suggested to the waiters they should all go and hunt up a speakeasy. Marita and her pal said they were going home.

"No, you come on along with us," said Jay.

"Not me. I gotta work tomorrow," said Marita.

"Me too. That don't make no difference," said the darkest waiter. The others joined him asking the two girls to change their minds; but the girls went home.

The fellows stood up, arguing just what they should do next, when Rosie elbowed through them and waved a bottle of gin in their faces.

"Le's have another round," said the mulatto waiter.

"You'd bettah," said Rosie. "Wha's this heah talk about you all going when is jest the time to start in on some real fun."

The boys sat down again, each waiter paying a round of drinks. The waiters had been paying all along. Jay and his friend had not paid for anything. The darkest waiter was soft. He began sifting a pack of cards, crying: "Coon-can!* Coon-can! Le's play coon-can!"

"Ahm feeling high, ahm feeling cocky," said Jay.

The bottle of gin was finished and they were now ready to leave, but Jay could not find his overcoat.

"Ain't nobody could take it 'cep'n' the one that done buys it." Rosie grinned maliciously.

Jay was mad and blew Mattie to hell with curses. Just a hussy trick to get me home to bed. Ain't got no shame nor pride, that woman. But I'll punish her some more.

Outside the snow had turned to sleet and a high wind was driving through the shivering naked trees.

"It'll be some sweet skating on the sidewalk tomorrow," said one of the waiters.

"And bitter cold, too," said Jay. And the thought of his overcoat gave him a comfortable, warm, and luxurious feeling.

The boys had decided to visit a certain speakeasy. They walked along Fifth Avenue, and Jay stopped before an apartment house.

"It's here, fellahs," he said.

"All right," said the chocolate boy. "Le's go on in and look the fair browns ovah."

Jay, with his hands in his pockets and his dress suit slightly damp, gleaming in the far-flung flare of the arc-light, was the picture of perfect aplomb.

"But, buddies, I ain't got no money on me," he announced.

"And I ain't got none, neither," said Jay's pal.

The waiters exchanged eye-flecks with one another.

"Well," said the mulatto waiter, "after Rosie she done ate up so much I ain't none so flush to treat anybody else again 'cep'n' mahself. What about you fellahs?"

His workmates took his cue and said they had just enough each for himself.

"Tell you what, then; we'll call this show off until some other night," said the mulatto.

The waiters said good night to Jay and his pal. They were unanimous about not treating them in the speakeasy. If Jay hadn't any money to pay in the speakeasy, let him go home to Mattie. They had seen and felt so much as servitors, that they had not wasted any pity on Mattie. There were women whose special problems made them stand for that kind of hoggishness. But, neither had they any servile praise for Jay's attitude.

The waiters saw Jay and his pal out of sight, then entered the apartment house and rang the bell of the speakeasy. They worked. Creatures of service, waiters—that moment serving up a rarebit, this moment a cocktail, next a high-ball; bellhops in livery with ridiculous buttons before and behind, leaping up like rabbits at the touch of a knob. And they were fool spenders having that curious psychology of some servants who never feel life such good living as when they are making a big splurge imitation of their employers. . . .

"Come on, buddies," said the mulatto. "We may be suckers all right in Rosie's joint, but we won't be suckers in a cat dog bite mah laig hear the player piano crying fair chile baby oh boy house."

Jay said good-by to his pal and hurried homewards, head bent against the sleety wind, his hands in his trousers pockets, and thinking aloud: Well I was setting for an all-night laying-off, but I guess I'll have to warm up the ole black hen tonight, after all.

But Mattie, too, had been thinking hard in the meanwhile.

"I don't know what love is, but I know what's a man!"

The cabaret song was singing in her head. She remembered when she first left Dixie and "went N'oth" to Philadelphia, how she had liked a yellow man and he had laughed in her ugly face and called her "black giraffe." She had forgotten the incident, it was so long ago, but Jay made her remember it now. She had hated that man deeply and wanted to do him real hurt. And now she felt the same kind of hatred for Jay.

She lay in bed without sleeping, waiting for Jay, but not in the mood he anticipated. Dawn was creeping along the walls when the bell rang. Mattie raked up a window and craned out her giraffe neck. She had on a white nightcap and looked like a scarifying ghost.

"Who's it?"

"It's me—Jay."

"Wait a minute."

Mattie opened the closet where she kept her soiled linen and took out the little bandanna bundle that she had made of Jay's rags of a suit, his old greasy cap, his old shoes, and the remains of his silk shirt.

"Theah's you' stuff. Take a walk."

The bundle fell against Jay, nearly knocking him over. Mattie raked down the window. The sleet blew hard in Jay's face and the wind sang round his rump. He turned up his collar and walked shivering toward Lenox Avenue.

From *Gingertown* (1932)

Courtesy of the Literary Representatives for the Works of Claude McKay, Schomburg Center for Research in Black Culture, the New York Public Library, Astor, Lenox and Tilden Foundations.

Crazy Mary

Miss Mary startled the village for the first time in her strange life that day when she turned herself up and showed her naked self to them. Suddenly the villagers realized that after many years of harmless craziness something was perhaps dangerously wrong with Mary, but before they could do anything about it she settled the matter herself.

For a long time she had been accepted as an eccentric village character. Ever since she had recovered from her long sad illness and started going round the village with a bunch of roses in her arms.

Before that she had been the sewing-mistress of the village school. She was a pretty young yellow woman then. Her parents, following the custom of those peasants with a little means, had sent her to a sewing-school in Gingertown. She had gone away in short frocks, with her hair down and a bright bow pinned to it.

When she returned for good after three years she was in long skirts, with her hair up in what the villagers called a "Chinese bump."

Her father bought her a Singer finer than those of the other peasant women, a foot-working one similar to that owned by the village tailor. She subscribed to *Weldon's Ladies' Journal* and the *Home Magazine,** and opened a little school in her home for girls to learn to sew and design and cut. Her girls called her Miss Mary, and a few superior folk, such as the parson and family, the schoolmaster, and the postmistress, called her Miss Dean.

The schoolmaster's wife was the sewing-mistress then. But two years later the schoolmaster left for a better-paying school. He was succeeded by a bachelor, and Miss Mary applied for and got the sewing-mistress's job. The sewing-mistress went to the school twice a week for two hours during the afternoon session.

Miss Mary sometimes took two or three of her bigger girls along to help teach the tots to sew.

Girls came from other villages to learn Miss Mary's art. She was much admired, for she was charming. She was nice-shaped, something like a ripened wild cane, and could look a perfect piece of elegance in a princess gown.

Naturally much of Miss Mary's spare time was spent with the schoolmaster. Often they went out walking together in the afternoon after school until twilight. And sometimes they rode horseback to Gingertown together. The villagers got to liking to see them together. The parson approved of it. So did Miss Mary's parents. And everybody thought the two would certainly get married. . . .

The schoolmaster was a pure ebony, shining and popular. He played cricket with the young men. He was of middle size, stocky, and an excellent underhand bowler. He organized a cricket club, and during the short days let school out earlier than usual to go to field practice.

Sometimes the schoolmaster and Miss Mary took tea together at the parsonage. And the schoolmaster would talk about the choir and new anthems with the minister's wife, who was the organist. Miss Mary was not in the choir, for she hadn't a singing voice nor any knowledge of music.

As a constant visitor to the Dean home the schoolmaster became almost like one of the family. The villagers indulged in friendly gossip about the couple, anticipating a happy termination of the idyll. Nothing could enrapture the people more than a big village wedding with bells and saddle horses and carriages.

But bang came the scandal one day.

The girls who attended Miss Mary's sewing-classes at home were nearly all girls just out of elementary school, between fourteen and fifteen years. There were a few younger who for some reason had not finished school, and also a few older who were considered and treated as young ladies.

Among those who accompanied Miss Mary to the school was a little bird-brown one plump as a squab, just turned thirteen, curiously cat-faced and forever smiling. They called her Freshy because she was precocious in her manners.

Sometimes the schoolmaster would tell one of the girls to do something in the teacher's cottage. To do a little cleaning up or prepare a beverage of bitter oranges or pineapple or a soursop-cup* during the recreation hours. And it seems that Freshy, always forward, had got herself asked to do things many times.

And one morning while the classes were humming with work, the schoolmaster at his desk, the mother of Freshy, with her bluejean skirt tucked high up and bandanna flying as if for war, rushed into the school and slapped the schoolmaster's face and collared and shook him, bellowing that he had ruined her little daughter.

The schoolmaster was in a pitiful state, trying to hold his dignity and the woman off, until the monitors interfered and the woman was at last mastered and put out.

The village was shaken as if by an earthquake. Of course, the schoolmaster denied that he had ruined Freshy, but the girl maintained by the mouth of her mother that he had.

The village midwife, after seeing Freshy, insisted that she had not been ruined. But the midwife was the sister of Miss Mary's father, who was a leader in the church.

The parson was constrained to relieve the schoolmaster of his duties and put his wife in temporary charge of the school. For the protection of his pastorate, he said. Then there was the religious side. The schoolmaster being a member of the church and lay preacher, a church meeting was called to air the affair.

The village was divided for and against the schoolmaster. Curiously, it was the older heads who were more favorable to him. The young folk and chiefly the bucks were already calling the man a rogue and tuning the whole thing into a salacious song. It began to be bruited* that the schoolmaster was secretly a wild one who abused the innocence of schoolgirls. But there were some who maintained that even at her age Freshy had already passed the age of innocence with the apples of her bosom so prettily tempting.

Freshy was very conscious of the notoriety she had attained, and, fortified by the aggressiveness of her mother, when she went about the village she tossed her head and turned her lips in scorn like a petulant little actress at those who whispered and stared at her.

The first church meeting, with the parson presiding, broke up in a babel of recriminations, when Freshy's mother became bellicose and abusive to those who had dared to insinuate that her daughter was not a mere child.

It was then that Miss Mary acted. Freshy had not returned to the sewing-school since the day the trouble began. Meeting her in the lane one afternoon, Miss Mary took her home. And alone with Freshy in a room she third-degreed her until the girl cried out that the schoolmaster had not touched her.

At the next church meeting Miss Mary gave an account of Freshy's confession. Speaking quietly in her refined way and holding all attention with her pretty personality, she was almost convincing the whole meeting. But Freshy's mother jumped up, interrupting her, and related how Miss Mary had prevailed upon her child to confess, accusing her of being a little woman and having been with the boys. In her turn Freshy's mother charged Miss Mary with being the schoolmaster's mistress, and in a rage she threatened to box her ears and made a rush for her. Women shrieked as if filled with the spirit for a public fight, but some men held back Freshy's mother and she was put out.

Again the church meeting broke up. The young men especially did not want to believe that a person so nice as Miss Mary could say dirty things to Freshy. But the women shook their heads dubiously and repeated the saying, "Still river run deep." The declaration of Freshy's mother started a big gossip, for it was locally conceded that Miss Mary was a virgin. There was nothing dishonorable in the fact that girls were deflowered at a tender age and young virgins were few in the country, nevertheless the village folk took a pride-like interest in any young woman of whom it could be said she was a virgin up until the time of her marriage.

It seemed as if the church and the village were going to rags over the affair, until a member named Jabez Fearon suggested taking the case to the law courts and having Freshy examined by a doctor from Gingertown. Jabez Fearon was the local tax-collector, commonly called the bailiff. His outstretched hand carried much weight among the peasants, but they had never considered his mind of any weight at all.

Now, however, his opinion appeared intelligent and worth acting upon. How strange that nobody had thought of the legal course before! After all the church-meeting bickering and disagreement! The younger church members thought that that was the most excellent way of settling the trouble. A doctor's examination and the decision of a judge.

But before any step was taken and another church meeting called, the schoolmaster quietly disappeared.

And a few weeks after his disappearance Miss Mary went to the city and stayed there a long time. Her people said that she had had a breakdown from nervous trouble and they had had to take her to a doctor in the city.

But the weeks became months before she returned. And then she was confined to the house for as many months more. The village thought she was surely consumptive. Especially when they glimpsed her so tiny and strange in the portico of the house or on the barbecue.

Then at long last, when she could not be detained at home and away from people any longer, she came out, and the village became aware that she was not consumptive, but a little crazy. Her parents stayed away from the church and were never the same charming folk again. Their village respectability became a sour thing.

Miss Mary went about with her hair down like a girl. And it was lovely hair, thick, black and frizzly. The first day she went out she gathered a bunch of flowers and took it to the schoolhouse and placed it on the teacher's desk without a word, and walked out. The new schoolmaster was a married man. The parson said that he would never engage an unmarried man again.

Miss Mary got rid of her shoes, too, and went about barefooted like a common peasant girl. Every day she gathered her flowers, and there was always plenty of red—hibiscus, poinsettias, dragon's-blood. And she had a strange way of holding the bouquet in her arm as if she were nursing it. Sometime she talked to herself, but never to anybody, and when anyone tried to talk to her she answered with a cracked little laugh.

Her people kept her clean. And the village folk settled down into familiarity with her as a strange character. Nobody thought that she should be sent to the madhouse, for she was harmless.

And the months turned into years, the village changed schoolmasters again, and even the parson was called to a church in a little town where he earned more money. The village had long ceased from wondering about the disappearance of the schoolmaster, and Freshy had had three children for three different black bucks before she was nineteen.

Then one day the schoolmaster returned. He had been away in Panama. He was a changed man after being so long free from semi-religious duties, a little dapper with a gait the islanders called "the Yankee strut." He was married to a girl he met over there, a saucy brown dressed in an extreme mode of the Boston dip of the day.

It was on a Sunday and they went to church. And after the service the schoolmaster and his wife stood in the yard, surrounded by an admiring group of old friends and young admirers who wanted to hear all about the life and prospects in Colon and Panama.

Nobody had thought of Miss Mary, poor crazy thing in that social center of the village, where new acquaintances were introduced and sweethearts met and children skipped about.

But she must have heard of his arrival somehow, for suddenly she appeared in the churchyard and, pushing through the folk around the schoolmaster, she threw the bouquet of flowers at him and, turning, she ran up the broad church steps and turned herself up at everybody, looking at them from under with a lecherous laugh.

There was a sudden bewildered pause. And then a young church member dashed up the steps after Mary and the church crowd recovered from the shock, remembering that she was crazy. But before he could reach and seize her she had jumped down the steps, shrieking strange laughter, and started running towards the graveyard.

Just outside the gate she turned again, repeated her act, and laughed. The young villager gave chase after her, followed by others. Mary ran like a rabbit in a mad zigzag. And whenever she saw herself at a safe distance from her pursuers she performed her act with laughter.

She ran past the graveyard and, striking the main road, she headed straight for the river. A little below where the river crossed the road there was a high narrow waterfall that from the churchyard looked like a gorgeous flowing of gold.

Mary ran down a little track leading to the waterfall. Her pursuers stopped in the road, paralysed by her evident intention, and began shouting to her to stop. And watching from the churchyard, the folk began to bawl and howl.

But Mary kept straight on. On the perilous edge of the waterfall she halted and did her stuff again, then with a high laugh she went sheer over.

From *Gingertown* (1932)

Courtesy of the Literary Representatives for the Works of Claude McKay, Schomburg Center for Research in Black Culture, the New York Public Library, Astor, Lenox and Tilden Foundations.

Eric D. Walrond

E ric Derwent Walrond was born in British Guiana, grew up in Barbados and Panama, and later migrated to the United States, France, and England. It was this peripatetic nature that was the driving force of his journalistic and fictional writings, which largely concern themselves with the lifestyle of the West Indian, whether in the Caribbean, the United States, or England.

Walrond was born on December 18, 1898, in Georgetown, British Guiana (now Guyana), though his parents were both natives of Barbados. Harsh economic conditions forced the family to depart for Barbados about 1907. Continuing financial strains led Walrond's father to head off to Panama in 1909, as part of a large contingent of West Indians working in the Canal Zone. After the father broke off contact with the family, they followed him to Colón two years later.

Once in Panama, young Walrond faced discrimination as a "Chumbo" (a Black West Indian). The Canal Zone had instituted a notorious system whereby Black workers were paid in silver whereas White workers were paid in gold. Walrond learned Spanish and worked as a reporter from 1916 to 1918 on the *Panama Star and Herald,* one of the most important papers in Latin America. Seeking his fortune, Walrond migrated to the United States on June 30, 1918.

Upon his arrival in the United States, Walrond worked at a variety of jobs but had difficulty gaining employment as a reporter, his chosen profession. His travails are recorded in his sketch "On Being Black," one of the earliest pieces by a Harlem Renaissance author to be published in a White-owned journal, the *New Republic.* Walrond was finally able to obtain work with the *Brooklyn and Long Island Informer* (1920–21) and Marcus Garvey's *Weekly Review.*

Walrond's real break came in winning a contest sponsored by Garvey's Universal Negro Improvement Association in the December 17, 1921, issue of the *Negro World*. Walrond soon became an assistant and then an associate editor with the periodical between 1921 and 1923, publishing numerous essays, reviews, and sketches. Garvey's emphasis on racial pride, Pan-Africanism, and resistance to racism appealed to Walrond, and these would remain central issues throughout his life. His initial praise of Garvey is evident in such pieces as "Marcus Garvey—A Defense." Walrond, however, was consistently at odds with the rest of the staff because of his emphasis on the importance of aesthetics rather than propaganda in literature. The furor over the federal investigation of Garvey's activities and the Jamaican leader's meeting with the Ku Klux Klan in 1922 further hastened the break between the two men.

Walrond's views on Black leadership are best seen in his essay "The New Negro Faces America." Here Walrond is critical of Booker T. Washington (as represented by his successor at Tuskegee, Major Robert Moton), W. E. B. Du Bois, and Garvey. Moton is rebuked for his emphasis on accommodation and for maintaining the need for learning "industrial efficiency." Du Bois is criticized for his arrogance and for his blindness toward the conditions of most Blacks. Garvey, though towering "head and shoulders above these two," is still seen as "a megalomaniac." In rejecting all the major Black leaders, Walrond offers his own hopeful view of the New Negro, recounting the economic progress made by the race.

In the early 1920s, disaffected with Black conditions in America, Walrond began to espouse an interest in socialism, signaled in part by his contributions to the *Messenger*. In "The Black City" Walrond forcefully speaks of the contradictions in Harlem, "a sociological *el dorado*" filled with vibrant creativity and crushing poverty. Walrond would become a contributing editor of the Communist publication the *New Masses* from 1926 to 1930, though he did not publish any work in the journal. Ultimately, however, Walrond abhorred any movement that he felt was doctrinaire, one that stressed politics over art. Inevitably, as he became more closely involved with different political, social, and literary movements, he became disenchanted with the dogma that frequently accompanied them.

After leaving the *Negro World*, Walrond also began writing (and working as business manager) for Charles S. Johnson's magazine

Opportunity, an organ of the National Urban League. Walrond began to hone his skills at fiction, writing six stories for *Opportunity*. "Vignettes of the Dusk" is a series of five short scenes portraying various forms of prejudice. The first piece, the most fully developed of the vignettes, is set in the middle of New York's financial district. The nameless narrator, flush with some money, seeks a more upscale eatery than is his usual wont. In awe of the fancy restaurant, he is almost afraid to enter. When he does, he feels he does not belong and is only able to whisper his order: "Oyster salad—and vanilla temptation." The "vanilla temptation" so tentatively ordered is symbolic of the "weirdly enchanting" lure of the restaurant and, to a larger extent, White America. The waiter hands him the bag "as if its contents were leprous." The man meekly leaves, but he realizes that he's been essentially "sho[o]ed out." The message seems to be that White America wants no part of integration between the races and that if Blacks aspire to the "vanilla temptation," they will only face rejection.

"The Stone Rebounds" is told from "the persona of a white writer who has been ostracized by his colleagues for bringing a black playwright to an all-white gathering. Later in the story the black playwright is implicitly and indirectly criticized by his black friends for bringing the white writer into a Harlem cabaret" (Berry 298). However, the story is more than just a tale of interracial intolerance. Kraus, the narrator, is an armchair radical who knows little about the people or causes he purports to advance. He revels in the "exotic" differences between Blacks and Whites and ultimately has a smug sense of superiority in being White. It is a fascinating piece, especially in a journal attempting to advance better relationships between the races. While working with *Opportunity*, Walrond often took Whites on tours of Harlem. One wonders if perhaps this story is an ironic reflection on Walrond's own excursions with people who often had no more understanding of Blacks than is exhibited by Kraus.

Although Walrond enjoyed socializing with Alain Locke, Charles Johnson, and others in the Talented Tenth, his fiction rarely deals with the lives of the New Negro elite. In his essay "The Negro Literati" (*Brentano's Book Chat* March/April 1925) Walrond advises the Black author to "paint pictures of people—of tantalizing black people—he knows." He heeded his own advice in his major literary work, *Tropic Death* (1926). Concerned with the lives of ordinary Caribbean folk, *Tropic Death* challenges the stereotypical American view of a monolithic Caribbean, instead depicting a complex area rich in linguistic and cultural diversity. As Carl Wade notes, "In its faithful re-recreation of the predicament of individual protagonists, mostly of the black peasant class, *Tropic Death* achieves a powerful indictment—however indirect—of the social, political, and economic arrangements under which this group subsisted" (416). In "Wharf Rats," for example, two young boys lose their lives while diving for quarters thrown by tourists, an indictment of the oppressive colonial system reinforcing the people's poverty.

Another effect of prejudice evident in Walrond's work is colorism, a frequent theme in his writing. Miss Buckner, in "The Palm Porch," a proud woman who prostitutes her daughters, exemplifies such intraracial prejudice, lamenting that two of the girls had run off with dark-complexioned "silver men." The mysterious Miss Buckner, whose past no one knows, is much like the Palm Porch she operates, which "shut out eyes effectively." The picture of decorum, she can murder a patron without letting it upset her lunch menu.

The generally favorable response of the critics to *Tropic Death* prompted Walrond's publisher, Boni and Liveright, to provide an advance for another book on the building of the Panama Canal. Walrond's success as an author may be measured by three major awards in 1927–28: a Harmon Award in Literature, a Zona Gale scholarship at the University of Wisconsin, and a Guggenheim Award. After winning the Guggenheim Award, Walrond traveled in the Caribbean before arriving in Paris in 1929, where he remained until 1932. During his years in France, Walrond shared an apartment for a time with Countee Cullen, became part of the entourage of Nancy Cunard, and wrote several magazine pieces.

Walrond moved to England in 1932 and, except for some years traveling, spent his remaining years there. It has commonly been assumed that Walrond virtually ceased writing once he left America, but this is not correct. In England, he was reunited with Garvey in the mid-1930s and wrote for Garvey's periodical, the *Black Man*, chronicling his disenchantment with the position of Blacks in England. Walrond also contributed articles to a number of journals and newspapers in the 1930s, 1940s, and 1950s and, along with Rosey E. Pool, selected poems for *Black and Unknown Bards: A Collection of Negro Poetry* (1958). The bulk of his published work, however, appeared in the *Roundway Review*, printed by the Roundway Psychiatric Hospital, where Walrond was a voluntary patient from 1952 to 1957. Walrond had long been plagued by fits of depression and felt enormous pressure to live up to his early promise. About fifteen stories and large sections of his work on the Panama Canal (titled "The Second Battle") were published in the *Review*. Even after his release from the hospital, Walrond was engaged in several projects including a planned reissuing of *Tropic Death* with revisions he had made over the years. His death of a heart attack on August 8, 1966, cut short these plans.

While Walrond may not have fulfilled the high expectations of him, his achievements, nonetheless, were considerable. His work as an editor and journalist and particularly as the author of *Tropic Death* placed him at the forefront of the Harlem Renaissance. His insistence on documenting Caribbean folklife, in all its aspects, helped to bring this rich cultural legacy to an American audience.

> There is no one repository of Walrond's papers. Letters and many of the *Roundway* pieces are available at Clark Atlanta University and the Devizes Museum (in Wiltshire, England). Small collections of letters are also available at Tulane University, the Schomburg Center, Howard University, Yale University, and through the Guggenheim Foundation.

BIBLIOGRAPHY

Agatucci, Cora. "Eric Walrond." *African American Authors 1745–1945: A Bio-Bibliographical Critical Sourcebook.* Ed. Emmanuel S. Nelson. Westport, CT: Greenwood P, 2000. 429–38.

Berry, Jay. "Eric Walrond." *Dictionary of Literary Biography, Volume 51: Afro-American Writers from the Harlem Renaissance to 1940.* Ed. Trudier Harris. Detroit: Gale, 1987. 296–300.

Bogle, Enid E. "Eric Walrond." *Fifty Caribbean Writers: A Bio-Bibliographical Critical Sourcebook.* Ed. Daryl Cumber Dance. Westport, CT: Greenwood P, 1986. 474–82.

Bone, Robert A. *Down Home: Origins of the Afro-American Short Story.* 1975. New York: Columbia UP, 1988.

Ikonné, Chidi. *From Du Bois to Van Vechten: The Early New Negro Literature, 1903–1921.* Westport, CT: Greenwood P, 1981.

Lewis, David Levering. *When Harlem Was in Vogue.* New York: Oxford UP, 1981.

Martin, Tony. *Literary Garveyism: Garvey, Black Arts and the Harlem Renaissance.* Dover, MA: Majority P, 1983.

Parascandola, Louis, ed. *"Winds Can Wake Up the Dead": An Eric Walrond Reader.* Detroit: Wayne State UP, 1998.

Ramchand, Kenneth. "The Writer Who Ran Away: Eric Walrond and *Tropic Death.*" *Savacou* 2 (September 1970): 67–75.

Wade, Carl A. "African-American Aesthetics and the Short Fiction of Eric Walrond: *Tropic Death* and the Harlem Renaissance." *CLA Journal* 42 (June 1999): 403–29.

Wade, Carl A., and Louis J. Parascandola. "In Search of Asylum: Eric Walrond's *Roundway Review* Writings, 1952–1957." *Journal of Caribbean Studies* 19 (Fall 2004–Spring 2005): 21–42.

Marcus Garvey—A Defense

The favorite parting shot of "dishonorably discharged" officers of the Universal Negro Improvement Association is to yelp and howl about the "dictatorship" of Mr. Marcus Garvey. "The Great I Am," "Imperialist," "Czar," etc., are epithets familiar to those editors and journalists who delight in wallowing in the mire of scandal and vituperation. Of the methods and administrative policies of Mr. Garvey they say a "mouthful." It is unfortunate that he is so iron-fisted and damning in his relations with his associates. For this reason the personnel of his organization is "inferior" in point of "culture" and "refinement" and "education." There is no comparison with it and other organizations with better trained men in them, with staffs which boast of college professors and competent experts.

All along the line criticism is directed against him because he demands of those about him 100 per cent loyalty above everything else. It is even gossiped that men of "brains" and "experience" have been passed up in preference to men who have shown a maximum of interest in Africa's redemption! Why not? This policy is the outgrowth—the direct psychological reaction—of the tragedy, as the black world knows, of appointing men of "brains" and "experience" to positions of trust and responsibility. From the beginning it was Mr. Garvey's rule to pick out the ablest men he could find and place them in executive office. Experience had taught him that to succeed, to carry out his monster program, brains, and brains of the highest order, had to be pressed into service. With that in mind, he went about the formation of a cabinet, examining, selecting, rejecting. In those days it mattered not where a man had come from, what church he attended, what association he was a member of. Only one thing counted—his fitness. After a rigorous investigation of his character and qualifications he was brought in, appointed according to his ability, and left to do his bit in the mighty cause of Africa's freedom. But what did the majority of them do? Did they start to work with the idea of rendering service to the cause, of subordinating personal greed and power to the larger interests of the movement? No. To them affiliation with it meant a means to a very definite personal end[.] Money, and as much of it as they could lay their hands on, was their purpose. Apart from that they had no interest in Mr. Garvey and his "crazy organization." In time exposures, expulsions and prosecutions followed.

The man's eyes began to open. Were all Negroes—so-called "educated" Negroes—crooks and liars? With his comparative analytical mind he dismissed that as Anglo-Saxon. That was the white man's way of summing up the whole race. But he had learned his lesson—a pretty dear one, indeed—and he was going to profit by it. What did he do? The fastidious smart-Aleck who drops into his office and overwhelms him with his "cultured" ways and courtly manners and his protestations of love for the Motherland is seen in his true colors. If necessary, czar-like methods are adopted to exclude rogues and traitors from the organization. "Once bitten, twice shy." Can you blame him?

From the *Negro World* February 11, 1922

The New Negro Faces America

The negro is at the crossroads of American life. He is, probably more than any other group within our borders, the most vigorously "led." On the one hand is the old-style leadership of Booker T. Washington's successor, Major Robert Moton, Principal of Tuskegee, who believes, like Christ, in "turning the other cheek," and in a maximum of industrial efficiency. On the other hand is the leadership of W. E. B. Du Bois of the National Association for the Advancement of Colored People, whose idea of salvation is in adequate political representation. This is the organization which is sponsoring the Dyer Anti-Lynching bill.

Towering head and shoulders above these two is Marcus Garvey, "Provisional President of Africa," and President General of the Universal Negro Improvement Association and African Committees [*sic*] League. This organization is otherwise known as the "Back to Africa" movement. It sprang into public notice a few years ago through the appealing oratory and historic abilities of its West Indian leader, Marcus Garvey. Garvey is a Jamaican, short, black, swaggering, muscularly built. As a printer and journalist in the West Indies he suffered from the injustices heaped upon members of his race. He went to South America, Europe and Africa. While in London he met Duse Mahomed Ali, the Egyptian editor of The African [*sic*] Times and Orient Review, from whom, it is said, he got his idea of an "Africa for the Africans."

Early in 1915 Garvey came to the United States and with a nucleus of seven formed in a dingy Harlem hall bedroom the most-talked-of negro movement in modern times. Just from the war, thousands of negro ex-service men, bitter, morose, disillusioned, fell into it. Stories of negro officers being stripped of their medals and epaulets and Croix de Guerres by "crackers" in the South stimulated recruiting in Garvey's African army. They dumped their money into it. The movement grew beyond Garvey's fondest hopes.

Early this year Garvey made a trip to Atlanta, Ga., where he interviewed the Imperial Wizard of the Knights of the Ku Klux Klan to find out, he said, "just what the Klan's attitude toward the negro was." Knowing the history of Ku Klux activities in reconstruction days in the South, the bulk of the American negroes who had faith in him, even after the colossal failure of the Black Star Line, viewed this as the last tie that linked them to the "American Emperor."

Just at this point it is well to observe that the negroes of America do not want to go back to Africa. Though Africa, to the thinking ones, means something racial, if not spiritual, it takes the same place in the negro's "colonization" plans as Jerusalem in the Jew's, for instance. This return, however, was the salient feature of Garvey's propaganda. In August of this year, at the Third International Convention of Negroes held at Garvey's Liberty Hall, a delegation of four was appointed, headed by G. O. Marke, a West African lawyer and editor, to go to Geneva to present a petition to the League of Nations asking it to turn over Germany's former African colonies to the Universal Negro Improvement Association. The delegation went and returned, and in glowing rhetoric at a riotously primeval festival at Liberty Hall told of the "impression" it made on the League delegates. The sending of this delegation, like most of Garvey's acts, was for theatrical effect.

Garvey, however, is paying dearly for these preposterous mistakes. A reaction has set in. The crowds who once flocked to hear how he was going to redeem Africa have begun to dwindle. The negroes have lost faith in Garvey. Still, in a thoroughly dispassionate survey of negro progress, one cannot deny that the idea of "Africa for the Africans" means a great deal to negroes in America. Some of them feel that with a strong native Government flourishing on the shores of Africa, evils like lynching in Georgia and exclusion laws in Australia would be dispensed with. Others, and these are in the majority, cannot see beyond the shores of the Hudson. They haven't any international vision. They, for the most part, are negroes of the agricultural regions, the very backbone of the South. To them Africa is a dream—an unrealizable dream. In America, despite its "Jim-Crow" laws, they see something beautiful.

On the other hand, there is the foreign negro to be considered. Yearly a certain percentage of West Indians come to America. On the whole the West Indian is intelligent. He is an indefatigable student. When the epic of the negro in America is written, it will show the West Indian as the stokesman in the furnace of negro ideals. What he lacks in political consciousness he makes up in industrial productivity. He works hard, saves his money, sends his children to the best schools and colleges, and does a little original thinking of his own.

The rank and file of negroes are opposed to Garveyism, dissatisfied with the personal vituperation and morbid satire of Mr. Du Bois, and prone to discount Major Moton's Tuskegee as a monument of respectable reaction. Even before the death of Booker T. Washington, Dr. W. E. B. Du Bois, Harvard Ph.D., was looked upon by the negroes as an intellectual icon. But there is now a revolt against Du Bois. The new negro feels that Mr. Du Bois is too far above the masses to comprehend their desires and aspirations. His "Darkwater,"* they feel, is a beautiful book, but it reveals the soul of a man who is sorry and ashamed he is not white. He hates to be black. In his writings there is a stream of endless woe, the sorrow of a mulatto whose white blood hates and despises the black in him. Clearly the issue is pretty well known on the fundamentals of present-day negro leadership. Garvey is a megalomaniac. Du Bois, unlike either Washington or the poet [Paul Laurence] Dunbar, suffers from the "superiority complex."

What, then, is the outlook for the new negro? Despite the handicaps of inadequate leadership, he is making tremendous headway in industry, to say nothing of art and literature. From 1900–1920 the value of farm property owned by negro farmers of the South has rapidly increased. This is true with reference to the value of the live stock, poultry, and implements and machinery owned. The value of land and buildings increased from $69,636,420 in 1900 to $273,501,665 in 1910, or 293 per cent [*sic*]. The value of land and buildings owned by the negro farmers of the South in 1920 was $522,178,137, an increase for the ten years of $248,676,472, or 91 per cent.***

According to the Negro Year Book for 1922 "negroes in South Carolina paid taxes on a property value of $53,901,018. In Virginia, negroes in 1921 owned 1,911,443 acres of land valued at $17,600,148."

It is estimated that the value of the property now owned by the negroes of the United States is over $1,500,000,000. The lands which they own amount to more than 22,000,000 acres, or more than 34,000 square miles, an area greater than that of the five New England States, New Hampshire, Vermont, Massachusetts, Connecticut and Rhode Island.

With this background of industrial prosperity what is the outlook for the negro? To give an adequate answer to this one must examine the negro's mental state. In the first place he is race-conscious. He does not want, like the American Indian, to be like the white man. He is coming to realize the great possibilities within himself, and his tendency is to develop those possibilities. He is looking toward a broader leadership. That which he has at present is either old-fashioned, unrepresentative of his spirit and desires, or stupid, corrupt, and hate-mad. Though there are thousands of college-bred negroes working as janitors and bricklayers and railroad porters, there are still more thousands who are fitting themselves to become architects, engineers, chemists, manufacturers. The new negro, who does not want to go back to Africa, is fondly cherishing an ideal—and that is, that the time will come when America will look upon the negro not as a savage with an inferior mentality, but as a civilized man. The American negro of today believes intensely in America. At times, when the train is whirling him back to dearly loved ones "below the line," he is tempted to be bitter and morose and, perhaps, iconoclastic. But he is hoping and dreaming. He is pinning everything on the hope, illusion or not, that America will some day find its soul, forget the negro's black skin, and recognize him as one of the nation's most loyal sons and defenders.

From *Current History* February 1923

The Black City

I

North of 125th Street and glowing at the foot of Spuyten Duyvil* is the sweltering city of Harlem, the "Black Belt" of Greater New York. With Negroes residing on San Juan Hill, on the East Side, in Greenwich Village, Harlem, undoubtedly, is the seething spot of the darker races of the world. As Atlanta, Georgia, is the breeding spot of the American Negro; Chicago, the fulfillment of his industrial hopes; Washington, the intellectual capital of his world; so is Harlem, with its 185,000 beings, the melting pot of the darker races. Here one is able to distinguish the blending of prodigal sons and daughters of Africa and Polynesia and the sun-drenched shores of the Caribbean; of peasant folk from Georgia and Alabama and the marsh lands of Florida and Louisiana. Here is banker and statesman, editor and politician, poet and scholar, scientist and laborer. Here is a world of song and color and emotion. Of life and beauty and majestic somnolence.

It is a sociological *el dorado*. With its rise, its struggles, its beginnings; its loves, its hates, its visionings, its tossings on the crest of the storming white sea; its orgies, its gluttonies; its restraints, its passivities; its spiritual yearnings—it is beautiful. On its bosom is the omnipresent symbol of oneness, of ethnologic oneness. Of solidarity! Hence its striving, its desperate striving, after a pigmentational purity, of distinctiveness of beauty. It is neither white nor black.

It is a city of dualities. Yonder, as the sun shoots its slanting rays across the doorstep of a realtor or banker or capitalist there is a noble son of Africa Redeemed on whose crown it shines. Well groomed, he is monocled or sprayed with a leaf of violet. By way of a boutonniere he sports a white or crimson aster—and in he goes. It is the beginning of his day as merchant or realtor or whatever he is. . . . Towards sunset, as his pale-faced prototype resigns himself to supper or home or cabaret or adoring wife or chorus girl he is seen, is this black son, this time in denim or gold-braided toga, on his way to that thing that puts bread in his and his wife's and his children's mouths, and steels that silver-like spot glowing at the bottom of him, so that day in and day out he doggedly goes on, striving, conquering, upbuilding.

It is the beginning of his day as a domestic.

II

It is a city of paradoxes. You go to the neighborhood theatre and there is a play of Negro life. It is sharp, true, poignant. In awe you open your mouth at the beauty, the majesty, the sheer Russian-like reality of it. Grateful, the house asks for the author, the creator, the playwright. He is dragged forward; there is an outburst of applause—emotion unleashed. Modestly bowing the young man is slowly enveloped in the descending shadows—and the crowd is no more.

Wonderful! You go home; on a roseate bed you sleep, dream, remember things. In the morning you get up. Slipping into a dressing robe you go down in answer to the postman's shrilling whistle. Out of eyes painted with mist you go and take the letter, take the letter from the postman. Wholly by accident you raise your eyes and find, find yourself looking at—the playwright!

It is a city of paradoxes. Along the avenue you are strolling. It is dusk. Harlem at dusk is exotic. Music. Song. Laughter. The street is full of people—dark, brown, crimson, pomegranate. Crystal clear is the light that shines in their eyes. It is different, is the light that shines in these black people's eyes. It is a light mirroring the emancipation of a people and still you feel that they are not quite emancipated. It is the light of an unregenerate.

As I say, you are walking along the avenue. There is a commotion. No, it is not really a commotion. Only a gathering together of folk. "Step this way, ladies and gentlemen . . . step this way. . . . There you are. . . . Now this Coofu medicine is compounded from the best African herbs . . ." East Fourteenth Street. Nassau Street. The Jewish ghetto. Glimpses of them whirl by you. Not of the Barnum herd, you are tempted to go on, to let the asses gourmandize it. Seized by a fit of reminiscence you pause. Over the heads of the mob you see, not the bushy black-haired head of the Hindu "fakir," the Ph.D. of Oxford and Cambridge (in reality the blatant son of the acacia soil of Constant Springs, Jamaica, still basking in the shadows of dialectical oppression); not the boomeranging Congo oil magnate; nor the Jew invader with his white, ivory white cheeks, hungry, Christ-like features, and flowing rabbinical beard. Instead you see a black man, of noble bearing, of intellectual poise, of undefiled English, a university man, selling at 900 per cent profit a beastly concoction that even white barbarians do not hesitate to gobble up.

And there is a reason, a mighty reason, for this, for the conversion, for the triumphs of this black charlatan; a reason that goes up into the very warp and woof of American life. Imagine it—think, think about it sometime.

III

It is a house of assignation, a white man's house of assignation, is this black city. It is voluptuously accessible to him. Before cabarets and restaurants, cabarets and restaurants that black folk cannot go into, he stops, draws up his limousine, takes his lady, bathed in shining silk, out; squeezes through the molting, unminding folk, tips the black pyramidal *major domo*, and skips up to the scarlet draped seraglio. Here is white morality, white bestiality, for the Negroes to murmur and shake their bronzing cauliflower heads at.

It is wise, is this black city.

From the *Messenger* January 1924

On Being Black

I go to an optician for a pair of goggles. My eyes are getting bad and my wife insists upon my getting them. For a long time I have hesitated to do so. I hated to be literary—that is, to look literary. It is a fad, I believe. On an afterthought I am convinced she is right; I need them. My eyes are paining me. Moreover, the lights in the subway are blindingly dark, and head swirling. Again, the glitter of spring sends needles through my skull. I need the things badly. I decide to go to the optician's. I go. It is a Jewish place. Elderly is the salesman. I put my cards on the table. . . . "Fine day, isn't it?" He rubs and twists his pigmy fingers and ambles back to the rear. A moment later he returns. With him is a tray of jewelry—lenses and gold rings, diamonds and silver frames. Fine, dainty, effeminate things.

"Here is a nice one," chirps the old gentleman in a sing-song tone, as he tries to fit it on to my nose. "Just the right kind of goggles to keep the dust from going into your eyes. Only the other day I sold—"

At first I feel as if it is one of these confounded new fangled things. Overnight they come, these new styles. Ideas! Here, I whisper to myself, is a new one on me. But I look again. It has a perforated bit of tin on either side of it like the black star-eyed guard on a horse's blinker.

"Oh, I can show you others, if you don't like that one. Want one with a bigger dust piece? I have others back here. Don't be afraid, I'll fix you up. All the colored chauffeurs on Cumberland Street buy their glasses here."

"But I am not a chauffeur," I reply softly. Were it a Negro store, I might have said it with a great deal of emphasis, of vehemence. But being what it is, and knowing that the moment I raise my voice I am accused of "uppishness," I take pains—oh such pains, to be discreet. I wanted to bellow into his ears, "Don't think every Negro you see is a chauffeur." But the man is overwhelmingly amused. His snow-white head is bent—bent over the tray of precious gold, and I can see his face wrinkle in an atrociously cynical smile. But I cannot stand it—that smile. I walk out.

II

I am a stenographer. I am in need of a job. I try the employment agencies. I battle with anaemic youngsters and giggling flappers. I am at the tail end of a long line—only to be told the job is already filled. I am ignorantly optimistic. America is a big place; I feel it is only a question of time and perseverance. Encouraged, I go into the tall office buildings on Lower Broadway. I try everyone of them. Not a firm is missed. I walk in and offer my services. I am black, foreign-looking and a curio. My name is taken. I shall be sent for, certainly, in case of need. "Oh, don't mention it sir. . . . Glad you came in. . . . Good morning." I am smiled out. I never hear from them again.

Eventually I am told that that is not the way it is done here. What typewriter do I use? Oh,—. Well, go to the firm that makes them. It maintains an employment bureau, for the benefit of users of its machine. There is no discrimination there; go and see them. Before I go I write stating my experience and so forth. Are there any vacancies? In reply I get a flattering letter asking me to call. I do so.

The place is crowded. A sea of feminine faces disarms me. But I am no longer sensitive. I've got over that—long since. I grind my teeth and confidently take my seat with the mob. At the desk the clerks are busy telephoning and making out cards. I am just one of the crowd.

One by one the girls, and men, too, are sent out after jobs. It has been raining and the air is frowsy. The Jewish girls are sweating in their war-paint. At last they get around to me. It is my turn.

I am sitting away down at the front. In order to get to me the lady is obliged to do a lot of detouring. At first I thought she was about to go out, to go past me. But I am mistaken. She takes a seat right in front of me, a smile on her wrinkled old-maidish face. I am sure she is the head of the department. It is a situation that requires a strong diplomatic hand. She does not send one of the girls. She comes herself. She is from Ohio, I can see that. She tries to make me feel at home by smiling broadly in my face.

"Are you Mr.———?"

"Yes."

"That's nice. Now how much experience you say you've had?"

She is about to write.

"I stated all that in the letter, I think. I've had five years. I worked for—"

"Oh yes, I have it right here. Used to be secretary to Dr.———. Then you worked for an export house, and a soap manufacturer. Also as a shorthand reporter on a South American paper. That is interesting; quite an experience for a young man, isn't it?"

I murmur unintelligibly.

"Well," continues the lady, "we haven't anything at present—"

"But I thought you said in your letter that there is a job vacant. I've got it here in my pocket. I hope I haven't left it at home—"

"That won't suit you. You see it—it—is a post that requires banking experience. One of the biggest banks in the city. Secretary to the vice-president. Ah, by the way; come to think of it, you're just the man for it. You know Mr.———of Lenox Avenue? You do! I think the number is———. Yes, here it is. Also one of his cards. Well, if I were you I would go and see him. Good day."

Dusk is on the horizon. I am once more on Broadway. I am not going to see the man on Lenox Avenue. It won't do any good. The man she is sending me to is a pupil of mine!

III

My wife's health is not very good and I think of sending her to the tropics. I write to the steamship company and in reply I receive a sheaf of booklets telling me all about the blueness of the Caribbean, the beauty of Montega Bay [*sic*], and the fine a la carte service at the Myrtle Bank Hotel. I am intrigued—I think that is the word—by a three months' cruise at a special rate of $150.00. I telephone the company in an effort to get some information as to sailing dates, reservations, and so forth.

"I understand," I say to the young man who answers the telephone. "I understand that you have a ship sailing on the tenth. I would like to reserve a berth at the $150.00 you are at present offering."

"White or colored?"

"Colored."

Evidently the clerk is consulting someone. But his hand is over the mouthpiece and I can not hear what he is saying. Presently—

"Better come in the office and make reservations."

"What time do you close?"

"Five o'clock."

"What time is it now, please?"

"Ten to."

"Good," I hurry, "I am at Park Place now. Do you think if I hop on a Broadway trolley I can make it before five?"

"I don't know," unconcernedly.

I am at the booking desk. It is three minutes to five. The clerks, tall, lean, light-haired youths, are ready to go home. As I enter a dozen pairs of eyes are fastened upon me. Murmuring. Only a nigger. Again the wheels of life grind on. Lots are cast—I am not speaking metaphorically. The joke is on the Latin. Down in Panama he is a government clerk. Over in Caracas, a tinterillo,* and in Mexico, a scientifico. I know the type. Coming to New York, he shuns the society of Spanish-Americans. On the subway at night he reads the New York Journal instead of La Prensa.* And on wintery evenings, you can always find him around Seventy-second Street and Broadway. The lad before me is dark, has crystal brown eyes, and straight black hair.

"I would like," I begin, "to reserve a passage for my wife on one of your steamers to Kingston. I want to get it at the $150.00 rate."

"Well, it is this way." I am positive he is from Guayaquil.* "It will cost you $178.00."

"Why $178.00?"

"You see, the passage alone is $170.00—"

"A hundred and seventy dollars! Why, this booklet here says $150.00 round trip. You must have made a mistake."

"You see, this $150.00 rate is for three in a room, and all the rooms on the ship sailing on the tenth are already taken up."

"All right," I decide. "the date is inconsequential. What I want is the $150.00 rate. Reserve a berth for me on any ship that is not already filled up. I don't care how late in the summer it is. I have brought a deposit along with me—"

I am not truculent. Everything I say I strive to say softly, unoffensively—especially when in the midst of a color-ordeal!

"Well, you'd have to get two persons to go with her." The Peruvian is independent. "There are only three berths in a stateroom, and if your wife wants to take advantage of the $150.00 rate, she will have to get two other colored persons to go with her."

"I s-e-e!" I mutter dreamily. And I did see!

"Come in tomorrow and pay a deposit on it, if you want to. It is five o'clock and—"

I am out on the street again. From across the Hudson a gurgling wind brings dust to my nostrils. I am limp, static, emotionless. There is only one line to Jamaica, and I am going to send her by it. It is the only thing to do. Tomorrow I am going back, with the $178.00. It pays to be black.

From the *New Republic* November 1, 1922

The Stone Rebounds

It is night. I am in dark Harlem. I am walking along Seventh Avenue, in company with a Negro playwright. I had met him at a radical forum downtown. I pride myself on being an intellectual anarchist; I haven't any prejudices. I am interested in the Negro problem. Interested in it the same as I am interested in Russia and India and Corea. I want to see Society take on a different shape. I am a radical. I stick to my Negro friend. I take him around with me. I run the risk of being ostracized. I remember once I took him to Barrett Manor. Barrett Manor is an art colony. Flappers and broken-down celebrities hang out there. It is a nice place. It is full of Dore's illustrations.* I like it. Always I am lionized by the crowd. Of love and death, poetry and pragmatism, sex and the eternal will—of all these things I would talk. They would hang around and anticipate the words as they came from my lips, especially the girls. I was such a favorite there. Then I took my Negro friend there. Why not? My friend is more intellectual than I. I realize it. I am big enough to admit it. In the old days as soon as I opened the wire-screened door they would all flock to greet me—but that day, I shall never forget it. I let my friend in first. I went in afterward. What a change! I was no longer the idol, the master conversationalist; no, I had fallen. Fallen from grace; fallen like Lucifer. That entire day I felt a pang of remorse at what it was to be white. Earl, superman that he is, did not seem to notice it. Why should he? It was his first visit there. But it galled me. I have tabooed Barrett Manor. I haven't been there since.

I think of all these things as I swing up the avenue. And my confession! As much as I had tried, I couldn't conceal it. At first I used to blame it on the bourgeoise; but Earl was wise. I could see it in the way he'd smile. Smiling out of the corner of his mouth!

So I decided to tell him. I laid my cards on the table. It is useless, I said, trying to run up against a stonewall—a Gibraltar of prejudice. Useless! I didn't have any difficulty bringing him to my point of view. Yes, he said, he had felt it all along—at the restaurant, the theatre, on the bus, in Greenwich Village; yes, it had followed us, like a starving wolf. But my friend, non-combatant that he is, suggested a way out. Why not let us meet up in Harlem, Black Harlem? Surely—. No, I hadn't any objection, I hastily assured him. Truth is, the idea thrilled me. I long wanted to visit the place. I had heard so much about it.

"It is in here."

I am jerked out of my reverie. I am on a dark, maple-shaded street. I don't know how Earl manages it, but I suppose he knows the place very well. I follow him. It is down in a basement. A sheet of purple is over everything. Dimly I make it out. Witch-like silhouettes belt it. Over the fireplace is a white peacock.* A majestic-looking bird. On the wall, over the piano, is a girl sitting on the bough of a huge cypress, playing a harp. Sunset shines thru the branches. Beside the piano is a bookcase, and on the center table is a medieval lamp. Its chimney is daubed with Oriental flowers. Quaint as can be. At once I take to it. I like the atmosphere. But the people in it! At a jut-like table is a girl, I don't know whether she is white or colored, talking to a man. I can not see his face—it is away from me. But his neck I can see. It is black. I am being introduced around. I can not always see their faces. The place is so romantically dark. It is a long time before I adjust my sight to the light. I am invited to a seat at the center table, and talk—group chatter—is resumed. A girl with pomegranate cheeks is on my right, and at my left is Earl. The girl is saying something to me.

"Well, Mr. Kraus,* how do you like it up here?"

"Oh, I think it is great," I whisper dreamily. "It is so—Bohemian."

The girl has creole eyes and I feast on them; but they are not magnetic enough to arrest the functioning of my other self—my sub-conscious self. I can hear Earl's soft musical voice as he leans over and talks to the lady with the cossack hat, at his left.

"No, he isn't colored. Jewish—a friend of mine. What? No, I don't think so. Kraus is a poet, not an anthropologist."

"What is he doing up here, then?"

"He just came along with me, that's all."

"Humph, that is funny."

"What's funny?"

"This white man coming up here—I don't understand it."

"Oh, don't be silly, Daisy. I thought you always say you haven't any prejudice."

I am talking to the dark-eyed girl at my elbow. Of course, it is about the race question. Everyone seems to be talking about it these days. I ask her what are her views on that eternal bugaboo—social equality.

"Well, it is this way," she begins, knocking off her cigarette. "I am colored, and self-conscious. Very much so; I can not get over it. It is part of me. I believe it ought to be so that if I want to marry a Dutchman, I can. I am of age, and I think I know what is best for me. More than the ignorant mob out on the street. Yes, I believe in social equality—if by social equality you mean intermarriage, and that is what it means nowadays."

I don't know what sort of look has crept into my eyes, but it must be an alarming one.

"Understand me clearly!" She hastened to add, "By that I do not mean that *I* personally wish to marry a white man. Get that straight."

I am conscious of an enveloping silence. I drink the tea that is put before me and try to think up clever things to say. I can not explain it. It is sepulchral—the silence. Even the girl beside me is taken with the string of Spanish beads around her neck. Occasionally I would glance over at the woman on Earl's right. She is toying with the Japanese ash tray on the table. But I am sure now and then she emits a grunt. Something ugh-ish. I am sure of it. I look around. On me a houseful of eyes is cast. I do not feel out of place. I rejoice in the reaction. I know why they are staring at me. I am white.

From *Opportunity* September 1923

Courtesy of the National Urban League.

Vignettes of the Dusk

I

It is lunch time. I am in the heart of America's financial seraglio. It is a lovely day. Spring. Oceans of richly clad people sweep by me. In my pocket I jingle coins of gold. Gold! I am tired of eating at Max's Busy Bee. The fellows who dine there are so—so—rough sometimes. Still it is the most democratic eating place I know. There is no class prejudice; no discrimination; newsboys, bootblacks, factory slaves, all eat at Max's.

Today I am "flush" and I think I ought to blow myself to a decent meal. My courage is bolstered up. Rich, I am extravagant today. I rub elbows with bankers and millionaires and comely office girls. Of seraphs and madrigals I dream—nut that I am. I look up at the sparkling gems of architecture and marvel at the beauty that is America. America!

I almost ran past it. There it is, the place with the swinging doors and the chocolate puffs in the show case. Myriads of Babbitts and elfin girls pour into it. Tremblingly I enter. It reminds me of a mediaevel palace. Mirrors, flowers, paintings, candelabra; waiters in gowns as white as alabaster; and at the table a row, two deep, of eager, bright faced youths and maidens.

I stand back in bewilderment. How efficient these waiters are! Don't they ever make mistakes? Don't they ever serve a frappe for a temptation, a soda for a sundae? Don't they ever—

The waiter's inquiring eyes are on mine. He has got round to me. I whisper my order to him.

"Oyster salad—and vanilla temptation."

I put both hands in my coat pockets and think of the beauty and romance to be found in this place. Up my sleeve I laugh at your intellectual immigrants who howl about the barrenness of America. To me it offers exhaustless possibilities. It opens up entirely new and unexpurgated editions to life. Yes, I say to myself, I must come back again. It is weirdly enchanting. The cuisine is so good. And the people here are such refined eaters! So unlike Max's, where everything is bolted down at a gulp!

Oh, why does he put himself to all that trouble? Couldn't he just hand it to me over there instead of having to come all the way round the counter to make sure that it gets into my hands? Couldn't he have saved himself all that trouble?

He is at my side. Stern and white-lipped he hands me a nice brown paper bag with dusky flowers on it. He holds it off with the tips of his fingers as if its contents were leprous.

"Careful," he warns farsightedly, "else you'll spill the temptation." I do not argue. Sepulchrally I pay the check and waltz out. It is the equivalent of being sho[o]ed out. And, listen folks, he was careful *not* to say, "No, we don't serve no colored here."

II

In 1918 he came to America. That means he is still a foreigner. He is not a citizen—yet. But he is going to be. It is going to be the Big Adventure of his life. But wait—

Sometimes he stops and thinks. He is a Negro. He is a foreign Negro. Every day he reads of lynchings in the South. He is besieged on all sides by vicious soul pricks. No, they'd say to him, you musn't go South; you won't like it down there. In some places, like Texas, you can't stand up under the same roof with a white man unless you take off your hat. You would rebel against it. You with your white man's point of view (don't you know the white nurse woman who attends his wife once told him, as she cocked her red head on one side and shut one of her ugly cross eyes, "I think English Negroes are more like white people in their point of view, don't you think so? They're so fine—and not so race conscious"). You, they say to him, you with your white man's ways and outlook will not stand for it. They'd string you up on a tree! They'd . . . .

"But I must go," he screams back at them. "I must! I can't be an American unless I am able to go South! I've got to go."

He thinks of his friend Williams. Williams is a Jamaican. But he is thoroly, spiritually, euph[em]istically American. Some dusky folks,

mistaking him for a native, so perfect is his philological assimilation—
I am referring to those Afro-Africans who speak of West Indians as
"monkey chasers"—come to him and say, "You know, Bill, dem monkey wimmin is de dummest—"

But Williams, who owns a lovely home in Jersey, and has a pretty
wife, a jewel of one of the best colored families of Baltimore, is not a
citizen. And he doesn't intend to be one. He has been here twenty
years. "America is all right," he'd say, "but I ain't taking no chances!"

III

I am a listening post. I am anchored in the middle of life's gurgling
stream. It is a stream that is anthropologically exotic. Up in the
Negro belt.

I am at a chop house on Lenox Avenue. It is a rendezvous for
Negro Bohemians. I am amazed at the conglomerateness of it. Quad-
roons, octoroons, gypsies, yellows, high and low browns, light and
dark blacks, of all shades and colors of shades.

"Well, what do you think of this young Negro generation?
Think they'll amount to anything?"

"Oh, they'll fizzle out like all the rest, Wind up as porters . . . elevator men . . . janitors . . . ."

Silence.

IV

I am thinking, thinking, thinking. Of white supremacy; of the Nordic
Renaissance . . . .

And again I don the armor of a listening post.

Right of me is a Negro, a very black Negro clarionetist, who, as
I take my seat, rises to go out. At the table from which he rose two
other men sit. One is a mullato; the other is fair, very fair, almost
white. He of the golden hair and thin lips leans back in his chair and
looks at the young man about to go out.

"Say," he whispered, "kin—kin ah come along?"

The other played with it. Slowly he took the tooth pick out of his
mouth and wagged his head decisively.

"Nope," he said, "I can't take you along, old top. Where I'm
going the folks don't like no yalla men."

V

Out on the street. I whine at the whirl of dust and dirt the wind blasts up on me. I am slowly going down the avenue. In front of me is a jet black trollop. Her hair is bobbed. I snort at the bumps—barber's itch— I am forced to see on the back of her scraped neck. Ugh! Glass bottle!

I stop at Archie's. I always stop at Archie's on the way down. Out on the steaming boulevard he is, as usual. Myriads of men—please don't tell me they all work at night—talk to him about horses, horses, horses. Coming up the avenue is a woman, an anthropological meta-morphosis . . . .

"May God strike me dead if I ain't telling you the truth," Archie is trying to convince a skeptic of something. "Eight years, I tell you. After me for eight long years. But I didn't bother. And talk about pretty, she was a dream. Her father was one of the richest colored men in Virginia. And she had a lovely bungalow on the South Side. Ober-lin graduate too. But I didn't marry her. And I didn't have anything against her. . . . She was so fine and thoughtful. Come any time at the house. I'll show you the little cuff links . . . things like that. . . . I didn't have anything against her. . . . Not a thing. Only thing she was too white. Her hair was a bit too much like old gold. . . . She was too white . . . ."

Coming up the avenue is the anthropological metamorphosis.

"Sure she ain't white, Archie?"

"Ah don't know . . . ."

"Seems lek she . . . ."

Goes the mystery by. Then . . . .

"Naw," Archie spits, "she ain't white. Can't you see her neck?"*

From *Opportunity* January 1924

Courtesy of the National Urban League.

The Wharf Rats

I

Among the motley crew recruited to dig the Panama Canal were arti-sans from the four ends of the earth. Down in the Cut drifted hordes of Italians, Greeks, Chinese, Negroes—a hardy, sun-defying set of white, black and yellow men. But the bulk of the actual brawn for the work was supplied by the dusky peons of those coral isles in the Caribbean ruled by Britain, France and Holland.

At the Atlantic end of the Canal the blacks were herded in box-car huts buried in the jungles of "Silver City"; in the murky tenements perilously poised on the narrow banks of Faulke's River; in the low, smelting cabins of Coco Té. The "Silver Quarters" harbored the inky ones, their wives and pickaninnies.*

As it grew dark, the hewers at the Ditch, exhausted, half-asleep, naked but for wormy singlets,* would hum queer creole tunes, play on guitar or piccolo, and jig to the rhythm of the *coombia*. It was a *brujer-ial* chant, for *obeah*,* a heritage of the French colonial, honeycombed the life of the Negro laboring camps. Over smoking pots, on black, death-black nights legends of the bloodiest were recited till they became the essence of a sort of Negro Koran. One refuted them at the price of one's breath. And to question the verity of the *obeah*, to dismiss or reject it as the ungodly rite of some lurid, crack-brained Islander was to be an accursed pale-face, dog of a white. And the *obeah* man, in a fury of rage, would throw a machette at the heretic's head or—worse—burn on his doorstep at night a pyre of Maubé bark* or green Ganga weed.

On the banks of a river beyond Cristobal, Coco Té sheltered a colony of Negroes enslaved to the *obeah*. Near a roundhouse, daubed with smoke and coal ash, a river serenely flowed away and into the guava region, at the eastern tip of Monkey Hill.* Across the bay from it was a sand bank—a rising out of the sea—where ships stopt for coal.

In the first of the six chinky cabins making up the family quarters of Coco Té lived a stout, pot-bellied St. Lucian, black as the coal hills he mended, by the name of Jean Baptiste. Like a host of the native St. Lucian emigrants, Jean Baptiste forgot where the French in him ended and the English began. His speech was the petulant *patois* of the unlettered French black. Still, whenever he lapsed into His Majesty's English, it was with a thick Barbadian bias.

A coal passer at the Dry Dock, Jean Baptiste was a man of intense piety. After work, by the glow of a red, setting sun, he would discard his crusted overalls, get in starched *crocus bag*,* aping the Yankee fore-man on the other side of the track in the "Gold Quarters," and loll on his coffee-vined porch. There, dozing in a bamboo rocker, Celestin, his second wife, a becomingly stout brown beauty from Martinique, chanted gospel hymns to him.

Three sturdy sons Jean Baptiste's first wife had borne him— Philip, the eldest, a good-looking black fellow; Ernest, shifty, cunning; and Sandel, aged eight. Another boy, said to be wayward and something of a ne'er-do-well, was sometimes spoken of. But Baptiste, a proud, disdainful man, never once referred to him in the presence of his children. No vagabond son of his could eat from his table or sit at his feet unless he went to "meeting." In brief, Jean Baptiste was a religious man. It was a thrust at the omnipresent *obeah*. He went to "meeting." He made the boys go, too. All hands went, not to the Catholic Church, where Celestin secretly worshiped, but to the English Plymouth Brethren* in the Spanish city of Colon.

Stalking about like a ghost in Jean Baptiste's household was a girl, a black ominous Trinidad girl. Had Jean Baptiste been a man given to curiosity about the nature of women, he would have viewed skeptically Maffi's adoption by Celestin. But Jean Baptiste was a man of lofty unconcern, and so Maffi remained there, shadowy, obdurate.

And Maffi was such a hardworking *patois* girl. From the break of day she'd be at the sink, brightening the tinware. It was she who did the chores which Madame congenitally shirked. And towards sundown, when the labor trains had emptied, it was she who scoured the beach for cockles for Jean Baptiste's epicurean palate.

And as night fell, Maffi, a long, black figure, would disappear in the dark to dream on top of a canoe hauled up on the mooning beach. An eternity Maffi'd sprawl there, gazing at the frosting of the stars and the glitter of the black sea.

A cabin away lived a family of Tortola mulattoes by the name of Boyce. The father was also a man who piously went to "meeting"— gaunt and hollow-cheeked. The eldest boy, Esau, had been a journeyman tailor for ten years; the girl next him, Ora, was plump, dark, freckled; others came—a string of ulcered girls until finally a pretty, opaque one, Maura.

Of the Bantu tribe Maura would have been a person to turn and stare at. Crossing the line into Cristobal or Colon—a city of rarefied gayety—she was often mistaken for a native *señorita* or an urbanized Cholo* Indian girl. Her skin was the reddish yellow of old gold and in her eyes there lurked the glint of mother-of-pearl. Her hair, long as a jungle elf's was jettish, untethered. And her teeth were whiter than the full-blooded black Philip's.

Maura was brought up, like the children of Jean Baptiste, in the Plymouth Brethren. But the Plymouth Brethren was a harsh faith to bring hemmed-in peasant children up in, and Maura, besides, was of a gentle romantic nature. Going to the Yankee commissary at the bottom of Eleventh and Front Streets, she usually wore a leghorn hat.* With flowers bedecking it, she'd look in it older, much older than she really was. Which was an impression quite flattering to her. For Maura, unknown to Philip, was in love—in love with San Tie, a Chinese half-breed, son of a wealthy canteen proprietor in Colon. But San Tie liked to go fishing and deer hunting up the Monkey Hill lagoon, and the object of his occasional visits to Coco Té was the eldest son of Jean Baptiste. And thus it was through Philip that Maura kept in touch with the young Chinese Maroon.

One afternoon Maura, at her wit's end, flew to the shed roof to Jean Baptiste's kitchen.

"Maffi," she cried, the words smoky on her lips, "Maffi, when Philip come in to-night tell 'im I want fo' see 'im particular, yes?"

"*Sacre gache!* All de time Philip, Philip!" growled the Trinidad girl, as Maura, in heartaching preoccupation, sped towards the lawn. "Why she no le' 'im alone, yes?" And with a spatter she flecked the hunk of lard on Jean Baptiste's stewing okras.

As the others filed up front after dinner that evening Maffi said to Philip, pointing to the cabin across the way, "She—she want fo'* see yo'."

Instantly Philip's eyes widened. Ah, he had good news for Maura! San Tie, after an absence of six days, was coming to Coco Té Saturday to hunt on the lagoon. And he'd relish the joy that'd flood Maura's face as she glimpsed the idol of her heart, the hero of her dreams! And Philip, a true son of Jean Baptiste, loved to see others happy, ecstatic.

But Maffi's curious rumination checked him. "All de time, Maura, Maura, me can't understand it, yes. But no mind, me go stop it, *oui*, me go stop it, so help me—"

He crept up to her, gently holding her by the shoulders.

"Le' me go, *sacre!*" She shook off his hands bitterly. "Le' me go—yo' go to yo' Maura." And she fled the room, locking the door behind her.

Philip sighed. He was a generous, good-natured sort. But it was silly to try to enlighten Maffi. It wasn't any use. He could as well have spoken to the tattered torsos the lazy waves puffed up on the shores of Coco Té.

II

"Philip, come on, a ship is in—let's go." Ernest, the wharf rat, seized him by the arm.

"Come," he said, "let's go before it's too late. I want to get some money, yes."

Dashing out of the house the two boys made for the wharf. It was dusk. Already the Hindus in the bachelor quarters were mixing their *rotie** and the Negroes in their singlets were smoking and cooling off. Night was rapidly approaching. Sunset, an iridescent bit of molten gold, was enriching the stream with its last faint radiance.

The boys stole across the lawn and made their way to the pier.

"Careful," cried Philip, as Ernest slid between a prong of oyster-crusted piles to a raft below, "careful, these shells cut wussah'n a knife."

On the raft the boys untied a rowboat they kept stowed away under the dock, got into it and pushed off. The liner still had two hours to dock. Tourists crowded its decks. Veering away from the barnacled piles the boys eased out into the churning ocean.

It was dusk. Night would soon be upon them. Philip took the oars while Ernest stripped down to loin cloth.

"Come, Philip, let me paddle—" Ernest took the oars. Afar on the dusky sea a whistle echoed. It was the pilot's signal to the captain of port. The ship would soon dock.

The passengers on deck glimpsed the boys. It piqued their curiosity to see two black boys in a boat amid stream.

"All right, mistah," cried Ernest, "a penny, mistah."

He sprang at the guilder* as it twisted and turned through a streak of silver dust to the bottom of the sea. Only the tips of his crimson toes—a sherbet-like foam—and up he came with the coin between his teeth.

Deep sea gamin,* Philip off yonder, his mouth noisy with coppers, gargled, "This way, sah, as far as yo' like, mistah."

An old red-bearded Scot, in spats and mufti, presumably a lover of the exotic in sport, held aloft a sovereign. A sovereign! Already red, and sore by virtue of the leaps and plunges in the briny swirl, Philip's eyes bulged at its yellow gleam.

"Ovah yah, sah—"

Off in a whirlpool the man tossed it. And like a garfish* Philip took after it, a falling arrow in the stream. His body, once in the water, tore ahead. For a spell the crowd on the ship held its breath. "Where is he?" "Where is the nigger swimmer gone to?" Even Ernest, driven to the boat by the race for such an ornate prize, cold, shivering, his teeth chattering—even he watched with trembling and anxiety. But Ernest's concern was of a deeper kind. For there, where Philip had leaped, was Deathpool—a sprawling place for sharks, for baracoudas!

But Philip rose—a brief gurgling sputter—a ripple on the sea— and the Negro's crinkled head was above the water.

"Hey!" shouted Ernest, "there, Philip! Down!"

And down Philip plunged. One—two—minutes. God, how long they seemed! And Ernest anxiously waited. But the bubble on the water boiled, kept on boiling—a sign that life still lasted! It comforted Ernest.

Suddenly Philip, panting, spitting, pawing, dashed through the water like a streak of lightning.

"Shark!" cried a voice aboard ship, "Shark! There he is, a great big one! Run, boy! Run for your life!"

From the edge of the boat Philip saw the monster as twice, thrice it circled the boat. Several times the shark made a dash for it endeavoring to strike it with its murderous tail.

The boys quickly made off. But the shark still followed the boat. It was a pale green monster. In the glittering dusk it seemed black to Philip. Fattened on the swill of the abattoir nearby and the beef tossed from the decks of countless ships in port it had become used to the taste of flesh and the smell of blood.

"Yo' know, Ernest," said Philip, as he made the boat fast to a raft, "one time I thought he wuz rubbin' 'gainst me belly. He wuz such a big able one. But it wuz wuth it, Ernie, it wuz wuth it—"

In his palm there was a flicker of gold. Ernest emptied his loin cloth and together they counted the money, dressed and trudged back to the cabin.

On the lawn Philip met Maura. Ernest tipped his cap, left his brother, and went into the house. As he entered Maffi, pretending to be scouring a pan, was flushed and mute as a statue. And Ernest, starved, went in the dining room and for a long time stayed there. Unable to bear it any longer, Maffi sang out, "Ernest, whey Philip dey?"

"Outside—some whey—ah talk to Maura—"

"Yo' sure yo' no lie, Ernest?" she asked, suspended.

"Yes, up cose, I jes' lef' 'im 'tandin' out dey—why?"

"Nutton—"

He suspected nothing. He went on eating while Maffi tiptoed to the shed roof. Yes, confound it, there he was, near the stand-pipe,* talking to Maura!

"Go stop *ee, oui*," she hissed impishly. "Go 'top ee, yes."

III

Low, shadowy, the sky painted Maura's face bronze. The sea, noisy, enraged, sent a blob of wind about her black, wavy hair. And with her back to the sea, her hair blew loosely about her face.

"D'ye think, d'ye think he really likes me, Philip?"

"I'm positive he do, Maura," vowed the youth.

And an ageing faith shone in Maura's eyes. No longer was she a silly, insipid girl. Something holy, reverent had touched her. And in so doing it could not fail to leave an impress of beauty. It was worshipful. And it mellowed, ripened her.

Weeks she had waited for word of San Tie. And the springs of Maura's life took on a noble ecstasy. Late at night, after the others had retired, she'd sit up in bed, dreaming. Sometimes they were dreams of envy. For Mama began to look with eyes of comparison upon the happiness of the Italian wife of the boss riveter at the Dry Dock—the lady on the other side of the railroad tracks in the "Gold Quarters" for whom she sewed—who got a fresh baby every year and who danced in a world of silks and satins. Yes, Maura had dreams, love dreams of San Tie, the flashy half-breed, son of a Chinese beer seller and a Jamaica Maroon, who had swept her off her feet by a playful wink of the eye.

"Tell me, Philip, does he work? Or does he play the lottery— what does he do, tell me!"

"I dunno," Philip replied with mock lassitude, "I dunno myself—"

"But it doesn't matter, Philip. I don't want to be nosy, see? I'm simply curious about everything that concerns him, see?"

Ah, but Philip wished to cherish Maura, to shield her, be kind to her. And so he lied to her. He did not tell her he had first met San Tie behind the counter of his father's saloon in the Colon tenderloin, for he would have had to tell, besides, why he, Philip, had gone there. And that would have led him, a youth of meager guile, to Celestin Baptiste's mulish regard for anisette which he procured her. He dared not tell her, well-meaning fellow that he was, what San Tie, a fiery comet in the night life of the district, had said to him the day before. "She sick in de head, yes," he had said. "Ah, me no dat saht o' man—don't she know no bettah, egh, Philip?" But Philip desired to be kindly, and hid it from Maura.

"What is it to-day?" she cogitated, aloud, "Tuesday. You say he's comin' fo' hunt Saturday, Philip? Wednesday—four more days. I can wait. I can wait. I'd wait a million years fo' 'im, Philip."

But Saturday came and Maura, very properly, was shy as a duck. Other girls, like Hilda Long, a Jamaica brunette, the flower of a bawdy cabin up by the abattoir, would have been less genteel. Hilda would have caught San Tie by the lapels of his coat and in no time would have got him told.

But Maura was lowly, trepid, shy. To her he was a dream—a luxury to be distantly enjoyed. He was not to be touched. And she'd wait till he decided to come to her. And there was no fear, either, of his ever failing to come. Philip had seen to that. Had not he been the intermediary between them? And all Maura needed now was to sit back, and wait till San Tie came to her.

And besides, who knows, brooded Maura, San Tie might be a bashful fellow.

But when, after an exciting hunt, the Chinese mulatto returned from the lagoon, nodded stiffly to her, said good-by to Philip and kept on to the scarlet city, Maura was frantic.

"Maffi," she said, "tell Philip to come here quick—"

It was the same as touching a match to the *patois* girl's dynamite. "Yo' mek me sick," she said. "Go call he yo'self, yo' ole hag, yo' ole fire hag,* yo'." But Maura, flighty in despair, had gone on past the lawn.

"Ah go stop *ee, oui*," she muttered diabolically, "Ah go stop it, yes. This very night."

Soon as she got through lathering the dishes she tidied up and came out on the front porch.

It was a humid dusk, and the glowering sky sent a species of fly—bloody as a tick—buzzing about Jean Baptiste's porch. There he sat, rotund, and sleepy-eyed, rocking and languidly brushing the darting imps away.

"Wha' yo' gwine, Maffi?" asked Celestin Baptiste, fearing to wake the old man.

"Ovah to de Jahn Chinaman shop, mum," answered Maffi unheeding.

"Fi' what?"

"Fi' buy some wash blue,* mum."

And she kept on down the road past the Hindu kiosk to the Negro mess house.

IV

"Oh, Philip," cried Maura, "I am so unhappy. Didn't he ask about me at all? Didn't he say he'd like to visit me—didn't he giv' yo' any message fo' me, Philip?"

The boy toyed with a blade of grass. His eyes were downcast. Sighing heavily he at last spoke. "No, Maura, he didn't ask about you."

"What, he didn't ask about me? Philip? I don't believe it! Oh, my God!"

She clung to Philip, mutely; her face, her breath coming warm and fast.

"I wish to God I'd never seen either of you," cried Philip.

"Ah, but wasn't he your friend, Philip? Didn't yo' tell me that?" And the boy bowed his head sadly.

"Answer me!" she screamed, shaking him. "Weren't you his friend?"

"Yes, Maura—"

"But you lied to me Philip, you lied to me! You took messages from me—you brought back—lies!" Two *pearls*, large as pigeon's eggs, shone in Maura's burnished face.

"To think," she cried in a hollow sepulchral voice, "that I dreamed about a ghost, a man who didn't exist. Oh, God, why should I suffer like this? Why was I ever born? What did I do, what did my people do, to deserve such misery as this?"

She rose, leaving Philip with his head buried in his hands. She went into the night, tearing her hair, scratching her face, raving.

"Oh, how happy I was! I was a happy girl! I was so young and I had such merry dreams! And I wanted so little! I was carefree—"

Down to the shore of the sea she staggered, the wind behind her, the night obscuring her.

"Maura!" cried Philip, running after her. "Maura! come back!"

Great sheaves of clouds buried the moon, and the wind bearing up from the sea bowed the cypress and palm lining the beach.

"Maura—Maura—"

He bumped into some one, a girl, black, part of the dense pattern of the tropical night.

"Maffi," cried Philip, "have you seen Maura down yondah?"

The girl quietly stared at him. Had Philip lost his mind?

"Talk, no!" he cried, exasperated.

And his quick tones sharpened Maffi's vocal anger. Thrusting him aside, she thundered, "Think I'm she keeper! Go'n look fo' she yo'self. I is not she keeper! Le' me pass, move!"

Towards the end of the track he found Maura, heartrendingly weeping.

"Oh, don't cry, Maura! Never mind, Maura!"

He helped her to her feet, took her to the stand-pipe on the lawn, bathed her temples and sat soothingly, uninterruptingly, beside her.

V

At daybreak the next morning Ernest rose and woke Philip. He yawned, put on the loin cloth, seized a "cracked licker"* skillet and stole cautiously out of the house. Of late Jean Baptiste had put his foot down on his sons' copper-diving proclivities. And he kept at the head of his bed a greased cat-o-nine-tails which he would use on Philip himself if the occasion warranted.

"Come on, Philip, let's go—"

Yawning and scratching Philip followed. The grass on the lawn was bright and icy with the dew. On the railroad tracks the six o'clock labor trains were coupling. A rosy mist flooded the dawn. Out in the stream the tug *Exotic* snorted in a heavy fog.

On the wharf Philip led the way to the rafters below.

"Look out fo' that *crapeau*,* Ernest, don't step on him, he'll spit on you."

The frog splashed into the water. Prickle-backed crabs and oysters and myriad other shells spawned on the rotting piles. The boys paddled the boat. Out in the dawn ahead of them the tug puffed a path through the foggy mist. The water was chilly. Mist glistened on top of it. Far out, beyond the buoys, Philip encountered a placid, untroubled sea. The liner, a German tourist boat, was loaded to the bridge. The water was as still as a lake of ice.

"All right, Ernest, let's hurry—"

Philip drew in the oars. The *Kron Prinz Wilhelm* came near. Huddled in thick European coats, the passengers viewed from their lofty estate the spectacle of two naked Negro boys peeping up at them from a wiggly *bateau*.*

"Penny, mistah, penny, mistah!"

Somebody dropped a quarter. Ernest, like a shot, flew after it. Half a foot down he caught it as it twisted and turned in the gleaming sea. Vivified by the icy dip, Ernest was a raving wolf and the folk aboard dealt a lavish hand.

"Ovah, yah, mistah," cried Philip, "ovah, yah."

For a Dutch guilder Philip gave an exhibition of "cork." Under something of a ledge on the side of the boat he had stuck a piece of cork. Now, after his and Ernest's mouths were full of coins, he could afford to be extravagant and treat the Europeans to a game of West Indian "cork."

Roughly ramming the cork down in the water, Philip, after the fifteenth ram or so, let it go, and flew back, upwards, having thus "lost" it. It was Ernest's turn now, as a sort of end-man, to scramble forward to the spot where Philip had dug it down and "find" it; the first one to do so, having the prerogative, which he jealously guarded, of raining on the other a series of thundering leg blows. As boys in the West Indies Philip and Ernest had played it. Of a Sunday the Negro fishermen on the Barbadoes coast made a pagan rite of it. Many a Bluetown dandy got his spine cracked in a game of "cork."

With a passive interest the passengers viewed the proceedings. In a game of "cork," the cork after a succession of "rammings" is likely to drift many feet away whence it was first "lost." One had to be an expert, quick, alert, to spy and promptly seize it as it popped up on the rolling waves. Once Ernest got it and endeavored to make much of the possession. But Philip, besides being two feet taller than he, was slippery as an eel, and Ernest, despite all the artful ingenuity at his command, was able to do no more than ineffectively beat the water about him. Again and again he tried, but to no purpose.

Becoming reckless, he let the cork drift too far away from him and Philip seized it.

He twirled it in the air like a crap shooter, and dug deep down the water with it, "lost" it, then leaped back, briskly waiting for it to rise.

About them the water, due to the ramming and beating, grew restive. Billows sprang up; soaring, swelling waves sent the skiff nearer the shore. Anxiously Philip and Ernest watched for the cork to make its ascent.

It was all a bit vague to the whites on the deck, and an amused chuckle floated down to the boys.

And still the cork failed to come up.

"I'll go after it," said Philip at last, "I'll go and fetch it." And, from the edge of the boat he leaped, his body long and resplendent in the rising tropic sun.

It was a suction sea, and down in it Philip plunged. And it was lazy, too, and willful—the water. Ebony-black, it tugged and mocked. Old brass staves—junk dumped there by the retiring French—thick, yawping mud, barrel hoops, tons of obsolete brass, a wealth of slimy steel faced him. Did a "rammed" cork ever go down that deep?

And the water, stirring, rising, drew a haze over Philip's eyes. Had a cuttlefish, an octopus, a nest of eels been routed? It seemed so to Philip, blindly diving, pawing. And the sea, the tide—touching the roots of Deathpool—tugged and tugged. His gathering hands stuck in mud. Iron staves bruised his shins. It was black down there. Impenetrable.

Suddenly, like a flash of lightning, a vision blew across Philip's brow. It was a soaring shark's belly. Drunk on the nectar of the deep, it soared above Philip—rolling, tumbling, rolling. It had followed the boy's scent with the accuracy of a diver's rope.

Scrambling to the surface, Philip struck out for the boat. But the sea, the depths of it wrested out of an aeon's slumber, had sent it a mile from his diving point. And now, as his strength ebbed, a shark was at his heels.

"Shark! Shark!" was the cry that went up from the ship.

Hewing a lane through the hostile sea Philip forgot the cunning of the doddering beast and swam noisier than he needed to. Faster grew his strokes. His line was a straight, dead one. Fancy strokes and dives—giraffe leaps . . . he summoned into play. He shot out recklessly. One time he suddenly paused—and floated for a stretch. Another time he swam on his back, gazing at the chalky sky. He dived for whole lengths.

But the shark, a bloaty, stone-colored mankiller, took a shorter cut. Circumnavigating the swimmer it bore down upon him with the speed of a hurricane. Within adequate reach it turned, showed its gleaming belly, seizing its prey.

A fiendish gargle—the gnashing of bones—as the sea once more closed its jaws on Philip.

Some one aboard ship screamed. Women fainted. There was talk of a gun. Ernest, an oar upraised, capsized the boat as he tried to inflict a blow on the coursing, chop-licking maneater.

And again the fish turned. It scraped the waters with its deadly fins.

At Coco Té, at the fledging of the dawn, Maffi, polishing the tin-ware, hummed an *obeah* melody.

> Trinidad is a damn fine place
> But *obeah* down dey. . . .

Peace had come to her at last.

From *Tropic Death* (New York: Boni & Liveright, 1926)

The Palm Porch

I

Below, a rock engine was crushing stone, shooting up rivers of steam and signaling the frontier's rebirth. Opposite, there was proof, a noisy, swaggering sort of proof, of the gradual death and destruction of the frontier post. Black men behind wheelbarrows slowly ascended a rising made of spliced boards and emptied the sand rock into the maw of a mixing machine. More black men, a peg down, behind wheelbarrows, formed a line which caught the mortar pouring into the rear organ of the omnivorous monster.

"All, all gone," cried Miss Buckner, and the girls at her side shuddered. All quietly felt the sterile menace of it. There, facing its misery, tears came to Miss Buckner's eyes and a jeweled, half-white hand, lifted gently to give a paltry vision of the immensity of it.

"All of that," she sighed, "all of that was swamp—when I came to the Isthmus. All." A gang of "taw"-pitching* boys, sons of the dusky folk seeping up from Caribbean isles, who had first painted Hudson Alley and "G" Street a dense black, and were now spreading up to the Point—swarmed to a spot in the road which the stone crusher had been especially cruel to, and drew a marble ring. Contemptibly pointing to them, Miss Buckner observed, "a year ago that would have been impossible. I can't understand what the world is coming to." Gazing at one another the girls were not tempted to speak, but were a bit bewildered, at this show of grossness on their mother's part. And anyway, it was noon, and they wanted to go to sleep.

But a light, flashed on a virgin past, burst on Miss Buckner, and she became reminiscent. . . .

Dark dense thicket; water paving it. Deer, lions, tigers bounding through it. Centuries, perhaps, of such pure, free rule. Then some khaki-clad, red-faced and scrawny-necked whites deserted the Zone and brought saws to the roots of palmetto, spears to the bush cats and jaguars, lysol to the mosquitoes and flies and tar to the burning timber-swamp. A wild racing to meet the Chagres* and explore the high reaches of the Panama jungle. After the torch, ashes and ghosts—bare, black stalks, pegless stumps, flakes of charred leaves and half-burnt tree trunks. Down by a stream watering a village of black French colonials, dredges began to work. More of the Zone pests, rubber-booted ones, tugged out huge iron pipes and safely laid them on the gutty bosom of the swamp. Congeries of them. Then one windy night the dredges began a moaning noise. It was the sea groaning and vomiting. Through the throat of the pipes it rattled, and spat stones—gold and emerald and amethyst. All sorts of juice the sea upheaved. It dug deep down, too, far into the recesses of its sprawling cosmos. Back to a pre-geologic age it delved, and brought up things.

Down by the mouth of a creole stream the dredges worked. Black in the golden mist, black on the lagoon.

With the aftermath there came a dazzling array of corals and jewels—jewels of the griping sea. Magically the sun hardened and whitened it. Sandwhite. Brown. Golden. Dross surged up; guava stumps, pine stumps, earth-burned sprats, river stakes. But the crab shell—sea crabs, pink and crimson—the sharks' teeth, blue, and black, and purple ones—the pearls, and glimmering stones—shone brightly.

Upon the lake of jeweled earth dusk swept a mantle of hazy blue.

II

"W'en yo' fadah wake up in de mawnin' time wid 'im marinah stiff out in front o' him—"

"Mek fun," said Miss Buckner, rising regally, "an' be a dam set o' fools all yo' life." She buried the butt in a Mexican urn, and strode by Anesta sprawling half-robed on the matted floor. "Move, gal, an' le' me go out dey an' show dis black sow how we want 'ar fi' stew de gunga peas* an' fowl."

"Oh, me don't wan' fi' go to no pahty," yawned Hyacinth, fingering the pages of a boudoir textbook, left her one evening by an Italian sea captain, "me too tiad, sah."

"An' me can't see how de hell me gwine mek up to any man if me got fi' fling in him face a old blue shif' me did got las' week. W'en is Scipio gwine bring me dat shawl him pramise fi' giv' me?"

"Me no fond ha-tall o' any 'Panish man," cried Anesta, "an' me don't see how me can—"

Miss Buckner swung around, struck. "Yo' t'ink so, he, his dat wha' yo' t'ink? Well, yo' bes' mek up unna* mind—all o' unna! Well, wha' a bunch o' lazy ongrateful bitches de whole carload of unna is, dough he?

Suddenly she broke off, anger seaming her brow, "Unna don't know me his hindebted to him, no? Unna don't know dat hif hit wasn't farrim a lot o' t'ings wha' go awn up yah, would be street property long ago—an' some o' we yo' see spo'tin' roun' yah would be some way else, an' diffrant altogaddah."*

"Ah know not me."

"Ah know Oi ain't owe nobody nothin'—"

"Yo' think yo' don't! But don't fool yourselves, children, there is more to make the mare go than you think—I see that now."

She busied herself gathering up glasses, flouncing off to the pantry.

The Palm Porch was not a canteen, it was a house. But it was a house of lavish self-containment. It was split up in rooms, following a style of architecture which was the flair of the Isthmian realtors, and each room opened out on the porch. Each had, too, an armor of leafy laces; shining dust and scarlet. Each had its wine and decanters, music and song.

On the squalid world of Colon it was privileged to gaze with hauteur, for Miss Buckner, the owner of the Palm Porch, was a lady of poise, charm and caution. Up around the ribs of the porch she had put a strip of canvas cloth. It shut out eyes effectively. Glancing up, one saw boxes of rosebush and flower vines, but beyond that—nothing. The porch's green paint, the opulent flower pots and growing plants helped to plaster on it the illusion of the tropical jungle.

There clung to Miss Buckner an idea of sober reality. Her hips were full, her hands long, hairy, unfeminine, her breasts dangling. She was fully seven feet tall and had a small, round head. Her hair was close to it—black, curly. Courageously she had bobbed and parted it at a time when it was unseasonable to do so, and yet retain a semblance of respect among the Victorian dames of the Spanish tropics.

Urged on by the ruthless spirit which was a very firm part of her, Miss Buckner was not altogether unaware of the capers she was cutting amid the few beings she actually touched. Among the motley blacks and browns and yellows on the Isthmus, there would be talk—but how was it to drift back to her? Via Zuline? Shame! "Who me? Me talk grossip wit' any sahvant gyrl, if yo' t'ink so yo' lie!" But the lack of an elfin figure and the possession of a frizzly head of hair, was more than made up for by Miss Buckner's gift of *manners*.

"Gahd, wha' she did got it, he?" folk asked; but neither London, nor Paris, nor Vienna answered. Indeed, Miss Buckner, a lady of sixty, would have been *wordless* at the idea of having to go beyond the dickty* rim of Jamaica in quest of *manners*. It was absurd to think so. This drop to the Isthmus was Miss Buckner's first gallop across the sea.

And so, like sap to a rubber tree, Miss Buckner's manner clung to her. Upon those of her sex she had slight cause to ply it, for at the Palm Porch few of them were allowed. Traditionally, it was a man's house. When Miss Buckner, beneath a brilliant lorgnette, was gracious enough to look at a man, she looked, sternly, unsmilingly down at him. When of a Sabbath, her hair in oily frills, wearing a silken shawl of cream and red, a dab of vermilion on her mouth, she swept regally down Bolivar Street on the way to the market, maided by the indolent Zuline, she had half of the city gaping at the animal wonder of her. Brief-worded, cool-headed, by a stabbing thrust or a petulant gesture, she'd confound any fish seller, any dealer in yampi or Lucy yam,* cocoanut milk or red peas—and pass quietly on, untouched by the briny babel.

In fact, from Colon to Cocoa Grove the pale-faced folk who drank sumptuously in the bowl of life churned by her considered Miss Buckner a woman to tip one's hat to—regal rite—a woman of taste and culture. Machinists at Balboa, engineers at Miraflores, sun-burned sea folk gladly testified to that fact. All had words of beauty for the ardor of Miss Buckner's salon.

Of course one gathered from the words which came like blazing meteors out of her mouth that Miss Buckner would have liked to be white; but, alas! she was only a mulatto. No one had ever heard of her before she and her five daughters moved into the Palm Porch. It was to be expected, the world being what it is, that words of murmured treason would drift abroad. A wine merchant, Raymond de la Croix, and a Jamaica horse breeder, Walter de Paz, vowed that they had seen her at an old seaman's bar on Matches Lane serving ale and ofttimes more poetic things than ale to young blond-headed Britons who would especially go there. But De Paz and De la Croix were men of frustrated idealism, and their words, to Miss Buckner at least, brutal though they were, were swept aside as expressions of useless chatter. Whether she was the result of a union of white and black, French and Spanish, English and Maroon—no one knew. Of an equally mystical heritage were her daughters, creatures of a rich and shining beauty. Of their father the less said the better. And in the absence of data tongues began to wag. Norwegian bos'n. Jamaica lover—Island triumph. Crazy Kingston nights. To the lovely young ladies in question it was a subject to be religiously high-hatted and tabooed. The prudent Miss Buckner, who had a burning contempt for statistics, was a trifle hazy about the whole thing.

One of the girls, white as a white woman, eyes blue as a Viking maid's, had eloped, at sixteen, to Miss Buckner's eternal disgust, with a shiny-armed black who had at one time been sent to the Island jail for the proletarian crime of prædial larceny.* The neighbors swore it had been love at first sight. But it irked and maddened Miss Buckner. "It a dam pity shame," she had cried, dabbing a cologned handkerchief to her nose, "it a dam pity shame."

Another girl, the eldest of the lot (Miss Buckner had had seven in all), had, O! ages before, given birth to a pretty, gray-eyed baby boy, when she was but seventeen and—again to Miss Buckner's disgust—

had later taken up with a willing young mulatto, a Christian in the Moravian Church. He was an able young man, strong and honest, and wore shoes, but Miss Buckner almost went mad—groaned at the pain her daughters caused her. "Oh, me Gahd," she had wept, "Oh, me Gahd, dem ah send me to de dawgs—dem ah send me to de dawgs." He was but a clerk in the cold storage; sixty dollars a month—wages of an accursed silver employee. Silver is nigger; nigger is silver. Nigger-silver. Why, roared Miss Buckner, stockings could not be bought with that, much more take care of a woman accustomed to "foxy clothes an' such" and a dazzling baby boy. Silver employee! Blah! Why couldn't he be a "Gold" one? Gold is white; white is gold. Gold-white! "Gold," and get $125 a month, like "de fella nex' tarrim, he? Why, him had to be black, an' get little pay, an' tek way me gal picknee from me? Now, hanswah [answer] me dat!" Nor did he get coal and fuel free, besides. He had to dig down and pay extra for them. He was not, alas! white. Which hurt, left Miss Buckner cold; caused her nights of sleepless despair. Wretch! "To t'ink a handsam gal like dat would-ah tek up wi' a dam black neygah man like him, he, w'en she could a stay wit' me 'n do bettah." But few knew the secret of Miss Buckner's sorrow, few sensed the deep tragedy of her.

And so to dam the flood of tears, Miss Buckner and the remaining ones of her flamingo brood, had drawn up at the Palm Porch. All day, the sun burning a flame through the torrid heavens, they would be postured on the porch. Virgin to the sun's gentle caresses, with the plants and flowers keeping the heat at bay, they'd be there. Slippers dangled on the tips of restive toes. Purple-lined kimonos falling away gave access to blushing, dimpled bodies. Great fine tresses of hair, the color of night, gave shadows to the revelations, gave structure.

III

"Come, Zuline,—hurry—it's getting late." The porch was vacant, dusk had fallen, and Miss Buckner wore an evening gown of white taffeta, fashioned in the Victorian epoch. It was tight and stiff and created a rustle, and there was a black bandeau pasted on to her skull.

Sullenly, the girl came, and gathered up the debris. "Sweep up dis ash, an cayh dis slip in Goldy's room, de careless t'ing," said Miss Buckner.

She went to one of the dusk-flooded rooms and seized a studded dagger which she stuck among the watches and brooches which shone on her bosom. She patted it, made sure it was safely a part of the glittering pattern, and ordered the night on.

"Get up, girls," she shouted, invading room after room, "it is late, get up!"

"Hello, Sailor Mack. Hit any home runs to-day?"

"An' you, you Kentucky millionaire—how many ships came through the locks to-day?"

"Bullocks—did you say?"

"Fie!"

"Oh, Mistah Council," she said, "how do you do?" Young Briton, red-faced, red-eyed, red-haired. Yellow-teethed, dribble-lipped, swobble-mouthed, bat-eared.

He kissed the proffered hand, and bowed low. He was gallant, and half-drunk. "Where's my girl, Anesta," he said, "by God, she is the sweetest woman, black or white—on the whole goddamned—"

"Sh, be quiet, son, come," and Miss Buckner led him to a chair among a group of men.

Constantly, Miss Buckner's hand kept fluttering to the diamond-headed pin stuck in her bosom.

Chaos prevailed, but Miss Buckner was quite sober. All about there were broken vases, overturned flower-pots, flowers, women's shoes. All the men were prostrate, the women exultant.

As midnight approached, the doorbell suddenly rang. And Miss Buckner rose, cautioning serenity. "All right, boys, let's have less noise—the captain's comin'."

In Anesta's lap there was an eruption, a young Vice-Consul staggered up—shaking her off, ready to face the coming of the visitor.

"Sit down, Baldy," she implored, "come back here to me—"

"Skipper, eh? Who is he? Wha' ya hell tub is he on?" He was tall and his body rocked menacingly.

"Put that goddam lime juicer to bed, somebody, will ya?"

"Yo' gawd dam American—why—"

Anesta rose, flying to him. "Now, Tommy," she said, patting his cheek, "that isn't nice."

"Let the bleddy bastard go to—"

But apparently an omnipotent being had invaded the porch, and a deep-throated voice barked sweetly down it, "Anesta, darling, take Baldy inside, and come here!"

"But, mother—"

"Do as you are told, darling, and don't waste any more time."

"No, Gawd blarst yo'—nobody will slip off these pants of mine. Lemme go!"

"Be a gentleman, sweet, and behave."

"What a hell of a ruction it are, eh?"

"Help me wit' 'im, Hyacinth—"

Ungallantly yielding, he permitted the girl to force him along on her arm. He stepped in the crown of Mr. Thingamerry's hat.* Only yesterday he had put on a gleaming white suit. Done by the Occupation, the starch on the edges of it made it dagger sharp. Now it was a sight; ugly drink stains darkened it. Booze, perspiration, tobacco weeds moistened it. His shirt, once stiff, was black and wrinkled. His tie, his collar, and trousers awry. His fire-red hair was wet and bushy and rumpled. Black curses fell from his mouth. But six months in the tropics and the nights and the girls at the Palm Porch had overpowered him. Held him tight. Sent from Liverpool to the British Consulate at Colon, he had fallen for the languor of the seacoast, he had been seized by the magic glow of the Palm Porch.

Seeing the Captain, Miss Buckner was as bright-eyed as a débutante. Instinctively her hands fled to her beaming bosom, but now the impulse was guided by a soberer circumstance.

The Captain was smiling. "Well, good lady," he said, "I see you are as charming and as nervous as usual. I hope you have good news for me to-day." He bowed very low, and kissed the jeweled hand.

"Oh, dear Captain," exclaimed Miss Buckner, touched by the Spaniard's gentility, "of course I have!" And she went on, "My renowned friend, it is so splendid of you to come. We have been looking forward to seeing you every minute—really. Was I not, Anesta, dear?" She turned, but the girl was nowhere in sight. "Anesta? Anesta, my dear? Where are you?"

It was a risky job, wading through the lanes of wine-fat men. As she and the Captain sped along, she was careful to let him see that she admired his golden epaulets, and the lofty contemptible way he'd step over the drunken Britons, but she in her own unobtrusive way was hurling to one side every one that came in contact with her.

"Christ was your color. Christ was olive—Jesus Christ was a man of olive—"

"Won't you wait a moment, Captain—I'll go and get Anesta." And she left him.

About him tossed the lime-juicers, the "crackers"— wine-crazed, woman-crazed. He turned in disgust, and drew out an open-worked handkerchief, blowing his nose contemptuously. He was a handsome man. He was dusky, sun-browned, vain. He gloried in a razor slash he had caught on his right cheek in a brawl over a German slut in a District canteen. It served to intensify the glow women fancied in him. When he laughed it would turn pale, stark pale, when he was angry, it oozed red, blood-red.

Miss Buckner returned like a whirlwind, blowing and applying a Japanese fan to her bosom.

In replacing it, a crimson drop had fallen among the gathering of emeralds and pearls, but it was nothing for her to be self-conscious about.

Very gladly she drew close to him, smiling. "Now, you hot-blooded Latin," she said, the pearls on the upper row of her teeth shining brighter than ever, "you must never give up the chase! The Bible says 'Him that is exalted'* . . . the gods will never be kind to you if you don't have patience. . . . No use . . . you won't understand . . . the Bible. Come!"

Pointing to the human wreckage through which they had swept, she turned, "In dear old Kingston, Captain, none of this sort of thing ever occurred! None! And you can imagine how profusely it constrains me!"

"Anesta, where are you, my dear? Here's the Captain—waiting."

Out of a room bursting with the pallor of night the girl came. Her grace and beauty, the tumult of color reddening her, excited the Captain. Curtseying, she paused at the door, one hand at her throat, the other held out to him.

It was butter in the Captain's mouth, and Miss Buckner, at the door, viewing the end of a very strategic quest, felt happy. The Captain, after all, was such a naughty boy!

The following day the *policia* came and got Tommy's body. Over the blood-black hump a sheet was flung. It dabbed up the claret. The natives tilted their chins unconcernedly at it.

Firm in the Captain's graces Miss Buckner was too busy to be excited by the spectacle. In fact, Miss Buckner, while Zuline sewed a button on her suède shoes, was endeavoring to determine whether she'd have chocolate soufflé or maidenhair custard for luncheon that afternoon.

From *Tropic Death* (New York: Boni & Liveright, 1926)

City Love

From a gulf in the dark low sea of rooftops there came mounting skyward the fiery reflexes of some gaudy Convention Night on Lenox Avenue. With the fate of a sinning angel the eye went *carombolling* 'cross the fizzing of a street lamp, caught the rickety vision of a bus, topheavy with a lot of fat, fanning Jews, tottering by on the cloudy August asphalt; flitted from the moon-shingled edges of elm and oak, onward, finally settling on the dark murmuring folk enlivening the park's green dusk rim.

"Quit that, honey!" warned the girl, softly. "I's skeert o' dirt, baby, don't you do that." She steered the lad's menacing hand out the way.

"No tellin' wheh some o' dat grabble might go," continued Nicey, making a pirate's cross bones of her legs.

A silence, dramatic to St. Louis, ensued. He was hurt, put out, ashamed of himself at Nicey's gently unanswerable rebuke.

He risked a pair of greedy, sun-red eyes round at her, and his courage took fresh impetus. "I know a place," he bristled suddenly with conviction, and Nicey's head turned involuntarily. "An' here Ah wuz—" he chuckled self-condemningly. "Come on, le's chance it."

"A nice place?" Nicey asked, quietly, not wishing to seem eager.

"Ah mean!" breathed Primus with deep-felt ardor.

"Yo' talk like yo' know it, like yo' done bin they orreadly," was what she was on the verge of saying, but large immediate interests possessed her, and she said instead, half-coyly, "No kiddin' now!"

"Honest," he said, getting up, "I ain't foolin'. I ain't green as I look. I bin there—"

"Oh yeah?" risked Nicey with surgical placidity.

"I mean," he stammered, admitting the error, but she checked the ripening flow of advances, and stood up. "That'll do," she said sagely, and walked, hips swinging, on down the hill in front of him. .

He kept a little ways behind, feeling insecure and moody at his silly measure of self-puffing.

A flower coursed by, and she caught it, pressing the white dewy petals to her mouth. Dissatisfied, she flung it in a curdle of nettles. "Ah likes flowers dat got pa'fune," she said, "dis one ain't got a bit o' smell."

As they sped out on the flaky stone flight of steps leading toward St. Nicholas, clots of lovers, in twos and more than twos, leaned against the bowing foliage, forcing the dicks, bronze and pale-faced ones, to take refuge upon their fobs and palms behind the dark viny hedge.

A big muddy touring car filled with a lot of drinking Bolita Negroes* skidded recklessly by into the gulch to One Hundred Thirty-fifth Street. Pebbly dust bombarded the lids of Nicey's and Primus' eyes.

". . . fur to go, baby?"

"Thutty fo'th . . . not fur . . . come . . . look out . . . you'll get run ovah, too."

A shanty, lodged beside an aerial railway track, with switches and cross ties, hovered dark and low above the street. A mob of Negroes passing underneath it hurried on as the trains rushed by, the lusty pressure chipping dust and rust off the girders.

Cars lurched in and out of side streets, assuming and unloading cargoes of vari-hued browns and blacks of conflicting shades of ebony splendor.

"How much furrer we got to go, honey," cried Nicey, dusty, eager, ill-at-ease.

"Not fur, honey, here we's at—"

They stopt before a brown stone dwelling. In the thickening night-light they glimpsed a fat butter-yellow Negress lolling in a rocker on the stoop and fanning herself with the long end of her apron.

There they stood, naked of pleats and tucks, frills and laces . . . orphans.

"Go on down t' the basement," the woman directed, with a wave of her heavy hand.

"You'd better wait here, Nicey," Primus said, with a show of manly vigor. Skipping to the basement the smells of a Negro cook shop came somersaulting at him. His senses were placid beside the sickening essences of corn and pork and candied yams.

The man who shared in this riotous obscenity was spotted by a kerosene torch swaying from a hook nailed in the wall. He was bald and tall and huge and spade black. He wore a shirt and flabby blue jeans and braces. Under such a low ceiling his fading oak skull threatened to violate the plumbing. In such a tiny passageway he seemed with his thick rotund figure to be as squat as an inflated bull frog.

He turned, at the shadow absorbing a length of the trembling light, and there was hair on both sides of his broad black face. He looked into Primus' eyes and a mist of mutuality sprang between them.

"Wha' yo' wife at?" he muttered in a whining Southern voice.

"I'll call 'er—"

"No, yo' don't hav' to call her," he assured him. "She outside?"

"Yeah."

"That's orright."

"Any bags? he plied further, eyeing St. Louis closely. "Wha' yo' bags at? Outside, too? Don't le' 'em stay dere. Bring 'em on down in yah."

"Bags?" cried Primus, quickly, "I ain't got no bags. Wha' kind o' bags?" He hung on eagerly for the rest.

"Ain't yo' know," the man said, with that faculty for understatement which seems to be the pride of Negroes of the late plantation class, "that yo' can't register at no hotel without bags? Go git yo'self a armful o' bags!"

He fled, breathless, to the girl on the pavement.

"Well!" Nicey said, both hands on her spreading hips.

He was excited and hurt, and he stuttered. "They—he—won't take us like this. I mean—we got to git weself* some bags—bags—bags—"

Nicey sighed, a plaintive sigh of relief—a sigh that was a monumental perplexity to him. "Don't look at me like that!" he swore, angry at his ineffectuality. "I did my darndest to git 'im to take us, but he won't do it. Says it's 'gainst the law."

"What yo' gwine do now?" she cut in, distrustful of self-defenses.

"Git me a bag, that's all! Ain't nothin' else to do. C'm awn!"

2

In the resistless languor of the summer evening the Negroes wandered restively over the tar-daubed roofs, squatted negligeed on shelterless window sills, carried on connubial pantomimic chatter across the circumscribed courts, swarmed, six to a square inch, upon curb and step, blasphemously jesting.

"I'll run up," he said, pausing before the portals of a greasy tower of flats. "You wait here, baby, I ain' gwine b' long."

And he cut a slanting passage through the mob, leaped up half a dozen crumbling steps, through a long narrow corridor, ending, blowing, before a knob on the sixth floor.

He rattled a key in the lock, and entered. A strip of oilcloth, dimly silvery in the shadowy interior, flashed at him. He put the strip behind him, flicked on the lights, and stared in Son Son's big starry eyes. The child was the browning purple of star apple* and was gorgeously animated. He was strapped in a ram-upholstered chair cocked against the window opening out upon a canyon of street. He jiggled at Primus a plumed African Knight of a doll.

The doll, profuse with bells and spangled half-discs, tinkled annoyingly. "Less noise, sah!" shouted Primus, descending on all fours and industriously examining the debris piled under the davenport which separated the cluttered room in two. Dimples of satanic delight brightened the child's face. He jiggled his toy, wagged his legs, carolling. He puffed his cheeks and booed, scattering mouth-mist about.

"Ain't I tell you to less noise, yo' lil' water mout'* imp yo'," cried St. Louis, flying up, seizing and confiscating the tasseled ebony knight and slapping the kid's dusk-down wrists. "Ain't I tell yo' not to botha' yo' pappy when 'e come 'ome, to less yo' noise?" The youngster's sudden recourse to imperturbability annoyed him. "Yo' ain't gwine cry no? Well, tek dat, an' dat, an' dat!" Cry, Uh say, Cry! Yo' won't open yo' mout', no, yo' won't buss loose, yo'—"

A pair of claws fell viciously on Primus' back, and, combined with the soaring quality of Tiny's voice, served to wheel him about-face with a swift downing jolt.

He had forgotten, alas! to push the bath room door when he came in.

"Look yah, man, wha' de hell yo' tink yo' his [is], hennyhow [anyhow]? Yo' tink yo' dey down in de Back Swamp whey yo' come from, wha' dem don' know nutton but fi' beat up people? Hey, dis yah sinting yo' Ah see 'tan' up yah, 'im tink 'im his back in Lucy a prog bout fi' yampies an' hunions in de picknee head. Come tumpin' de po' picknee roun' like him hone him!"

A fit of conquering rage narrowed and hardened and glistened Tiny's small, tight, mole-flecked face.

From the piano she flew to Son Son's side. The child was bashful, and in a dazed, defensive mood. "Hit dis yah picknee a next* time 'n see if me don' cahl a policeman fi' yo' hay. Hey, yo' na'h ashame' o' yo'self, no, fi' come down pon' a puny liggle picknee like dis 'n a show arf yo' strengt'? Why yo' didn't knock de man de oddah day when 'im bruk 'im wheel barrow 'cross yo' neck back 'pon de wharf? Why yo' didn't ram yo' hook in 'im gizzard, yo' dutty old cowrd yo', yo' can't fight yo' match, but yo' must wait till yo' get 'ome an' tek it out pon' me po' boy picknee."

He was on his knees, ransacking the amassing litter.

"Yo' a prowl 'bout now," Tiny went on, hugging Son Son to her bosom, "like a cock sparrow, but go 'long. Me na'h say nutton to yo', me jes' ah wait till de cole weddah come roun' again. An', boy, me will see yo' faht blue hice* fuss befor' yo' get anyt'ing from me to shub in yo' stinkin' guts! The day yo' say yo' got de back ache, an de foot ache, an' de turrah ache, don't le' me hear yo' wit' me name 'pon yo' mout', yo' hear? Fo' if yo' tink yo' gwine get me fo' go out fi' scrub me finger nail dem* white fi' cram bittle* down a neygah man troat like yo', yo is lie! Yo' bes' mek up yo' mine now it warm 'n get yo'self a helevator job fo' when de winter come. Fo' so 'elp me Gawd me will see yo' in holy hell fuss befo' yo' a see me trudge hup an' down dem yah stair' like I is any whore fi' do as yo' dam well please."*

"Oh, woman," he chuckled, unconcernedly, "tun yo'self out o' me way, yo' smell bad." He banged the door after him, a frayed valise under his arm.

3

He espied her, not leaning toward the frog-ringed moon rising out of the river, against the red-spotted rods barricading the way to the cellar, where he had left her; but standing facing him, a speck in the dusk, on the opposing piazza, in an arrow of shadow in the court. He crossed the street, and was inside the marbled sink.

Nicey detached herself from the wall and waved a red, exacting mouth before his tense, sweating face. "Got any idea o' de time," she asked, impatiently.

He had taken a virgin pride in the valise, and was wrestling with it. "Le' me see—" He yanked out the coruscant* disc, and Nicey's calm was star-cut. "Ten nine," he said, looking full and composed at her. It broke him up to be there facing her with the lamplight, stealing past her clouded face, giving an added lustre to the curves and brackets of her body.

"Well," she cried, aroused, "I'll be jail housed! You mean to tell me you had me waitin' down here fo' you fo' nearly a hour, yo' lanky suck egg son of a bitch!" She swung herself free of his grovelling embraces.

"Oh, Nicey," he begged, running after her, "don't go, sweet, I got de bag—"

"An' now yo' got it," she turned, interrogatively, "Wha' yo' expect to do with it?"

"Tek it on back there!" he avowed in one of his recurrent moments of self-assertiveness.

"Like hell we do!" she swore, "I'm gwine home."

"Oh, don't go, Nicey," he cried, swinishly, "I know a place. Don't let's go home after all the trouble we bin to."

"Aw, hell, boy, yo' give me a pain in the hip. Yo' know a place me eye! Where is this place at?"

"Come awn, I'll show yah! Don't be skeert, I know what I'm talkin' 'bout—"

"Like hell you do."

". . . it ain't the same one we bin to orready."

"Fur?" she perked up, with returning curiosity.

"Oh, no, jes' roun' de corner, I'll show yo'. Yo' tink it's fur? It ain't fur." His lurid efforts at self-assertion were taking a strange weight with her.

And so they peddled on. The dust, the city's dissoluteness, the sensory pursuits, gave a rigorous continuity to themselves, and to their needs, sent them burning against the sinister sovereignty of Upper Fifth Avenue.

Here there was a cluster of figures aloft. "Come on up," cried the man, "look out, lady, fo' dat ole runnin' hoss. Little Bits, ain't I tell you not to leave yo' things knockin' 'bout like dat? Come 'n tek 'em in miss . . . look out, mistah, get up there, Mignon, an' let the gemman pass."

As a sort of imposed ritual the woman remarked, with a friendly frown suggestive of a discovery of startling import, "Ain't it hot tonight."

"Ain't it though?" returned Nicey, flopping grandly by.

"This way, folks," cried the man, showing them to the parlor.

Passing the opulent hangings, sinking ankle deep in the rugs, Nicey was moved to observe, "Gee, I'd like to sleep in a swell place like this." As the female of the occasion she was led to the reddest plush couch in the room. Outside by the coat rack the two men stopt.

Primus' head bared, he was dabbing for the sweat sizzling in the rim of his hat. He put the valise down and went through his pockets for the money.

A princely urbanity governed the man. He edged the light behind him and scanned the most vagrant impulses lurking in Primus' eyes.

"Why don't you people come right?" he scolded in fatherly fashion. "Yo' don't come right," he insisted, trusting to the fleetness of the young man's mind.

Of the two listening there was no doubt that Nicey's ears were cocked nearer the big man's voice.

"Now take the lady," he went on, with disarming felicity, "Why—why don't she wear a hat?"

With the feet of a deer, the girl shot out the parlor, sped past St. Louis, through the vestibule and out into the Harlem night.

"I keep on tellin' 'em they won't come right," he said, as Primus trotted, valise in hand, down the stairs. "Don't they know that folks don't travel that-a-way?"

As she was about to merge in with the dusk saturating Lenox Avenue, he caught up with her.

"Jee, you're an unlucky bastard!"

"I'm sorry, Nicey."

"I never heard o' anybody with your kind o' luck. Yo' must o' spit on a hot brick or somethin'."

"I'd give anything to prove to you, Nicey, that I ain't nobody's simp."

"You're a long time provin' it, big boy."

"Oh, honey, giv' me time!"

"Say, big fellah, go to the judge, don't come to me. I can't giv' yo' any mo' time."

"I'd do anything—"

"Go stick yo' head in a sewer then."

"Let's go back, sweet, come, let's."

"Go back where?"

"I mean—with a hat. I'll go git yo' a hat."

"Christ, what next, buyin' me a hat. All I got to do is stick roun' you long enough an' you'll be buyin' me a teddy aftah awhile."

At a Hebrew hat shop on the Avenue they stopt and when they came out again Nicey was none the worse for a prim little bonnet with bluebells galloping wildly over it.

Crowds of high-hitting Negroes, stevedores from the North River docks—Cubans prattling in sugar lofts on the Brooklyn water front—discarding overalls and gas masks and cargo hooks—revelling in canes and stickpins and cravats—strutting light browns and high blacks—overswept the Avenue. And the emotion of being part of one vast questing whole quickened the hunger in Nicey's and Primus' breasts.

Waddling down the long moldy corridor, he let the girl go on ahead of him. The man was behind him, carrying the candle and jingling keys, ready to exact the casuallest ounce of tribute. "Don't forget," he said, "that if you want hot water in the morning, it'll be fifty cents extra."

From *The American Caravan* (New York: Macaulay, 1927)

Eulalie Spence

E ulalie Spence was born in Nevis on June 11, 1894, and came in 1902 to the United States, where she would go on to become one of the pioneers of the Black theater, part of a group that, as Nellie McKay writes, "were interested in producing images that represented the lives of black people as honestly as they could" (164). Such a portrayal was obviously Spence's goal, and she wrote about a dozen one-act plays and had several plays produced, reflective of her strong abhorrence of plays meant to be read, not performed.

Spence has been largely ignored in most studies of the Harlem Renaissance, perhaps because her medium was drama, an area rarely treated in studies of Harlem Renaissance literature. There are several reasons for this relative neglect of the genre, chiefly because many of the plays dealing with Black life in the 1920s were written by Whites (e.g., Paul Green's *In Abraham's Bosom*, 1927, Eugene O'Neill's *The Emperor Jones*, 1920, and *Showboat*, 1927, adapted by Jerome Kern and Oscar Hammerstein from a novel by Edna Ferber).

This does not mean that Blacks were not writing plays; indeed, before 1930, well over one hundred African Americans had written plays for the nonmusical stage (Gray 109). Most of these plays were produced in Black churches and little theaters. The plays that were produced in larger venues were frequently musicals, often performed with the support of White patrons. Such plays include *Strut, Miss Lizzie* (1922), *Chocolate Dandies* (1924), and *Shuffle Along* (1924). As Christine Rauchfuss Gray points out, "By staying within the Black community and by writing for it, black dramatists relinquished the fame or popularity that their works might have had and if they had written for white producers and publishers and, by extension, white audiences and readers" (43). Therefore, their plays often remain unpublished and unstaged, with manuscripts either discarded or yellowing in archives and their work still to be explored by literary historians.

Drama was viewed, however, as an important vehicle for conveying Black culture by such leaders as W. E. B. Du Bois, Alain Locke, and Carter Woodson. These race leaders wanted to use drama to present a true picture of Black life in contrast to the stereotypical stage "darky." Periodicals proved to be an effective way to encourage Black drama. The *Crisis*, *Opportunity*, the *Crusader*, the *Messenger*, and the *Negro World* all regularly published reviews of plays, and the *Crisis* and *Opportunity* sponsored contests for one-act plays. Spence won five awards in the *Crisis* and *Opportunity*, exceeding any other dramatist.

From 1925 to 1928 Spence was affiliated with Du Bois's Krigwa Players, a company meant to exemplify the race leader's belief that plays be "About us [Black Americans] . . . By us . . . For us . . . Near us" (Du Bois 447). Spence's play *Fool's Errand* was produced by the Krigwa Players in 1927 shortly before being entered in the National Little Theatre Tournament, where it was presented at the Frolic Theatre, making her the first Black woman to have her work seen on Broadway. The play won the $200 Samuel French prize, which was accepted by Du Bois, angering Spence and contributing to the demise of the New York branch of the Krigwa group. Spence also had philosophical differences with Du Bois, whose affinity for propaganda plays did not always correspond with Spence's own interest in folk drama. Her credo is laid out clearly in her essay "A Criticism of the Negro Drama": "We go to the theatre for entertainment, not to have old fires and hates rekindled." This does not mean, however, that Spence was merely a writer of "whimsical comedy," as Lorraine Elena Roses and Ruth Elizabeth Randolph suggest (295). Rather, as Yvonne Shafer observes, "Her works are shot through with the social issues surrounding her" (282).

Spence, alone among the Harlem Renaissance women playwrights, focuses on Harlem life. Her plays concentrate on typical Harlem folk, both saints and sinners. Her female characters especially are often "independent, willful, and challenging individuals with their own tastes and aspirations" (Watkins-Owens 154). This is demonstrated by Georgia, who refuses to be sweet-talked by her lover in *The Starter*; feisty Martha and the vengeful spirit in *Her*; and particularly Fanny in *Hot Stuff*.

All three of Spence's plays contained in this anthology are set in New York. "The Starter," winner of third prize in the *Opportunity* contest awards, concerns an idealistic young man (an elevator starter) and the more practical woman, Georgia, he hopes to marry. Despite its seemingly lighthearted tone, the play touches on issues such as gender and class; furthermore, its focus on the failure of communication between the two lovers, a frequent concern in Spence's work, deviates from the happy ending of most popular plays.

Perhaps *Hot Stuff*, winner of a third prize *Crisis* award, best illustrates Spence's concern with the problems of urban life. In "A Criticism of the Negro Drama," Spence remarks that in novels like Claude McKay's *Home to Harlem* it is possible to put "the most revolting detail between the covers of a book." Yet her work, like that of McKay, is often told in Harlem Black vernacular (her speech training proved an asset to her dialogue) and frequently provides a gritty portrayal of Harlem life. Fanny is a numbers runner, a seller of stolen goods, a prostitute, and a cheat, both on her husband and on her clients. Even after her husband catches her in a compromising position and beats her and her companion, she refuses to change her ways. Still, the play never condemns Fanny. As Elizabeth Brown-Guillory points out,

> Spence seems to be mirroring a society in which blacks do what they have to do in order to survive and to secure material things. Some of them . . . place all of their trust in the numbers game, hoping to win enough to make ends meet. Some make a living by stealing from corporate America. Some prostitute their bodies in order to live and to have the finer things in life. What permeates the play is a sense of urban poverty and the con games that are enacted in order to survive in a fast-paced, uncaring world. (*Wines in the Wilderness* 40–41)

Her is one of the few plays by Spence that is not a comedy. Ostensibly a ghost story (perhaps influenced by the Caribbean "duppy" stories of vengeful spirits told to her by her mother), the play also looks at a serious issue: the abuse of women. Notably, the murdered woman in this play is a Filipino, an outsider, who has been victimized by her "yellow"-complexioned husband, Kinney. Eventually, his cruelty drives her to hang herself. In her sympathetic rendering of the foreigner, "Spence is perhaps speaking of her own family, particularly of her father's alienation in the United States" (Perkins 106). As Spence stated in a 1973 interview, "West Indians were not popular in this country." The ghost in the play gains its just revenge. The success shared by Spence and her sisters in America, too, has in a sense provided vindication to Spence's immigrant father.

The market for theater, as with the other arts, went into decline after the onset of the Depression. Spence's only work after 1930 was her lone full-length play, *The Whipping* (1932), adapted from Roy Flannagan's novel of the same name. Spence also wrote a screenplay loosely based on the play and sold to Paramount Pictures (produced but never released) for $5,000. Sadly, this was the only drama for which Spence received any monetary compensation. Despite the cessation of her writing after this point, Spence maintained a lifelong interest in the arts through teaching and involvement in school and community theater. She taught English and elocution at Eastern District high school in Brooklyn from 1927 to 1958, where one of her students was producer Joseph Papp of Public Theater fame.[1] In 1937 Spence, who never married, received a B.S. from New York University, and she received an M.A. in speech from Columbia University in 1939. She died in Gettysburg, Pennsylvania, on March 7, 1981.

NOTES

Spence's papers are available at the Schomburg Center.

1. For a discussion of Spence's influence on the future producer, see Helen Epstein's *Joe Papp: An American Life* (Boston: Little, Brown, 1994).

BIBLIOGRAPHY

Brown-Guillory, Elizabeth. *Their Place on the Stage: Black Women Playwrights in America.* 1988. New York: Praeger, 1990.

Brown-Guillory, Elizabeth, ed. and intro. *Wines in the Wilderness: Plays by African American Women from the Harlem Renaissance to the Present.* New York: Praeger, 1990.

Burton, Jennifer, ed. and intro. *Zora Neale Hurston, Eulalie Spence, Marita Bonner, and Others: The Prize Plays and Other One-Acts Published in Periodicals.* New York: G. K. Hall, 1996.

Du Bois, W. E. B. "Krigwa Players Little Negro Theatre: The Story of a Little Theatre Movement." *Lost Plays of the Harlem Renaissance 1910–1940.* Ed. James V. Hatch and Leo Hamalian. Detroit: Wayne State UP, 1996. 446–52.

Giles, Freda Scott. "Willis Richardson and Eulalie Spence: Dramatic Voices of the Harlem Renaissance." *American Drama* 5 (Spring 1996): 1–22.

Gray, Christine Rauchfuss. *Willis Richardson: Forgotten Pioneer of African-American Drama.* Westport, CT: Greenwood P, 1999.

McKay, Nellie. "'What Were They Saying?': Black Women Playwrights." *Harlem Renaissance Re-Examined: A Revised and Expanded Edition.* Ed. Victor A. Kramer and Robert A. Russ. Troy, NY: Whitston P, 1997. 151–66.

Perkins, Kathy A., ed. and intro. *Black Female Playwrights: An Anthology of Plays Before 1950.* Bloomington: Indiana UP, 1989.

Peterson, Bernard L. Jr. *Early Black American Playwrights and Dramatic Writers: A Biographical Directory and Catalog of Plays, Films, and Broadcasting Scripts.* New York: Greenwood P, 1990.

Roses, Lorraine Elena, and Ruth Elizabeth Randolph. *Harlem Renaissance and Beyond: Literary Biographies of 100 Black Women Writers, 1900–1945.* Boston: G. K. Hall, 1990.

Shafer, Yvonne. *American Women Playwrights, 1900–1950.* New York: Peter Lang, 1995.

Spence, Eulalie. Taped interview with James V. Hatch. August 22, 1973. Hatch-Billips Archives, Schomburg Center.

Watkins-Owens, Irma. *Blood Relations: Caribbean Immigrants and the Harlem Renaissance.* Bloomington: Indiana UP, 1996.

The Starter*

A Comedy of Harlem Life

CHARACTERS

T. J. KELLY

FIRST WOMAN

SECOND WOMAN

GEORGIA

Scene: *Present-day Harlem.*

Time: *A summer evening.*

AT RISE: THOMAS JEFFERSON KELLY *is sprawled upon the bench, his straw hat on one side, his coat on the other.* T. J. KELLY *as he signs himself, is reading a copy of "The News." From time to time, he chuckles, mutters aloud, whistles or hums in a low baritone.* T. J. KELLY'S *face is the most important thing that ever happened to him. For the rest,* T. J. *is tall, dapper and in love.*

T. J. KELLY. Holy gee! What d'ye know 'bout that! (*He stares a bit, then turns the page*) Um! Some looker! Hello! "Woman gives Birth To Four Healthy Sons"! Gee! A male quartet! Four! . . . "Father Overjoyed!" Like hell, he is! (T. J. *throws the paper on the ground in disgust.*) Gee! Suppose something like that was to happen to me! (T. J. *grabs his coat and hat and prepares for flight. Suddenly he stops short, laughing sheepishly. He resumes his seat. He takes his hat off and places it on the bench.*) Reckon them things only happen to furriners. Sure! (T. J. *whistles a few lines from "'Tain't Gonna Rain No Mo.'" Two tired looking women trudge into view. They stop short and look at* T. J. *in exasperation.*)

FIRST WOMAN. (*Mopping her face with a handkerchief*) Any wonder we kain't find no place tuh set? Looka him sprawlin' on dat bench, will yuh? Gawd, it's hot!

SECOND WOMAN. (*Addressing* T. J. KELLY) Say, move up, will yuh? Yuh ain't go' no lease on dat bench. . . .

T. J. KELLY. (*With a provoking grin*) Reserved! (*He spreads both arms along the back of the bench.*)

FIRST WOMAN. (*With a snort*) Reserved! Kin yuh beat dat fer nerve, Mis' Clark?

SECOND WOMAN. Ah should say not! (*To* T. J. KELLY) Take yo' arms off dat bench, you loafin' nigger!

T. J. KELLY. (*Calmly*) Now, see here Angel face, and you too, Grape Nuts! Ah know you're both dying for a real live hug from an honest tuh goodness he-man. Well, come on an' get it. I won't charge you nothing.

FIRST WOMAN. (*Indignantly*) Kin yuh beat it?

SECOND WOMAN. (*Angrily*) Ah like yo' gall!

T. J. KELLY. (*Pleasantly*) They all do! You're not the only one!

FIRST WOMAN. A woman kain't walk tru dis park no mo', 'thout bein' insulted!

SECOND WOMAN. Aw, come on, Mrs. Henry! Ah would'n' set thar now ef he was tuh scrub de whole bench—

FIRST WOMAN. Me neither. (*They turn scornfully away and walk on.*)

T. J. KELLY. (*Hums audibly*)

> Honey! Say doan' yuh know
> Honey! Ah love yuh so—
> Yuh's cute, yuh's sweet
> Yuh's mighty fine—
> Sweeter dan de watermelon hangin' on de vine.

(*A pretty brown girl in a light dress comes along the path from the direction in which the women are walking. She merely glances at their angry faces and passes on. They stop and look back at her. As she approaches* T. J. KELLY, *he rises, makes an elaborate bow and sweeps his belongings to one side. Then* T. J. KELLY *kisses the girl, Valentino-fashion. The women stand and stare.*)

FIRST WOMAN. Brazen!

SECOND WOMAN. Hussy! (*They pass on.*)

GEORGIA. (*With her very first breath*) Say, T. J. did yuh see them ole hens stare?

T. J. KELLY. No. I couldn't see nothin' but you, then, Honey.

GEORGIA. Well, they sure did stare! Reckon they was jealous all right!

T. J. KELLY. Not a doubt of it!

GEORGIA. Say, yuh doan' hate yuhself, do you?

T. J. KELLY. Naw! 'Tain't no use hating the person you have to live with.

GEORGIA. Meanin' who?

T. J. KELLY. Meaning me—Thomas Jefferson Kelly—at your service.

GEORGIA. Oh! (*She moves away, the length of the bench.*)

T. J. KELLY. Say, what's the idea of moving down there?

GEORGIA. Yuh gets along pretty well by yuhself—doan' yuh?

T. J. KELLY. Sure, but I gets along better when you're around. (*He reaches out and draws her close to him.*)

GEORGIA. (*Leaning against his shoulder*) 'Twas a helluva day, T. J.

(*She sighs.*)

T. J. KELLY. It sure was! Ninety in the shade! To see the way people shop in all this hot weather! I don't see how they do it! I have to stand there by that cage till I'm ready to drop! An' talk about dumbbells! Why those birds can't read, some of them. They stand by an elevator marked "down" an' expects it to go up—and other way 'round! An' the fool questions they asks! Gee! To think of all my education being lost on those people!

GEORGIA. Poor T. J. Yuh's had too much schoolin'—that's whut's the matter with yuh—

T. J. KELLY. (*Fully launched upon his grievances*) Two terms in High School, and don't you forget it. . . . Funny—me standing there in a Palm Beach suit with brass buttons, an' a hat to match with more brass buttons! Sometimes a man gets to thinkin'—Here I am a starter—a starter—just one step better'n the man who runs the cage—Gee! *That's* a helluva job!

GEORGIA. It sure is! I'm glad yuh's a starter, T. J.

T. J. KELLY. (*Bitterly*) Yeh! But there's something about the name that don't just hit me right. Starter! Starter! It seems to get over into a man's life—somehow—starter!

GEORGIA. (*Sitting up wide-eyed*) Gee! That's funny!

T. J. KELLY. Is it? Well, I don't just see the point—that's all.

GEORGIA. Why T. J.—yuh knows Ah does sewin' doan yuh? (T. J. *nods*) Well, Ah ain't never tole yuh 'bout mah place 'cause it's so low-down. Eyetalians and Jews and colored—all in tergether. It's a dump. Well, I'm what they calls a Finisher. Finisher on dresses! See? That's whut Ah meant—You bein' a Starter and me a Finisher!

T. J. KELLY. (*Giving a loud laugh*) Holy gee! That's a good one! Say, Georgia, we'd make a good team—we would. (*He gives her a tight hug.*)

GEORGIA. (*Pleased*) Quit yuh kiddin'.

T. J. KELLY. No kiddin'. Y'know, kid, I bin thinkin'—Say, why don't we get married? Huh?

GEORGIA. Ah dunno, 'cept yuh never mentioned it befo'.

T. J. KELLY. Well, I'm mentioning it now. See? Think it over, kid. Well, what's the answer?

GEORGIA. (*Slowly*) Has yuh got any money, T. J.?

T. J. KELLY. (*With an injured air*) Money! Say! Have a heart! That's a fine question.

GEORGIA. (*Slyly*) Fer a starter!

T. J. KELLY. (*Suspiciously*) Say—are you making fun of me?

GEORGIA. Co'se not, T. J.!

T. J. KELLY. Well, you're taking your time 'bout answering—ain't yuh?

GEORGIA. How much yuh got saved, T. J.?

T. J. KELLY. (*Frowning*) Ain't that a little personal, Honey?

GEORGIA. Ah don't think so—but co'se ef yuh doan' feel like sayin'—

T. J. KELLY. I have fifty-five dollars! That's not so bad for—

GEORGIA. Fer a *starter!* (*She draws away from him coldly*) Yuh mean yuh ain't got mo'n fifty-five dollars an' you wukin' steady?

T. J. KELLY. An' me dressing like a gentleman an' paying dues in a club an' two Societies an' a Lodge? An' taking you to the theatre twice a week—

GEORGIA. *Movies*—an' doan' yuh ferget it!

T. J. KELLY. (*Angrily*) So, that's how you feel about it—is it? Don't I take you to dances? Didn't we go to Coney last week and a cabaret Monday night? How the devil you expect me to have money?

GEORGIA. (*Coldly*) Nobuddy asked yuh nothin' 'bout marryin'—you's the one mentioned it—

T. J. KELLY. Sure, but that don't give you no right to ask 'bout my bank account. Reckon you wouldn't say how much *you've* got in your bank.

GEORGIA. Well, sence yuh's dyin' tuh fine out—

T. J. KELLY. (*Angrily*) Who—me?

GEORGIA. Sence yuh's dyin' ter know—Ah's got two hundred dollars!

T. J. KELLY. Whew! (*Almost immediately he recovers his air of superiority*) Well, that ain't so much!

GEORGIA. Mo'n you's got!

T. J. KELLY. (*Reflectively*) Two hundred dollars! Say, you know what, Georgia? That's enough money to start on. We could get a nice room—Why I've got a peachuva room. An' we could get new fixings—pay down a deposit, you know. I could arrange all that at the store. They know me—Two hundred dollars ain't so bad! Say! Say—many a man's got married on less!

GEORGIA. Yuh ain't sayin' nuthin' 'bout yo' fifty-five—

T. J. KELLY. Fifty-five's all right—as a starter—but it ain't nothing for a man to talk about.

GEORGIA. An' whut 'bout a ring, T. J.?

T. J. KELLY. A ring! (*He looks the picture of dismay.*)

GEORGIA. (*Sarcastically*) Yuh ain't never heard 'bout that befo' has yuh?

T. J. KELLY. Sure—but—Well,—Oh, all right! I'll get you a ring—a beauty, too, get me?

GEORGIA. See here, boy friend! Ah'm a regular girl! An' Ah knows a Woolworth Special when Ah sees one!

T. J. KELLY. (*Indignantly*) Say, d'you think I'd put a Woolworth over on you? How d'you get that way?

GEORGIA. Reckon it's frum 'sociatin' wid them Jews an' Eyetalians. Say, those folks sure wears diamonds.

T. J. KELLY. (*Incredulously*) To work?

GEORGIA. Sure!

T. J. KELLY. Fake, that's all!

GEORGIA. Fake nuthin'!

T. J. KELLY. Well, kid, what d'you say?

GEORGIA. Ah dunno, T. J. (*She sighs once more*) Ah was reckonin' on that two hundred fer rainy weather—(T. J. *whistles a bar or two from* "*Tain't Gonna Rain No Mo.*'") In mah business thar's plenty rainy weather. Las' year Ah was outa wuk altogether four months.

T. J. KELLY. (*Aghast*) What? How come?

GEORGIA. Laid off. Nuthin' doin'—It's a reg'lar thing in my line—dull season—strikes—union dues—

T. J. KELLY. But you could always find something else, couldn't you?

GEORGIA. Naw. Wuk's slack every place. An' then's the time Ah needs mah savin's.

T. J. KELLY. How 'bout waitress in some nice—

GEORGIA. Nuthin' doin'. Ah ain't no hash slinger!

T. J. KELLY. You're mighty fussy ain't you?

GEORGIA. Ef we got married yuh would'n' mind mah stayin' home when things was slow, would yuh, T. J. (T. J. *swallows painfully*) Gee, it would be great tuh be able tuh stay in bed mornin's. Yuh know, T. J., the thought uh hittin' de chillies has driv' plenty into matrimony befo' now. Gee! Tuh lie in bed on a cole winter mornin' when de sleet an' rain er batterin' at de winders!

T. J. KELLY. (*Impatiently*) Fer Gawd's sake, woman—

GEORGIA. (*Startled out of her dreaming*) What the matter, T. J.?

T. J. KELLY. (*Irritably*) Say—all this talk 'bout cold and sleet—an' stayin' in bed—Gee! It's enough to give a man cold feet.

GEORGIA. Cole feet! Well, if yuh has cole feet, now's the time tuh say so! (*She rises.* T. J. KELLY *grasps her hand. He draws her down again.*)

T. J. KELLY. Say, it's a fine way to spoil a good night—talkin' 'bout winter mornings—(*He kisses her*) Looka there, Honey!

GEORGIA. (*Reluctantly*) Whar?

T. J. KELLY. (*Pointing*) Over there. Going to be a moon to-night.

GEORGIA. Sure 'nuff.

T. J. KELLY. Not so bad! An' looka there Honey!

GEORGIA. Whar?

T. J. KELLY. (*Pointing*) Down there! All those lights an' those people an' this park—We owns the whole show!

GEORGIA. Quit yuh kiddin'.

T. J. KELLY. Gawd, Harlem sure is great! Looka them lights!

GEORGIA. Say, T. J.? (*She sits upright as though she has just remembered something.*)

T. J. KELLY. What you thinkin', Honey?

GEORGIA. Is we engaged?

T. J. KELLY. (*Annoyed*) Lawd! Do we have to go all over that? (*In a kindlier tone*) Keep yuh eyes on them lights, Honey an'—an' forget it. (*The park is very much darker now.* GEORGIA's *head snuggles up against* T. J.'s *shoulder. His arm slips about her waist. The Moon-man hangs his lantern in the heavens, and we do the only kindly thing we can think of. We draw the Curtain.)*

CURTAIN

From *Plays of Negro Life* (New York: Harper, 1927)

Her*

A Mystery Play in One Act

PERSONS IN THE PLAY
MARTHA
PETE
JOHN KINNEY
ALICE
SAM

Time: *About 8 o'clock one rainy night in spring.*

Scene: *Martha's living room.*

(*To describe this, we must describe* MARTHA—*old, black, Martha who takes in washing for some "very old families," who is, herself, always immaculate in her grey dress and white apron. Martha, who takes care of Pete, her husband—crippled and an idler for more than fifteen years—Martha, who irons in the living room—eats there for the accommodation of Pete, and spreads her clothes horse there on rainy days. Martha, who is the oldest tenant in the house—who rents the rooms for John Kinney, and collects the rentals, as well.*

We must also describe old PETE *in his invalid chair—his steel rimmed spectacles and his Bible lying open on his knees.*

No modern living room, this—just Martha's room—with her cheap prints on the walls—religious, every one of them—and her odd tables and cast off chairs—hand-me-downs from the "white folks." All we really need to know about the construction of the room is that a door at back, left, opens upon the hallway.)

MARTHA. (*Picking up some of the clothes from the horse, rolling them into a bundle, and putting them into a pillow case on the chair beside her ironing board.*) They's most as wet as they was when Ah hung 'em out. Ef this weather keeps up Ah doan see how Ah's goin' git these clothes out by Saturday. Weather what's good fer farmers doan help us washwimmin none.

PETE. (*Looking up, surprised*) 'Tain't lak yuh, Martha, complainin! Reckon yuh back's bad ter-night.

MARTHA. (*Who punctuates her remarks with little emphatic clamps of her iron*) No wuss'n usual.

PETE. Then somethin's on yuh mind.

MARTHA. Mebbe.

PETE. Yuh wuks too hard, Martha. Ah wish—(*He ends with a sigh.*)

MARTHA. (*Looking up, quickly*) What yuh wishin' fer, Pete?

PETE. In them magazines yuh brung home last week there was a piece 'bout some cripple fellers—how they's learned how ter make money—plenty money. Ah ain't read nuthin' so mirac'lus in a long time, Martha, an' Ah get ter thinkin'—Ah might er bin helpin' yuh all these years, ef Ah'd knowed how.

MARTHA. (*Clamping her electric iron down with alarming energy*) Pete Alexander, ef yuh ain't got no better sense than ter pick out pieces 'bout cripples, Ah'm goin' stop bring' home them no 'count books. Now doan lemme hear no more er that trash.

PETE. (*Humbly*) Ah was only thinkin'—

MARTHA. (*Still irate*) Yuh ain't got no business thinkin'—'bout sech trash. Yuh's puttin' yourself with these here young fellers what's bin hurt in the War. It's nigh on fifteen years yuh bin settin' there an' Ah ain't done no complainin's Ah knows uv.

PETE. (*Proudly*) That ain't no woman lak yuh, Martha, nowhar. Ah knows it an' Ah thanks Gawd fer yuh, day an' night.

MARTHA. (*Somewhat mollified*) Well, doan lemme hear no more talk 'bout yuh earnin' money. (*After a few seconds*) Ah ain't slep' good these two nights, Pete.

PETE. Ah heard yuh movin' long 'bout five this mornin'.

MARTHA. Five! Ah didn' close mah eyes all night.

PETE. (*Anxiously*) What's the mattuh, Martha?

MARTHA. Pete. (*Martha lowers her voice which is pregnant with meaning*) Ah seen Mr. Kinney this mornin'. He's got some folks fer up above.

PETE. Fer upstairs? (*Pete's voice, like Martha's, has acquired a new note, not unmixed with dismay.*)

MARTHA. They's ter come ter-night ter see the rooms.

PETE. Ter-night?

MARTHA. Ah'm ter show them 'round—so he said. Reckon ef it keeps on rainin' they won't come.

PETE. (*Uneasily*) Reckon they won't. . . . Martha, did yuh tell him?

MARTHA. Yuh bet Ah tole him. But it didn' do no good, Pete. Nobuddy ain't goin' change him.

PETE. Ah reckon yuh's right, Martha.

MARTHA. (*Significantly*) 'Lessen it's *Her*.

PETE. Her?

MARTHA. She's kep' me awake these two nights.

PETE. (*Moving restlessly in his chair*) It ain't natural—this talk 'bout Her.

MARTHA. 'Course it ain't natural, but it's *real*. What yuh hears is *real*, ain't it?

PETE. (*Stubbornly*) Ah ain't never heard nothin', Martha.

MARTHA. But they's them what has heard. Yuh knows that, doan yuh?

PETE. So they says, but mah ears jes' good's yours, Martha. Ah ain't never heard nothin'.

MARTHA. (*Scornfully*) Then they ain't so good's yuh thinks, Pete.

PETE. Yuh ain't heard Her in more'n a year.

MARTHA. The place ain't bin rented in more'n a year.

PETE. 'Tain't honest rentin' them rooms after what's happened.

MARTHA. Ah tole Mr. Kinney's much.

PETE. An' what he said ter that, Martha?

MARTHA. He says ef Ah doan want ter show them rooms ter people, he kin git somebuddy else. 'Course Ah needs the money, little's it is.

PETE. (*Clinging to a forelorn hope*) It's rainin' so hard Ah reckon they won't come ter-night.

MARTHA. Ah 'spec not, 'lessen they wants 'em real bad.

PETE. (*Resentfully*) Ef Mr. Kinney's so set on rentin' them rooms he oughta show 'em himself.

MARTHA. (*With one of her energetic swoops on the ironing board*) Him! He ain't bin near them rooms in eighteen years, an' Ah reckon he ain't never goin' up thar!

PETE. Ah reckon not, sence he doan never go higher'n the ground floor.

MARTHA. He's lookin' powerful bad. Looks' though he bin worryin' plenty 'bout somethin'.

PETE. (*with a rare chuckle*) Worryin' 'bout how he kin spen' some er that money uv his.

MARTHA. More likely worryin' 'bout Her.

PETE. *Her?* What good'll it do him ter worry 'bout Her, *now?*

MARTHA. Yuh kin call it conscience, or yuh kin call it HER! 'Tis one and the same thing, Ah reckon. But he's worryin' powerful hard. (*A loud peal of the door bell. Martha and Pete exchange glances. Martha puts down her iron*) Ah reckon it's the folks ter see the rooms. (*Pete nods. Martha opens the door. Standing upon the threshold, silent, gaunt, austere, is* JOHN KINNEY. *His yellow face is seamed and somewhat haggard. His eyes are burning with a strange fire. Martha, evidently astonished, just stands there gasping. Pete fumbles for his spectacles, finds them, puts them on—and still no word is spoken.*)

JOHN KINNEY. Well, are you going to let me in? (*Such a cold ironic voice with a world of weariness behind it. Martha silently draws back and the visitor enters. Pete recovers his wits a full second before Martha does.*)

PETE. Take a seat, suh! 'Tis a bad night, Ah reckon.

MARTHA. (*Placing a chair for John Kinney*) Ah's powerful 'sprised ter see yuh, Mr. Kinney. Ah stared lak Ah'd seen a ghost, sure 'nuff. (*The moment the words are out, Martha recognizes her blunder. Pete looks at her reproachfully. John Kinney, however, merely smiles his little mocking smile.*)

JOHN KINNEY. No ghost, this time. (*Takes a seat*) And that brings me to the subject of my visit. I'm expecting a young couple here, this evening. They ought to be here at any minute. (*Looks at his watch*) They wish to see the rooms above.

MARTHA. Yes suh. Yuh's tole me 'bout showin' 'em.

JOHN KINNEY. Well, I've changed my mind. When they come I'll show them the rooms myself.

MARTHA. Yuh going up *thar?* (*Consternation is plainly written on her face.*)

JOHN KINNEY. Yes. If you will give me the keys—

MARTHA. But, good Lawd, suh! Yuh ain't bin up thar goin' on twenty years!

JOHN KINNEY. Then it's time I did go up. The place may need a few repairs.

MARTHA. Yuh did it over last year for them other folks. They didn' stay more'n a month.

JOHN KINNEY. Ah! To be sure. Well, I'll just take a look around and see for myself. I told Mrs. Smith to bring her husband and meet me here at eight o'clock. Don't let me interrupt your work, Martha. I see you are busy.

MARTHA. (*Returning to her ironing board, reluctantly*) Ah ain't so busy but what Ah kin show them rooms fer yuh, suh. Ah hopes you ain't mad 'count uv what Ah said this mornin'. Ah's allus done mah best 'bout rentin' them rooms.

JOHN KINNEY. Perhaps you have, in the past. But you don't want to do your best *now*. (*Martha is silent.*) That, however, is not my real reason for wanting to see those rooms. Looking back over the years, twenty you say—Twenty! I can see what a fool I've been—what a fool you've helped me to be. (*Nothing moves in the room now—not even Martha's iron.*) You—with your talk of signs and omens— sound and night alarms. You've filled my mind with superstitious fears. I, who used to laugh at fears! (*An additional sternness creeping into his voice*) Well, you've frightened away my tenants long enough with your gossip and your fancies. I won't say that you've done these things out of malice, but—By God! Some men might!

MARTHA. (*Slowly*) Then—Then yah doan believe nothin' Ah's ever tole yuh?

JOHN KINNEY. (*Grimly*) I did, once. Now I know they're lies or fancies.

PETE. (*Moved to resentment*) Martha ain't no liar! Ef she says she's heard goins on, she's heard 'em!

JOHN KINNEY. I suppose you've also heard these goings on, as you call them?

PETE. (*Reluctantly*) No. Ah ain't never heard nothin'. But Lawd, Ah ain't got the ears Martha's got. Thar ain't a tenant what's lived up thar that ain't left, 'cause uv *Her.*

JOHN KINNEY. (*With a faint smile*) But *you've* slept—

PETE. (*Stoutly*) Mah ears ain't nowhere ez good's Martha's.

JOHN KINNEY. Nor mine. How is it that in all these years she's never bin back to disturb my slumbers? How do you account for that?

MARTHA. (*Angrily*) Ah ain't no call ter account fer nothin' but what Ah knows 'bout.

JOHN KINNEY. Very good. Now with the best of intention, perhaps, you've frightened away my tenants. The power of suggestion is a greater force than we realize. I can forgive this, but I can't forgive your filling your mind with your fancies. I've come to the conclusion that the only way to wipe the incident clean from my mind—except as we have occasion to remember some unfortunate happening—is to go up there tonight and show Mrs. Smith those rooms myself.

MARTHA. 'Tain't fer me to say yuh shouldn't go up thar. Only Ah doan lak it none. Thar's bin plenty goin' on up thar these two nights. Ah doan lak it none (*with a shake of her head*). Ah reckon it means somethin's going ter happen.

JOHN KINNEY. Something is going to happen. I'm going to brush a thousand cobwebs from my brain. I haven't felt happier about anything in a long time. I ought to have done this years ago instead of avoiding the place.

PETE. Mebbe yuh's right suh. Mebbe yuh's right.

JOHN KINNEY. Of course I'm right. (*Looking at his watch*) Eight on the minute. I hope they don't keep me waiting—Oh, by the way, I may as well tell you good people that I expect to sell this house.

PETE. (*Almost dropping his spectacles in surprise*) Sell this house!

MARTHA. Ef yuhs goin' sell it suh, why yuh wants to bother goin' up thar?

JOHN KINNEY. (*With his one-sided smile*) Just to prove to you that you've been wrong and that I've been as gullible as a child. It's my one chance of being a free man and I'm not going to lose it. (*The door bell rings.*) Ah! Here they are. (*Martha opens the door. On the threshold stands* ALICE SMITH, *a good-looking brown girl, and her husband* SAM, *somewhat browner. Alice wears a tricky little felt hat and yellow raincoat. Sam wears—well—brown hat, coat, and shoes, a very trying harmony for one of his complexion.*)

ALICE. (*Nodding to Martha, but addressing herself to John Kinney*) Ah reckon we ain't more'n a minute late. (*To Sam*) Sam this's Mr. Kinney. Mr. Kinney this's mah husband, Mr. Sam Smith.

JOHN KINNEY. (*Shaking hands with Sam, a cordiality which surprises Martha*) Glad to meet you. You're certainly on time.

SAM. (*Pleased*) We's colored through an' through, Alice an' me 'sceptin' that we's allus on time. When we says eight, we means eight, not half past nine. (*Sam chuckles as if at a huge joke.*)

JOHN KINNEY. Well, as a man of business I appreciate that. This— (*Waving his hand in the direction of Pete and Martha*) This is Mrs. Alexander and her husband. (*Nodding in Martha's direction*) Mrs. Alexander usually rents my rooms—shows them to visitors—But I'll show you these myself. Martha, if you'll get me the key—(*Martha dives into an old jug and produces the key. Very slowly she hands it to John Kinney who pockets it.*) (*To the Smiths*) I have a powerful search light (*tapping his coat pocket*). So if you're ready, we'll go up and inspect the rooms. (*Martha and Pete exchange glances. Perhaps the smile on John Kinney's lips is just a shade more mocking than usual as he turns to Martha.*) I will stop in on my way down, Martha. There is a little matter I want to see you about. (*In about another second Martha and Pete are left alone. Martha spreads another garment on the board and takes up her iron. Pete looks at her timidly and clears his throat.*)

PETE. I reckon he's right 'bout goin' up thar. A man ain't got no right actin' so scared 'bout nothin' (*Hastily*) Ah mean 'bout—(*His voice dies away under the fierce glare in Martha's eyes*)

MARTHA. Yuh doan need say nothin' more. Yuh's allus bin a disbeliever, Pete, an Ah reckon yoh'll never change 'lessen yuh's give a sign.

PETE. (*Uneasily*) Ah doan need no sign, Martha.

MARTHA. (*Pointing to the Bible on Pete's knees*) Yuh ain't read that thar Book from cover to cover 'thout comin' cross signs an' wonders a-plenty.

PETE. Sure they's signs. But—

MARTHA. 'Taint *you* Ah'm thinkin' uv, Pete, nor John Kinney. It's that girl Ah'm thinkin' uv—her an' that young feller. She's got a sweet face. Ah took ter her right off. She ain't a bit older than *she* was when she come here. They ain't goin' have no happiness up thar.

PETE. Ah hope yuh ain't right 'bout that Martha.

MARTHA. Pete Alexander! (*Perhaps Martha's iron as well as her tone causes Pete to draw himself up with a start.*) Pete Alexander. Ah ain't never tole a soul 'bout what happen up thar. Yuh knows that.

PETE. Sure. Ah knows that.

MARTHA. Mr. Kinney thinks Ah's tole all them other folks an' that scared 'em way frum here.

PETE. Ah reckon he does.

MARTHA. Well, Ah ain't never tole nobuddy, but Ah'm goin' tell that little gal 'fore she moves up thar. 'Taint fair lettin' 'em move in.

PETE. (*Curiously*) When yuh goin' tell her Martha? Yuh ain't goin' tell her 'fore Mr. Kinney?

MARTHA. Ah doan know. Ah reckon the Lawd'll 'pint the time. (*A knock on the door, and John Kinney and the Smiths come in once more. Perhaps Kinney's face is a bit more pale, but his mocking smile is more pronounced as his eyes encounter Martha's.*)

JOHN KINNEY. Everything is quite ship shape, Martha.

ALICE. It's jes' lovely. Gimme large rooms every time. Everything looks nice an' clean, too.

SAM. Ah reckon we'll settle fer them rooms now. How 'bout it, Alice?

ALICE. Sure. We'll pay a deposit right now.

JOHN KINNEY. Half a month, please.

SAM. Right. (*He takes a wallet from his pocket, extracts two bills and hands them to Kinney. Pete glances anxiously at Martha, but the latter is standing downcast, her eyes on the floor. Kinney seats himself at one of the little tables, reaches into an inner pocket, produces a receipt book, then jumps up with an exclamation of annoyance.*)

JOHN KINNEY. My wallet! I'm afraid I've dropped it! (*He searches his other pockets feverishly—but the missing wallet is not forthcoming. Everyone looks at him uncomfortably.*)

SAM. (*Sympathetically*) That sure is tough!

JOHN KINNEY. (*Angrily*) Tough! There were over five hundred dollars in that wallet! And what's more, I had it when I came in here tonight!

MARTHA. In here!

PETE. (*Echoing Martha's words blankly*) In here!

ALICE. You might uv dropped it in the hall, or upstairs.

JOHN KINNEY. A note-book! I wonder if I could have dropped my wallet then!

SAM. It doan do no harm lookin'. Ah'll go with yuh ef yuh wants.

JOHN KINNEY. (*Sharply*) No, thank you. Wait here a few minutes, if you don't mind. I prefer going alone.

SAM. Sure we'll wait.

ALICE. It's too bad. But yuh'd better look upstairs. Yuh might er dropped it sure 'nuff. (*Kinney goes out, giving the door an angry slam.*)

SAM. Ah hope he doan think *we* found his ole wallet. Gee! Five hundred dollars! Bet that guy's got money ter burn!

ALICE. (*With a little laugh*) Bet he doan burn none, though.

MARTHA. (*In a tone of suppressed excitement*) Listen! He'll be back any minute, an' Ah's got somethin' powerful important ter say. (*Paying no heed to the surprised glances of Sam and Alice*) Yuh musn' take them rooms, 'lessen yuh wants ter have more trouble than yuh knows 'bout. They's—they's haunted!

ALICE. (*In a shrill voice*) What's that yuh said?

SAM. Good Lawd!

MARTHA. (*Her voice containing a deadly seriousness*) Haunted! They ain't nobuddy bin able ter live in them rooms longer'n they could git out!

ALICE. (*In a faltering voice*) Yuh ain't jokin'?

MARTHA. Before the good Lawd, Ah's tellin' yuh the truth!

SAM. But—listen here! Ef what yuh says is true—Does this landlord know 'bout what yuh's tellin' us?

MARTHA. He knows alright. Ah reckon he'll tell us ter leave, when he knows Ah's tole yuh. Well, Ah'm thinkin' 'tis time we did quit. Doan yuh think so, Pete?

PETE. (*Loyally*) Ah thinks same's you does, Martha.

ALICE. I can't believe it.

SAM. Nor me. (*Becoming suddenly suspicious*) Say. Yuh ain't tryin' ter scare us outer them rooms in favor uv somebuddy else, are yuh?

MARTHA. (*Tensely*) Listen. It's nigh on twenty years ago when we first seen Her. She was one of these here Philippine gals. John Kinney met her when he was soljerin' in them parts. He was young then, an' handsome. She was pretty's a picture, with her big, black eyes an' a head of hair lak we doan never see no more. An' she had plenty money. Well, John Kinney marries her an 'bout a year later they comes ter New York. He quits the army, then, an' goes inter real estate. He tole Her he's goin' buy her a beautiful house—an' he takes her money—she was only a furriner—an' young. She didn' know no better. But he doan buy the pretty house he tole her 'bout. He buys this apartment house. That's when she first commence ter see through him. He uster live then in two little rooms back uv his dingy office. 'Tweren't no place fer the likes uv Her. She pined fer the country an' the grass and the flowers. She wanted him ter fix up one uv these floors so's she could have some place ter breathe in. But he figgered on the rent from them apartments, an' he wouldn't let her have one.

SAM. Gee! What a brute! (*Alice slips her hand into his.*)

MARTHA. She uster come here ter collect the rents. Many's the time Ah's seen her big, black eyes a-swimming in tears. She jes' took ter me right off—An Pete an me thought the world uv her. We didn't always understan' what she said. She didn't speak no good English lak Pete an' me, but we could make out she was lonesome an' scared uv New York—scared too, uv that husband uv hers. She missed her folks back home powerful bad. She was jes' a little wild bird, caught an' put in a cage in a dark room. Well, seems lak John Kinney tole her one time that she could have the next floor that got vacant. She runs up here ter tell me—jes' laughin' an' cryin' all together. She uster come here whenever she got a chance—an' sit here an' plan how she'd fix them rooms. Such funny ideas she had, too, 'bout fix-ins—but pretty. Well, 'bout three months later, the folks on the top floor move away an' she tole John Kinney 'bout her plans. She was all ready ter move in. (*Martha pauses just long enough to wipe a tear with the corner of her apron.*) If the ole devil didn't up an' tell her he'd changed his mind. Seems he'd done forgot all about it. He tole her he needed the money real bad ter pay some bills. Ah ain't never forgot how she look when she tole me 'bout it. Her heart was nigh breakin', Ah reckon. She tole me that them rooms was hers—an' she was goin' ter move in. Ah thought she was jes' talkin wild—but she weren't.

ALICE. (*Breathlessly*) What happened?

MARTHA. The next afternoon John Kinney found her up thar hangin' between the parlor an' the bedroom.

ALICE. (*With a little moan*) Oh, my Gawd! She'd—

MARTHA. (*Nodding confirmation*) An' she ain't never moved away from up thar—jes' lak she said.

SAM. (*Mopping his face with a hand that shakes perceptively*) Ah reckon they ain't no rooms fer us, Alice.

ALICE. (*In a voice bordering on the hysterical*) Let's go, Sam. Quick 'fore he comes back!

SAM. (*With clarity*) Sure. Ah doan never want ter see nothin' more uv him. Reckon he's still lookin' fer that wallet. (*A loud crash is heard. Everyone starts violently—Pete, so violently that his Bible falls to the floor. A moment of petrified silence*)

MARTHA. It's upstairs.

SAM. Somebuddy fell down! (*He swallows convulsively.*)

ALICE. (*Bursting into tears*) Oh, Sam, let's get outer here, quick 'fore somethin' happens!

MARTHA. Ah 'spec somethin' *has* happened. (*To Sam*) Reckon we'd better go up an' see ef Mr. Kinney's hurt.

SAM. (*Drawing back*) Who, me? Yuh ain't talkin' ter me, sister!

ALICE. (*Clinging tightly to his arm*) Doan yuh do it, Sam. Doan leave me!

SAM. Sam Smith ain't never goin' near them rooms no more!

MARTHA. Well, Ah reckon Ah'd better go up an' see what's happened.

SAM. (*Looking [in] horror at the mere suggestion*) Yuh's crazy, woman. Let me outer here!

MARTHA. Ah reckon Ah'll ask the people downstairs ter go with me.

PETE. (*Anxiously*) Doan yuh go by yuhself, Martha!

MARTHA. (*Reassuringly*) Ah'll jes' step downstairs an' ask Mr. Brown ter go thar with me.

SAM. An, we'll jes hop on downstairs with yuh. This ain't no place fer comfort! (*Alice, who has Sam tightly by the arm, stoops to lift her umbrella which has fallen to the floor. At that moment, Martha, who has opened the door and gone out into the hall, hurries back into the room, shutting the door precipitously behind her. She rushes over to Pete, grasping him by the arm, and giving him a little shake.*)

MARTHA. Pete! Pete! yuh wanted a sign! Ah jes seen John Kinney walkin' down the stairs with *Her*! She had him by the hand an' she was laughin'! (*The curtain starts to descend just as Alice's piercing scream rings through the room.*)

THE END

1927. Reprinted in Perkins, ed. *Black Female Playwrights* (1989)

Hot Stuff*

CHARACTERS

FANNY KING	The "Red Hot" Mama
MARY GREEN	Fanny's Friend
JOHN COLE	A Numbers Addict
JENNIE BARBOUR	John's Girlfriend
ISADORE GOLDSTEIN	A Jew
WALTER KING	The "Red Hot" Mama's "Daddy" (Husband)

Scene: *The living room in Fanny's flat. The furnishings are simple and in good taste. A full length mirror is at left, and a door opening upon the hallway. At right, two windows overlook the street. Heavy portieres at center back separate the living room from the bedroom.*

Time: *The present. About eight o'clock on a winter's night.*

AT RISE: FANNY *is sitting at a table busily assorting slips of paper. Her friend,* MARY GREEN, *is sitting close by waiting patiently for* FANNY *to finish what she is doing.* FANNY's *beauty is a kind called "striking." Large, flashing black eyes, small mouth, regular features and slick bobbed head. Her skin is a golden brown; her figure sensuous to a fault.* MARY GREEN *is very good-looking, slender and very fair. Although she is rouged and painted every bit as much as* FANNY, *she lacks the warmth and vividness of the latter's personality.*

FANNY. (*looking at a slip*) Reg'lar Dumb Dora—this one! Plays high everyday, never sticks to a number and raises a helluva noise when they come the day she drops 'em! (*She adds the slip to her little pile.*) Say, there's easy money in this game, Mary. I'm thinkin' uh droppin' the other, pretty soon if my luck keeps up! An' talk 'bout suckers! Believe me, it's here you find them.

MARY. Guess nobuddy can put anything over on you, Fanny.

FANNY. I'd like to see 'em try—just once!

MARY. I ain't got no luck in this game. It gets me how some people make out so well!

FANNY. I don't lose nuthin'; you take it from me. (*She slaps the last slip on the pile.*) Well, that's that! Good day for little Fanny.

MARY. How much?

FANNY. Two hundred fifty!

MARY. My Gawd! Ain't you a lucky kid! Gee! It makes me sick hearing you rattle off hundreds like that! How d'ye do it?

FANNY. Secrets of the trade. You gotta be on the inside! Say . . . who was that six foot sheik you was with at Craig's last night?

MARY. Bill Hogan! Met him in Atlantic City . . . doctor's convention last summer.

FANNY. I know it's the truth! He ain't a doctor, is he?

MARY. He ain't nothing but! Dr. Bill Hogan!

FANNY. Well, what d'ye know! Some looker!

MARY. An' that ain't all!

FANNY. I know he don't hang out round here . . .

MARY. Naw. No such luck. He comes from out West. He's only here for a week on business.

FANNY. Well, I know you're steppin' fast while he's here. I tried to get to your table but I didn't have a ghost of a chance. Walter was along an' you know what that means. A wasted evening! Try an' have some fun with a husband like mine dangling at your elbow.

MARY. Where's Walter tonight?

FANNY. He's gone to Brooklyn to see a feller 'bout a deal. He won't be back till late.

MARY. Well, I got a date myself. Gimme twenty-five pair, Fanny. Ten flesh, five black an' ten nude.

FANNY. Right! Don't know if I got ten flesh, though. (*She opens the drawer of a cabinet in the room and takes out a quantity of silk stockings.*) No, I ain't got but five flesh. You better take five uh these parchment. They're the latest.

MARY. All right. (*She examines the stockings.*) Reg'lar two fifty or I'm a liar.

FANNY. Nothing but! One thing about you, Mary, you sure does know good stuff when you see it!

MARY. An' it don't stop at stockings. I'll tell the world. (*She hands* FANNY *some bills.*) Twenty-five!

FANNY. Right! (*She tucks the bills in her dress.*) How much you lettin' 'em go at, Mary? I get a dollar sixty-five for the one's I sell.

MARY. That ain't hot enough for my customers. I can't charge more'n a dollar fifty. If I do, they say the price is cold—an' won't buy. Too much competition in this line. (*She puts the stockings in a small black satchel.*)

FANNY. Well, I have a side line, so it's different for me! I don't sell a single dress less'n fifteen.

MARY. An' they're worth forty every one of 'em. Well, kid, I'm off. Dr. Bill ain't got but one more day.

FANNY. What you done with Jack this last week?

MARY. Jack's outta town. Back Sunday!

FANNY. I get you.

MARY. S'long.

FANNY. S'long kid!

(*As the door closes on* MARY, FANNY *picks up the stockings and returns them to the cabinet. The telephone rings.* FANNY *sits beside the table, takes the phone from beneath the rose taffeta flounces of a tall white-haired doll.*) Hello? Yes, this is Mis' King. What number you say? 429? Yes. 429. Ten cents on the combination. That's sixty cents. All right, Mis' Harris! No, I won't forget! Goodbye! (*She writes the number on a pad and is about to turn away when the phone rings once more.*) Who is it? Oh, that you honey? Not tonight! I'm tired, kid! ... Well ... Where we goin'? Half past nine at the usual place! Gone to Brooklyn, won't be back till eleven. I'll leave a note. Oh, Walter won't mind! I'll tell him Mary and me have gone to the theater. Naw ... Walter don't snoop! If he did I wouldn't live with him five minutes. S'long, kid! (*She hangs up the receiver. There is a knock at the door, and* FANNY *admits* JOHN COLE. COLE *is a rather short, dark fellow with a jerky, nervous way of speaking.* FANNY *freezes instantly at the sight of him and closes the door with a little slam.*) Well? You got my message, didn't you?

COLE. Yes, Mis' King, but I couldn't believe it.

FANNY. Well, it's true. Of course, I'm awful sorry. If I knew any way I could help you out I sure would.

COLE. But ... (*He swallows convulsively.*) Mis' King, I don't want to make no trouble, but ...

FANNY. You better not! The idea!

COLE. Two hundred an' fifty dollars! You can't mean it.

FANNY. See here, I'm sorry, darned sorry. If I'd a seen your slip, I'd a played it. Why wouldn't I? I ain't no thief, am I? I dropped that paper. I don't know how I coulda done it! It ain't never happened before. Of course, I'll give you back your fifty cents.

COLE. (*with a gesture of protest*) Fifty cents! Don't talk of fifty cents! I gotta have that money. Mis' King! I gotta have my winnings!

FANNY. (*harshly*) See here! I know you're excited an' all that, but I won't stand fer no funny talk! You gotta have your money! What money! You ain't got no money! You ain't got no winnings!

COLE. (*fiercely*) I believe you took 'em! You ain't honest! You're lyin'! They told me you was like that, but I didn't believe 'em.

FANNY. Now you get outa here! Get right out! The very idea! (*She opens the door.*) You get right out!

COLE. (*walking to the door*) I'll go, but I ain't done with this. (*He plucks desperately at the band of his hat.*) Nobuddy's gonna rob me an' get away with it. (FANNY *slams the door after him.*)

FANNY. Well, if he ain't got gall! Hm. His two hundred and fifty! Try'n collect, you nut! (*She goes into the adjoining room and returns with an evening gown. She places it over a chair. The doorbell rings.* FANNY *goes close to the door and calls.*) Who is it?

FEMALE VOICE FROM WITHOUT. Customer, Mis' King.

FANNY. (*opening the door*) Hello! I can't seem to remember you.

(*She looks keenly at the newcomer.*)

JENNIE. I ain't bin here before! A friend uh mine told me you had some pretty dresses. Have you got any more left?

FANNY. Sure. Come in. I got some just your size. (*She closes the door and motions toward the bedroom.*) Step right in here, will you?

JENNIE. (*She is a small dark girl with a sharp decisive quality about her voice.*) Just a minute, Mis' King. You're a numbers agent, ain't you?

FANNY. Yes. You want to play a number?

JENNIE. (*coldly*) Listen, I didn't come here 'bout no dresses . . .

FANNY. (*slowly*) Oh! Well, what the devil did you come fer?

JENNIE. John Cole's a friend uh mine—

FANNY. (*with a slight sneer*) Oh! Very interesting! He sent you to collect for him, did he?

JENNIE. No. I told him I'd come and collect. An' what's more, I'm goin' to keep my promise.

FANNY. (*sharply*) I ain't got no time to waste on you.

JENNIE. You'se got time to hand over that money.

FANNY. Try an' get it! You make me laugh, you do! (*She takes a seat, crosses her legs in a leisurely fashion and surveys the other insolently.*)

JENNIE. Mebbe yuh won't laugh when yuh hears what I gotta say.

FANNY. Say, are you as looney as your boyfriend?

JENNIE. (*angrily*) Yuh can steal all the silk dresses an' stockings yuh wants—I don't care! But when it comes to stealin' cold cash what don't belong to yuh, that's where I take a hand!

FANNY. Well, of all th—

JENNIE. Listen to me! I work in the same building with Walter King. I know the name of the firm he works for. Want to know their name? See yuh don't. Well, yuh shipping clerk daddy ain't pinin' to go up the river, is he?

FANNY. (*springing to her feet*) How dare you! Get outa here, right now, you dirty little . . .

JENNIE. Cut that! I know two people who bought dresses from yuh. They're friends uh mine. Do yuh want 'em to go down to twenty-eighth street with me as witnesses?

FANNY. That kinda bluff won't go here. You got some nerve, I'll tell the world!

JENNIE. Not more'n you'se got.

FANNY. Get outa here! You don't know nothing! Think you're smart, don't you?

JENNIE. Saltzberg and Olinsky. Fifth floor—I work on the sixth. If you don't come across, I'll be there first thing in the mornin'.

FANNY. You can go to hell for all I care—

JENNIE. (*walking over to the door*) All right. I see it suits you if your daddy takes a long rest in the cooler. But lemme tell yuh somethin' kid: he won't go alone. You're his accomplice an' yuh'll get yours same ez him! (*She opens the door, but* FANNY, *after a moment's hesitation, runs up to her and lays a detaining hand on her arm.*)

FANNY. Close that door.

JENNIE. What fer?

FANNY. I want to tell you somethin'.

JENNIE. (*closing the door*) Well? There's only one thing I'm willin' to hear.

FANNY. I'll give you the money. I can't afford to have you squeal. How do I know you won't tell no how?

JENNIE. Yuh don't know. But you got my word that I won't. I ain't no liar.

FANNY. You might. Just to get even.

JENNIE. I ain't got no love fer Saltzberg and Olinsky, an' I ain't got none fer you. But just the same, I ain't one fer doin' my own people like some folks I know.

FANNY. (*opens the cabinet once more. She takes out a roll of money and hands it to* JENNIE.) Just like it come in.

JENNIE. All right! I'll give it to John. This is a losin' game anyhow, but it could be played on the level. (*She goes out.*)

FANNY. (*closes the cabinet with a slam. She taps impatiently with her neatly slippered foot.*) Dirty little shine! She'd a done it too! (*She snatches up the evening dress and moves toward the bedroom. There is a discreet knock at the door.* FANNY *throws the dress over the chair once more and opens the street door with an angry jerk. On the threshold stands* ISADORE GOLD-STEIN,* *a Jewish peddlar of questionable reputation. He is good-looking, sleek, possessing an ingratiating smile and a familiar manner. In his hand he carries a briefcase.*)

FANNY. (*shortly*) Well?

GOLDSTEIN. I got something what you should see.

FANNY. Beat it. I don't want nuthin'. (*She makes a movement to slam the door.*)

GOLDSTEIN. (*staying the door with his hand*) Why you should be so mean to me? A good friend of yours, Miss Green, she tells me . . .

FANNY. I ain't got no money to buy nothing.

GOLDSTEIN. I ain't ask you should buy what you don't see.

FANNY. (*stepping aside*) Well, come in an' be quick about it. I gotta go out.

GOLDSTEIN. (*opening his suitcase*) I got something here what is such a bargain you never see. Now, wait! I know you know good stuff. Miss Green she tell me you good picker. Now . . . What you say? (*He shakes out a beautiful ermine wrap.*) I see already you like it. Well, try it on.

FANNY. Gee, it's a beauty! (*She strokes the fur lovingly.*)

GOLDSTEIN. Try it on. It don't cost you nuthin' to try it on. (*He places the wrap about* FANNY's *shoulders. She glides up to the mirror and preens herself, like a bird.* GOLDSTEIN *watches her with a gleam of admiration in his eye.*) You look like one queen. Ain't a man wouldn't fall dead fer you in such a coat. Turn round. So. You don't need I should tell you nuthin'. You got eyes in your head. Well, what you say?

FANNY. (*unable to tear her eyes away from her image in the mirror*) How much?

GOLDSTEIN. Cheap. Dirt cheap. If I would sell this coat you couldn't buy it. I give it away, that's all.

FANNY. How much?

GOLDSTEIN. You want to know how much you pay for this coat in Jaeckels? In any big house?

FANNY. I ain't buyin' it from Jaeckels', see?

GOLDSTEIN. I know that. Now that coat—I am givin' it away fer two hundred fifty. I gotta have cash tonight. If I would wait till tomorrow, I could get twice that easy. But I can't wait, see? I gotta get rid of it tonight. Two hundred fifty an' it's a present. What you say?

FANNY. (*derisively*) Know any more good jokes?

GOLDSTEIN. You think I'm jokin'?

FANNY. I know you're jokin'. (*She takes off the wrap and hands it to* GOLDSTEIN.) Here. I ain't crazy if you is. Say, do I look like two hundred fifty spot cash?

GOLDSTEIN. You look like a million dollar kid to me. Say, would you pass up such a coat like this? It don't suit nobody but you.

FANNY. Then you better give it to me. Make it a present like you said.

GOLDSTEIN. That's just what I'm doin'.

FANNY. Come off!

GOLDSTEIN. Mebbe we can make it a good business. How much you got?

FANNY. A clean hundred an' not another cent.

GOLDSTEIN. (*shaking his head*) Think again, kid.

FANNY. Pack up yuh coat! Reckon we can't do no business.

GOLDSTEIN. (*coming close to her and stroking her arm*) Mebbe you got something what ain't money.

FANNY. What you mean?

GOLDSTEIN. You know what I mean. (*He places his arms about* FANNY's *waist.*)

FANNY. (*without drawing away*) Get out. I'm a respectable, married woman, an' don't you forget it.

GOLDSTEIN. Who said you ain't? If you wasn't respectable, I wouldn't make no bargain with you. Get me?

FANNY. I got a husband.

GOLDSTEIN. Well, why not? A fine looking girl what you is don't have no trouble getting husbands. Mebbe we make a bargain. What you say? How much you got over a hundred?

FANNY. Not a red cent.

GOLDSTEIN. (*hesitating*) If you could make fifty more. (FANNY *shakes her head.*) Twenty-five? (FANNY *shakes her head.*)

FANNY. You said yourself, I was a million dollar kid. (*She goes up close to him, puts her arms slowly about his neck and kisses him.* GOLDSTEIN *holds her close, returning her kisses hotly.*) Well?

GOLDSTEIN. (*thickly*) You win, you little brown devil. (*He takes the coat and wraps it around* FANNY.) Well, where's the money? When do I get paid?

FANNY. C. O. D. (*She goes into the bedroom. The portieres close behind her.* GOLDSTEIN *hesitates and then follows her.*)

THE VOICE OF GOLDSTEIN. You say you got a husband?

THE VOICE OF FANNY. Sure.

THE VOICE OF GOLDSTEIN. He wouldn't come in now an' go for getting excited, would he?

THE VOICE OF FANNY. Naw. He's in Brooklyn. (*The living room door opens slowly. A tall, dark fellow enters. He closes the door and replaces the key in his pocket. He notices the suitcase, frowns in a puzzled fashion and then passes in his same quick manner into the bedroom. There is a loud exclamation, another and another. The sound of a blow and fall.* GOLD-STEIN *dashes wildly out of the room,* WALTER KING *in full pursuit.* GOLDSTEIN *grabs his hat and suitcase, but fumbles at the door.* KING *yanks him away, opens the door and with a well aimed kick sends the Jew sprawling. The latter scrambles to his feet and plunges out of the room.* KING *picks up the suitcase and hurls it after the peddlar, slamming the door. Breathing rapidly and heavily, he re-enters the bedroom.*)

VOICE OF FANNY. Lemme alone! I didn't do nuthin'. (*She utters a loud scream. There is the sound of scuffling and other loud screams, sobs and moans. There is never a word from* KING.) Yuh's killing me! Gawd! Oh! Murder! Murder! (*Shriek after shriek rents the air. There is a loud knocking on the hall door. The shrieks cease.* KING *comes out. He walks up to the mirror and adjusts his tie and collar. He flicks a bit of thread from his coat and puts it on. He takes up his hat and puts that on. He listens for a moment to the loud sobs and moans in the adjoining room. Then he walks to the hall door, opens it and goes out, banging the door behind him. The moans become noticeably fainter. There is a silence. The portieres are parted and there stands* FANNY *in a most disheveled condition. Dangling from one hand is the beloved ermine wrap. She places the wrap close to her face, stroking it with her cheek. She braces up suddenly. She slips the coat about her shoulders. She walks across the floor, painfully, and then as she reaches the mirror, a little sob breaks from her.)*

FANNY. The dirty brute! Glad he didn't scratch my face none. (*She smoothes her hair. She turns around and around.*) Some bargain! (*She walks to the telephone.*) Bradhurst 2400. Hello! Jim? Jim, this is Fanny. Yes, I'm home. Can't make it tonight, kid. Of course, it's Walter. Tomorrow night, same time. O.K. Say, honey, I just bought some coat. It's a peach! You'll see me strut tomorrow night, all right. I don't mean maybe. Goodbye, honey. Goodnight. (*She hangs up the receiver with a sigh.*)

CURTAIN

1927. Reprinted from Brown-Guillory, ed., *Wines in the Wilderness* (1990)

A Criticism of the Negro Drama as It Relates to the Negro Dramatist and Artist

Yes, we have our colored artists. We have our Robeson, Rose McClenndon [*sic*], our Wilson* and various others who have reached an undeniable place of prominence in the realm of the theatre. And we have had our Florence Mills.*

Even the most casual theatre-goer to-day is familiar with one or more of these stars in the theatrical firmament. But alas, the same cannot be said of the Negro dramatist.

Negro drama does not of necessity include the work of the Negro dramatist. Strictly speaking, Negro drama is any drama or theatrical production which essays to portray the life of the Negro. Where, then, is the Negro dramatist?

Who are the writers that have provided the vehicle for Gilpin, Robeson, Rose McClenndon and Bledsoe?* Frankly, yet reluctantly, too, we may name them, and never a Negro will be found among them.

Suppose there had been no *Emperor Jones*, and no *Porgy*; no *In Abraham's Bosom* and no *Show Boat*? What then? Ask the Negro artist, he knows.

Some there are who have shuddered distastefully at these plays; been affronted by Paul Green, degraded by Du Bose Hayward, and misunderstood by Eugene O'Neill. But ask the Negro artist if he is grateful to these writers. He will tell you. And ask the Negro dramatist what he feels about it. If he is forward-thinking, he will admit that these writers have been a great inspiration; that they have pointed the way and heralded a new dawn.

The drama, more particularly, the American drama, is from twenty to thirty years behind the novel and short story in point of subject matter. There is almost no subject to-day that cannot be discussed with the most revolting detail between the covers of a book. If there are any who doubt this, let them read *Home to Harlem* by Claude McKay. Not so with our drama. Here we have elected to be squeamish, and perhaps advisedly so. Nevertheless, this does not imply that the theatre has not made enormous strides ahead. The drama has developed a new technique, new ways and means, a new genius of mechanism and a new direction.

Unfortunately, almost everyone thinks that he can write a play. Writers will grant the poet his form and the novelist his; the essayist his mould and the writer of short stories his. However, when it comes to the play, why—one merely takes one's pen in hand and presto! we have Dialogue! I have seen plays written by our Negro writers with this caption: To Be Read, Not Played!

A play to be read! Why not the song to be read not sung, and the canvas to be described, not painted! To every art its form, thank God! And to the play, the technique that belongs to it!

Here it is then that our Negro dramatists have failed to reach a larger and more discriminating public. They have labored like the architect who has no knowledge of geometry and the painter who must struggle to evolve the principles of perspective.

May I advise these earnest few—those seekers after light—white lights—to avoid the drama of propaganda if they would not meet with certain disaster? Many a serious aspirant for dramatic honors has fallen by the wayside because he would insist on his lynchings or his rape. The white man is cold and unresponsive to this subject and the Negro, himself, is hurt and humiliated by it. We go to the theatre for entertainment, not to have old fires and hates rekindled.

Of course, if we have a Shaw or Galsworthy among us, let him wander at will in the more devious by-paths of race dissection. Let him wander wheresoever he will—provided he has no eye for the box-office. For even as far-famed a dramatist as Galsworthy could not keep his recent play, *The Forest,** more than a very limited time on the London stage. Why? It dealt with propaganda, and as beautifully written and staged as it was, it had to be withdrawn.

What, then, is left to the Negro dramatist? Let him portray the life of his people, their foibles, if he will, and their sorrows and ambition and defeats. Oh, yes, let us have all of these, told with tenderness and skill and a knowledge of the theatre and the technique of the times. But as long as we expect our public, white and colored, to support our drama, it were wise to steer far away from the old subjects.

A little more laughter, if you please, and fewer spirituals!

From *Opportunity* June 1928

Courtesy of the National Urban League.

5
HISTORIANS

Arthur A. Schomburg

A rthur (Arturo) Alfonso Schomburg, the famous bibliophile and champion of Black culture, was born in San Juan, Puerto Rico, on January 24, 1874. His mother, a Black migrant worker from the Virgin Islands, raised him with little assistance from his father, the son of a Puerto Rican woman and a German immigrant. The nurturing influence of his mother and his maternal grandparents seems to have been the shaping factor in his life (James 201–02). Schomburg gained some formal education in Puerto Rico and the Virgin Islands but he was largely self-taught. His interest in Black culture dates back to his school days in Puerto Rico, when the taunting of his White teachers and classmates that Blacks had no significant achievements pushed him to seek out as many works by Black authors as he could. While in Puerto Rico, Schomburg also took an active interest in the Cuban and Puerto Rican independence movements.

Schomburg arrived in the United States on April 17, 1891, soon finding employment in a law office. While in America, he continued his interest in Cuban and Puerto Rican independence. In 1892, he published his first article, a description of a political club he had helped form, in *Patria*, a journal founded by Cuban revolutionary and author Jose Martí.

Schomburg took a position at Bankers Trust Company in 1906. During his years as a law clerk and banker, he explored Black culture, making trips to Central America, the Caribbean, and throughout the United States, where he collected materials. He was also one of the founders of the Negro Society for Historical Research in 1911 and became president of the American Negro Academy in 1922.

By 1926 he had amassed a collection of several thousand items—books, pamphlets, prints, and manuscripts—which the New York Public Library purchased for $10,000 through a grant from the Carnegie Corporation. This was to be the basis for the Schomburg Center for Research in Black Culture (a part of the New York Public Library), the largest collection of materials on the subject in the world. The cost paid for the collection was a fraction of the expense incurred by Schomburg, a man of limited financial resources, in assembling it. As Schomburg said, "Because I have a lot of books does not mean that I have a lot of money" (qtd. in Walrond 6). Still, the materials had long outgrown the space available for them at his residence in Brooklyn, and he was happy to have the collection housed at the 135th Street Library, in the center of Harlem. The library quickly became a meeting place for many of the rising young talents and greatly facilitated the flowering of the Harlem Renaissance. The vast resources Schomburg compiled provided aid and assistance, not always acknowledged, to many authors and researchers, including James Weldon Johnson, Langston Hughes, Jessie Fauset, Alain Locke, and Claude McKay.

In 1929, Schomburg retired from Bankers Trust on a medical pension (he had been suffering from chronic headaches and nosebleeds) and became curator of the Negro Collection at Fisk University, greatly adding to their library. Due to diminishing resources at Fisk, however, Schomburg was forced to leave his position. In 1932, the Carnegie Corporation provided funding for Schomburg to return to New York City and curate his own collection at the 135th Street Library. He held this position until his death on June 10, 1938, following complications from a tooth infection.

Schomburg's lifelong interest in Black culture throughout the diaspora is reflected not only in the research center that bears his name but also in his published work. Although he was not the most skillful author in either English or Spanish (the essays in English required frequent editing before publication), his writings never failed to reflect his erudition. This is best illustrated by "The Negro Digs Up His Past" (first published in the Harlem edition of *Survey Graphic* March 1925 and reprinted in Locke's *The New Negro*), where Schomburg acknowledges the desire for Blacks to claim their racial identity, concomitantly stressing the need for scrupulous accuracy in studying Black history.

He fervently believed that "[h]istory must restore what slavery took away." Schomburg admired Garvey, a fellow Pan-Africanist and staunch Black nationalist, and, like him, felt the way to achieve Black liberation was through the education of the Black masses.

Despite his lack of formal education, Schomburg was an astute collector of Black heritage, utilizing whatever means he could to acquire materials. He made frequent appeals to booksellers and friends to track down Black artifacts. The result of his relentless efforts was the creation of a collection of unparalleled scope and breadth. This is the legacy by which he will be best remembered.

The bulk of Schomburg's papers are at the Schomburg Center. Other materials are located at the Moorland-Spingarn Research Center at Howard University and the Charles S. Johnson Collection at Fisk University.

BIBLIOGRAPHY

Allen, James Egert. *The Legend of Arthur A. Schomburg.* Cambridge, MA: Danterr, 1975.

Gubert, Betty Kaplan. "Schomburg, Arthur Alfonso." *American National Biography.* Ed. John A. Garraty and Mark C. Carnes. New York: Oxford UP, 1999. 422–24.

James, Winston. *Holding Aloft the Banner of Ethiopia: Caribbean Radicalism in Early Twentieth-Century America.* New York: Verso, 1998.

Kaiser, Ernest. "Schomburg, Arthur Alfonso." *Dictionary of American Negro Biography.* Ed. Rayford W. Logan and Michael R. Winston. New York: Norton, 1982.

Ortiz, Victoria. "Arthur A. Schomburg: A Biographical Essay." *The Legacy of Arthur A. Schomburg: A Celebration of the Past, a Vision for the Future.* New York: New York Public Library, 1986.

Piñeiro de Rivera, Flor. *Arthur A. Schomburg: A Puerto Rican's Quest for His Black Heritage.* San Juan: Centro de Estudios Avanzados de Puerto Rico y el Caribe, 1989.

Rogers, J. A. "Arthur A. Schomburg: 'The Sherlock Holmes of Negro History.'" *World's Great Men of Color.* Vol. 2. 1947. New York: Simon & Schuster, 1996. 449–53. 2 vols.

Sinnette, Elinor Des Verney. *Arthur Alfonso Schomburg: Black Bibliophile & Collector.* New York: New York Public Library, 1989.

Sinnette, Elinor Des Verney, W. Paul Coates, and Thomas C. Battle, eds. *Black Bibliophiles and Collectors: Preservers of Black History.* Washington, D.C.: Howard UP, 1990.

Walrond, Eric. "Visit to Arthur Schomburg's Library Brings Out Wealth of Historical Information." *Negro World* April 22, 1922: 6.

The Negro Digs Up His Past

The American Negro must remake his past in order to make his future. Though it is orthodox to think of America as the one country where it is unnecessary to have a past, what is a luxury for the nation as a whole becomes a prime social necessity for the Negro. For him, a group tradition must supply compensation for persecution, and pride of race the antidote for prejudice. History must restore what slavery took away, for it is the social damage of slavery that the present generations must repair and offset. So among the rising democratic millions we find the Negro thinking more collectively, more retrospectively than the rest, and apt out of the very pressure of the present to become the most enthusiastic antiquarian of them all.

Vindicating evidences of individual achievement have as a matter of fact been gathered and treasured for over a century: Abbé Gregoire's* liberal-minded book on Negro notables in 1808 was the pioneer effort; it has been followed at intervals by less known and often less discriminating compendiums of exceptional men and women of African stock. But this sort of thing was on the whole pathetically over-corrective, ridiculously over-laudatory; it was apologetics turned into biography. A true historical sense develops slowly and with difficulty under such circumstances. But to-day, even if for the ultimate purpose of group justification, history has become less a matter of argument and more a matter of record. There is the definite desire and determination to have a history, well documented, widely known at least within race circles, and administered as a stimulating and inspiring tradition for the coming generations.

Gradually as the study of the Negro's past has come out of the vagaries of rhetoric and propaganda and become systematic and scientific, three outstanding conclusions have been established:

First, that the Negro has been throughout the centuries of controversy an active collaborator, and often a pioneer, in the struggle for his own freedom and advancement. This is true to a degree which makes it the more surprising that it has not been recognized earlier.

Second, that by virtue of their being regarded as something "exceptional," even by friends and well-wishers, Negroes of attainment and genius have been unfairly disassociated from the group, and group credit lost accordingly.

Third, that the remote racial origins of the Negro, far from being what the race and the world have been given to understand, offer a record of credible group achievement when scientifically viewed, and more important still, that they are of vital general interest because of their bearing upon the beginnings and early development of human culture.

With such crucial truths to document and establish, an ounce of fact is worth a pound of controversy. So the Negro historian to-day digs under the spot where his predecessor stood and argued. Not long ago, the Public Library of Harlem housed a special exhibition of books, pamphlets, prints and old engravings, that simply said, to skeptic and believer alike, to scholar and school-child, to proud black and astonished white, "Here is the evidence." Assembled from the rapidly growing collections of the leading Negro book-collectors and research societies, there were in these cases, materials not only for the first true writing of Negro history, but for the rewriting of many important paragraphs of our common American history. Slow though it be, historical truth is no exception to the proverb.

Here among the rarities of early Negro Americana was Jupiter Hammon's Address to the Negroes of the State of New York, edition of 1787, with the first American Negro poet's famous "If we should ever get to Heaven, we shall find nobody to reproach us for being black, or for being slaves." Here was Phyllis Wheatley's Mss. [sic] poem of 1767 addressed to the students of Harvard, her spirited encomiums upon George Washington and the Revolutionary Cause, and John Marrant's St. John's Day eulogy to the "Brothers of African Lodge No. 459" delivered at Boston in 1789. Here too were Lemuel Haynes' Vermont commentaries on the American Revolution and his learned sermons to his white congregation in Rutland, Vermont, and the sermons of the year 1808 by the Rev. Absalom Jones of St. Thomas Church, Philadelphia, and Peter Williams* of St. Philip's, New York, pioneer Episcopal rectors who spoke out in daring and influential ways on the Abolition of the Slave Trade. Such things and many others are more than mere items of curiosity: they educate any receptive mind.

Reinforcing these were still rarer items of Africana and foreign Negro interest, the volumes of Juan Latino, the best Latinist of Spain in the reign of Philip V, incumbent of the chair of Poetry at the

University of Granada, and author of Poems printed there in 1573 and a book on the Escurial published 1576; the Latin and Dutch treatises of Jacobus Eliza Capitein, a native of West Coast Africa and graduate of the University of Leyden, Gustavus Vassa's celebrated autobiography that supplied so much of the evidence in 1796 for Granville Sharpe's attack on slavery in the British colonies, Julien Raymond's Paris exposé of the disabilities of the free people of color in the then (1791) French colony of Hayti, and Baron de Vastey's *Cry of the Fatherland*, the famous polemic by the secretary of Christophe* that precipitated the Haytian struggle for independence. The cumulative effect of such evidences of scholarship and moral prowess is too weighty to be dismissed as exceptional.

But weightier surely than any evidence of individual talent and scholarship could ever be, is the evidence of important collaboration and significant pioneer initiative in social service and reform, in the efforts toward race emancipation, colonization and race betterment. From neglected and rust-spotted pages comes testimony to the black men and women who stood shoulder to shoulder in courage and zeal, and often on a parity of intelligence and talent, with their notable white benefactors. There was the already cited work of Vassa that aided so materially the efforts of Granville Sharpe, the record of Paul Cuffee,* the Negro colonization pioneer, associated so importantly with the establishment of Sierra Leone as a British colony for the occupancy of free people of color in West Africa; the dramatic and history-making exposé of John Baptist Phillips, African graduate of Edinburgh, who compelled through Lord Bathhurst in 1824 the enforcement of the articles of capitulation guaranteeing freedom to the blacks of Trinidad. There is the record of the pioneer colonization project of Rev. Daniel Coker in conducting a voyage of ninety expatriates to West Africa in 1820, of the missionary efforts of Samuel Crowther* in Sierra Leone, first Anglican bishop of his diocese, and that of the work of John Russwurm, a leader in the work and foundation of the American Colonization Society.

When we consider the facts, certain chapters of American history will have to be reopened. Just as black men were influential factors in the campaign against the slave trade, so they were among the earliest instigators of the abolition movement. Indeed there was a dangerous calm between the agitation for the suppression of the slave trade and the beginning of the campaign for emancipation. During that interval colored men were very influential in arousing the attention of public men who in turn aroused the conscience of the country. Continuously between 1808 and 1845, men like Prince Saunders, Peter Williams, Absalom Jones, Nathaniel Paul, and Bishops Varick and Richard Allen, the founders of the two wings of African Methodism, spoke out with force and initiative, and men like Denmark Vesey (1822), David Walker (1828) and Nat Turner* (1831) advocated and organized schemes for direct action. This culminated in the generally ignored but important conventions of Free People of Color in New York, Philadelphia and other centers, whose platforms and efforts are to the Negro of as great significance as the nationally cherished memories of Faneuil and Independence Halls. Then with Abolition comes the better documented and more recognized collaboration of Samuel R. Ward, William Wells Brown, Henry Highland Garnett [sic], Martin Delaney [sic], Harriet Tubman, Sojourner Truth, and Frederick Douglass with their great colleagues, Tappan, Phillips, Sumner, Mott, [Harriet Beecher] Stowe and Garrison.*

But even this latter group who came within the limelight of national and international notice, and thus into open comparison with the best minds of their generation, the public too often regards as a group of inspired illiterates, eloquent echoes of their Abolitionist sponsors. For a true estimate of their ability and scholarship, however, one must go with the antiquarian to the files of the *Anglo-African Magazine*, where page by page comparisons may be made. Their writings show Douglass, McCune Smith, Wells Brown, Delaney, Wilmot Blyden and Alexander Crummell* to have been as scholarly and versatile as any of the noted publicists with whom they were associated. All of them labored internationally in the cause of their fellows; to Scotland, England, France, Germany and Africa, they carried their brilliant offensive of debate and propaganda, and with this came instance upon instance of signal foreign recognition, from academic, scientific, public and official sources. Delaney's *Principia of Ethnology* won public reception from learned societies, Pennington's* discourses an honorary doctorate from Heidelberg, Wells Brown's three year mission the entreé of the salons of London and Paris, and the tours of Frederick Douglass, receptions second only to Henry Ward Beecher's.*

After this great era of public interest and discussion, it was Alexander Crummell, who, with the reaction already setting in, first organized Negro brains defensively through the founding of the American Negro Academy in 1897 at Washington. A New York boy whose zeal for education had suffered a rude shock when refused admission to the Episcopal Seminary by Bishop Onderdonk,* he had been befriended by John Jay and sent to Cambridge University, England, for his education and ordination. On his return, he was beset with the idea of promoting race scholarship, and the Academy was the final result. It has continued ever since to be one of the bulwarks of our intellectual life, though unfortunately its members have had to spend too much of their energy and effort answering detractors and disproving popular fallacies. Only gradually have the men of this group been able to work toward pure scholarship. Taking a slightly different start, The Negro Society for Historical Research* was later organized in New York, and has succeeded in stimulating the collection from all parts of the world of books and documents dealing with the Negro. It has also brought together for the first time co-operatively in a single society African, West Indian and Afro-American scholars. Direct offshoots of this same effort are the extensive private collections of Henry P. Slaughter of Washington, the Rev. Charles D. Martin of Harlem, of Arthur Schomburg of Brooklyn, and of the late John E. Bruce, who was the enthusiastic and far-seeing pioneer of this movement. Finally and more recently, the Association for the Study of Negro Life and History has extended these efforts into a scientific research project of great achievement and promise. Under the direction of Dr. Carter G. Woodson,* it has continuously maintained for nine years the publication of the learned quarterly, *The Journal of Negro History*, and with the assistance and recognition of two large educational foundations has maintained research and published valuable monographs in Negro history. Almost keeping pace with the work of scholarship has been the effort to popularize the results, and to place before Negro youth in the schools the true story of race vicissitude, struggle and accomplishment. So that quite largely now the ambition of Negro youth can be nourished on its own milk.

Such work is a far cry from the puerile controversy and petty braggadocio with which the effort for race history first started. But a general as well as a racial lesson has been learned. We seem lately to have come at last to realize what the truly scientific attitude requires, and to see that the race issue has been a plague on both our historical houses, and that history cannot be properly written with either bias or counterbias. The blatant Caucasian racialist with his theories and assumptions of race superiority and dominance has in turn bred his Ethiopian counterpart—the rash and rabid amateur who has glibly tried to prove half of the world's geniuses to have been Negroes and to trace the pedigree of nineteenth century Americans from the Queen of Sheba. But fortunately to-day there is on both sides of a really common cause less of the sand of controversy and more of the dust of digging.

Of course, a racial motive remains—legitimately compatible with scientific method and aim. The work our race students now regard as important, they undertake very naturally to overcome in part certain handicaps of disparagement and omission too well-known to particularize. But they do so not merely that we may not wrongfully be deprived of the spiritual nourishment of our cultural past, but also that the full story of human collaboration and interdependence may be told and realized. Especially is this likely to be the effect of the latest and most fascinating of all of the attempts to open up the closed Negro past, namely the important study of African cultural origins and sources. The bigotry of civilization which is the taproot of intellectual prejudice begins far back and must be corrected at its source. Fundamentally it has come about from that deprecation of Africa which has sprung up from ignorance of her true rôle and position in human history and the early development of culture. The Negro has been a man without a history because he has been considered a man without a worthy culture. But a new notion of the cultural attainment and potentialities of the African stocks has recently come about, partly through the corrective influence of the more scientific study of African institutions and early cultural history, partly through growing appreciation of the skill and beauty and in many cases the historical priority of the African native crafts, and finally through the signal recognition which first in France and Germany, but now very generally, the astonishing art of the African sculptures has received. Into these fascinating new vistas, with limited horizons lifting in all directions, the mind of the Negro has leapt forward faster than the slow clearings of scholarship will yet safely permit. But there is no doubt

that here is a field full of the most intriguing and inspiring possibilities. Already the Negro sees himself against a reclaimed background,
in a perspective that will give pride and self-respect ample scope, and
make history yield for him the same values that the treasured past of
any people affords.

From *The New Negro* (New York: Albert & Charles Boni, 1925)

J. A. Rogers

B orn in Negril, Jamaica, on September 6, 1883,[1] Joel Augustus Rogers migrated to the United States in 1906, studying art in Chicago while working as a Pullman porter before settling in New York City in 1921. In Jamaica, Rogers had been brought up to think of himself in terms of class rather than color. Upon arriving in America, he was shocked by the discrimination he was forced to endure because of his race, causing some friends to advise him, because of his light complexion, to "pass" for White. Instead, Rogers, an avid reader from his youth, educated himself about both African and European history and went on to become an early champion of Black studies.

Rogers published his findings in a number of periodicals, including the *Messenger*, the *Negro World*, *American Mercury*, and the *Pittsburgh Courier*, where for years his illustrated column "Your History" was a favorite of many readers. Rogers's experience as a porter is partly fictionalized in *From Superman to Man* (1917). The Black porter, Dixon, (ironically named after the racist author of *The Clansman*, Thomas Dixon) bravely and very cleverly refutes all of a passenger's arguments about Black inferiority. That even such a hard-core racist as the passenger can finally recognize his own ignorance demonstrates one of Rogers's fundamental beliefs: that racial prejudice can be eradicated through education. He believed that if Blacks learned of their past achievements, which had been omitted by most historians, they would look at themselves with pride, and if Whites learned about these achievements, they would not treat Blacks in an inferior manner.

Rogers attempted this process of education in two ways: "The first was his biographical research . . . [and] [t]he second . . . involved race-mixing and intermarriage" (Turner 36). The best examples of his biographical work, documenting the achievements of Blacks, are his two-volume *The World's Great Men of Color 3000 B.C. to 1946 A.D.* (1946) and *One Hundred Amazing Facts about the Negro* (1934). Rogers believed that the Egyptians were a Black race and that Western civilization simply continued this tradition. Rogers felt that biography, which shows the best and worst of people, "will ever be the highest and most civilizing form of literature" (*World's Great Men of Color* 7) and that racism could be combated only by demonstrating that there are no "pure" racial groups and that we are all of one race, the human race. This is evident in the essay "Is Black Ever White?" in which Rogers disputes the whole notion of race: "I see but one American people, speaking a common language, and at bottom having a common ideal, shading in color by imperceptible degrees from white to black, or black to white, as you will." Several of Rogers's works, including *As Nature Leads* (1919) and the three-volume *Sex and Race* (1941–44), speak of the benefits of racial mixing. In these works Rogers "contends that it is inevitable that black and white will have the urge to mix, and always will do so, despite the most virulent opposition and stringent legislation" (Sandoval 6)

Rogers's optimism about the eventual blending of the races did not mean that he was blind to racial prejudice. Like Dixon in *From Superman to Man*, Rogers was well aware of the bigotry that would need to be overcome. In his essay "Who Is the New Negro, and Why?" he praises the courage and pride of the New Negro, tracing this fighting spirit back to Nat Turner and Denmark Vesey. The New Negro is unafraid of being labeled "rebel, atheist, pagan, infidel, Socialist, Red, heathen, radical . . . [.] He will be anything else but a sheep."

Because he was not formally trained, having no postsecondary schooling, some historians have questioned the results of Rogers's research. This has particularly been the case where Rogers has taken controversial positions (e.g., claiming Black ancestry for several American presidents and other notable people or his views on racial mixing). However, Rogers was an able scholar who taught himself Spanish, French, German, and Portuguese to aid his painstaking research in European, African, and American archives. He was affiliated with the Paris Society of Anthropology, the American Geographical Society, and the Academy of Political Science. He was one of the earliest Black war correspondents, reporting on the Italian-Ethiopian War in 1935. Over the years he was able to garner support from a wide array of sources, including Garvey (both men appealed to the masses, though they differed in their views on race-mixing), Harrison, Malcolm X, George Schuyler, and even Du Bois, who, in an offhanded compliment, said that "no man living has revealed so many important facts about the Negro race as has Rogers. His mistakes are many and his background narrow, but he is a true historical student" (qtd. in Turner 38). Perhaps the greatest testimonial to Rogers, however, comes from the common readers, who have kept his works, all of which were originally self-published, in print for years. Most have gone through numerous editions. He was and still remains their historian, which is fitting since "his purpose was to popularize black history and to reach the 'man in the street'" (Sandoval 6).

Before his death on September 6, 1966, in New York City shortly after suffering a stroke, Rogers made great strides in his mission to teach common people about Black history. Rogers's work is testimony to the need to include the achievements of all people in literary, cultural, and political histories, and to the fact that the omission of these achievements from our histories can lead to an incomplete and inaccurate perception of events.

NOTES

Rogers's papers are largely found at Fisk University in Nashville, Tennessee.

1. Rogers's wife, Bertha, records his birth date as September 6, 1880, and his death date as March 26, 1966. However, most sources list his year of birth as 1883 and his death date as September 6, 1966.

BIBLIOGRAPHY

Hutchinson, George. *The Harlem Renaissance in Black and White.* Cambridge: Harvard UP, 1995.

Jones-Ford, Jacqueline. "J. A. Rogers." *Notable Black American Men.* Ed. Jessie Carney Smith. Detroit: Gale, 1999. 1029–30.

Logan, Rayford W. *Dictionary of American Negro Biography*. Ed. Rayford W. Logan and Michael R. Winston. New York: W.W. Norton, 1982.

Peters, Linda Ray. "The Life and Works of Joel Augustus Rogers." M.A. thesis, Northern Illinois U, 1978.

Pinckney, Darryl. *Out There: Mavericks of Black Literature*. New York: Basic Civitas Books, 2002.

Rogers, J. A. "How and Why This Book Was Written." *World's Great Men of Color*. Vol. 1. 1947. New York: Simon & Schuster, 1996. 1–24. 2 vols.

Sandoval, Valerie. "The Bran of History: An Historiographic Account of the Work of J. A. Rogers." *Schomburg Center for Research in Black Culture Journal* 1 (Spring 1978): 5–7, 16–19.

Turner, W. Burghardt. "J. A. Rogers: Portrait of an Afro-American Historian." *Black Scholar* 6 (January–February 1975): 32–39.

From Superman to Man

The limited was speeding on to California over the snow-blanketed prairies of Iowa. On car Bulwer, the passengers had all retired, and Dixon, the porter, his duties finished, sought the more comfortable warmth of the smoker, where he intended to resume the reading of the book he had brought with him—Finot's "Race Prejudice."*

***

"Your book, George?"*

"Yes, sir."

"What is it about?"

"Oh, only a scientific work," said the other, carelessly, not wishing to broach the subject of racial differences that the title of the book suggested.

Dixon's evident desire to evade a direct answer seemed to sharpen the other's curiosity, for he suggested off-handedly, but with ill-conceived eagerness: "Pretty deep stuff, eh?" Then in the same manner, he inquired, "Who's the author?"

Dixon noted his curiosity, and deciding to gratify it, handed him the book, which he took with feigned indifference. He opened it near the beginning, and, moistening his fore-finger, began turning over the leaves. Now and then he would stop to read a marked passage, each time muttering half-audibly, "Nonsense, ridiculous!"

After glancing through the book the passenger* turned back to the frontispiece in a search for the author's name. When he found it, he blurted out with ill-concealed disgust, "Just as I thought! Written by a Frenchman," then, before he could recollect to whom he was talking—so full was he of what he regarded the absurdity of Finot's view—he again blurted out, "Do you believe all these impossible views about the equality of the races?"

Now Dixon's policy was to carefully avoid any topic that was likely to produce a difference of opinion with a passenger, provided that the avoidance did not entail any sacrifice of his self-respect. In this instance, he regarded his questioner as one to be humored, rather than vexed, for just then the following remark, made by this same man that afternoon, recurred to him.

"The Jew, the Frenchman, the Dago and the Spaniards are all 'niggers' to a greater or less extent. The only white people are the Anglo-Saxon, Teutons and Scandinavians." This, Dixon surmised, accounted for the remark he had made about Finot's adopted nationality, and it amused him.

Dixon pondered his question for a few minutes, then there occurred to him a method by which he could retain his own opinion, even while in apparent accord with the views of the other. He responded accordingly:

"No, sir, I do not believe in the equality of the races. As you say, it is impossible."

The passenger looked up from his book as if he had not been expecting a response, but seemingly pleased with Dixon's acquiescence continued.

"Writers of this type don't know what they are talking about. They write from mere theory. If they had to live among 'niggers,' they would sing an entirely different tune."

Dixon felt that he ought not to let this remark go unchallenged. He protested courteously: "Yet, sir, M. Finot has admirably proved his arguments. I am sure if you were to read his book you would agree with him, too."

"Didn't you just say you differed with the views in this book?" questioned the other sharply.

"I fear you misunderstand me, sir."

"Didn't you say you did not believe in the equality of races?"

"Yes, sir."

"Then why?"

"Because as you said, sir, it is impossible."

"Why? Why?"

"Because there is but one race—the human race."***

[During the rest of the trip, Dixon has consistently been out-witting the passenger, who is slowly being won over to the porter's arguments.]

Dixon now consulted his watch and informed the other that they would arrive at the next station in fifteen minutes and would stay there ten minutes. Remembering that he would probably not have another chance to speak with this man, he decided to summarize his argument, and as the other did not speak, he continued:

"Looking back on the conversation we have had, sir, and sup-ported by a mass of other information gathered from various sources, I am confident that every argument brought forward to prove Negro inferiority, of which I have heard, is wrong; that there is no bad trait possessed by the Negro which cannot be paralleled by the white man. In short, 'that black is not so very black, nor white so very white'; that the Negro is disliked, not so much for his features, his criminality and his imputed bad traits, as for the color of his skin and the nature of his hair."

"But is that the real reason," he continued, in a spirit of raillery. "For instance, if a Negro has money, he will find any number of whites to kowtow to him. Foreign Negroes, too, or any Negro who can pass off as Spanish, French—in short, anything else but United States cit-izens, are better treated though these persons are of the same mixture of black and white. Many of the most prejudiced whites, too, have Negro intimates. Really, this prejudice, habit, affectation, whim or whatever it is, is so ridiculous, so utterly opposed to everything bor-dering on intelligence, that it is a wonder these persons never happen to see themselves in their true light and have a hearty laugh at their own expense."

"What do yo think would offer a solution to the problem?" asked the passenger seriously.

"A sense of humor."

"Something easier than that."

"Then I should like to see the formation of a national commis-sion for an inquiry into the subject and to ascertain the best means for adjusting the relationship between these two bodies of our citizens. There are also three methods which I have always thought would help a great deal: First, text-books in the public schools, teaching in a sim-ple manner the latest scientific findings in this matter, without making any special reference to the situation here in America; second, the establishment of federal schools in those parts of the South where the Negroes abound; and third, a non-political provision for a certain number of Negro congressmen. I consider the matter sufficiently serious to be taken in hand by the federal government, and the stoppage of the evil now might—indeed, I am sure it would—save future generations a great deal of trouble."

Excerpt from *From Superman to Man* (1917)

Jazz at Home

Jazz is a marvel of paradox: too fundamentally human, at least as modern humanity goes, to be typically racial, too international to be characteristically national, too much abroad in the world to have a special home. And yet jazz in spite of it all is one part American and three parts American Negro, and was originally the nobody's child of the levee and the city slum. Transplanted exotic—a rather hardy one, we admit—of the mundane world capitals, sport of the sophisticated, it is really at home in its humble native soil wherever the modern unsophisticated Negro feels happy and sings and dances to his mood. It follows that jazz is more at home in Harlem than in Paris, though from the look and sound of certain quarters of Paris one would hardly think so. It is just the epidemic contagiousness of jazz that makes it, like the measles, sweep the block. But somebody had to have it first: that was the Negro.

What after all is this taking new thing, that, condemned in certain quarters, enthusiastically welcomed in others, has nonchalantly gone on until it ranks with the movie and the dollar as a foremost exponent of modern Americanism? Jazz isn't music merely, it is a spirit that can express itself in almost anything. The true spirit of jazz is a joyous revolt from convention, custom, authority, boredom, even sorrow—from everything that would confine the soul of man and hinder its riding free on the air. The Negroes who invented it called their songs the "Blues," and they weren't capable of satire or deception. Jazz was their explosive attempt to cast off the blues and be happy, carefree happy, even in the midst of sordidness and sorrow. And that is why it has been such a balm for modern ennui, and has become a safety valve for modern machine-ridden and convention-bound society. It is the revolt of the emotions against repression.

The story is told of the clever group of "Jazz-specialists" who, originating dear knows in what scattered places, had found themselves and the frills of the art in New York and had been down to the gay Bohemias of Paris. In a little cabaret of Montmârt[r]e they had just "entertained" into the wee small hours fascinated society and royalty; and, of course, had been paid royally for it. Then, the entertainment over and the guests away, the "entertainers" entertained themselves with their very best, which is always impromptu, for the sheer joy of it. That is jazz.

In its elementals, jazz has always existed. It is in the Indian war-dance, the Highland fling, the Irish jig, the Cossack dance, the Spanish fandango, the Brazilian *maxixe*, the dance of the whirling dervish, the hula hula of the South Seas, the *danse du vêntre* of the Orient, the *carmagnole** of the French Revolution, the strains of Gypsy music, and the ragtime of the Negro. Jazz proper, however, is something more than all these. It is a release of all the suppressed emotions at once, a blowing off of the lid, as it were. It is hilarity expressing itself through pandemonium; musical fireworks.

The direct predecessor of jazz is ragtime. That both are atavistically African there is little doubt, but to what extent it is difficult to determine. In its barbaric rhythm and exuberance there is something of the bamboula, a wild, abandoned dance of the West African and the Haytian Negro, so stirringly described by the anonymous author of *Untrodden Fields of Anthropology,** or the *ganza* ceremony so brilliantly described in Maran's *Batouala.** But jazz time is faster and more complex than African music. With its cowbells, auto horns, calliopes, rattles, dinner gongs, kitchen utensils, cymbals, screams, crashes, clankings and monotonous rhythm it bears all the marks of a nerve-strung, strident, mechanized civilization. It is a thing of the jungles— modern man-made jungles.

The earliest jazz-makers were the itinerant piano players who would wander up and down the Mississippi from saloon to saloon, from dive to dive. Seated at the piano with a care-free air that a king might envy, their box-back coats flowing over the stool, their Stetsons pulled well over their eyes, and cigars at an angle of forty-five degrees, they would "whip the ivories" to marvellous chords and hidden racy, joyous meanings, evoking the intense delight of their hearers who would smother them at the close with huzzas and whiskey. Often wholly illiterate, these humble troubadours knowing nothing of written music or composition, but with minds like cameras, would listen to the rude improvisations of the dock laborers and the railroad gangs and reproduce them, reflecting perfectly the sentiments and the longings of these humble folk. The improvised bands at Negro dances in the South, or the little boys with their harmonicas and jews'-harps, each one putting his own individuality into the air, played also no inconsiderable part in its evolution. "Poverty," says J. A. Jackson of the *Billboard*, "compelled improvised instruments. Bones, tambourines, make-shift string instruments, tin can and hollow wood effects, all now utilized as musical novelties, were among early Negroes the product of necessity. When these were not available 'patting juba'* prevailed. Present-day 'Charleston' is but a variation of this. Its early expression was the 'patting' for the buck dance."

The origin of the present jazz craze is interesting. More cities claim its birthplace than claimed Homer dead. New Orleans, San Francisco, Memphis, Chicago, all assert the honor is theirs. Jazz, as it is to-day, seems to have come into being this way, however: W. C. Handy,* a Negro, having digested the airs of the itinerant musicians referred to, evolved the first classic, "Memphis Blues." Then came Jasbo Brown, a reckless musician of a Negro cabaret in Chicago, who plays this and other blues, blowing his own extravagant moods and risqué interpretations into them, while hilarious with gin. To give further meanings to his veiled allusions he would make the trombone "talk" by putting a derby hat and later a tin can at its mouth. The delighted patrons would shout, "More, Jasbo. More, Jas, more." And so the name originated.

As to the jazz dance itself: at this time Shelton Brooks,* a Negro comedian, invented a new "strut," called "Walkin' the Dog." Jasbo's anarchic airs found in this strut a soul mate. Then as a result of their union came "The Texas Tommy,"* the highest point of brilliant, acrobatic execution and nifty footwork so far evolved in jazz dancing. The latest of these dances is the "Charleston," which has brought something really new to the dance step. The "Charleston" calls for activity of the whole body. One characteristic is a fanatic fling of the legs from the hip downwards. The dance ends in what is known as the "camel-walk"—in reality a gorilla-like shamble—and finishes with a peculiar hop like that of the Indian war dance. Imagine one suffering from a fit of rhythmic ague and you have the effect precisely.

The cleverest "Charleston" dancers perhaps are urchins of five and six who may be seen any time on the streets of Harlem, keeping time with their hands, and surrounded by admiring crowds. But put it on a well-set stage, danced by a bobbed-hair chorus, and you have an effect that reminds you of the abandon of the Furies. And so Broadway studies Harlem. Not all of the visitors of the twenty or more well-attended cabarets of Harlem are idle pleasure seekers or underworld devotees. Many are serious artists, actors and producers seeking something new, some suggestion to be taken, too often in pallid imitation, to Broadway's lights and stars.

This makes it difficult to say whether jazz is more characteristic of the Negro or of contemporary America. As was shown, it is of Negro origin plus the influence of the American environment. It is Negro-American. Jazz proper, however, is in idiom—rhythmic, musical and pantomimic—thoroughly American Negro; it is his spiritual picture on that lighter comedy side, just as the spirituals are the picture on the tragedy side. The two are poles apart, but the former is by no means to be despised and it is just as characteristically the product of the peculiar and unique experience of the Negro in this country. The African Negro hasn't it, and the Caucasian never could have invented it. Once achieved, it is common property, and jazz has absorbed the national spirit, that tremendous spirit of go, the nervousness, lack of conventionality and boisterous good-nature characteristic of the American, white or black, as compared with the more rigid formal natures of the Englishman or German.

But there still remains something elusive about jazz that few, if any of the white artists, have been able to capture. The Negro is admittedly its best expositor. That elusive something, for lack of a better name, I'll call Negro rhythm. The average Negro, particularly of the lower classes, puts rhythm into whatever he does, whether it be shining shoes or carrying a basket on the head to market as the Jamaican women do. Some years ago while wandering in Cincinnati I happened upon a Negro revival meeting at its height. The majority present were women, a goodly few of whom were white. Under the influence of the "spirit" the sisters would come forward and strut—much of jazz enters where it would be least expected. The Negro women had the perfect jazz abandon, while the white ones moved lamely and woodenly. This same lack of spontaneity is evident to a degree in the cultivated and inhibited Negro.

In its playing technique, jazz is similarly original and spontaneous. The performance of the Negro musicians is much imitated, but seldom equalled. Lieutenant Europe, leader of the famous band of the "Fifteenth New York Regiment," said that the bandmaster of the Garde Republicaine, amazed at his jazz effects, could not believe without demonstration that his band had not used special instruments. Jazz has a virtuoso technique all its own: its best performers, singers and players, lift it far above the level of mere "trick" or mechanical effects. Abbie Mitchell, Ethel Waters, and Florence Mills; the Blues singers, Clara, Mamie, and Bessie Smith; Eubie Blake, the pianist; "Buddy" Gilmore,* the drummer, and "Bill" Robinson, the pantomimic dancer—to mention merely an illustrative few—are inimitable artists, with an inventive, improvising skill that defies imitation. And those who know their work most intimately trace its uniqueness without exception to the folk-roots of their artistry.

Musically jazz has a great future. It is rapidly being sublimated. In the more famous jazz orchestras like those of Will Marion Cook, Paul Whiteman, Sissle and Blake, Sam Stewart, Fletcher Henderson, Vincent Lopez* and the Clef Club units, there are none of the vulgarities and crudities of the lowly origin or the only too prevalent cheap imitations. The pioneer work in the artistic development of jazz was done by Negro artists; it was the lead of the so-called "syncopated orchestras" of Tyers and Will Marion Cook, the former playing for the Castles of dancing fame, and the latter touring as a concertizing orchestra in the great American centers and abroad. Because of the difficulties of financial backing, these expert combinations have had to yield ground to white orchestras of the type of the Paul Whiteman and Vincent Lopez organizations that are now demonstrating the finer possibilities of jazz music. "Jazz," says Serge Koussevitzky, the new conductor of the Boston Symphony, "is an important contribution to modern musical literature. It has an epochal significance—it is not superficial, it is fundamental. Jazz comes from the soil, where all music has its beginning." And Leopold Stokowski says more extendedly of it:

Jazz has come to stay because it is an expression of the times, of the breathless, energetic, superactive times in which we are living, it is useless to fight against it. Already its new vigor, its new vitality is beginning to manifest itself. . . . America's contribution to the music of the past will have the same revivifying effect as the injection of new, and in the larger sense, vulgar blood into dying aristocracy. Music will then be vulgarized in the best sense of the word, and enter more and more into the daily lives of people. . . . The Negro musicians of America are playing a great part in this change. They have an open mind, and unbiased outlook. They are not hampered by conventions or traditions, and with their new ideas, their constant experiment, they are causing new blood to flow in the veins of music. The jazz players make their instruments do entirely new things, things finished musicians are taught to avoid. They are pathfinders into new realms.

And thus it has come about that serious modernist music and musicians, most notably and avowedly in the work of the French modernists Auric, Satie and Darius Milhaud, have become the confessed debtors of American Negro jazz. With the same nonchalance and impudence with which it left the levee and the dive to stride like an upstart conqueror, almost overnight, into the grand salon, jazz now begins its conquest of musical Parnassus.

Whatever the ultimate result of the attempt to raise jazz from the mob-level upon which it originated, its true home is still its original cradle, the none too respectable cabaret. And here we have the seamy side to the story. Here we have some of the charm of Bohemia, but much more of the demoralization of vice. Its rash spirit is in Grey's popular song, "Runnin' Wild":*

> Runnin' wild; lost control
> Runnin' wild; mighty bold,
> Feelin' gay and reckless too
> Carefree all the time; never blue
> Always goin' I don't know where
> Always showin' that I don't care
> Don' love nobody, it ain't worth while
> All alone; runnin' wild.

Jazz reached the height of its vogue at a time when minds were reacting from the horrors and strain of war. Humanity welcomed it because in its fresh joyousness men found a temporary forgetfulness, infinitely less harmful than drugs or alcohol. It is partly for some such reasons that it dominates the amusement life of America to-day. No one can sensibly condone its excesses or minimize its social danger if uncontrolled; all culture is built upon inhibitions and control. But it is doubtful whether the "jazz-hounds" of high and low estate would use their time to better advantage. In all probability their tastes would find some equally morbid, mischievous vent. Jazz, it is needless to say, will remain a recreation for the industrious and a dissipater of energy for the frivolous, a tonic for the strong and a poison for the weak.

For the Negro himself, jazz is both more and less dangerous than for the white—less, in that he is nervously more in tune with it; more, in that at his average level of economic development his amusement life is more open to the forces of social vice. The cabaret of better type provides a certain Bohemianism for the Negro intellectual, the artist and the well-to-do. But the average thing is too much the substitute for the saloon and the wayside inn. The tired longshoreman, the porter, the housemaid and the poor elevator boy in search of recreation, seeking in jazz the tonic for weary nerves and muscles, are only too apt to find the bootlegger, the gambler and the demi-monde who have come there for victims and to escape the eyes of the police.

Yet in spite of its present vices and vulgarizations, its sex informalities, its morally anarchic spirit, jazz has a popular mission to perform. Joy, after all, has a physical basis. Those who laugh and dance and sing are better off even in their vices than those who do not. Moreover, jazz with its mocking disregard for formality is a leveller and makes for democracy. The jazz spirit, being primitive, demands more frankness and sincerity. Just as it already has done in art and music, so eventually in human relations and social manners, it will no doubt have the effect of putting more reality in life by taking some of the needless artificiality out. . . . Naturalness finds the artificial in conduct ridiculous. "Cervantes smiled Spain's chivalry away," said Byron.* And so this new spirit of joy and spontaneity may itself play the rôle of reformer. Where at present it vulgarizes, with more wholesome growth in the future, it may on the contrary truly democratize. At all events, jazz is rejuvenation, a recharging of the batteries of civilization with primitive new vigor. It has come to stay, and they are wise, who instead of protesting against it, try to lift and divert it into nobler channels.

From *The New Negro* (New York: Albert & Charles Boni, 1925)

Is Black Ever White?

Walter White,* author of "The Fire in the Flint," in an interesting article on his mental reactions to criticisms of his latest book, "Flight," says among other things:

"Then there are amusing editorials like that which came to me from a Florida paper—the *Miami News*, which scored me for 'drawing upon my imagination in trying to picture the experiences of a Negro who passes for white.' The writer goes on to intimate that there is no such thing as a Negro successfully passing himself off as a white person and, therefore, I wrote of things wholly foreign to my own experience. I was tempted sorely to send him a photograph—being somewhat laden with work just now prevents my paying a personal visit upon the editor in Miami—and let it convince the Florida Horace Greely that there WERE Negroes who could, if they chose to do so, might [*sic*] cross the line."

For once I find myself agreeing with a cracker. I, too, insist that you cannot find any human being of any color passing off for another color, unless he stains his face, or possesses the qualities of a chameleon, or the people he goes among are color-blind. If a man has a coloring that among human beings is known as white, he is white regardless of what his ancestry may be. He certainly isn't blue, or green, or yellow or red, not if I am to go by the color-chart, and use my own eyes, and commonsense instead of the eyes of American race prejudice.

Because of the prejudiced idea that one can be white and black in complexion at the same time, every one of known Negro ancestry has a common interest. But at the same time it is high time that we learn to use our own eyes and own judgment about things, and not to accept the biased views of others. The white man, wishes to maintain a separate exploiting caste, and when we use his phraseology—a phraseology that is two hundred and fifty years behind the time—we but help to keep the chains fastened on ourselves.

If one is dark-brown, or brown, or yellow, or white-skinned, he is that color, that's all. It is a simple fact, possessing neither honor nor disgrace. If one is mixed Caucasian or Negro or Indian he is that as a fact, no matter how much prejudiced whites, or blacks, who use the eyes of white men to look at themselves, may say to the contrary. No matter what others may say, I, for one, cannot see two races, or a dozen in America. I see but one American people, speaking a common language, and at bottom having a common ideal, shading in color by imperceptible degrees from white to black, or black to white, as you will—this variety of coloring being of as little moment to the real human value as the variety of hair coloring.

Yes, I agree with the writer of the *Miami News*, though I fancy he won't thank me for the endorsement, that a Negro cannot successfully pass off as a white person. A white cow or mouse; a white dog or louse hasn't to "pass off" as white: *they are white.*

One of the first things towards "solving" this so-called race problem is to learn to call things by their right name.

Mr. White's point of view is no doubt due to the fact that he is not ashamed of his ancestry—a fact, which I, for one, have ample proof. He is one of the few, regardless of complexion, who has taken up the cudgels for justice for conviction's sake rather than money's sake. He believes in the group to which, logically and biologically, he belongs least—believes in it to the extent of having in it hostages to fame and fortune, by which I mean if he were to send a photograph of his children to the editor of the *Miami News*, little as that worthy is likely to know which of his associates are white and which "colored," he would know that the children are colored.

Mr. White's attitude in this last mentioned respect is clearly a rebuke to many, obviously colored, nevertheless I, for one do not call him a Negro. In "Flight" he speaks of his heroine, Mimi, as belonging to the Negro race. There is but one race—the human race—and in so far as Mimi belonged to any variety of it, she belonged to the so-called white race. I regard any other point of view as too big a concession to the Bourbons, who insist that if one is thirty-one parts of one thing and only one of another, he belongs to the one, because of some magical, or heaven-only-knows what quality involved. Now I am not going to accept that though all the crackers in Christendom shouted it in my ear.

I recognize, moreover, that right here is the fountain-head of the so-called color line, to which I am totally and unalterably opposed particularly when there is such a large percentage of citizens of the same descent as Mr. White and either do not know or wouldn't acknowledge it.

From the *Messenger* September 1926

Who Is the New Negro, and Why?

One hears much these days about the New Negro. Who is he, and who knows him? In slavery times there was a type of Negro, who worshipped his master and his family. He was a tattle-tale also, and whenever he saw one of his fellow-slaves do anything, he ran to the master, for which he would be rewarded with a ham knuckle, or a suit of old clothes. The betrayers of Nat Turner and John Brown were Negroes. The first person killed by John Brown was Hayward Shepard, a Negro.

This type was also made a slave-driver, then he became a tyrant of tyrants. When he became a slave-holder, as many did, he was even more exacting than the whites. When the Civil War broke out, this dog-like creature stayed at home protecting his master's family and property while the master was fighting to keep him enslaved, or he joined the ranks of the Confederacy. Benjamin Tillman* later introduced a bill, to make these black Confederates and slaveholders "white," a quite unnecessary step, internally.

On the other hand there was a type of slave—stubborn, rebellious, liberty-loving—who, like Nat Turner and Denmark Vesey, kept his master awake at nights, worrying lest they should rise up, massacre him and his family, plunder the plantation and take to the woods, as was so often the case, particularly in Hayti, Jamaica and Guiana.

The Old Negro is the present-day type of the first; the New of the second. Faces, like styles, may change but the human nature underneath remains practically unchanged.

One may recognize the difference between Old and New in their bearing. The former, respecting color more than qualification, is apologetic when dealing with white people. He acts as if he were always in the way, as if he had no right to be on earth. One can hear the clank of the slave's chain in all that he says and does.

The New is erect, manly, bold; if necessary, defiant. He apologizes to no one for his existence, feeling deep in his inner being that he has just as much right to be on earth and in all public places as anyone else. He looks the whole world searchingly in the eye, fearing or worshipping nothing nor no one. Self-possessed, he makes himself at home wherever circumstances place him. In a word, he respects himself, first of all.

The Old Negro, on the other hand, worships the white man, because of his absence of pigment. He is like the old colored mammy, who seeing the Minister from Hayti at a social function in Washington was horrified that a black man should be associating on terms of equality with white people, many of whom were his inferiors.

The Old Negro has a contempt for his own people, and in speaking of them he uses the same terms of contempt that his spiritual predecessors did. Shut your eyes when he speaks, and you'll hear a cracker talking.

The New Negro wastes no time worrying about his color. He realizes that a human being if he is to be visible at all must have a coloring of some sort, hence to him, one shade of coloring is the equal of every other. If light-complexioned he does not deem himself better than his darker brother.

The Old Negro when insulted, grins and apologizes; the New either ignores it or acts in a way to make his manliness felt. The Old submitted supinely to massacre as in the New York and Philadelphia riots, and the Palestine, Springfield and East St. Louis ones. The New arms himself and prepares to exact as many lives as possible, as in Washington, Chicago, Longview, Houston, Brownsville. All of which makes it clear that the possession of a college degree or of polish and refinement does not necessarily make a New Negro. Also he may be old or young. Manliness is a quality that inheres in the very fibre of one's being—a quality that like wine, improves with age.

The New Negro would rather lose his tongue than betray his people in their struggle for freedom and equality. Should any amelioration come to him because of superior talent, it turns to gall in his mouth when he remembers the sufferings of the rest of his people.

The Old, hat in hand, is always begging white people, a sort of glorified cripple with a can. Because of this he always has two different messages, one which he gives to white people, the other to colored ones. He is a living lie.

The New Negro supports movements conducted by his own people, because he realizes that these are the only ones that are ever going to speak out frankly and forcefully on his grievances. White persons, in such matters as economics, religion, politics, range all the way from the rabid radical to the rank conservative. So far as race is concerned, however, the vast majority is but of one complexion—the conservative, hence organizations supported by them for Negroes, have at bottom, the same Nordic goal, that is keeping the Negro "in his place," or at best a little lower than the angels. The New Negro realizes that the finest work, the real work for the advancement of the group will have to be done by its own members. It's an old saying: The man that pays the piper calls the tune.

The Old Negro is too thankful for small mercies; he believes that the employer does him a favor by hiring *him*. He is always praising enemies of the race like Cole Blease or Tillman or Vardaman,* because of some trifling sop given by these individuals to some isolated group or person, while doing all they can to keep back the group, as a whole. The New Negro, on the other hand, is satisfied with no concessions or patronage of any sort. He wants neither more nor less than his rights as a man and a citizen. And this difference between the Old and the New enters into their respective attitudes toward the times in which they are living. While the New Negro prepares to live, to live vigorously, and dangerously, if necessary, to make the whole weight of his presence felt while he moves on this earth; the Old prepares to die, and go to heaven where he will at least be a white man in complexion. "Wash me," he sings, "and I shall be whiter than snow." He tries to get a corner on religion, and sinks his money in churches, which brings no returns and are shut four-fifths of the week. He is as priest-ridden as the Italians of the Middle Ages, and enjoys it. The New on the other hand, invests his money in homes and factories. He tries to get a corner on business and education that will fit him to compete successfully with the whites, while the Old is singing psalms and repeating like parrots the religious nonsense that the enslavers of his forefathers used also to enslave their primitive minds.

The Old Negro is chiefly interested in what Abraham, Moses, David, Jehosaphat and other fictitious and semi-fictitious creatures of a barbarous tribe did in Palestine thousands of years ago. So far as his thinking is concerned he is a walking mummy. The New Negro relegates all these things to their proper, infinitesimal place in the scheme of things, and is interested most of all in life as it stirs around him. He jettisons Matthew for Marx; David for Darwin; and prefers Douglass to Lincoln. He studies economics instead of wasting his time with epistles.

The New Negro joins unions either of his own, or forces the whites to take him in, and once in never rests until he gets fairplay. He realizes that if white men have to create unions in order to get justice from white men like themselves, then this step is even more necessary for Negroes. The Old Negro, on the other hand, is an individualist. He pulls off to himself and begs the employer for work, thus paving the way for his being used, not as a union, but as an individual, to break strikes.

The Old Negro, once having reached what he believes to be the top of the ladder, spends a great deal of his time kicking off other climbers. He wants to rule the roost alone, to be greatest in the kingdom of heaven, while the New Negro, remembering his own hard struggle, is eager to give other aspirants a helping hand, even though the newcomer gives promise of eclipsing him. In other words, he is a good sport. He is, further, not afraid of contradiction, and does not believe he is an oracle on what will solve this so-called race problem. He is ever eager for new information.

The Old Negro falls glibly for all the agencies used by white friends to sidetrack the mind of the Negro group from its real problems such as over-stressing of Negro art, spirituals, piffling poetry, jazz, cabaret life, and the puffing into prominence of mediocre Negroes. The New Negro again relegates these to their proper place. He realizes that the race question is almost solely an economic one, and is satisfied with nothing less than equal opportunity for employment with equal wages. He sees that in all those things that make for the benefit of the nation, as a whole, there is no color discrimination. That is, as in paying taxes, no one asks his color; it is only in getting a return that there is discrimination. In short that in all those things that make for the white man's benefit, he is a white man, but in those that make for his, he is only a Negro.

The Old Negro is also more interested in "high-yallers," football, boxing, handball, in mastering the intricacies of the black bottom and the Charleston, in making signs in "frats" and lodges and splitting hairs about points of order in such places, in parading in gaudy uniforms, and in slicking his hair than in doing something vital towards getting himself and his group out of the rut of semi-slavery. Improving his mind by reading good books and acquiring a knowledge of the history of his racial group, is to the Old Negro, a real pain.

The Old Negro protests that he does not want social equality; the New, seeing that this is but another phrase for social justice, demands it. No social inequality for him. He feels that the first and foremost of all duties is to seek freedom, hence he has a perfect right to take any step, however violent, to rid himself of tyranny. With Thomas Jefferson he repeats: "Resistance to tyranny is obedience to God." Like the five colored immortals, Anderson, Copeland, Green, Leary and Newby,* who joined John Brown in his raid on Harper's Ferry, he stands ever ready to head or to join any movement that will strike for freedom.

The New Negro is not afraid of such bogey labels as rebel, atheist, pagan, infidel, Socialist, Red, heathen, radical, realizing that what they really connote is "thinker." He will be anything else but a sheep.

And where is the New Negro of whom we have been hearing so much? Is he an ideal or a reality? This much is evident, that many who have been making a noise like New Negroes have proved to be but asses in lion's skins. When a lion appeared they took to the woods.

From the *Messenger* March 1927

NOTES

GARVEYITES

56 Pan-African Congress: organized by Du Bois in 1919.

56 Senator MacCullum: T. G. MacCallum, state senator for Mississippi, 1932–36.

56 Senator France of Maryland: Joseph Irwin France, U.S. senator, 1917–23.

56 Dr. Heinrich Schnee: governor of German East Africa, 1912–18.

62 Whatsoever you give, in like measure it shall be returned to you: "For with the same measure that ye mete withal it shall be measured to you again" (Luke 6:38).

62 An eye for an eye, a tooth for a tooth: "Ye have heard that it hath been said, An eye for an eye, and a tooth for a tooth" (Matthew 5:38).

63 Samson brought down the temple upon his head and upon the heads of the Philistines (Judges 16:29–30).

64 Hitch your hopes to the stars: "hitch your wagon to a star," Ralph Waldo Emerson from the essay "Civilization" in *Society and Solitude* (1870).

64 For a discussion of Garvey's position on communism, see Rupert Lewis's *Marcus Garvey: Anti-Colonial Champion* (Trenton, NJ: Africa World Press, 1988), 125–51.

66 Morefield Storey, Joel Spingarn, Julius Rosenwald, Oswald Garrison Villard, Congressman Dyer and Mary White Ovington: Morefield Storey was a former president of the American Bar Association and president of the NAACP. Joel Elias Spingarn (1875–1939), writer, editor, humanitarian, professor of comparative literature at Columbia University, long involved with the NAACP, was the organization's president from 1915 until his death. Julius Rosenwald, chief shareholder of Sears, Roebuck & Company, was a backer of the National Urban League. The Rosenwald Fund supported many Negro educational and cultural endeavors. Grandson of abolitionist William Lloyd Garrison,

Oswald Garrison Villard was a founding member of the NAACP and owner and editor of the *Nation*. Representative L. C. Dyer of Missouri, with the backing of the NAACP, sponsored an anti-lynching law in 1921–22. The bill passed the House but lost in the Senate due to a filibuster by southern lawmakers. Mary White Ovington (1865–1951), political activist and author, helped found the NAACP.

70 "Up from Slavery," by Booker T. Washington: his autobiography, published in 1901.

70 Basutoland: Present-day Lesotho, a landlocked country in southern Africa. Basutoland became a British protectorate in 1868 and was granted independence in 1966.

73 Edwin P. Kilroe: (1883–1953) was assistant district attorney of New York from 1916 to 1923. He and Garvey quarreled repeatedly over Garvey's business ventures. When Garvey published a scathing piece on Kilroe in the August 2, 1919, *Negro World*, Kilroe sued for libel. Garvey retracted his claims after the case reached trial in August 1920.

84 Burrell and Ford: Benjamin E. Burrell (1892–1959), a Jamaican-born poet and songwriter, was associate secretary of the UNIA in 1917–18. He later became a member of the African Blood Brotherhood and published regularly in the *Crusader*. Rabbi Arnold Josiah Ford (1877–1935) was born in Barbados. He composed several songs for the UNIA collected in the *Universal Ethiopian Hymnal* (1920). He later founded the congregation for Beth B'nai Abraham, a synagogue for Ethiopian Jews. In a *Negro World* article from August 25, 1923, Ford explains the origins of the anthem (Ted Vincent, *Keep Cool* [London: Pluto P, 1995, 139–41]).

88 Riffian: An inhabitant of the Rif, along the Mediterranean coast of Morocco.

90 Original headline omitted: How Marcus Garvey Lays Down the Principles Which Must Guide the Race in Its Struggle for a Place in the Sun. The piece is best known as "African Fundamentalism."

90 Crispus Attucks and George William Gordon: Crispus Attucks (ca. 1723–70) was among a group of American patriots that confronted British troops in Boston on March 5, 1770. He was the first to die in the skirmish, later known as the Boston Massacre. George Gordon (ca. 1820–65), son of a wealthy White slave owner and a Black slave, was a leading Jamaican activist. A harsh critic of colonial policies, he was opposed to governor Edward John Eyre, who resisted any reform. On October 11, 1865, protesters in Morant Bay clashed with police. Gordon, though not directly involved, was hanged twelve days later.

92 "This above all—to thine own self be true, and it must follow, as the

night the day, thou canst not then be false to any man." Shakespeare, *Hamlet* 1.3.78–80.

95 Omitted is a long review of *Home to Harlem* published in *John O'London's Weekly*. The review celebrates the novel "as a social document" in which Whites are amazed by the decadent portrayal of Harlem life.

96 The "Century Magazine" in 1920: Garvey is probably thinking of *Back to Africa*, which was actually published in February 1923.

101 [*sic*] is in the source.

102 Antonio Maceo: Antonio Maceo y Grajales (1845–96). Black Cuban who was killed while fighting for Cuban independence.

103 Westwood: A training school designed to teach domestic science to young women.

104 Ashanti: Yard describes Ashwood's experience in Ghana at some length, pp. 162–81.

111 Shakespeare: Jacques Garvey slightly misquotes the lines:

> Famine is in thy cheeks,
>
> Need and oppression starvest in thine eyes,
>
> Contempt and beggary hangs upon thy back:
>
> The world is not thy friend, nor the world's law;
>
> *Romeo and Juliet* (V, i, 69–72)

118 Madam Kemal: Latife Hanim, who married Mustafa Kemal Atatürk (first president of Turkey, 1923–38) on January 29, 1923. They were divorced on August 5, 1925.

127 splendid article: "The Negro Artist and the Racial Mountain," published on June 23, 1926. In it, Hughes urged Black artists and intellectuals to liberate themselves from White standards of beauty and artistry.

127 Winold Reiss: Fritz Winold Reiss (1886–1953), German artist famous for his sketches of Native Americans and African Americans. He provided illustrations for *The New Negro* (1925).

SOCIALISTS

138 "those juggling fiends": Shakespeare, *Macbeth* (V, viii, 19–22). The first line of the quotation should be "And be these juggling fiends no more believ'd."

138 the Brownsville affair: Protesting their treatment, Black soldiers raided Brownsville, Texas, on August 13–14, 1906. One White resident was killed and two wounded. President Theodore Roosevelt dismissed 167 enlisted Black soldiers despite little evidence of their guilt.

139 one of these papers: The conservative African American *New York Age*.

139 A Texas paper: The *Rebel*.

141 Edgar Grey: A newspaperman and government informant who infiltrated both the UNIA and the ABB. Grey was a native of Liberia but grew up in Antigua.

141 W. Monroe Trotter: William Monroe Trotter (1872–1934) was a fierce opponent of Booker T. Washington.

146 Emmett Scott: Chief assistant to Booker T. Washington.

146 "Just Crabs": The title alludes to an essay by Booker T. Washington.

147 Just-So Stories: Children's fables by Rudyard Kipling, published in 1902.

147 "Subsidized Sixth": An attack on Black editors of *The Emancipator* as well as an allusion to Du Bois's "Talented Tenth."

148 "Scientific radicalism": A reference to the *Messenger* magazine, which its editors stated was the "Only Magazine of Scientific Radicalism in the World Published by Negroes."

149 Lester Ward . . . Stevenson: Lester Ward (1841–1913) was an American sociologist and educator who advocated against social Darwinism and for more government involvement in social problems. Archibald Ewing Stevenson (1884–1961) was a conservative lawyer who was highly critical of Marxism.

153 D'Artiguenave: Phillipe Sudre D'Artiguenave, a weak president installed by the United States shortly after its occupation of Haiti in 1915. He was forced to sign a treaty giving the United States broad control over the country.

154 Revelation 3:16: God indicates he will reject the indecisive, "because thou art lukewarm, and neither cold nor hot, I will spew thee out of my mouth."

156 At least one president of the United States: probably Warren G. Harding.

157 The "Fighting Fifteenth": The 369th Infantry Regiment, nicknamed the "Harlem Hellfighters," was awarded the French Croix de Guerre.

158 George E. Wibecan . . . William Stanley Braithwaite: George E. Wibecan was a Republican politician and longtime activist. William Stanley-Braithwaite (1870–1962) was a conservative but highly influential poet and critic who was a professor at Atlanta University.

159 "The American Cavalryman" . . . "The Vengeance of the Gods": *The American Cavalryman*, a novel published in 1917 and set in Liberia by Henry F. Downing (1851–1921), dramatist and author of several books about Liberia, where he had spent several years; *The Leopard's Claw*, an adventure novel by George W. Ellis (1875–1919) published in 1917; *The Veiled Aristocrats*, a novel dealing with race relations by

White author Gertrude Sanborn (1881–1928) and published in 1923; *The Vengeance of the Gods*, four stories of the color line by William Pickens (1881–1954), published in 1922.

159 Alrutheus Ambush Taylor . . . "Lenox Avenue": Taylor (1891–1954) was the author of such works as *Revitalized Slavery Curbed;* William Ferris (1874–1941) was literary editor of *Negro World* and author of *The African Abroad* (1913); *Sidelights on Negro Soldiers* was a history by Charles H. Williams (1886–?) and published in 1923; *Two Colored Women with the American Expeditionary Forces*, by Addie W. Hunton and Kathryn M. Johnson, was published in 1920; "Lenox Avenue" was a poem by Sidney Alexander (b. 1886).

159 Major Wilson . . . T. Thomas Fortune: Joseph T. Wilson (1836–1891) was the author of such works as *The Black Phalanx: A History of the Negro Soldiers of the United States in the War of 1775–1812, 1861–65* (1888); William C. Neill (178?–1860) was a leading Presbyterian minister; Rufus L. Perry (1833?–1895) was the author of *The Cushite: Or the Descendants of Ham as Found in the Sacred Scriptures, and in the Writings of Ancient Historians and Poets from Noah to the Christian Era* (1893); Atticus G. Haygood (1839–1896) was the author of *The Case of the Negro, as to Education in the Southern States* (1885); T. Thomas Fortune (1856–1928) was a prominent Black journalist, founder in 1883 of the *New York Age* and chief editorial writer for several years for the *Negro World*.

160 perfectly well known to him: The author is Harrison. The article is "The Real Negro Problem," *Modern Quarterly* 3 (September–December 1926): 314–21.

160 William Lonsdale Brown: Perhaps Harrison means William Wells Brown, a well-known author and abolitionist.

160 Walter Everette Hawkins: (1883–?) Author of the volume of poetry *Chords and Discords* (1920).

161 the Van Vechten matter: The controversial *Nigger Heaven* (1926), which examined the seamier side of Harlem life.

161 "The Chipwoman's Fortune" . . . "Lulu Belle": *The Chip Woman's Fortune* was written by Willis Richardson (1889–1977), the first African American to have a nonmusical production on Broadway, in 1923; *Lulu Belle* was a play by Edward Sheldon and Charles MacArthur first performed at the Belasco Theatre on February 9, 1926, and published the same year.

161 Sinclair Watkins: William A. Sinclair (1858–?), author of *The Aftermath of Slavery: A Study of the Condition and Environment of the American Negro* (1905); John Wesley Cromwell (1846–1927), author of *The*

Negro in American History (1914) and editor of the weekly paper *The Peoples's Advocate*, founded in 1876; Lucian Watkins (1879–1921) author of the poetry collection *Voices of Solitude* (1907) and a regular contributor to *Negro World*.

161 Edward Byron Reuter . . . Percy Amaury Talbot: Reuter, (1880–1946), author of *The Mulatto in the United States* (1918); Talbot, (1877–1945), author of *In the Shadow of the Bush* (1912).

162 Ernest Just: Just (1883–1941) received a Ph.D. in biology from Dartmouth and taught for years at Howard University. He was given the first Spingarn Medal from the NAACP in 1915.

162 a journalist who slings niftier prose: Probably J. A. Rogers. Harrison wrote two highly favorable commentaries on Rogers's *From Superman to Man* (*Negro World* [July 31, 1920]: 8; *Negro World* [January 1922]: 10.)

162 David's sow: Apocryphal story of a tavern owner named David Lloyd who had a sow with six legs, which was an object of public curiosity. After David's wife drank too much one day, she fell asleep in the sty. When David brought some customers around to see the sow, instead they saw the barman's wife, whereupon one shouted, "That is the drunkenest sow I ever saw."

168 Come unto me all ye who are weary: "Come unto me, all ye that labor and are heavy laden, and I will give you rest" (Matthew 11:28).

168 Senators Hoke Smith of Georgia and Overman of North Carolina: Senator Hoke Smith (1855–1931); Senator Lee Slater Overman (1854–1930), conservative senator from North Carolina for almost twenty-eight years.

168 Vandervelde: Emile Vandervelde, a socialist lawyer who made an impassioned speech in defense of Black American missionary William Shepherd, a sharp critic of King Leopold of Belgium's rule in the Congo.

169 Keir Hardie and Philip Snowdon: Keir Hardie (1856–1915), first leader of the Labour Party; Philip Snowdon (1864–1937), First Viscount, chancellor of the exchequer. Both men were pacifists and opposed British involvement in World War I.

169 "Yea, though I walk through the valley of the shadow of death, I will fear no evil: For thou art with me; thy rod and thy staff they comfort me" (Psalms 23:4).

170 Those who live by the sword shall perish by the sword: "All they that take the sword shall perish with the sword" (Matthew 26:52).

171 ryots: Peasants, or tenant farmers.

175 The "Call," the "Liberator" and "Pearson's": well-known Socialist publications.

178 the first . . . to publish a newspaper in this country: Russworm was like-

ly not the first Black college graduate in the United States (James, *Holding Aloft* 296n7).

181 Reverend E. Ethelred Brown: Pastor at the Harlem Community Church and author of a number of political pieces, including "Labor Conditions in Jamaica Prior to 1917," *Journal of Negro History* 4 (October 1919): 351–58, written before his arrival in America in 1920. For more on him see Mark D. Morrison-Reed's *Black Pioneers in a White Denomination* (Boston: Skinner House Books, 1994), 30–111.

187 Howard Carter, Lord Carnarvon: Howard Carter (1874–1939) led the expedition in search of King Tut's tomb (1922); Lord George Carnarvon (1866–1923) financed the expedition.

188 Babbittry: Dull-witted middle-class mindset typified by the title character in Sinclair Lewis's novel *Babbitt* (1923).

195 Anent: With regard to.

COMMUNISTS

204 Moton: Robert R. Moton (1867–1940) succeeded Booker T. Washington as principal at Tuskegee Institute.

204 Bourbon Burleson: Albert Sidney Burleson (1863–1937), Democratic congressman from Texas. He was appointed postmaster general in 1913 and held that position until 1921. During that time, he banned a number of anti-war periodicals.

204 Nyassaland: present-day Malawi.

205 *Requiescat en Pace*: Rest in Peace.

206 Col. Robins and Mr. Bullitt: Colonel Raymond Robins went to Russia in 1917 as a member of the Red Cross mission. William C. Bullitt was appointed as assistant secretary of state in 1917. He was a strong advocate for United States recognition of the new Soviet regime, a position not shared by President Wilson. Bullitt resigned from his post in 1919 in protest of the proposed terms of the Treaty of Versailles. He later served as U.S. ambassador to France and the Soviet Union.

208 Kolchak and Denikine: Aleksandr Kolchak, a Russian naval officer and political leader who briefly gained power among the counter-revolutionary forces. He was executed by the Bolsheviks in 1920. Denikine: Russian General Anton Denikine (1872–1947).

211 This piece also appeared in an almost identical form in the *Crusader* in October 1921.

214 Sinn Fein: Irish nationalistic movement begun in 1905 that gained great popularity after the British suppression of the Easter Rebellion in 1916. The name itself means "we ourselves."

214 Senussi: a nomadic North African Islamic group.

219 Decorated tomfoolery: This paragraph is an attack on Garveyism.

221 Domingo: "Figures Never Lie, But Liars Do Figure" *Crusader* (Oct. 1921): 13–14.

221 Catered for: A Caribbean Creole idiom meaning "expect."

222 Defection of Bishop McGuire: George Alexander McGuire (1866–1934) was born in Antigua. He became involved with the Garvey movement in 1919. Disillusioned by racism he had witnessed within the Episcopal Church, McGuire felt the need to establish a separate Black church, a view he promulgated within the UNIA. McGuire's quarrels with Garvey over the use of UNIA membership lists led him to bolt the UNIA for the ABB in 1921. He rejoined the UNIA in 1924.

222 T.U.U.L.: Trade Union Unity League, organized 1n 1929 to counter the more conservative American Federation of Labor. The Cleveland Convention attracted almost seven hundred delegates.

223 Negro radicals: The Negro radicals referred to Richard B. Moore, Otto Huiswood, W. A. Domingo, Cyril Briggs, and Hubert Harrison.

223 Mention of the Communist International is not made in the *Negro Worker* reprint of the article (titled "How Garvey Betrayed the Negro" in August 1932). The two paragraphs "The betrayal of these aspirations . . ." and "To-day as the result of large-scale migrations . . ." were also dropped from the *Negro Worker,* possibly showing a split within the Black community over the Black Belt plan.

225 Heywood Broun: Broun (1888–1939) was a leading newspaper columnist and a key figure in the Socialist Party.

225 Norman Thomas: Thomas (1884–1968) was the leader of the Socialist Party and under its banner made several unsuccessful attempts at the presidency of the United States.

226 fourteenth and fifteenth amendments: The Fourteenth Amendment, ratified in 1868, ensured equal citizenship rights for "all persons born or naturalized in the United States." The Fifteenth Amendment, ratified in 1870, barred voting discrimination "on account of race, color, or previous condition of servitude."

230 Published with a brief "Introduction of Resolution on the Negro Question" in *Proceedings of the Congress* (Berlin, 1927), 126–30; reprinted in Turner and Turner as "Statement at the Congress of the League against Imperialism and for National Independence, Brussels, February, 1927." Unsigned but credited to Moore by Turner and Moore, 135.

232 Anglo-Italian Pact: Concluded April 16, 1938. Great Britain agreed to recognize Italian sovereignty over Ethiopia while Italy respected

Spanish territory and was to withdraw its "volunteers" at the conclusion of the civil war, when the agreement was to come into force.

232 A Wall Street corporation: Firestone Rubber Company.

232 corvee system: Forced labor.

234 Wm. Green: William Green (1873–1952) became AFL president in 1924.

236 John L. Lewis: Lewis (1880–1969) served as president of the United Mine Workers of America from 1920 until 1960. He led the movement to establish the CIO in 1935.

237 Mayor Walker and the Tammany Hall politicians: James Walker, charismatic mayor of New York from 1926 to 1932, who was forced to resign because of evidence of corruption. Tammany was the name for the Democratic machine in New York City. A powerful political force begun as a reformist movement in the eighteenth century, Tammany gradually became corrupted under such bosses as William M. Tweed. It had lost most of its strength by 1932.

239 Salvation of the race: Changed to "the salvation of the black and white workers" in the *Daily Worker* reprint of the article, published Sept. 17, 1928, under the title "Housing Vital Problem of Negro Workers."

240 thirteenth amendment: The Thirteenth Amendment, abolishing slavery, was passed in 1865.

241 Angelo Herndon, Tom Mooney: Angelo Herndon joined the Communist Party in 1929. After distributing flyers for a march in Atlanta on June 30, 1932, demanding relief for the jobless, Herndon clashed with the police. He was arrested and found guilty of insurrection and was sentenced to eighteen to twenty years on a Georgia chain gang. His case became a cause célèbre among communists. See Foner and Shapiro, *American Communism and Black Americans: A Documentary History, 1930–1934* 320–51; Thomas J. Mooney (1882–1942) was a socialist and a member of the International Molders Union. He was convicted of complicity in a bombing in San Francisco in 1916 and was imprisoned until 1939, when he was pardoned. Mooney was thought by many to have been set up by anti-labor forces. See Richard H. Frost, *The Mooney Case* (Stanford, CA: Stanford UP, 1968).

241 William L. Patterson: Patterson (1891–1980) was an attorney and a Communist Party leader. As executive director of the International Labor Defense, he helped prepare the legal defense for the Scottsboro Boys. See his autobiography, *The Man Who Cried Genocide* (New York: International P, 1971).

241 *Mr. President: Free the Scottsboro Boys:* The president being appealed to is Franklin D. Roosevelt.

254 Gastonia: The National Textile Worker's Union, led by Fred Beal, struck at the Loray Mill, in Gastonia, North Carolina, on April 1, 1929. Of the 2,200 workers at the mill, 1,800 struck. The workers' cause suffered as a result of the murders of police chief O. F. Adderholt in June 1929 and labor organizer Ella May Wiggins in September 1929. For more on the strike, see John Salmond, *Gastonia 1929: The Story of the Loray Mill Strike* (Chapel Hill: U of North Carolina P, 1995) and Liston Pope, *Millhands and Preachers: A Study of Gastonia* (New Haven: Yale UP, 1942). See also George Padmore's "Gastonia: Its Significance to Negro Labor" in this volume.

262 Otto Hall: Hall and his younger brother Harry Haywood were leading Black American communists. Unlike his brother, Otto was opposed to the Black Belt republic proposal.

265 anarcho-syndicalists: Anarcho-syndicalists were supporters of a movement attempting to transfer the means of industrial production to the workers.

268 Matthew Woll: Woll (1880–1956), an AFL vice-president in 1919, was strongly anti-communist.

269 Depriest: Oscar DePriest (1871–1951), a Republican from Chicago, was the first Black member of Congress elected from a northern district in 1928.

LITERARY FIGURES

280 Peace, O my rebel heart!: the words are inscribed on McKay's tombstone.

280 Reg: McKay's brother.

281 The trades: Easterly winds.

281 purple apples: Star apples, small, round fruit, purple when ripe.

282 pimento's flowering: allspice. The tree bearing this flower is known in Jamaica as pimento.

282 honey-fever grass: Used to treat fevers.

282 Ping-wing: Shrub about six feet high resembling a pineapple plant.

282 painted ladies: Butterflies "with brownish black and orange wings" (McKay, *Complete Poems* 317).

282 rose-apple: A small, round yellowish fruit.

282 alligator pears: A rough-skinned variety of avocado.

284 "Baptism": As Françoise Charras observes, this poem "can be viewed as a subversion of the melting pot theme" ("The West Indian Presence in Alain Locke's *The New Negro* [1925]," *Temples for Tomorrow: Looking Back at the Harlem Renaissance*, ed. Geneviève Fabre and Michel Feith [Bloomington: Indiana UP, 2001], 286n26).

284 "Exhortation: Summer 1919": This poem, like many of the McKay poems included in this anthology, was first published in slightly different form in the *Liberator*. See Claude McKay, *Complete Poems* (ed. and intro. William J. Maxwell, Urbana: U of Illinois P, 2004) for variants. "Exhortation: Summer 1919" is an apocalyptic poem, like "If We Must Die," inspired by the Red Summer of 1919. The East has several references in poem (the rising sun, the fledgling Soviet Union, the star signaling the birthplace of Christ). The call for Ethiopia to awake in line 17 likely harkens, as Maxwell suggests (McKay, *Complete Poems* 331), to Psalms 68:31: "Princes shall come out of Egypt; Ethiopia shall soon stretch out her hands unto God."

285 "The White House": When the poem was published in *The New Negro*, Locke changed the title to "White Houses." McKay vehemently objected, claiming that the title "White Houses" "changed the whole symbolic intent and meaning of the poem, making it appear as if the burning ambition of the black malcontent was to enter white houses in general" (*A Long Way from Home* 313–14).

287 Carpenter: Edward Carpenter (1844–1929), a British author whose most notable work was *Love's Coming of Age* (1896), a commentary on human sexuality.

288 McKay was extremely circumspect about his failed restaurant and the friend with whom he opened it.

288 McKay married fellow Jamaican Eulalie Imelda Lewars on July 20, 1914, in Jersey City. By 1918, the marriage had ended. They had one child, Rhue Hope McKay, whom McKay would never see, though he corresponded with her. The marriage was apparently doomed because of McKay's Bohemian lifestyle and his bisexuality. See Wayne Cooper, *Claude McKay: Rebel Sojourner in the Harlem Renaissance* (Baton Rouge: Louisiana State UP, 1987), 29–32, 70–76, 149–51.

288 The poems are "To the White Fiends," "The Conqueror," "The Park in Spring," "Is It Worth While?" and "Harlem Shadows."

289 Bedwardism: Alexander Bedward (1859–1930) was the leader of a messianic group in Jamaica in the early years of the twentieth century.

292 Part 1 was published in *Crisis* (December 1923).

293 Siki: A flamboyant boxer, Battling Siki (1897–1925) was once the light heavyweight champion. His birth name was Baye Phal, and he was a native of French West Africa (in what is now Senegal).

294 menshevists: Initially members of the moderate branch of the Social Democratic Party at odds with the more radical Bolsheviks. After November 1917, those who opposed the Soviet government.

294 Boris Pilnyak (1894–1937), a popular Russian novelist. "Okonoff" and "Feodor" have not been identified.

294 Chukovsky . . . Zamiatan . . . Maishack: Korney Chukovsky, a well-established literary figure; Yevgeny Zamyatin (1884–1937), a novelist; Daniel Maishack, a minor poet.

300 The dean of Negro critics: William S. Braithwaite (1878–1962), cited in "The Negro in Literature," *Crisis* (September 1924): 208.

302 Jakes . . . Madam Lauras: characters in *Home to Harlem.*

308 Sweetman: The lover of a woman, often married, who receives gifts and money from her.

308 Grass widow: A woman separated from her husband.

309 Brilliantine: A preparation for the hair to make it smooth and shiny.

315 Coon-can: A card game derived from the Spanish game *conquian.* Variations of the game in America would lead to such popular forms as rummy and canasta.

318 *Weldon's Ladies' Journal* and the *Home Magazine:* Popular magazines publishing household hints, fashion news, and fiction.

319 bitter oranges . . . sour-sop cup: Bitter oranges are also called sour oranges and are the Seville variety with a bitter pulp. A sour-sop cup is a thick, milky drink sweetened with the sweet-sour pulp of the soursop.

320 Bruited: Made known.

332 "Darkwater": *Darkwater: Voices from Within the Veil* (1920) a work of fiction, autobiography, and poetry.

334 Spuyten Duyvil: Located in the Bronx, separated from Manhattan by the Harlem River.

339 Tinterillo: A low-level clerk; also a shyster lawyer.

339 La Prensa: *El Diario, La Prensa,* a widely read New York–based Spanish newspaper.

339 Guayaquil: The largest city in present-day Ecuador.

340 Dore's illustrations: Gustave Dore (1832–83), a popular French painter and illustrator.

341 A white peacock: The White Peacock Café was a meeting place in Harlem often frequented by Walrond while he was working for the *Negro World.* He writes of it in his column "Books" (the *Negro World* May 20, 1922: 4).

342 Kraus: a White poet, Joseph Kraus, who worked with Walrond at the *Negro World.*

346 "Can't you see her neck?": Robert Bone discusses how Walrond connects the back of people's necks (the area where the hair is hardest to straighten) with their racial identity (*Down Home: Origins of the Afro-American Short Story* [1975; New York: Columbia UP, 1988], 181).

347 Pickaninnies: A term for a young child (usually of Black or East Indian

heritage). While it is a pejorative term in the United States, it can be used with affection in the West Indies.

347 Singlet: A man's undershirt.

347 *Coombia:* Popular dance in Panama. *Brujerial* chant refers to practitioners of magic. *Obeah* is a belief in supernatural forces used to achieve or defend against evil ends.

347 Maubé bark: Bittersweet drink made from the mauby tree.

347 Monkey Hill: common name for the city of Mount Hope.

347 *crocus bag:* Brown sack made out of jute, often used in making clothing.

348 The English Plymouth Brethren: an austere Christian fundamentalist group of which Walrond's mother was a devout follower.

348 Cholo: Indian of Spanish American ancestry.

349 leghorn hat: Hat plaited from a distinctive wheat straw, chiefly imported from Leghorn, Italy.

349 Fi': to, for.

350 *Rotie* (roti): Baked, unleavened bread made from flour.

350 Guilder: Dutch coin. It was also used as currency in British Guiana, once settled by the Dutch.

350 Gamin: A street urchin.

351 Garfish: A grey, saltwater fish with a long, narrow, spearlike snout.

352 Stand-pipe: Short for standard pipe. The pipe was mounted on a concrete stand and placed at the side of the road for public usage of water.

353 Fire hag: In folklore an old woman who sheds her skin at night and becomes a ball of fire seeking victims whose blood she sucks. Also known as a *soukouyan* in several islands and as an *old-higue* in Guyana and Jamaica.

354 Wash blue: Bleachlike additive to whiten clothes but also used in *obeah* rituals.

355 "Cracked licker" skillet: A pan used in processing sugar cane.

355 *Crapeau:* A large toad whose glands contain toxins; a Creole variation of the French *crapaud.*

356 *Bateau:* (French) A flat-bottomed boat.

359 "Taw"-pitching: Marble shooting. A *taw* is the largest marble shot.

359 Chagres: A river in Panama that flows into the Caribbean Sea.

360 Gunga peas: Dark green peas often cooked in stews; also known as pigeon peas.

360 Unna: you all, your.

360 Unna don't know: /h/ in initial position tends to be dropped or added in Jamaican English. When "h" is dropped "home" is pronounced "ome." Word-initial additions of "h" occur, for example, in "hif" ("if"). Miss Buckner's speech here can be translated as follows: "Don't you know that I am indebted to him? Don't you know that if it weren't

for him a lot of the things [sexual activity] that go on here would be out on the street [they would be street prostitutes]—and some of us that are having a good time here would be someplace else altogether."

361 Dickty: High-toned.

362 Yampi or Lucy yam: Varieties of yams. A Lucy yam is also known as a white yam.

362 Prædial larceny: Stealing produce from someone's land.

365 Mr. Thingamerry's hat: Thingamerry is a substitute for a person's name who is either forgotten or thought of as being unimportant.

366 "Him that is exalted": This is a reference to Christ. "Him that God exalted with his right hand to be a Prince and a Savior for you to give repentance to Israel, and forgiveness of sins" (Acts 5:31).

368 Bolita Negroes: Bolita (or bolito) was a popular illegal gambling game using numbers. West Indians were prominent in the business, including Casper Holstein.

369 weself: In Caribbean Creole, subject, object, and possessive pronouns are used in various sentence positions.

370 Star apple: A purplish-brown fruit with a sweet pulp and seeds arranged in a star pattern.

370 Water mout': Dribbling.

371 A next: Another.

371 faht blue hice: Fart blue ice (i.e., to do something impossible).

371 finger nail dem: Fingernails. "Dem" either before or after the noun often denotes plurality in Caribbean Creole.

371 bittle: Bickle, food.

371 Yo' bes mek up yo' mine . . . : Tiny's words can be translated as follows: "You'd better make up your mind now that it's warm to get yourself an elevator job for when the winter comes. For so help me God I will see you in holy hell before you will see me trudging up and down stairs as if I am any whore for you to do with as you damn well please."

371 Coruscant: glittering.

379 *The Starter*: Won third prize in the *Opportunity* contest, 1927. The play had several amateur productions according to Bernard L. Peterson Jr., *Early Black American Playwrights and Dramatic Writers: A Biographical Directory and Catalog of Plays, Films, and Broadcasting Scripts.*

386 *Her*: According to Peterson, the play was produced "by the Krigwa Players at the 135th St. Library Theatre in Harlem, for 3 perfs, Jan. 7, 19, and 24, 1927; again presented April 20, 25, and 27, 1927, dir. by Charles Burroughs" (179).

397 *Hot Stuff*: Won third prize in the *Crisis* contest, 1927. There is no indication that it has ever been produced.

403 Isadore Goldstein: Although connections between Jews and Caribbean

immigrants were frequently made (e.g., Walrond's essay "The Hebrews of the Black Race," *International Interpreter* July 14, 1923: 468–69), negative views of Jews are not infrequent. Goldstein, the stereotypic Jewish peddlar (as with several of Walrond's pieces), represents the often ambivalent relationships between Blacks and Jews at the time.

406 Rose McClendon, Wilson: Rose McClendon (1884–1936), a well-known actor and theatrical promoter; Eric Arthur ("Dooley") Wilson (1894–1953), a drummer and an actor. He is best known for playing the pianist, Sam, in the film *Casablanca* (1942).

406 Florence Mills: A popular singer and dancer in such shows as *The Plantation Revue*. Her death in 1927, at the age of thirty-two, was deeply mourned in Harlem.

406 Gilpin, Bledsoe: Charles Gilpin (1878–1930), a well-known actor who starred in Eugene O'Neill's *The Emperor Jones* at the Provincetown (New York) Theatre in 1920, winning the NAACP's Spingarn medal; Julius C. (Jules) Bledsoe (1898–1943), a baritone who originated the role of Joe in *Show Boat* (1927).

408 *The Forest:* 1924 play by John Galsworthy (1867–1933), a Nobel Prize–winning author (1932) known for his social satire.

HISTORIANS

414 Abbé Gregoire: Henri Grégoire (1750–1831), radical French constitutional bishop of Blois. He is the author of *De la Littérature des Nègres, ou Recherches sur leurs Facultés Intellectuelles, leurs Qualité Morales, et leur Littérature* (1808).

415 Jupiter Hammon . . . Peter Williams: Hammon (1711–c.1806) was the author of the first known published work by an African American author, the poem "An Evening Thought, Salvation by Christ with Penitential Cries" (1761); Phyllis Wheatley (c.1753–84) was a poet whose work Schomburg was especially proud to have in his collection. The poem to Harvard is "To the University of Cambridge, in New England" and the one to Washington is "To His Excellency General Washington" (1776); John Marrant (1755–91) wrote *A Narrative of the Lord's Wonderful Dealings with John Marrant, a Black* (1785); Lemuel Haynes (1753–1833) was a New England minister who ministered to White and Black congregations, and was the author of the sermon "Universal Salvation" (1806); Rev. Absalom Jones (1746–1818) was co-founder of the Free African Society and minister of St. Thomas's African Episcopal Church; Peter Williams (1780–1840) founded the abolitionist *Freedom's Journal* (1827).

416 Juan Latino . . . Christophe: Latino (c. 1518–94); Escurial, a palace and monastery outside Madrid; Capitein (1714–47), the first African ordained in a Protestant church; Vassa, Olaudah Equiano (1745–97), author of *The Interesting Narrative of the Life of Olaudah Equiano or Gustavus Vassa the African* (1789); Granville Sharp (1735–1813), a leading British abolitionist; Vastey (d. 1820), author of *Le Cri de la Patrie* (1815); Henri Christophe (1767–1820), hero of the Haitian Revolution and King of Haiti, 1811–20.

416 Cuffee: Paul Cuffe (1759–1817), free-born African American who advocated the migration of Blacks to Africa.

416 Rev. Daniel Coker . . . Samuel Crowther: Coker (1780–1840) was the first African Methodist Espicopal (AME) missionary to Africa in 1820; Crowther (1806–91) was born in Yorubaland (present-day Nigeria) and was the first African Anglican bishop.

417 Prince Saunders . . . Nat Turner: Saunders, also spelled Sanders, (1775–1839) was an African American who traveled extensively. He lived in Haiti for several years and published the *Haytian Papers* (1818–20); Nathaniel Paul (1775–1834); James Varick (1750–1827) was the founder of the African Methodist Episcopal Zion Church; Richard Allen (1760–1831) was the founder of the AME Church; David Walker (c.1785–1830) was the abolitionist author of the militant pamphlet *David Walker's Appeal in Four Articles; Together with a Preamble, to the Coloured Citizens of the World* (1829); Nat Turner (1800–31) led a slave rebellion in Virginia in 1831 that galvanized both the anti-slavery and pro-slavery movements.

417 Samuel R. Ward . . . Garrison: Samuel R. Ward (b. 1817) was the author of *Autobiography of a Fugitive Negro, his anti-slavery labours in the United States, Canada and England* (1855); Henry Highland Garnet (1815–82) was a former slave minister and abolitionist who called for an uprising to end slavery in 1843; Martin Delany (1812–85) was a Black nationalist, abolitionist, and author; Arthur Tappan (1786–1865), Wendell Phillips (1811–84), Lucretia Mott (1793–1880), and William Lloyd Garrison (1805–79) were all leading White abolitionists. Charles Sumner (1811–74) was a radical Republican during Reconstruction.

417 McCune Smith . . . Alexander Crummell: James McCune Smith (1813–65); Wilmot Blyden (1832–1912), born in the Virgin Islands, was a pioneer Pan-Africanist and a Liberian nationalist; Alexander Crummell (1819–98) was a clergyman and an early Pan-Africanist.

417 Pennington: James Pennington (1809–70) author of *The Fugitive Blacksmith, or, Events in the History of James W. C. Pennington* (1849).

417 Henry Ward Beecher (1813–87), leading White abolitionist.

418 Benjamin Onderdonk (1791–1861), a New York City Episcopal bishop.

418 Negro Society for Historical Research: founded by Schomburg and John E. Bruce (1856–1924).

418 Henry P. Slaughter . . . Dr. Carter G. Woodson: Henry Procter Slaughter (1871–1958) was a journalist and prominent collector of Black books; Reverend Charles Douglass Martin was a Moravian minister who was an important Black book collector. Carter G. Woodson (1875–1950) founded the *Journal of Negro History* (1915) and was the author of *The Miseducation of the Negro*. Schomburg faulted his scholarship in his review of Woodson's *The Negro in Our History* in the *Negro World*, Nov. 4, 1922: 3.

424 Finot's "Race Prejudice": Jean Finot (1858–1922), author of *L'agonie et la mort des races* (*The Death-Agony of the "Science" of Race*), 1911.

424 George: Generic name for all Black porters, derived from George Pullman, inventor of the cars.

424 the passenger: In later editions the passenger is described as a U.S. senator from Oklahoma.

428 *Maxixe . . . carmagnole*: *maxixe*, known as the Brazilian Tango, was popular in café society in the early 1910s; *danse du vêntre*, belly dancing; *carmagnole* was a popular song heaping scorn upon Marie Antoinette and her supporters.

428 *Untrodden Fields of Anthropology*: published in 1896 under the pseudonym Dr. Jacobus X.

428 Maran's *Batouala*: A novel by René Maran (1887–1960), born in Martinique. He won the prestigious Goncourt Prize for the 1921 novel, a stinging rebuke of colonialism.

429 "Patting juba": Complex rhythmic foot stomping and slapping the hands, thighs, and knees.

429 W. C. Handy: William Christopher Handy (1873–1958), composer, musician, bandleader, author of such hits as "Memphis Blues" (1912) and "St. Louis Blues."

429 Shelton Brooks: A native of Canada, Brooks (1886–1975) composed such popular hits as "Some of These Days," "Darktown Strutters' Ball," and "Walkin' the Dog."

429 "The Texas Tommy": Thought to be the first swing dance, introduced in San Francisco in 1909.

431 Abbie Mitchell . . . Buddy Gilmore: Mitchell (1884–1960) was a singer and actress, the wife of Will Marion Cook; Clara Smith (1894–1935) was a blues singer with such hits as "Every Woman's Blues" and "Whip It to a Jelly"; Mamie Smith (1883–1946) was the first African American woman to record the blues, with her best-selling record "Crazy Blues" (1920); "Buddy" Gilmore was a member of James Reese Europe's Society Orchestra.

431 Cook . . . Lopez: Will Marion Cook (1869–1944) was the author, with Paul Laurence Dunbar, of the musical *Clorindy, or the Origin of the Cakewalk* (1898). Fletcher Henderson (1897–1952) was a pianist, bandleader, and arranger who helped usher in the big band swing sound. Vincent Lopez (1895–1975) was a bandleader and pianist popular on the New York hotel scene.

432 Grey's popular song "Runnin' Wild," composed by Jerry Grey, Leo Wood, and Arthur H. Gibbs.

433 "Cervantes smiled Spain's chivalry away," said Byron: *Don Juan*, canto xiii, stanza xi.

434 Walter White: (1893–1955), civil rights leader, NAACP official, and author of the novels *The Fire in the Flint* (1924) and *Flight* (1926).

436 Benjamin Tillman: Governor (1890–94) and senator (1895–1918) from South Carolina. A staunch supporter of Jim Crow laws and lynching.

438 James Kimble Vardaman (1861–1930) conservative governor (1904–08) and senator (1913–19) from Mississippi.

440 Anderson, Copeland, Green, Leary, Newby: Osborn Perry Anderson, John A. Copeland Jr., Shields Green, Lewis Sheridan Leary, and Dangerfield Newby. These were the five slain Blacks who were among the twenty-one men led by John Brown on October 16, 1859.

INDEX

Harlem Twenty-First District
Club of the Socialist Party, 242
Harrison, Hubert Henry, 28,
131–34; arrival in U.S., 9; as
collector of Black books, 26;
"The Descent of Du Bois," 133,
144–46; "Hands across the
Sea," 153–54; "Just Crabs," 133,
146–48; "Launching the Liberty
League," 132, 141–42; and
McKay, 274, 277n4; "The
Negro and Socialism," 131; *The
Negro and the Nation*, 37n2, 131;
and *Negro World*, 30, 227n4;
"No Negro Literary
Renaissance," Says Well Known
Writer, 159–62; as pioneering
radical, 18, 19, 25, 448n;
"Prejudice Growing Less and
Co-operating More, Says
Student of Question," 155–58;
"Race Consciousness," 154–55;
and Rogers, 423; "Socialism and
the Negro," 131, 135–41; "Two
Negro Radicalisms," 132,
148–51; *When Africa Awakes*,
26, 131; "The White War and
the Colored World," 133,
151–52
Hart-Cellar Immigration and
Nationality Act, 11
Hathaway, Heather, 4
Haywood, Harry, 23, 450n
Haywood, William "Big Bill," 132
Hendrickson, Elizabeth, 19, 39n12
Henke, Holger, 11
Henry, Keith, 14
Hey! Hey!, 98
Hillquit, Morris, 19, 163
Holstein, Casper, 8, 28, 37n5, 157
Howell, Howard Adolph, 8, 38n10
Huggins, Nathan, 274
Hughes, Langston, 7, 27, 35, 127,
276, 412
Huiswoud, Otto E., 242–44; and
ABB, 22; and ANLC, 22; at

Fourth Congress of Communist
International, 20, 275; and
Jamaican Trades and Labor
Union, 23; "The Negro
Problem Is Important," 243,
245–46; as pioneering radical,
20, 21, 227, 448n; and Soviet
Communist resolution
concerning Black Americans,
23; "World Aspects of the
Negro Question," 243, 246–55
Hurston, Zora Neale, 27, 35

Ikonné, Chidi, 35
Immigration Act of 1924, 10
indentured labor, 2
Industrial Workers of the World
(IWW), 132, 207
International Colored Unity
League (ICUL), 133
International Congress against
Colonial Oppression and
Imperialism, 228, 230–34
International Ladies Garment
Workers Union, 185
International Trade Union
Committee of Negro Workers
(ITUC-NW), 23, 243, 257

Jacques, Amy. *See* Garvey, Amy
Jacques
James, C. L. R., 98, 257
James, Kelvin Christopher, 36
James, Winston, 8–9, 25, 38n10,
273
jazz, 29, 30, 427–33
Jekyll, Walter, 288; *Jamaican Song
and Story*, 273
Jim Crow laws, 12, 33
Jim Crow unions, 261, 268
Johnson, Charles S., 27–28, 325,
326
Johnson, James Weldon, 27, 38n7,
412
Jones, Absalom, 415, 417, 455n
Jones, Claudia, 39n12